Poor Relief and Protestant

Poor Relief and Protestantism

The Evolution of Social Welfare
in Sixteenth-Century Emden

TIMOTHY G. FEHLER

Aldershot • Brookfield USA • Singapore • Sydney

© Timothy G. Fehler, 1999

Published by
Ashgate Publishing Limited
Gower House
Croft Road
Aldershot
Hants
GU11 3HR
England

Ashgate Publishing Company
Old Post Road
Brookfield
Vermont 05036–9704
USA

The author has asserted his moral right under the Copyright, Designs and Patents Act, 1988, to be identified as the author of this work.

British Library Cataloguing in Publication Data

Fehler, Timothy G.
    Poor Relief and Protestantism: The Evolution of Social Welfare in
    Sixteenth-Century Emden
    (St Andrews Studies in Reformation History)
    1. Public welfare—Germany—Lower Saxony—Emden—History
    —16th century.   2. Public welfare—Religious aspects.
    3. Protestantism.
    I. Title
    362.5'8'09435917

Library of Congress Cataloging-in-Publication Data

Fehler, Timothy G.
    Poor relief and Protestantism: the evolution of social welfare in
    sixteenth-century Emden/Timothy G. Fehler.
        (St Andrews Studies in Reformation History)
        Includes bibliographical references and index.
        ISBN 1-85928-378-0 (hardback)
        1. Public welfare—Germany—Emden (Lower Saxony)—History—16th
    century. I. Title. II. Series.
    HV280.E45F44   1999
    362.5'8'09435917—dc21   98–52490
                                                       CIP

ISBN 1 85928 378 0

This book is printed on acid free paper

Typeset in Sabon by Manton Typesetters, 5–7 Eastfield Road, Louth, Lincs, LN11 7AJ
Printed and bound in Great Britain by MPG Books Ltd, Bodmin, Cornwall

Contents

List of Figures, Maps and Tables

Figures

Maps

Tables

Acknowledgements

As I sit to acknowledge the assistance and encouragement that I have received over the course of this project, I am both pleased and overwhelmed. At virtually every stage of research and writing, multitudes of friends, colleagues, mentors and family have substantially helped shape this book. My indebtedness begins with my Doktorvater Robert Kingdon whose demands for careful and thorough engagement with the sources have constantly challenged me and allowed me to attempt to tell this story. I have prized his encouragement and profited from his contacts over the past decade. His contacts with Professor Heinz Schilling, then at the Universität Gießen, now at the Humboldt Universität in Berlin, helped me define my topic in its earliest stages, and the forum which Professor Schilling offered me in his Oberseminars in both Gießen and Berlin were crucial in helping me interpret my initial findings from the Emden archives in 1991–93.

I was so well received in Emden that it would be impossible to mention all our friends and those who made our stay rewarding both personally and professionally. I am grateful for the constant thoughtfulness that was shown to Jacquelyn and me during our stay, as so many people made sure that we became integrated into the community. Dr Menno Smid served as mentor for my earliest work in Emden; it was his advice and encouragement that got my research off the ground, and he kept me going always in the right direction. He placed his invaluable knowledge of Emden's history at my beck and call, with enthusiastic conversations that often continued into the wee hours of the morning. He and his wife Margo always made us feel at home in their house; their hospitality and their help in finding housing cannot be repaid. I am also grateful to Walter Schulz, the director of the Johannes a Lasco Bibliothek Grosse Kirche Emden, who with Frau Dringenberg, Frau Braams, and the rest of the staff have gone out of their way to accommodate me and were always willing to interrupt their own work in order to deal with my many questions and queries. Walter Schulz opened up the full resources of the Bibliothek to me, and his wife Hedwig and family have opened up their home to us on subsequent visits to Emden. Frau Dr Hildegard Baege went above and beyond the call of duty at the Archiv der Grossen Kirche. She was always sure that I had the materials I needed, and she worked diligently to ensure that Jacquelyn and I were well integrated into Emden and East Frisian culture. I would also like to express my appreciation to the staffs at both the Stadtarchiv Emden and the Staatsarchiv Aurich. Henning Jürgens, at the JAL Bibliothek, has served as a critical link in the final stages of editing as he has checked and rechecked my many long-distance queries during the past year. We are grateful for the friendliness and encouragement given by the Van Koningsvelds and the Fasts ... . The list is already long, but is still incomplete: I hope that all of our Emden friends will recognize and accept the depth of my gratitude for their encouragement and assistance.

The insights and criticisms of many colleagues and friends have substantially improved the text at various stages. I am especially grateful to Andrew Pettegree, Marshall Crossnoe, Ronald Granieri, and Gene Fehler for kindly sacrificing to read the entire manuscript as it evolved (Andrew and my father more than once!).

Jacquelyn's steadfast love, patience, and support have made this possible and fun. From her readings of initial drafts to her tolerance of me as deadlines approached (and sometimes passed), I could not have finished this without her; nor would I have wanted to. This book is dedicated to her.

Timothy G. Fehler
Furman University
1999

Abbreviations

ArchGK	Archiv der Grossen Kirche in Emden
ARG	*Archiv für Reformationsgeschichte*
BRN	*Bibliotheca Reformatoria Neerlandica*, ed. S. Cramer and F. Pijper, 10 vols (The Hague, 1903–14)
EJb	*Emder Jahrbuch* (Jahrbuch der Gesellschaft für bildende Kunst und vaterländische Altertümer zu Emden)
EKP	Emder Kontrakten-Protokolle; STAA, Rep. 234
Fremdlingen I	Account book of the *fremdlingen* deacons, 1558–68
Fremdlingen II	Account book of the *fremdlingen* deacons, 1569–75
KRP	Emden Kirchenratsprotokolle; Heinz Schilling and Klaus-Dieter Schreiber (eds), *Die Kirchenratsprotokolle der reformierten Gemeinde Emden 1557–1620* (2 vols, Cologne, 1989–92); the pages are numbered sequentially in the two volumes (vol. i=pages 1–553; vol. ii=pages 556–1200)
OUB	*Ostfriesisches Urkundenbuch*, ed. Ernst Friedlaender, 2 vols (Emden, 1878–81); vol. 3, ed. Günther Möhlmann (Aurich, 1975)
Quer.	Querimoniale Civitatis Emedense; STAA, Rep. 241, Msc. A168
QuF	Quellen und Forschungen zur Ostfriesischen Familien- und Wappenkunde
SCJ	*Sixteenth Century Journal*
StaE	Stadtarchiv Emden
STAA	Niedersächsisches Staatsarchiv Aurich
TRE	*Theologische Realenzyklopädie* (Berlin: Walter de Gruyter)

CHAPTER ONE

Introduction

If only we too fulfilled the gospel in our time! In the past one gave to churches and cloisters; now one gives to poor institutions, which were not around then.

Emden's Reformed church bookkeeper (*c.* 1590)[1]

Around 1590, in the German port city of Emden, the bookkeeper of the Reformed church sat down to look through the church's old account books. After noting some of his discoveries on the opening pages of the current account book, he bemoaned the fact that people were presently contributing too much for the poor, while the last recorded bequest of land or property directly to the church had been in 1541. This discouraged church official's complaint surprisingly demonstrates the dramatic changes that Emden's social welfare institutions and attitudes toward poor relief underwent during the course of the sixteenth century. That Emden's social welfare system changed will come as no surprise to historians who study early modern poor relief. Yet the tremendous acceleration of Emden's urban, social, religious and economic development in the sixteenth century provides an unusual context in which to study the evolution of early modern social welfare.

Historians have described the systems of poor relief emerging in the sixteenth century as 'the beginning of modern social welfare' and 'a radical departure from the beaten paths of medieval charity'.[2] Such innovation has thus not surprisingly inspired an explosion of scholarly research on poverty and social welfare over the past three decades. Debates have developed around two key issues. First, scholars have tried to map out precisely the nature of late medieval charity in order to gauge the 'newness' of early modern poor relief methods. Second, analysis of the motivations behind the welfare reforms has been a hotbed in the historiography of early modern poverty: the new theology of Protestantism, the intellectual climate of humanism, socio-economic changes, and a growing state interest in control and discipline have all been considered as driving forces behind poor relief changes. The debate over the significance of the Protestant Reformation in the reform of poor

---

[1] ArchGK no. 364, *Liber Expensarum (1572–95)*, p. 2.

[2] Elsie McKee, *John Calvin on the Diaconate and Liturgical Almsgiving* (Geneva, 1984), p. 93; Robert Jütte, *Poverty and Deviance in Early Modern Europe* (Cambridge, 1994), p. 2.

relief has re-intensified in recent years. Ole Peter Grell has, in fact, called 'urgently' for a 'revisionist interpretation ... which emphasises the significance of the Reformation for bringing about these changes'. Grell wants to replace the dominant historiographic viewpoint which sees the Reformation's significance as 'negligible' and which sees the poor relief changes 'as inspired by civic leaders and Christian humanists who were responding not to religious reforms, but to the economic and demographic changes of the period'.[3] That the refashioning of poor relief was influenced by the climate of religious change is indisputable. What remains to be seen, however, is the extent to which the religious changes can be extracted from their socio-economic context. This complex relationship between religious ideology and practical reality makes up an important facet of the history of the Reformation. Emden's story will thus provide a more balanced understanding of Reformation change by a diachronic analysis of one of the most prominent Protestant cities of the period, the 'Geneva of the North'.[4]

Emden experienced significant religious, social, and communal changes in the first half of the sixteenth century, but in the 1550s the velocity of the changes increased. The most significant of these changes was the arrival of thousands of Dutch refugees fleeing the war against Spain in the Netherlands. The city's population doubled within the course of a few years; and as the city attracted many wealthy refugees, its shipping economy reached an unprecedented level. During the second half of the sixteenth century, Emden had grown from a small provincial German town into Europe's busiest shipping port, if only temporarily. One study has placed the shipping capacity of the fleet of ships registered in Emden in 1570 as greater than that of the entire kingdom of England.[5] The city's equally rapid fall from European prominence beginning at the end of the sixteenth century has had the effect of obscuring Emden from the sight of most modern viewers, but Emden's economic significance was not hidden to contemporaries. In Marlowe's *Doctor Faustus*, two angels approached Faustus in his study. The Good Angel entreated him to think of heaven and heavenly things; the Bad Angel, of honour and

---

[3] Grell's review article, 'The religious duty of care and the social need for control in early modern Europe', *The Historical Journal*, 39 (1996) pp. 257, 263; Grell, 'The Protestant imperative of Christian care and neighbourly love', in *Health Care and Poor Relief in Protestant Europe 1500–1700*, eds O. P. Grell and A. Cunningham (London, 1997), p. 43.

[4] For an overview of these issues in Emden, see Timothy Fehler, 'The Burden of Benevolence: Poor Relief and Parish Finance in Early Modern Emden', in Beat Kümin (ed.), *Reformations Old and New* (Aldershot, 1996), pp. 219–36.

[5] Bernhard Hagedorn, *Ostfrieslands Handel und Schiffahrt im 16. Jahrhundert* (Berlin, 1910), p. 251.

wealth. Faustus responded, 'Of Wealth! Why, the signiory of Embden shall be mine. When Mephistophilis shall stand by me, what god can hurt thee, Faustus? thou art safe.'[6] Emden's sudden economic boom, the wealth of which Faustus dreamed, resulted to a large extent from the influx of refugees from the Dutch Revolt, many of whom were rich and brought their business ventures and expertise with them to Emden. Many other refugees, however, arrived in Emden with nothing. As we will see, Emden's poor relief institutions evolved dramatically to deal with the new social and economic climate.

The flood of exiles affected more than just Emden's economy. Virtually all of the Dutch refugees who came to Emden were members of the Reformed church, fleeing their homeland to escape religious persecution. Emden's significance for the development of Reformed Protestantism in the Netherlands – as a city of refuge, a missionary centre, and a hub of printing, propaganda and advice – led to its designation as 'Moederkerk' (Mother Church).[7] Its influence on the Netherlands has been compared to Geneva's influence on France, and 'of the two [Reformed cities], Emden was the more successful'. While the northern Netherlands, the country toward which Emden directed its primary energy, largely followed Emden's ecclesiastic institutional model and adopted a Calvinist form of Protestantism, France, the focus of Geneva's activities, did not.[8] Nor should the influence of the Dutch refugees on Emden's own ecclesiastical development be underestimated. The exiles instigated an ever-growing interest in church discipline as well as a firming up of Emden's own Reformed institutions. In the last quarter of the century, Emden underwent an intense phase of confessional development – Heinz Schilling has called this phase in Emden's development a 'Calvinization' – which ultimately, when combined with the growing communal mentality and increasing self-assurance of the citizenry, resulted in the establishment of a Calvinist city church.[9]

---

[6] Christopher Marlowe, 'The Tragical History of Dr. Faustus, Scene V' in John Gassner (ed.), *A Treasury of the Theatre* (3rd edn, New York, 1967), p. 226. Marlowe's 'Dr Faustus' was first performed successfully in England in the winter of 1588/89. For an example of the close economic connections between England and Emden/East Frisia, see the following works by G. D. Ramsay: *The Politics of a Tudor Merchant Adventurer: A Letter to the Earls of East Friesland* (Manchester, 1979); *The City of London in International Politics at the Accession of Elizabeth Tudor* (Manchester, 1975), p. 240.

[7] On this issue, see Andrew Pettegree, *Emden and the Dutch Revolt. Exile and the Development of Reformed Protestantism* (Oxford, 1992).

[8] Robert M. Kingdon's review of *Die Kirchenratsprotokolle der reformierten Gemeinde Emden 1557–1620* (ed. Heinz Schilling) in *Göttingische Gelehrte Anzeigen*, 246 (1994), pp. 134–5.

[9] Schilling, *Civic Calvinism in Northwestern Germany and The Netherlands* (Kirksville, MO, 1991), p. 9.

The organisation of poor relief is a point of convergence for the interests of early modern politics, religion and society. Thus social welfare administration provides a window to many issues of central importance to the Reformation. The development of Emden's system of poor relief is an impressive story. For a town hurled from a sleepy obscurity into the centre of European affairs, the creation of so elaborate and effective a structure of poor relief is an amazing achievement. It sheds a fascinating light on the capacities of a civic élite in a part of Europe which more sophisticated contemporaries considered slow-witted and rude. The city's responses to the needs of the poor are highly interesting because they combine so many currents: the need to preserve good order in urban space, the new theoretical and theological view of the indigent inspired by Protestantism, and the application of practical good sense to pressing immediate problems. Emden exhibits all these strands to a high degree and thus makes a fascinating case study.

A key characteristic of the system of social welfare in the Middle Ages was its lack of centralisation. Poor relief was usually administered by means of parish, monastic, confraternal and hospital foundations.[10] Wealthy and generous people often contributed money or land in return for masses and prayers for their souls after their deaths. Also, in most cities institutions called 'spitals' or hospitals were established to help the poor and needy. Generally smaller than modern hospitals, these institutions were not meant to provide medical aid but rather to give assistance and housing to pilgrims, orphans, the elderly, invalids or other disadvantaged.[11] By the thirteenth century charitable institutions, spurred on in part by the early work of the new Franciscan and Dominican mendicant orders, had proliferated across much of Europe and had adapted to fit better into the social and economic conditions of an increasingly urban life based ever more upon cash economies.[12] In fact, ecclesiastical poor law seems to have worked 'tolerably well' until about the fourteenth century.[13] This 'flourishing of charitable institutions' was interrupted by

---

[10] The most extensive survey of medieval poor relief institutions and methods alongside their impact upon the poor and descriptions of the daily circumstances of the medieval poor themselves is Michel Mollat, *Les Pauvres au Moyen Age* (Hachette, 1978), translated by Arthur Goldhammer, *The Poor in the Middle Ages* (New Haven, 1986).

[11] Although hospitals also sheltered sick people, the sick generally 'stayed home and died in their own beds'; Jeannine Olson, *Calvin and Social Welfare; Deacons and the Bourse française* (Selinsgrove, 1989), pp. 19–20.

[12] Mollat, *The Poor in the Middle Ages*, pp. 135–57.

[13] For instance, see Brian Tierney, *Medieval Poor Law: A Sketch of Canonical Theory and its Application in England* (Berkeley, 1959), esp. pp. 109ff.

the rise of pauperism and other social unrest beginning around the middle of the fourteenth century.

The limited centralisation in the administration of charity created many gaps in social welfare. With the coming of the Black Death, the Hundred Years' War, and greater challenges to ecclesiastic and feudal authorities, social problems multiplied across Europe. Plague, famine and war (and the poverty consequent on these crises) contributed to the growing social unrest of the later Middle Ages. While Michel Mollat probably overemphasises the role of the 'angry poor' in social uprisings, he argues convincingly that 'nostalgia for a better time, rancour, and misery combined to produce something like a festering abscess: all it took was an accident to puncture the abscess and release the built-up poisons'.[14] The number of welfare organisations and stricter regulations increased in many localities to try to curtail the rise of pauperism and plug the welfare gaps. The common perception of medieval charity is that the merit of good works associated with Catholic theology caused many people to give indiscriminately to the poor without necessarily discriminating as to the worthiness of the recipient. Some historians have demonstrated, however, that canon law did, in fact, pronounce the importance of (and provide a method for) discriminating between the poor who should and should not be given alms, and that many almsgivers in the Middle Ages distinguished between the worthy and the undeserving poor.[15] In any case, when scattered organised charity failed to provide relief to those in need, the poor were left on their own to try to alleviate their poverty.

In medieval towns, begging was already a problem: 'It became the unorganised all-pervasive form of welfare in the new urban centres.'[16] The lack of an organised church response led to localised reactions.[17]

---

[14] Mollat admits that 'it would be misleading to try to pinpoint the role of the poor in these disturbances by looking for some typical underlying process', *The Poor in the Middle Ages*, p. 212.

[15] Tierney, *Medieval Poor Law*, pp. 46ff, and 'The Decretists and the "Deserving Poor"', *Comparative Studies in Society and History*, 1 (1958/59), pp. 360–73; Pullan, *Rich and Poor in Renaissance Venice* (Cambridge, MA, 1971), pp. 11f, 197ff; and 'Catholics and the Poor in Early Modern Europe', *Transactions of the Royal Historical Society*, 26 (1976), pp. 15–34; Paul Fideler, 'Christian humanism and poor law reform in early Tudor England', *Societas*, 4 (1974), pp. 272f.

[16] Olson, *Social Welfare*, p. 20. Jean-Pierre Gutton, *La société et les pauvres en Europe* (Paris, 1974), pp. 94f, describes the increasing hostility toward vagabonds in the last century of the Middle Ages due to their rising numbers.

[17] Natalie Zemon Davis, 'Poor Relief, Humanism, and Heresy', in *Society and Culture in Early Modern France* (Stanford, 1975), pp. 37f. Here she considers the failure of medieval parish assistance and the fragmented nature of medieval poor relief. Tierney, *Medieval Poor Law*, pp. 128ff also points to the 'breakdown of parish relief' but feels that the failure has been overstated.

Increasingly, individuals and communities began to establish institutions and confraternities in order to express their concern for the poor as well as for their own souls.[18] Soon, civil authorities began to follow the lead of these lay associations and take control of social welfare, and by the early sixteenth century the magistrates of many municipalities had begun to assume at least partial responsibility and supervision of poor relief.[19]

The numbers of poor people and the varieties of poverty increased. The traditional groups had included such poor as orphans, widows, the sick, and the blind. By the end of the Middle Ages, new forms of poverty became prevalent:

> As a large number of urban wage-earners, cottagers and day-labourers lived in circumstances which even contemporaries admitted to be extremely precarious, larger, structural and cyclical changes, such as economy, war, [and] climate, could accelerate the impoverishment processes which had attained such enormous proportions in the sixteenth century and which remained at work throughout the early modern period.[20]

Furthermore, by the sixteenth century, as a result of economic difficulties and enormous population growth, vagrancy and poverty became monumental problems, especially for the cities.[21]

Of course, significant changes in the kinds of poverty and the dramatic increase in numbers of poor necessitated modifications in the medieval approach to charity; there was some tinkering and some radical change. In spite of lingering disagreements between historians over the pace of change and the character of the new methods of social welfare in the sixteenth century, there is general acknowledgement that

---

[18] For instance, see Mollat, *The Poor in the Middle Ages*, pp. 273ff; Maureen Flynn, *Sacred Charity: Confraternities and Social Welfare in Spain, 1400–1700* (Ithaca, 1989), pp. 16f.

[19] Indeed, urban magistrates began involving themselves in matters of poor relief during the Middle Ages. For instance, Strasbourg's magistrates wielded increasing direct control over the collection of alms as well as the hospitals, orphanages, and officials elected to distribute such alms, from 1263 onward; Miriam Usher Chrisman, *Strasbourg and the Reform: A Study in the Process of Change* (New Haven, 1967), p. 275; Otto Winckelmann, 'Über die ältesten Armenordnungen der Reformationszeit (1522–1525)', *Historische Vierteljahrschrift*, 17 (1914/15), p. 190.

[20] Jütte, *Poverty and Deviance in Early Modern Europe* (Cambridge, 1994), p. 2.

[21] See Robert Jütte, 'Poor Relief and Social Discipline in Sixteenth-Century Europe', *European Studies Review*, 11 (1981), p. 25; Olson, *Social Welfare*, pp. 20f; Abel Althouguia Alves, 'The Christian Social Organism and Social Welfare: The Case of Vives, Calvin and Loyola', *SCJ*, 20 (1989), p. 3; Harold Grimm, 'Luther's Contribution to Sixteenth-Century Organization of Poor Relief', *ARG*, 61 (1970), pp. 222f, points out the decline in medieval giving and the need for new approaches to poor relief.

social welfare took on a new appearance.[22] Many recent studies identify several common features or tendencies in poor relief reforms in cities across sixteenth-century Europe: centralisation of administration, a professionalisation and laicisation (e.g. a shift from clerical to lay administration), and a rationalisation of organisation.[23]

In the 1520s, some centralised municipal poor relief institutions emerged, especially in south Germany and the southern Netherlands. These gradually spread throughout north-western Europe. The trend toward intervention on the part of the magistrates in matters of poor relief had begun in the late Middle Ages, but the actual creation of centralised social welfare institutions sponsored by the civil authorities came to fruition in the 1520s.[24] Nuremberg's Poor Ordinances centralised the city's relief in 1522. Similar civic ordinances bringing about a centralisation of social welfare were adopted in Strasbourg in 1523, and in Mons and Ypres in the southern Low Countries in 1525.[25]

A typical strategy for centralisation in the German cities was the creation of a 'common chest'. This 'common chest' fund typically received the assets from the previously existing hospitals and charitable institutions, from donations and endowments, and, in Protestant cities, from the monastic and church properties that were secularised. Indeed, most Protestant cities seem to have adopted some sort of centralised 'common chest' to administer the former monastic properties along with the assets of the confraternities.[26] The fund would then be

---

[22] Both Pullan (*Rich and Poor*, pp. 198f) and Tierney (*Medieval Poor Law*, p. 132), argue that sixteenth-century social welfare practices grew out of a 'single developing tradition' (Tierney), and thus there is no distinct difference between sixteenth-century and medieval social welfare. Jütte (*Poverty and Deviance in Early Modern Europe*, p. 2), on the other hand, emphasises 'a radical departure from the beaten tracks of medieval charity'.

[23] Jütte provides a thorough overview of the various features of the sixteenth-century reorganisation of poor relief in *Poverty and Deviance*, pp. 100–142.

[24] Civic intervention should not necessarily be seen as a 'secularisation' of poor relief. Such actions by the civil authorities often had the support of the religious leadership. For instance, the Strasbourg Cathedral preacher Johannes Geiler von Kayserberg frequently advocated – as early as 1498 – that the magistrate should be responsible for the poor and poor relief; some of his writings (for instance his '11 Articles' of 1501) have been edited by Léon Dacheux, *Die ältesten Schriften Geilers von Kaysersberg* (Freiburg im Breisgau, 1882; reprinted Amsterdam, 1965).

[25] Lille followed with such a centralisation in 1527; Jean-Pierre Gutton, *La société et les pauvres en Europe (XVIe–XVIIIe siècles)* (Paris, 1974), p. 105; Thomas Fischer, *Städtische Armut und Armenfürsorge im 15. und 16. Jahrhundert* (Göttingen, 1979), pp. 266–70; for a partisan discussion, see Otto Winckelmann, 'Über die ältesten Armenordnungen der Reformationszeit', esp. part II.

[26] One need not go so far as Jütte, however, who makes the blanket claim: 'All the Protestant systems of poor relief had certain points in common: all were based upon the

administered by a specified number of laymen elected to oversee the poor and distribute the alms.[27] The authority of the magistrates over the 'common chest' varied from city to city, and the centralisation of administration did not necessarily mean complete abolition of the older institutions. For instance, in Ypres several other relief institutions survived the establishment of the 'common chest' (*bourse commune*). Indeed, three hospitals continued to function, and the administrators of the *bourse commune* co-operated with the overseers of the 'Tables of the Holy Ghost', organisations which had provided parish relief since the later Middle Ages.[28]

Another common form of centralisation was the creation of a central hospital or similar type of institution. In 1535, there were eight social welfare institutions in Geneva (seven of them hospitals) which were responsible for taking care of the city's social problems. With the creation of the Hôpital-Général in 1535, all these institutions were combined into one foundation for the care of the sick and the poor. The control of the Hôpital-Général was given to laymen, who were responsible for both administration of the hospital and the actual care of the poor. These civic officials became 'deacons' after the return of Calvin in 1541.[29]

A prototype for this kind of centralised, municipal poor relief institution originated in the 1530s. The establishment of the Aumône générale in Catholic Lyon in 1534 began a trend which quickly spread to other French cities (perhaps also inspiring Geneva's Hôpital-Général).[30] Natalie Zemon Davis examined the establishment of the Aumône générale and pointed out that although it was initially instituted temporarily to meet

---

idea of a 'common chest", *Poverty and Deviance*, pp. 105f. The claim of universality here is inaccurate, as will be illustrated in the case of Emden.

[27] For the development of the 'common chests' in various German and Dutch cities, see Winckelmann, 'Über die ältesten Armenordnungen der Reformationszeit', and 'Die Armenordnungen von Nürnberg (1522), Kitzingen (1523), Regensburg (1523) und Ypern (1525)', *ARG*, 10 (1913), pp. 242–80 and 11 (1914), pp. 1–18; for specific case studies, see, for instance, Stefan Oehmig, 'Der Wittenberger Gemeine Kasten in den ersten zweieinhalb Jahrzehnten seines Bestehens (1522/23 bis 1547)', *Jahrbuch für Geschichte des Feudalismus*, 12 (1988), pp. 229–69; William Wright, 'A Closer Look at House Poor Relief through the Common Chest and Indigence in Sixteenth-Century Hesse', *Archiv für Reformationsgeschichte*, 70 (1979), pp. 225–37.

[28] J. Nolf, *La réforme de la bienfaisance publique à Ypres au XVIe siècle* (Ghent, 1915), pp. xli–xlii.

[29] Robert Kingdon, 'Social Welfare in Calvin's Geneva', *American Historical Review*, 76 (1971), esp. pp. 52–6; Olson, *Social Welfare*, pp. 21f.

[30] R. Gascon, 'Economie et pauvreté aux XVI et XVII siècles. Lyon exemplaire et prophétique', in Michel Mollat (ed.), *Etudes sur l'histoire de la pauvreté* (Paris, 1974), pp. 747–60.

extreme needs, this institution soon became the chief method of poor relief in Lyon. The break with the earlier social welfare system is seen in Davis's description of its founding:

> Henceforth, all charitable distributions in Lyon, and most charitable services, were to be performed by a new government body, the *Aumône générale*, or by the hospitals run by the Consulate ... All the various alms given out at Saint Jean and other churches and monasteries during the year were now to be paid as a lump sum to the *Aumône*. No one was to give any handout of any kind in front of his house or in any public place (though no penalty was created for doing so), but contributions were to be given to an *Aumône générale* canister or collector. All begging was prohibited under pain of whipping and banishment.[31]

Lyon's hospital, the Hôtel Dieu, survived the creation of the Aumône générale, which co-ordinated the pre-existing relief practices.[32] A similar centralised system of municipal relief with an *aumône générale* was created in 1555 in Orléans, one of several French cities to follow the model of Lyon.[33]

Recent studies have focused on some areas which have long been considered outside the domain of centralised social welfare in the early modern period, including Catholic Italy and Spain. In Venice, the city magistrates gradually appropriated the poor relief duties of the confraternities, taking over the principal charitable institutions by the seventeenth century.[34] Bologna's confraternal hospitals (*ospedali*) underwent a process of consolidation and politicisation in the course of the fifteenth and sixteenth centuries.[35] The Spanish cities of Toledo and Zamora also experienced a gradual centralising of their charitable agencies, even if not to the extent undergone in other parts of Europe.[36] The new Europe-wide trend toward centralisation coupled

---

[31] Natalie Davis, 'Poor Relief', p. 39.

[32] Ibid., pp. 38–42.

[33] Leslie Goldsmith, *Poor Relief and Reform in Sixteenth-Century Orléans* (Ph.D. thesis, University of Wisconsin-Madison, 1980), esp. pp. 30–46, 180–206. Other French areas created aumônes généraux on the heels of Lyon's establishment, for instance, Rouen (1534), Troyes (1545), Châlons-sur-Marne (1564), Amiens (1565), Abbeville (1565), Beauvais (1573); Camille Bloch, *L'Assistance et l'état en France à la veille de la Revolution* (Geneva, 1909), p. 44. The Paris Aumône générale, most often called the Grand bureau des pauvres, was created in 1544; Barbara Diefendorf, *Beneath the Cross: Catholics and Huguenots in Sixteenth-Century Paris* (Oxford, 1991), p. 20.

[34] Pullan, *Rich and Poor*, pp. 239ff.

[35] Nicholas Terpstra, *Lay Confraternities and Civic Religion in Renaissance Bologna* (Cambridge, 1995), esp. pp. 179–216.

[36] Linda Martz, *Poverty and Welfare in Hapsburg Spain. The Example of Toledo* (Cambridge, 1983), pp. 61–158; Flynn, *Sacred Charity*, pp. 82–94, 102–10, 117–27.

with a rationalisation of organisation created a 'premeditated system' of social welfare.[37]

Such a 'premeditated system' demanded that the methods of the more fragmented and complicated system of medieval almsgiving be rationalised. In general, this meant the creation of new procedures of recordkeeping and of supervision of the poor. New rules carefully regulated bookkeeping procedures, and auditors or supervisors were regularly to oversee the accounts of expenditures and income. Furthermore, officials generally visited the poor, drawing up lists of deserving and undeserving poor. The poor could also make requests for aid on particular occasions.[38] Administrators separated those who were invalids or dependent into two groups: those needing institutional care (for instance, orphans or the sick) and those who could receive aid in their homes. For those receiving aid from home, a ticket or token was provided which allowed them to receive their weekly dole (often bread and money).[39]

Closely connected with this rationalisation of poor relief was an emphasis on social discipline.[40] Healthy and able poor were to work. In fact, new industries were often developed in order to provide occupation and promote self-support. For instance, Lyon's city government financed the rector of the Aumône générale in order to establish the silk industry in Lyon. The magistrates intended it to train not only orphan girls, but also the daughters of families on the relief rolls.[41] Furthermore, the children were to be educated and apprenticed.[42] This education included moral training, to which was tied a strong concern for the salvation of impoverished vagrants and beggars.

As a result of the movement toward more rationalised and centralised social welfare, a professionalisation of the position of poor relief administrator occurred. In order to provide better supervision of the poor, and better administration, the overseers made frequent visits to the

---

[37] The humanist cleric Jean de Vauzelles had claimed in his sermons that this kind of rationalised system would cost no more than spontaneous handouts in the street; Davis, 'Poor Relief', p. 40.

[38] For instance, Kingdon, 'Social Welfare', pp. 56–9; Davis, 'Poor Relief', pp. 40ff; Jütte, *Poverty and Deviance*, p. 102.

[39] Davis, 'Poor Relief, Humanism and Heresy', pp. 39ff, describes the procedure in Lyon.

[40] See, especially, Alves, 'Christian Social Organism' and Jütte, 'Poor Relief and Social Discipline'. Both articles stress the emphasis placed on the education and work of the poor in attempts to maintain social order.

[41] A similar arrangement was made for the cotton industry; Davis, 'Poor Relief', pp. 43f.

[42] Jütte, 'Poor Relief and Social Discipline', esp. pp. 40f; Davis, 'Poor Relief', pp. 42f; Pullan, *Rich and Poor*, pp. 402ff.

poor throughout the town. The move away from the traditional relief provided in the hospitals also led to the increased professionalisation of these relief officers. As outdoor relief was expanded, systematised and rationalised, the administrators began to attempt detailed investigations into the circumstances of each poor recipient.

Most reform statutes of the sixteenth century placed social welfare under lay control. This change often involved giving direct control of hospitals, orphanages, collection and distributions of the alms to magistrates, though poor relief administration involved the civil government to varying extents in different regions. Usually they would also have some control over the choice of officials to supervise or carry out these poor relief functions. The choice of the word 'laicisation' to describe this process is intended to distinguish a particular aspect of the overused term 'secularisation'. 'Laicisation' emphasises the sanctioning of the role of the laity in previously clerical functions. This process needs to be distinguished from other processes that are usually subsumed under the term 'secularisation': for instance, to take from the religious sphere and place in the civil sphere. Indeed, despite changes in religious values associated with charity, social welfare reforms of the sixteenth century, whether Catholic or Protestant, retained fundamentally religious foundations and significance. Especially in Reformed Protestant regions, certain relief administrators were given the church office of 'deacon'; they remained laymen, since the clergy were generally removed from a direct role in Reformed poor relief.[43] In some regions, new statutes created a complete break with the traditional methods of church control.[44] Despite this authority given to laymen, some cities still reserved some functions for the clergy. Such functions could range from assisting the administrators by exhorting donors to almsgiving to serving in administrative positions within the new charitable organisations.[45]

---

[43] Elsie McKee, *John Calvin on the Diaconate and Liturgical Almsgiving* (Geneva, 1984), pp. 120–23, discusses these meanings. Robert Henderson has argued that Calvin actually 'resacralised' (rather than 'secularised') social welfare by making it a function of an ecclesiastical office which was run by laymen; 'Sixteenth-Century Community Benevolence: An Attempt to Resacralize the Secular', *Church History*, 38 (1969), pp. 421–8. See also Kingdon, 'Calvin's Ideas about the Diaconate: Social or Theological in Origin?', in Carter Lindberg (ed.), *Piety, Politics and Ethics: Reformation Studies in Honor of George Wolfgang Forell* (Kirksville, MO, 1984), pp. 169ff.

[44] Kingdon, 'Social Welfare', p. 51. Natalie Davis, 'Poor Relief', pp. 32ff, discusses the new administration of Lyon's Aumône générale by laymen. She points out the justifications given for lay control in this Catholic city: corruption of the clergy and high evaluation of the laity.

[45] For instance, Brian Pullan, 'The Famine in Venice and the New Poor Law, 1527–1529', *Bollettino dell' Istituto di Storia della Società e dello Stato Veneziano*, 5/6 (1963/64), pp. 143f.

Perhaps the most pressing social problem facing the social reformers of the sixteenth century was that of beggars and vagrants.[46] All areas of Europe, whether Protestant or Catholic, had to try to solve the problem, and discussions about the merits and harm of begging dominated much of the intellectual debate on the subject of social welfare reform. While most writers, especially the humanists and Protestant theologians, argued for a prohibition of begging, a few – primarily some Catholic theologians – supported continued begging with some limitations.[47] Consequently, when poor relief reforms were initiated, the question of how to control begging generally came up in one form or another. A common belief which seems to have guided most of the reforms was that each city or parish should have to provide only for its own residents. Thus hostility toward foreign vagrants grew in the fifteenth century, as vagrants were increasingly seen as a social danger and a cause of criminality and brigandage.[48] This 'suspicion' of vagrants and non-residents found its way into many sixteenth-century ordinances. Most legislation, however, was not very successful.[49] Contemporary debates over the problem of begging in Catholic towns proved especially troublesome, primarily resulting from the mendicant orders' opposition to any prohibitions.[50] So, although Protestant towns usually outlawed begging entirely, Catholics often retained some form of licensed begging.

Humanists were among the most active advocates working for changes in the perception of the poor and in social welfare. Juan Luis Vives, Jean de Vauzelles, Thomas More and Thomas Starkey articulated new methods of dealing with the poor, including the ideas of centralisation and rationalisation of the relief institutions, and education of the poor.[51] Perhaps the most eloquent call for poor relief reform in the sixteenth

---

[46] Natalie Davis, 'Poor Relief', pp. 24–7, contains a striking portrayal of begging.

[47] Jütte, *Poverty and Deviance*, p. 101.

[48] Gutton, *La société et les pauvres en Europe*, p. 94.

[49] See, for instance, Natalie Davis, 'Poor Relief', p. 39; Wright, 'A Closer Look', pp. 225, 231; McKee, *Diaconate*, pp. 96f; Olson, *Social Welfare*, pp. 22–3; Jütte, *Poverty and Deviance*, p. 167.

[50] Natalie Davis, 'Poor Relief', p. 17.

[51] Juan Luis Vives, *De subventione pauperum* (1526), in F. R. Salter (ed.), *Some Early Tracts on Poor Relief* (London, 1926); ibid., also translated ('On Assistance to the Poor') by Alice Tobriner in *A Sixteenth-Century Urban Report*, Part II (Chicago, 1971). Davis, 'Poor Relief, Humanism, and Heresy', pp. 231–6. Fideler, 'Christian humanism and poor law reform in early Tudor England'; Geoffrey Elton, 'An Early Tudor Poor Law', *Economic History Review*, 2nd series, 6 (1953), pp. 55–7, questions the humanist influence on the English statute of 1536; see also Elton's 'Reform by Statute: Thomas Starkey's *Dialogue* and Thomas Cromwell's Policy', *Proceedings of the British Academy*, 54 (1968), pp. 165–88.

century was Vives's *De subventione pauperum*. Published in 1526, it was written at the request of the mayor and city council of Bruges. As a backdrop to his innovative organisational proposals, including a centralisation and rationalisation of institutions and a prohibition of begging, Vives advocated a new vision of the poor.

Vives wrote that his plan 'will not prevent a man from becoming a pauper but will prevent him from remaining long in that condition, by promptly stretching forth a hand to help him to his feet'. Indeed, the importance of education was central to Vives's vision, especially for poor children; without such training, the children would learn only on the streets. Vives ended his treatise by listing the material and spiritual advantages that would result from his measures. Theft and acts of violence would decrease, greater concord would prevail, and it would be 'safer, healthier, and pleasanter to attend churches and to dwell in the city'. Beyond these civic advantages, however, would be, most importantly, the profit to the poor themselves:

> [the former poor] will regain judgement, sensibility, piety. They will live among men like citizens, disciplined, observant of human laws; they will keep their hands pure from acts of violence; they will serve God truly and honestly; they will be men; they will be what they are called, Christians. What else is this, I ask, than to have restored many thousands of men to themselves and to have won them for Christ?

'They will be men.' Such was the goal of the humanist's call for poor relief reforms. Not only would the new methods relieve many of the social ills associated with poverty, they would go even further to restore the individual to proper values and Christian duty through education. Such moral training was necessary because poverty could never be completely eliminated. Thus, as Vives insisted, 'Students should learn to live frugally, but neatly and cleanly, and to be content with little.'[52]

Intellectual fervour abounded on the topic of social welfare in the sixteenth century, as writers from all persuasions – humanist and secular writers, alongside Protestant and Catholic theologians – clamoured for poor relief reform.[53] Calls for reform did not, however, always go uncriticised. Fierce debates raged between writers with differing visions of the poor and of the necessary reform methods.[54]

---

[52] Vives, *De subventione pauperum*, in Salter (ed.), pp. 36, 44–7, 21.

[53] Jütte provides a very useful appendix with short biographical sketches of several of the important poor relief reformers of the sixteenth century; *Poverty and Deviance*, pp. 204–16, compare p. 101.

[54] See Flynn's discussion of welfare reform in Spain, *Sacred Charity*, pp. 75–114 (esp. pp. 91–9 for the intense argument between Domingo de Soto and Juan de Medina).

The exact relationship between Vives's humanistic writings and the emergence of new social welfare methods is a matter of debate. The argument that the poor relief reforms in the Netherlands and northern Europe were initiated by Vives and other Christian humanists has been generally discredited.[55] Vives's treatise was not published in the Low Countries until 1526; the reforms in Mons and Ypres had been initiated in 1525. Vives's treatise can, therefore, be viewed in part as a confirmation of the reform changes already under way in the Low Countries.[56] Nevertheless, the values and ideas represented by Vives and other northern humanists promoted poor relief reform after 1526 as Vives's plan circulated widely across Europe.[57] The significance given to Christian humanists as the driving force behind poor relief change often relates inversely to the emphasis a scholar places on the Protestant Reformation in reshaping medieval charity.

Certain interpretations about sixteenth-century poor relief stem from overstated generalisations about the medieval church's role in social welfare. For instance, Ernst Troeltsch associated the entire welfare operations of the medieval church with the practice of mere 'charity'.[58] He described Catholic social welfare simply as indiscriminate individual action in giving alms. In addition to emphasising the unsystematic nature of medieval poor relief, he saw medieval social welfare's fundamental nature as ecclesiastical, with church control of the various endowed charitable institutions. Furthermore, many Protestant polemicists criticised Catholic poor relief because of the Catholic doctrine that good works contribute to the salvation of those who give alms.[59]

---

[55] See Otto Winckelmann, 'Über die ältesten Armenordnungen', pp. 376–84. Winckelmann's goal in discrediting the humanist initiative was to make the case for a German influence, in order to emphasise the impact of Protestant ideas on poor relief organisation.

[56] Kingdon, 'Social Welfare', p. 68, points out that from time to time 'rather than initiating change, intellectuals often justified the changes engineered by the practical business leaders of the community'. Calvin's *Ecclesiastical Ordinances* of 1541 for Geneva can be viewed in a similar way.

[57] Vives's treatise was soon translated into French, Spanish, and Italian; Tobriner, *A Sixteenth-Century Urban Report*, p. 18. The English Poor Law 1536 was almost definitely influenced by Vives's work; Fideler, pp. 280–85. Franz Ehrle, *Beiträge zur Geschichte und Reform der Armenpflege* (Freiburg im Breisgau, 1881), p. 29; Winckelmann, 'Über die ältesten Armenordnungen', pp. 387.

[58] The church's 'reaction [to social suffering] did not take the shape of social reform, or of organic change: it was simply and solely the work of charity'; Troeltsch, *The Social Teaching of the Christian Churches*, trans. by Olive Wyon (2 vols, New York, 1931; original German published 1911), I, 134.

[59] Troeltsch, I, 133–8. Tierney, *Medieval Poor Law*, pp. 46ff.

These traditional characterisations of medieval charity have generally been contrasted with descriptions of Protestant attitudes toward poor relief. Again according to Troeltsch, Protestant leaders and churches achieved a far-reaching 'social policy'. Protestantism developed a much more rational form of state intervention in social welfare, one that was concerned with the welfare of the poor themselves.[60] According to these arguments, then, the poor relief changes of the sixteenth century resulted from the spread of Protestantism.

Such arguments had their origins in the sixteenth century. Luther and other Protestant polemicists had railed against Catholic charity with its doctrine of good works and thus denounced the benevolent man for being primarily concerned with himself. Moreover, some sixteenth-century critics sometimes associated poor relief reforms with Protestantism. Some contemporaries in Catholic cities like Lyon and Ypres viewed their own social welfare reforms as being tainted with heresy. For instance, Vives wrote in 1527 that the Bishop of Tournai's vicar was attacking his treatise *De subventione pauperum*: 'he rules that it is heretical and Lutheran'. In 1532, the Inquisitor of Lyon attacked a sermon by the French cleric and humanist Jean de Vauzelles, who urged sweeping new welfare measures (which were eventually adopted). The Inquisitor said it was filled with errors and was 'pernicious to Catholic piety', and he further argued that Lyon had more to fear from a host of heretics than it did from an excess of poor vagrants.[61] Some Catholic regions were even hesitant to pass laws prohibiting begging on the grounds that such laws were 'Lutheran'.[62]

Throughout most of the nineteenth century, historians and theologians saw the theology of the Lutheran Reformation as the initial force which motivated the reform of the traditional methods of poor relief. In the last quarter of the nineteenth century, however, some Catholic scholars began to question that conventional view. Most significant among them were Franz Ehrle and Georg Ratzinger.[63] They argued that in many instances Catholic poor relief reforms had been attempted before Protestant reforms, and distinguished between what they saw as a two-fold movement in the reform of poor relief at the beginning of the

---

[60] Troeltsch, II, 557, 565ff.

[61] Natalie Davis, 'Poor Relief', pp. 17, 52–5. Although mendicant orders denounced the Ypres 'common chest' as heretical, the fundamental principles of the city's relief changes were upheld by the Sorbonne in 1531; Salter (ed.), *Some Early Tracts*, pp. 32–4.

[62] Olson, *Social Welfare*, pp. 22f.

[63] Ehrle's *Beiträge* and his 'Die Armenordnungen von Nürnberg (1522) und von Ypern (1525)', *Historisches Jahrbuch*, 9 (1888), pp. 450–79; Georg Ratzinger, *Geschichte der Kirchlichen Armenpflege* (2nd edn, Freiburg im Breisgau, 1884).

sixteenth century: one purely socio-economic and originating in the fifteenth century, and one specifically Protestant (that is 'Lutheran') reform based on the Saxon Church Ordinances.[64]

Otto Winckelmann gave the most comprehensive argument in response to these claims in the early twentieth century.[65] He disputed Ehrle's claims that there was no recognisable influence of Lutheran theology upon the Nuremberg poor relief reforms and that the earliest reforms (1522) were simply continuations of previous reform efforts. Winckelmann was also upset by the utilisation of Ehrle's perspective by other scholars.[66] Winckelmann countered with an analysis of the earliest poor relief ordinances of the Reformation period in order to argue that the original reforms were Lutheran. He claimed that they had arisen out of Lutheran Nuremberg and spread, through Strasbourg, to Ypres.[67] After displacing Vives's treatise as the initial spark for reform, Winckelmann then supplanted the theory of a northern humanist inspiration of the poor relief reforms in the Low Countries with a theory of German, specifically Lutheran, influence. In the mid-1920s, the Catholic historian Paul Bonenfant carefully assessed this argument.[68] Noting both the temporal and qualitative closeness between the German reforms and those in the Netherlands, Bonenfant cautiously accepted some of Winckelmann's schema. He went on to make the case, however, that the Ypres city leaders did not perceive any 'Lutheranness' in the Nuremberg social welfare reforms.[69]

The recent outpouring of historical research on early modern social welfare has gone a step further in demonstrating the flaws in assuming

---

[64] Ehrle, 'Die Armenordnungen', p. 479. Ehrle ends his second essay with the phrase, 'muß die 1521 und 1522 in Nürnberg erstandene Armenordnung aus ersterer Bewegung [in other words, the purely socio-economic reforms] hergeleitet werden'. These certainly were the fighting words which inspired Winckelmann's work.

[65] 'Die Armenordnungen von Nürnberg', pp. 242–72; 'Über die ältesten Armenordnungen', pp. 187–228, 361–440.

[66] Winckelmann complained that the economic historian Ludwig Feuchtwanger 'accepted the interpretation of Ehrle without deliberation' and that Feuchtwanger's work 'provokes [one] very much toward criticism in its complete interpretation as well as in the details'; 'Die Armenordnungen von Nürnberg', pp. 242f, 'Über die ältesten Armenordnungen', pp. 187f. See Feuchtwanger, 'Geschichte der sozialen Politik und des Armenwesens im Zeitalter der Reformation', *Jahrbuch für Gesetzgebung, Verwaltung und Volkswirtschaft*, 32 (1908), pp. 167–204 and 33 (1909), pp. 191–228.

[67] 'Über die ältesten Armenordnungen', esp. the discussion on pp. 373–6, 385–7.

[68] 'Les origines et le caractère de la réforme de la bienfaisance publique aux Pays-Bas sous le règne de Charles-Quint', *Revue Belge de Philosophie et d'Histoire*, 5 (1926), pp. 887–904 and 6 (1927), pp. 207–30; see also 'Un aspect du régime calviniste à Bruxelles au XVIième siècle: la question de la bienfaisance', *Bulletin de la Commission Royale d'Histoire*, 89 (1925), pp. 265–358.

[69] 'Les origines et le caractère', esp. pp. 216, 220–23.

a direct relationship between Luther's theological reforms and the reforms of poor relief in the sixteenth century. These studies have analysed
local charitable institutions in their religious, cultural and municipal or
regional contexts, and have demonstrated that the common poor relief
reforms of the sixteenth century cut across confessional boundaries.[70]
Pullan, for instance, has called into question the assumptions about the
'Lutheranness' of the early sixteenth-century reform plans. He demonstrated that Nuremberg's poor relief organisation was modelled upon
the *Monti di Pietà* which had emerged in Italy.[71] Although many of the
southern German towns which initiated reforms were Lutheran or had
a number of Lutheran sympathisers, there was nothing inherently Lutheran or Protestant about the reform programmes; the acceptance of
these reforms in Catholic territories substantiates this argument. Natalie
Davis's study of the previously mentioned Aumône générale of Lyon has
demonstrated that co-operation existed between Catholics and Protestants in organising the newly centralised poor relief institution, and that
even during the Religious Wars the Aumône continued to receive contributions from both confessions. Her conclusion has been largely confirmed
by recent case studies of early modern social welfare:

> Protestant and Catholic cities and cities of mixed religious compo-
> sition initiated rather similar reforms, usually learning from each
> other's efforts. Lyon is an example of a religious coalition for
> welfare reform dominated by Catholics. Is Nuremberg an example
> of welfare reform by a religious coalition dominated by Protes-
> tants? The fact that reform in poor relief cut across religious
> boundaries and that Protestants and Catholics worked together on
> it shows the extent to which it rested on values and insights com-
> mon to both groups.[72]

---

[70] For example, Terpstra, *Lay Confraternities and Civic Religion in Renaissance Bologna* (Cambridge, 1995); Brian Pullan, *Rich and Poor in Renaissance Venice* (1971), and
'Catholics and the Poor in Early Modern Europe', *Transactions of the Royal Historical
Society*, 26 (1976), pp. 15–34; Natalie Davis, 'Poor Relief, Humanism, and Heresy'
(1975); Linda Martz, *Poverty and Welfare in Hapsburg Spain: The Example of Toledo*
(Cambridge, 1983); Robert Jütte, *Obrigkeitliche Armenfürsorge in deutschen Reichsstädten
der frühen Neuzeit: Städtisches Armenwesen in Frankfurt am Main und Köln* (Cologne,
1984); Kathryn Norberg, *Rich and Poor in Grenoble, 1600–1814* (Berkeley, 1985);
Martin Dinges, *Stadtarmut in Bordeaux 1525–1675. Alltag, Politik, Mentalitäten* (Bonn,
1988); Jeannine Olson, *Calvin and Social Welfare* (London, 1989); Maureen Flynn,
Sacred Charity: Confraternities and Social Welfare in Spain, 1400–1700 (Ithaca, 1989);
Lee Palmer Wandel, *Always Among Us: Images of the Poor in Zwingli's Zürich* (Cambridge, 1990).

[71] The *Monte di Pietà* was a new type of loan institution intended to protect poor
people from usurers; *Rich and Poor*, pp. 254ff, 281.

[72] Davis, 'Poor Relief', pp. 56–60.

The process of rationalisation, centralisation and politicisation – trends frequently linked to the Protestant Reformation – can be found in Catholic cities as well. There were certainly differences between Catholic and Protestant poor relief systems, but a simple explanation based solely upon theological factors does not fully grasp the local nature of poor relief reforms.[73] Even the typical differences between Protestants and Catholics with respect to approaches to begging, for example, do not fall neatly across confessional lines in practice. For instance, the Protestant Elizabethan Poor Law allowed certain licensed begging, while the Catholic cities of Lyon and Ypres banned begging completely, and Catholic Emperor Charles V authorised prohibitions of begging in territories of the Holy Roman Empire in 1531.[74]

Historians generally agree that the reforms of the sixteenth century, taken as an entire system, mark a distinctly new approach to the previous methods of poor relief, but some scholars have been careful to emphasise that many of the common features of the sixteenth century had precursors in the Middle Ages. Thus they have debated the origins of laicisation (in particular, the role of the laity in medieval confraternal charity), and the occasional attempts in the Middle Ages to prohibit begging and to centralise charitable activities under civil control. For instance, canon law provided a discrimination against able-bodied beggars which was legislated in England in 1349 and 1388; Brian Pullan argues that these English laws and similar prohibitions in medieval Spain contributed to the ease with which sixteenth-century laws were adopted. Both Brian Tierney and Pullan have traced and emphasised the development of social welfare through medieval theory/canon law and practice.[75] Hence, these historians see the sixteenth-century reforms as continuations or accelerations of past trends.[76] The rationalised organisation and centralised administration so common in the sixteenth-century

---

[73] Some recent studies have, however, continued to point to the importance of Protestant ideas in the early poor relief reforms. See Ole Peter Grell and Andrew Cunningham, 'The Reformation and changes in welfare provision in early modern Northern Europe', in *Health Care and Poor Relief in Protestant Europe* (London, 1997), pp. 1–42; Grell, 'Religious duty', pp. 257–63; Grell, 'Protestant imperative', pp. 43–65; Grimm, 'Luther's Contribution', pp. 222–34 (esp. pp. 222–3); Carter Lindberg, '"There Should Be No Beggars Among Christians": Karlstadt, Luther, and the Origins of Protestant Poor Relief', *Church History*, 46 (1977), pp. 313–34.

[74] Gutton, *La société et les pauvres en Europe*, p. 105.

[75] Tierney, *Medieval Poor Law*, pp. 128–9, 132; Tierney, 'The Decretists and the "Deserving Poor"'; Pullan, *Rich and Poor*, pp. 197–201.

[76] Michel Mollat, *Les Pauvres au Moyen Age*, traces the development of poor relief and attitudes toward the poor throughout the Middle Ages. He notes a shift in attitudes taking place in the late Middle Ages. Antecedents to many common sixteenth-century reforms occurred at that time.

reform programmes were often simply 'superimposed' on to the 'old' system of medieval social welfare.[77]

Pullan has come up with an interesting notion which attempts to resolve this historiographic question regarding the 'newness' of sixteenth-century welfare reforms. He argues that even if no single feature of sixteenth-century poor relief was without medieval roots, the combination of features which made up the reforms and the widespread adoption of the reforms can be considered 'new':

> In general, poor relief in western Europe in the fourteenth and fifteenth centuries fails in many respects to conform to the image created by later historians ... Many changes once supposedly located in the sixteenth century were anticipated, at least in theory and in principle, by earlier generations. Very likely, some sixteenth-century changes in philanthropy and social legislation were changes in degree rather than in kind; quantitative changes, rather than changes in principle; changes stimulated by graver economic needs, rather than by radical alterations in intellectual attitudes ... To say this is not to belittle the achievements of sixteenth-century Europeans, for much significant historical change is quantitative rather than qualitative, and much revolution is accomplished by revival.[78]

Thus the sheer quantity of change makes the sixteenth century a vital period for the study and comparison of social welfare institutions and attitudes toward the poor.

The broad scope of Emden's social welfare system as it developed in the sixteenth century and the fact that five of its sixteenth-century institutions survived well into this century have contributed to a sense of local pride in Emden regarding the city's poor relief institutions. Among the institutions that we will see in the coming chapters, the Clementiner Shipper's Brotherhood, the Reformed deacons of the local poor (so-called *haussitzenden*, or house-sitting, poor), and the deacons of the refugee poor (so-called *fremdlingen*, or foreign, poor), continue to the present; the town's hospital (the Gasthaus) burned down in 1938 and was never rebuilt; the Grain Reserve slowly ceased to function in the two decades after World War II. Indeed, in the last 150 years local historians have written a number of brief descriptions

---

[77] In Orléans, for instance, the medieval Hôtel-Dieu was retained with a variety of administrative reforms during the course of the sixteenth century, and it complemented the newly centralised system of the Aumône générale; Goldsmith, 'Poor Relief', pp. 57–179, esp. 76–82. The examples of Ypres and Lyon, which illustrate the survival of some of the traditional institutions, have been mentioned above.

[78] Pullan, *Rich and Poor*, pp. 198f.

of the sixteenth-century development of these institutions.[79] Yet, none of
these goes beyond a 'local history' (*geschichtliche Heimatskunde*) approach of praising ancestors for founding such enduring institutions.
Little attempt has been made to describe exactly how or why they were
formed and organised and how they functioned.[80] A recently published
prosopographic analysis of the administrators of Emden's five major
poor relief institutions provides a useful description of the overlapping
networks of welfare, church and civic administrators from the late sixteenth into the eighteenth century, though its reliance on incomplete lists
of names and almost total dependence on the incomplete secondary
literature to describe poor relief operations and administrations lead to
some inaccuracies.[81] The example of Emden's *Becken* diaconate provides
an instructional example of the limitations of previous work on Emden's
poor relief. The *Becken*, as we will see in Chapter 4, was one of the city's
important innovations in the mid-sixteenth century, as Emden's church
leaders attempted to create a separate diaconate with a specifically restricted function: to provide solely for poor people who were members of
the Reformed congregation. Yet it is never mentioned in any of the 'local
history' articles on the city's poor relief institutions, probably because the
Becken diaconate survived only two decades and these articles have been
interested essentially in describing the centuries-old origins of Emden's
existing institutions. The only mention of the *Becken* in any secondary
literature appears in the prosopographic analysis of relief administrators,
but the failure even here to investigate the origins or motivations of the
diaconate led to a number of inaccuracies and an incomplete understanding of Emden's sixteenth-century social welfare developments.[82]

---

[79] Pastor J. Conrad, *Gedenkschrift zur Gasthaus- und Gasthauskirchefrage* (type-
script, ArchGK no. 120; Emden, 1919); [no name], 'Emdens Einrichtungen zu wohlthätigen
Zwecken', *Ostfriesisches Monatsblatt für provinzielle Interessen*, 2 (1874), pp. 165–73,
371–5, 400–404; Leo Fürbringer, *Die Stadt Emden in Gegenwart und Vergangenheit*
(Emden, 1892), pp. 134–8; O. G. Houtrouw, *Ostfriesland. Eine geschichtlich-ortskundige
Wanderung gegen Ende der Fürstenzeit* (Aurich, 1889), pp. 47ff; Hermann Meier, 'Das
Gasthaus und das Privilegium der 'Särgemacherei'', *Ostfriesisches Monatsblatt für
provinzielle Interessen*, 1 (1873), pp. 480–87; M. Minolts, 'Die Clementiner Brüderschaft
in Emden', *Ostfreesland. Ein Kalender für Jedermann*, 20 (1933), pp. 151–2, and his
'Emdens Bysejaager', *Ostfreesland. Ein Kalender für Jederman*, 23 (1936), pp. 157–8; J.
Mülder, *Die Diakonie der Fremdlingen-Armen 1558–1858* (Emden, 1858; reprint Emden,
1958); [no name], 'Ursprung des Fremdlingen-Armen-Institutes zu Emden', *Frisia*, III
(1844), pp. 162–3.

[80] An exception to this generalization must be made for Mülder's narrative of the
fremdlingen deacons, the most detailed of these studies, which does utilize the surviving
account books in order to describe the operations of the diaconate.

[81] Marion Weber, 'Emden – Kirche und Gesellschaft in einer Stadt der Frühneuzeit' (2
parts), *EJb*, 68 (1988), pp. 78–107 and 69 (1989), pp. 39–81.

[82] Weber, 'Kirche und Gesellschaft', I, 91–2.

The present study corrects many misconceptions about Emden's social welfare system in order to present a comprehensive picture of the way poor relief was administered in the sixteenth century, taking advantage of Emden's remarkable story to shed additional light on social welfare and provision for the poor as an aspect of the social history of the Reformation period. The various institutions which emerged in the middle of the century provided a complex net of sometimes competing, sometimes co-operating services. This book emphasises the administrators of those institutions, how they functioned and the types of relief they provided. Indeed, we will witness how the institutions evolved throughout the period – at times due to religious ideals, at times due to the necessities of economics, famine and plague, and at times due to civic pride, political struggles and warfare.

While Emden's surviving medieval and early modern sources are not complete for any institution, the exceptional quality of several important sources allows the reconstruction of many aspects of the city's evolving system of poor provision. The sources before 1500 are scanty, but the town's very rich notarial collection of contracts and testaments begins in 1509 and continues throughout the period.[83] The notebook of criminal complaints in Emden provides additional insights into the period from 1510 to 1557.[84] From the second half of the century, six exceptionally important and useful sources survive. Three account books of the local *haussitzenden* deacons and two account books of the refugee *fremdlingen* deacons provide a wonderful means by which to view some of the actual institutional workings of poor provision; the minutes of the Emden church consistory meetings begin in 1557 and offer the church's perspective on a number of poor relief matters.[85] Finally, the scattered correspondence and accounting records in the church and city archives help to reveal some of the motivations and concerns of the administrators of the poor relief institutions.[86]

---

[83] Almost all surviving pre-1500 sources have been collected in the *Ostfriesisches Urkundenbuch*, 3 vols (Emden, 1878, 1881; Aurich, 1975), (cited as OUB). The contracts and testaments are in the *Emden Kontraktenprotokollen*, in STAA, Rep. 234 (cited as EKP).

[84] *Querimoniale Civitatis Emedense*, in STAA, Rep. 241, Msc. A168 (cited as Quer.).

[85] ArchGK nos 1117, 1118, 3001, 3194 for the *haussitzenden* deacons; *Fremdlingen I* and *Fremdlingen II* for the *fremdlingen* deacons. The *fremdlingen* books list over 6 000 refugee poor who received alms from the deacons – often with the recipient's name, place of origin, trade, age, and family status. An additional account book for the *Gasthaus* survives after 1595, too late for this study, but it allows for some useful comparisons: in StaE, GII/3/1. The church consistory minutes have recently been edited by Heinz Schilling, *Die Kirchenratsprotokolle der reformierten Gemeinde Emden 1557–1620* (2 vols, Cologne and Vienna, 1989–92), (cited as KRP).

[86] For a complete list of the archival sources see Section I of the Bibliography.

Thus the quality of Emden's surviving (though incomplete) sources allows the modern reader to understand not only the extent of the organisational system of relief but the painstaking care given to individual cases of poor provision later in the sixteenth century. Though not all poor relief recipients were enthusiastic about such individual attention, the administrators strove to maintain social order and reduce poverty by spending much time emphasising education, training, work and discipline, as well as provision for the poor. Emden's amazing, though previously untold, story of social welfare developments will help delineate more clearly the complex and varied interplay of religious, socio-economic and political forces motivating social welfare changes of the early modern period. Emden's leaders imaginatively confronted newly emerging poor relief problems, yet their effective innovations were often tempered by a continuity with traditional methods and institutions of provision – methods and institutions which first appeared in Emden's surviving sources around the turn of the sixteenth century. The next chapter will investigate poor provision in Emden during the opening decades of the sixteenth century and lay out the pre-Reformation social welfare landscape. This will then enable the subsequent chapters to depict more clearly the evolution of the city's social welfare in the light of the religious changes and practical problems later in the century.

CHAPTER TWO

Pre-Reformation Poor Relief in Emden

> Before the Reformation, the poor sought aid from a plethora of institutions, some providing alms, in food or coin, and some providing shelter as well ... A variety of these institutions in differing combinations could be found in any town. Frequently they competed for resources, and their responsibilities to the poor overlapped. The poor could and often did seek aid from a number of institutions within the same town or same region.
>
> 'Social Welfare', *The Oxford Encyclopedia of the Reformation*[1]

Though perhaps not a plethora, Emden's combination of social welfare institutions and activities apparently met the poor relief needs of the small town during the fifteenth century. Mendicant orders in East Frisia, particularly the Franciscans in the Emden suburb of Faldern, collected alms specifically for the poor. Several lay confraternities and trade guilds provided relief for their members. The town also had a hospital or two, a plague house, and a number of institutions of a very local character, such as *Gotteskammern*, which were individual one-room apartments to provide in-house support for the poor in need of short- and long-term housing and care. An apparent increase in lay poor relief institutions in the opening decades of the sixteenth century indirectly implies a growing need for social welfare provision in Emden. The town's population increased with its regional economic and political significance, and the periphery of town, especially, became home to growing numbers of poor (or those perched precariously at the precipice of poverty). Although the social welfare developments of the early sixteenth century were not as dramatic as those to come, they corresponded to Emden's late medieval rise as the economic and political centre of East Frisia.

Emden's Medieval Setting

A sleepy, backwater village at the beginning of the sixteenth century, Emden was catapulted to the forefront of European affairs during the second half of the century. The rapid evolution of the city later in the

---

[1] Lee Palmer Wandel, 'Social Welfare', *The Oxford Encyclopedia of the Reformation*, ed. Hans Hillerbrand (Oxford, 1996), vol. 4, pp. 78–9.

Map 2.1   Emden in around 1574 (from Georg Braun and Frans Hogenberg's *Civitates orbis terrarum*)

sixteenth century makes Emden important for scholars of the Reformation and early modern Europe. Although Emden's gradual rise to local
economic and political prominence during the fifteenth century provides no foreshadowing of the town's later sudden boom, it helps explain
the shape of its later developments.

The territory of East Frisia lay in the north-western hinterland of the
Holy Roman Empire. Separated from the rest of Germany by a belt of
marsh and moor which made travel difficult during much of the year,
the East Frisian 'half-island', as it is sometimes called, maintained a
close economic and cultural relationship with the neighbouring Netherlands. Beginning in the late Middle Ages, East Frisia followed the same
linguistic development as Groningen and the eastern Netherlands with
the gradual replacement of the traditional Frisian with Middle Low
German.[2]

East Frisia's peculiar religious development in the Middle Ages resulted
largely from the territory's partitioning between the bishoprics of Münster,
Oldenburg, and the archdiocese of Bremen (see Map 2.2). The south-
west corner of East Frisia, which included Emden, belonged to the diocese
of Münster. Emden was more than 100 miles from the bishop in Münster,
and this Frisian portion of the bishopric was separated entirely from the
rest of the bishopric by the diocese of Oldenburg. The boundaries formed
by the medieval religious situation are strikingly similar to the confessional lines formed after the Reformation: the area around Emden became
predominantly Calvinist; the north-eastern portion of East Frisia was
Lutheran, while Catholicism survived along the southern edge of the
territory. The relative isolation of the Frisian region of the diocese of
Münster from the bishop in Münster resulted in a certain independence
within its medieval ecclesiastical organisation. For instance, the bishops
of Münster allowed control of the provost, who was a layman here, to be
transferred to the ruling local families (*Häuptlinge*).[3] In the local region

---

[2] Louis Hahn, *Die Ausbreitung der neuhochdeutschen Schriftsprache in Ostfriesland*
(Leipzig, 1912), pp. 1–5.

[3] On the typical duties and functions of the provosts in the Frisian region of the
bishopric of Münster, see Gerda Krüger, *Die münsterische Archidiakonat Friesland in
seinem Ursprung und seiner rechtsgeschichtlichen Entwicklung bis zum Ausgang des
Mittelalters* (Hildesheim, 1925), pp. 58–66; the role of the Frisian provost in Münster
was also described in a document from Pope Alexander VI from 1492, *OUB* no. 1304.
The importance of the provosts' lay character is stressed and the variances within the
territory are discussed by Menno Smid, *Ostrfriesische Kirchengeschichte* (Pewsum, 1974),
pp. 28–37, 40–51; also, Smid, 'Zur Geschichte und Bedeutung des Ostfriesischen
Interessentenwahlrechts', *Jahrbuch der Gesellschaft für niedersächsische Kirchengeschichte*,
68 (1970), pp. 39–58; Bernd Kappelhoff, 'Die Reformation in Emden', part I, *EJb*, 57
(1977), pp. 94f; Hajo van Lengen, *Geschichte des Emsiger Landes vom frühen 13. bis
zum späten 15. Jahrhundert* (Aurich, 1973), pp. 198ff.

Map 2.2 Medieval East Frisian ecclesiastical boundaries (after Menno Smid, 'Ostfriesland', p. 162)

including Emden, for example, the ruling Abdena family received the office of provost in the thirteenth century, and they possessed the lay office as an inheritable family holding for five generations until they were ousted in the fifteenth century. The Abdena's provost selected the senior priest in Emden's parish church (the so-called Grosse Kirche). In 1485 the pope granted the count the right to appoint all benefices in East Frisia.[4]

---

[4] *OUB* no. 614.

The economic importance of Emden's position at the mouth of the Ems river had begun to grow in the early fifteenth century.[5] The town's authorisation in 1412 to charge customs on certain products and its right to hold a market (*Stapelrecht*) led to a gradual migration of many merchant families into Emden from market cities farther up the Ems. At this time, most of the settlement in Emden was centred on Pelzerstrasse, the oldest street in Emden, and extended northward, perhaps as far as Grossestrasse (see Map 2.3). Even into the first decades of the sixteenth century, the area north of Grossestrasse was referred to as 'outside the northern gates'. The Emden markets offered products of the rural East Frisian hinterland: local East Frisian cattle, butter and cheese were exchanged at the Emden markets for products which were not produced locally in the countryside, especially rye, beer, wood and other raw materials. East Frisian farmers primarily raised livestock and only secondarily grew crops. Their main crop was barley, but farmers also occasionally grew oats and beans, some wheat, and a little rye (beer could not be brewed locally because of the impurity of the water).[6] Dependence on imported rye to make bread continued throughout the sixteenth century and had noticeable effects on mid-sixteenth-century poor relief. For instance, deacons had to arrange for frequent purchases of rye, and local citizens formed the Grain Reserve to ensure the availability of inexpensive grain.

Throughout the Middle Ages, East Frisia had no centralised political authority. Instead, numerous chieftains (*Häuptlinge*) exercised power in each of the local regions within East Frisia.[7] Only in the mid-1400s did the Cirksena family, from the western coast of East Frisia, gain control of Emden and begin an attempt to exert authority over all East Frisia. The chieftain Ulrich Cirksena saw Emden as a natural governmental seat for East Frisia and began to expand the city by financing large construction projects, including an enlargement of the Grosse Kirche with a gothic choir. Ulrich built his own castle in Emden (to replace the castle of the earlier Abdena family), and he and his descendants took up residence in the town. Gradually, over the second half of the fifteenth century, the Cirksena's title grew from *Häuptling* to 'count *in* East Frisia' to 'count *of* East Frisia'.[8] In 1493 the Cirksena Count

---

[5] For the development of shipping and trade in fifteenth-century East Frisia, see Bernhard Hagedorn, *Ostfrieslands Handel und Schiffahrt im 16. Jahrhundert*, vol. I (Berlin, 1910), pp. 1–60.

[6] Ibid., I, 2.

[7] On the emergence of the *Häuptlinge*, see van Lengen, *Geschichte des Emsiger Landes*; Heinrich Schmidt, *Politische Geschichte Ostfrieslands* (Leer, 1975), pp. 62–76.

[8] *OUB* no. 807 (1 October 1464); ibid. no. 1433 (5 April 1495).

Map 2.3 Key locations in Emden (detail from map of Emden around 1610)

Edzard I (ruled 1491–1528) signed treaties in which the Hanseatic city of Hamburg and the bishop of Münster ceded their rights over Emden to the Cirksena family.[9] Hamburg additionally recognised Emden's right to collect customs and duties on passing ships (*Vorbeifahrtsrecht*) as an old custom.[10] Having thus secured his own authority over Emden and the town's economic independence from Hamburg and religious autonomy from Münster, Count Edzard I further sought to expand his own dynastic rights as well as the commercial rights of Emden. The Holy Roman Emperor Maximilian officially ratified Emden's privilege of *Vorbeifahrts- und Stapelrecht* in 1494, and the next year he granted Emden the use of his imperial coat of arms.[11] Edzard then spent the last three decades of his reign consolidating his gains and enforcing his preeminence over the local nobility and other chieftains in East Frisia.[12]

Thus it can be seen that the small town of Emden with its 1 000–3 000 inhabitants received increased significance and legitimisation through the territorial politics of the East Frisian count.[13] Emden's civic constitution and communal development, nevertheless, did not keep pace with the gradually growing economic success of the city and its major merchant families. The 1493 treaties between Count Edzard and Hamburg and the bishop, which recognised the commercial rights of the city as part of the count's rights of dominion in the town, did not even mention the rights of the town's citizens; Emden was the residence and possession of the count.[14]

---

[9] Ibid. no. 1361 (26 May and 1 June 1493); Hagedorn, I, 15f, 19.

[10] Ibid. no. 1361, p. 388. Although the right had never been officially granted to Emden, there is evidence that Emden had, in fact, exercised the *Vorbeifahrtsrecht*; see, for instance, ibid. nos 1095–7, 1117, 1159. Further proof of Emden's practice of collecting customs can be seen in the attempt in 1483 from the principal interests in Groningen and Münster to link the two with a canal which bypassed Emden and the northern portion of the River Ems. The attempt failed due to technical difficulties; Hagedorn, I, 11.

[11] *OUB* no. 1414 (4 November 1494), nos 1449, 1450 (20 July and 10 August 1495).

[12] On the attempts at territorial expansion by the Cirksenas under Count Edzard I, see Schmidt, *Politische Geschichte Ostfrieslands*, pp. 117–36; Heinrich Reimers, *Edzard der Grosse* (Aurich, 1910). On Edzard's political consolidation, see Schmidt, pp. 136–50; Reimers, *Edzard d. Gr. und seine Feinde*, supplement from *Der Kalender 'Ostfreesland'* (Norden, 1933).

[13] A reliable estimate of Emden's population around 1500 cannot be made – it was probably somewhere between 1 000 and 3 000. An estimate of 5 000 for 1550 has been made; Hermann de Buhr, 'Die Entwicklung Emdens in der zweiten Hälfte des 16. Jahrhunderts' (Ph.D. diss., Hamburg, 1967), p. 53. Hagedorn, *Ostfrieslands Handel und Schiffahrt im 16. Jahrhundert*, vol. II (Berlin, 1912), p. 3, has estimated that Emden's population increased by more than six times, perhaps by as much as ten times, in the first eight decades of the century.

[14] Hagedorn, I, 19.

Since the mid-fifteenth century, a council of eight advisers and four Burgermeisters had existed in the town, but these civic positions were completely in the hands of the count.[15] The town council could not, therefore, be considered a communal institution. The count's appointed town councillors met together with, and were dominated by, the count's permanent representative in the town, the bailiff (*Drost*), who ran the count's administration from the castle.[16]

The citizenry in Emden, therefore, had little voice in the political administration of the town, and in 1500 Emden lacked many of the corporate institutions and indeed the communal mentality which had developed in other late medieval cities. After the first decade of the century, however, the city's account books depict a small degree of growing financial independence from the count and bailiff on the part of the town council.[17] Yet the degree of the citizenry's involvement in this princely council remained low into the 1540s when only one-quarter of the posts were even filled.[18] Beyond the count's town council, no additional outlets existed for support of or opposition to the count's civic policies. Given the weakness of the town council, it is hardly surprising that we can find no civic oversight of the town's hospitals or other poor relief funds, as was common in many other late medieval towns. A study of fourteenth- and fifteenth-century hospitals in the Holy Roman Empire found that one-quarter were endowed by city governments. Moreover, city governments assumed control of at least one-quarter of the hospitals they had not endowed.[19] Administration of Emden's poor relief institutions was in the hands of influential citizens

---

[15] Johannes Stracke, 'Zur Genealogie und Soziologie des Emder Rates im Mittelalter 1442–1528', *Ostfriesland*, 3 (1952), pp. 28–33.

[16] Christian Lamschus, *Emden unter der Herrschaft der Cirksena* (Hildesheim, 1984), has compiled a massive prosopographic analysis of the officials of the county, the city, and the church from about 1470 to 1528 and has demonstrated the very close connections to the ruling house within the circles of power in Emden at the start of the sixteenth century. For a critical review of Lamschus's methodology, see Bernd Kappelhoff, 'Über die Grenzen sinnvoller Anwendung moderner theoretischer Begriffe auf historische Sachverhalte: Bemerkungen zu einer Neuerscheinung zur Emder Stadtgeschichte', *EJb*, 66 (1986), pp. 94–111.

[17] Heinz Schilling, *Civic Calvinism* (Kirksville, MO, 1991), pp. 14f; his chapter 'Calvinism and Urban Republicanism: The Emden Experience', pp. 11–39, provides an overview of Emden's constitutional development from the late Middle Ages to the Emden Revolution of 1595 in its religious, social, communal and political contexts. H. Schnedermann, 'Emder Stadtrechnungen aus den ersten Jahrzehnten des 16. Jahrhunderts', *EJb*, 1, 3 (1874), pp. 107–20.

[18] Schilling, *Civic Calvinism*, p. 15.

[19] Michel Mollat, *Poor in the Middle Ages*, trans. Arthur Goldhammer (New Haven, 1978), pp. 275f, 282ff.

of the town, several of whom were at times civic officials, but Emden's magistracy did not take control of these affairs.

The office of the churchwarden (*Kirchenvögte* or *Kirchengesch-worenen*) allowed for some lay civic participation within the church organisation. The four churchwardens administered the church proper-ties and buildings and took part along with the pastors in the ecclesiastical court (*Sendgericht*), which handled cases of morals, marriage, and dis-order in the church community.[20] In the Frisian region of the diocese of Münster, authority to select the churchwardens was placed in the hands of the provost. Since Emden's provost was, in fact, an official of the Cirksena counts, the churchwardens too fell under the indirect control of the count.[21] Nevertheless, the institution of the churchwardens of-fered some of Emden's more influential citizens real opportunities for responsibility within the administration of church matters.[22]

Expressions of late medieval piety also enabled some opportunity for civic participation in ecclesiastical matters.[23] While sometimes outside the primary organisation of the church, such expressions provided a means for the citizenry to take an active part in matters of faith. During the last quarter of the fifteenth century, at least five lay confraternities were formed. Having lay members administer the confraternities ex-panded opportunities for involvement in religious activities in Emden to a larger circle of people. Additionally, a hospital (*Gasthaus*) was organ-ised and operated with apparent independence from the count and the church. Thus these lay corporations, coupled with donations to support the benefices and altars of the minor clergymen in Emden, were the primary outlets for participation of Emden's citizenry in church and civic affairs in the early sixteenth century.[24] Donations to support the poor were also common pious activities among Emden's citizens.

---

[20] Smid, *Kirchengeschichte*, pp. 44–51; H. Deiter, '"Dat Seentrecht" der sieben Münsterschen Probsteien in Ostfriesland', *Jahrbuch des Vereins für niederdeutsche Sprachforschung*, 8 (1882), pp. 86–96. For the jurisdiction of the Sendgericht, see the text of the Sendrecht in Borchling, *Niederdeutschen Rechtsquellen*, pp. 143ff.

[21] Lamschus, *Herrschaft der Cirksena*, pp. 321, 464–8.

[22] For a prosopographic analysis of the churchwardens up to 1527, see Lamschus, *Herrschaft der Cirksena*, esp. pp. 434–48.

[23] Kappelhoff, 'Reformation in Emden', I, 111–15.

[24] For a discussion of the altars in the Grosse Kirche and those who held the rights to the election of their priests, see Kappelhoff, 'Reformation in Emden', I, 97–101.

Piety, Charity, and the Emergence of Institutional Poor Relief

Organised distribution of alms in medieval Emden took place primarily
in conjunction with the brothers of the Franciscan monastery in nearby
Faldern, just on Emden's outskirts. Very little information, in Emden or
elsewhere, has survived about the charitable activities of the mendicant
orders like the Franciscans. Themselves poor, the Franciscans kept no
records of the alms they received, and we are left mostly with indirect
evidence.[25] By the mid-fifteenth century, however, sources in Emden
begin to document three new types of institutions which practised
charity around the town: confraternities, hospitals (*Gasthaus*, plural
Gasthäuser), and individual apartments (*Gotteskammer*, plural *Gotteskammern*). Emden's confraternities were lay brotherhoods founded
primarily for mutual spiritual assistance. In order to meet their religious
goals, the confraternities sponsored masses and prayers for their dead
members and feast celebrations honouring their patron saint. These
brotherhoods also played a large role in poor relief, supplementing the
charitable work of the Franciscans. Gasthäuser of the later Middle Ages
served as both poor houses and hospitals, superintended by a married
couple or a steward who lived in or near the Gasthaus. In Emden, the
late medieval Gasthäuser were organised similarly to the confraternities
with an independent, lay foundation. Gotteskammern, or small rooms
in which the poor could live, were numerous in Emden.

People in Emden established Gotteskammern to provide long-term
housing for a poor person or family, and were by definition one-room
apartments. Such poor relief provision appears to be quite unusual in
late medieval and early modern Europe. Perhaps such small-scale institutions have left few traces, or donors in larger towns had more
opportunities than in Emden to leave their bequests to established
institutions or hospitals rather than creating new, individual foundations. Or perhaps such small foundations have slipped through the
cracks in studies that are primarily interested in questions of emerging
centralisation and civic control. Whatever the reason, other studies of
early modern social welfare offer few descriptions of Gotteskammer-
like poor relief.[26] Along these lines, then, Emden's extensive use of such
Gotteskammern appears to be unusual, if not unique. These small apartments were generally owned and operated by a confraternity, a Gasthaus,
or the church, although some wealthy residents of Emden created

---

[25] On the activities of the mendicants and their role in poor relief, see Mollat, *Poor in
the Middle Ages*, pp. 123–34.

[26] Peter Gabrielsson, *Von den Gottesbuden zum Wohnstift. Die Geschichte der
hamburgischen Stiftung 'Dirck Koster Testament' 1537–1977* (Hamburg, 1980).

Gotteskammern that had their own independent administrations and functioned as private foundations.

The earliest charitable foundation on record in Emden is a private Gotteskammer. The story surrounding its creation sheds light on several facets of life in Emden, including familial obligations and late medieval piety including donations to both the church and charity. The example is therefore worth investigating in some detail. Vicar Herr Engelke had private property at his disposal in addition to the income from his benefice from the Altar of Our Lady. In 1462, he had purchased the remaining two-thirds of a house.[27] Six years earlier, the owners of the house had made a pious donation of one-third of the house 'so that it always shall remain by Our Lady's Altar in Emden'.[28] With his purchase, Engelke now had control over the entire house: unrestricted authority over the two-thirds in his private possession and rights of usufruct over the one-third that was part of his benefice. This enabled him, in 1469, when his son Hinrick was in some distress, to give the house to his son and daughter-in-law.[29] As an illegitimate son of a priest, Hinrick would have been deprived of inheritance rights. Hence Engelke wanted to provide for his son by means of a legal transaction before his death. Engelke stipulated that if Hinrick and his wife should die without surviving children, then the house would belong 'for ever and ever to the Altar of Our Lady, priest after priest'. This provision prohibited Hinrick and his wife from selling the house. Engelke went on, however, to reinforce his familial obligations by allowing an exception that if they should 'come into great poverty' and have no other goods – for instance, if Hinrick ended up in prison or was killed, and his wife should not have enough goods – they could then sell the house in order to 'protect against affliction and distress'.[30]

Yet one-third of the house which Engelke had just given to his son actually belonged to the Altar of Our Lady. In order to recompense the Altar, Engelke financed the construction of a new house, which had at least four apartments and was to be built near the churchyard. Engelke would live in one section of the house, and after his death so could his successors as prebendaries of the Altar of Our Lady. This action is noteworthy because not only did he compensate his benefice, he also demonstrated his own piety by making additional donations. Finally, we find that the new house was to have apartments in the southern end

---

[27] 8 June 1462, ArchGK no. 59; copied in *OUB* no. 781.

[28] The original donation letter no longer exists; a transcription can be found in a compilation of church properties from *c.* 1546, ArchGK no. 315, p. 8.

[29] A copy of this transaction contract was made *c.* 1546, ArchGK no. 315, pp. 7v–8.

[30] Ibid., p. 7v.

for 'two poor people who serve God to live in for God's sake, the one after another for ever and ever'. 'Engelke's friends' would choose the poor people to live in this house. He even went beyond this charitable foundation to allocate to the church one final portion of the house: in the apartment above the one for the poor, a 'good, honourable priest should live, priest after priest'. The inhabitant of this room should pay the token sum of one gulden rent per year to go for requiems.[31]

Although Engelke's contract does not use the term Gotteskammern, this was in effect the first recorded instance of their creation. Almost a century later a portion of Engelke's house by the churchyard was still used as, and called, a Gotteskammer.[32] To create a Gotteskammer, an individual usually bequeathed a house or portion of a house to be used as living quarters for poor people. In this case, Engelke established two Gotteskammern before his death, constructing a new house specifically for this purpose. Unfortunately, Engelke did not specify the names of the 'friends' who would decide who would live in the Gotteskammern; whether these administrators were laymen or fellow clerics cannot be determined.

Although this first recorded Gotteskammer was a private foundation, it was essentially connected with the ecclesiastical estate. Herr Engelke, the priest of the Altar of Our Lady, donated the house to the Altar and provided virtually free housing for future prebendaries of the Altar, two poor people, and an additional priest of Emden's church. Thus, two priests would reside alongside the poor in the Gotteskammern. Moreover, at the roots of Engelke's pious donation was his intention to safeguard members of his family against poverty. In spite of Engelke's status as a relatively wealthy member of the ecclesiastical estate, his story provides us with an example which is not atypical. Examples abound in Emden which illustrate the religious nature of poor relief and the integral connection between piety, charity and familial obligations in the later Middle Ages.

Despite numerous and varied trends in collective and individual piety during the later Middle Ages, one characteristic was common throughout Europe: the promotion of spiritual welfare. People were concerned with their salvation and sought to ensure their soul's place in heaven. Throughout this period, Europeans displayed a tremendous zeal for making bequests and donations to benefit their souls after death.[33] In

---

[31] Ibid., p. 8.

[32] See the comment written after the transcription of Engelke's contract in 1546; ibid.

[33] For a short analysis of piety in Germany, see Bernd Moeller, 'Frömmigkeit in Deutschland um 1500', *Archiv für Reformationsgeschichte*, 56 (1965), pp. 5–47. For discussions on the expressions of piety in Emden, see Kappelhoff, 'Reformation in Emden', I, 111–15; and Lamschus, *Herrschaft der Cirksena*, pp. 449–59.

East Frisia during the last third of the fifteenth century, no testament was composed without some allocation being given to the benefit of the church.[34] This trend continued into the first decades of the sixteenth century, and has been shown to include donors from all social strata.[35]

While the individual wealth of the donors varied greatly, the motivation for the donations was largely uniform: 'for the salvation of their souls', as the bequests usually read. In 1470, Emden citizen Beneke van Aurike left all his goods to the church, including his considerable landholdings, in order to ensure 'his soul's salvation in the glory of God, because he had often obtained the goods dangerously against the commandments of God'. Beneke's fear of damnation over his business dealings did not mollify the anger of his relatives at losing their entire inheritance to this act of piety. They challenged the testament, and the judges rendered a decision which gave to Beneke's relatives two houses and 400 gulden out of the large estate.[36] Such gifts to the church were often also connected with acts of charity. Wolter and Stine Kremer's 1453 testament afforded the surviving spouse all the couple's possessions along with the responsibility to provide for the spiritual welfare of the deceased spouse by financing masses for the soul of the dead spouse and by giving alms.[37]

Even the very rich sought spiritual protection by aiding the poor. The hard-dealing businessman, Hompo Hayen, was one of Emden's Burgermeisters from 1472 until his death in 1511. Hompo had been probably the richest citizen of Emden, with holdings of more than 800 hectares of rich marshland around Emden and an estimated yearly rent income from his properties of around 1 000 gulden.[38] In 1512, a year after his death, Hompo's widow Fosse endowed a weekly mass 'to the glory of God, salvation [of] her dearly departed husband's and her ... souls'. Fosse selected a particularly interesting site for the prayers for her husband's soul. She chose to endow Herr Eyllert, the 'headpriest in St Gertrude's *Gasthaus*', to read the masses every Friday before the altar in the Gasthaus.[39] Given their wealth, Hompo and Fosse could have endowed masses with any number of priests before several altars in the

---

[34] Kappelhoff, 'Reformation in Emden', I, 111.

[35] Ernst Kochs, 'Die Anfänge der Ostfriesischen Reformation', part I, *EJb*, 19, 1 (1916), p. 143, note 4.

[36] *OUB* no. 888 (badly damaged original is in ArchGK no. 7). On Beneke's landed wealth, see Lamschus, *Herrschaft der Cirksena*, p. 454, note 274.

[37] *OUB* no. 656 (the original in ArchGK no. 11 is badly damaged).

[38] Heinrich Reimers provides a description of Hompo's life and family in 'Aus Emder Bürgermeisterhäusern um 1495', *EJb*, 24 (1936), pp. 12–41 (p. 15 for references to his income and landholdings).

[39] EKP 1/55.

parish church or in the Franciscan monastery, as many less wealthy people did. But they obviously felt that the efficacy of the prayers of the poor and of the priest of the Gasthaus poor would have the most benefit to the 'salvation of their souls'.[40]

The creation of religious confraternities resulted from just such individual zeal for good works, charity and religious patronage in order to ensure one's salvation.[41] By the later Middle Ages, these spiritual assistance societies existed all over Europe and included all sectors of the population in their membership rolls.[42] Although they were sometimes organised around specific trades, the lay brotherhoods differed from trade guilds in their spiritual goals. They were created in order that their members, in pursuit of their own salvation, might collectively appropriate the treasury of meritorious deeds of past saints. As described by Maureen Flynn,

> By joining a confraternity, individuals gained communal protection and fortified their spiritual well-being with ties of fellowship. The confraternities designed requiem masses, prayer services, vigils over tombs and almsgiving programs to assist the friendship with saints for assistance in salvation. By setting themselves up under the protection of special saints and honouring their feast days with masses, public processions and dancing, they established patronage relationships with heavenly beings capable of bestowing grace.[43]

Members of confraternities were, in a sense, able to pool their spiritual resources to ensure the salvation of everyone.

Confraternities existed in various regions throughout Europe by the thirteenth century, and began to proliferate during the second half of the fifteenth century.[44] The study of the Spanish town of Zamora with

---

[40] Fosse also included a clause at the end of her endowment which was not commonly found in donations of the time. Should the successors to Herr Eyllert in the future not wish to hold the masses as prescribed, the heirs of Hompo and Fosse would have the right to move the endowment to a church where the masses would be said 'for ever and ever'. The three administrators of the Gasthaus signed the endowment contract as witnesses. EKP 1/55.

[41] Mollat, *Poor in the Middle Ages*, pp. 99f, 142f, 273ff.

[42] See, for example, Gabriel le Bras, 'Les confréries chrétiennes. Problèmes et propositions', *Revue historique de droit français et étranger* (Paris, 1940–41), pp. 310–63, esp. 324–5.

[43] *Sacred Charity: Confraternities and Social Welfare in Spain, 1400–1700* (Ithaca, 1989), p. 13.

[44] The activities especially of the Franciscans and Dominicans 'were responsible for extending confraternities throughout many parts of Italy and France by the fourteenth century', Flynn, *Sacred Charity*, p. 16. See Giles-Gérard Meersseman, 'Etudes sur les anciennes confréries dominicaines', *Archivum Fratrum Praedicatorum*, 22 (1951), pp. 275–93.

its astounding number of confraternities – 150 in a population of 8 600 by the second half of the sixteenth century – shows that the dramatic growth of its confraternities began during the last two decades of the fifteenth century.[45] While this proportion is not to be found in other parts of Europe, confraternities clearly blossomed across the continent.[46] In Germany, the small town of Wittenberg possessed 21 confraternities among a population of about 2 100 (not counting students or residents of the castle).[47] Confraternal activities were similar, if proportionally less intense in larger northern German harbour towns. More than 70 confraternities can be documented for Lübeck, which had a population of about 25 000; at the beginning of the Reformation, Hamburg, with a population of 16 000 to 18 000 residents, had 99 confraternities, most of which were founded after 1450.[48]

At least five confraternities existed in Emden by the end of the fifteenth century.[49] Documentation describing the activities of four of the five – the Confraternities of Our Lady, St Clement, St Ann, and St Antonius – is extant, while an additional brotherhood, St Jurgen's, is identified in one source with no further references.[50] Given the lack of surviving sources, it is possible that additional confraternities were also

---

[45] Flynn, *Sacred Charity*, pp. 16f. She also cites the results of studies of larger Spanish cities: Valladolid had at least 100 confraternities for an estimated population of 30 000, and Toledo had 143 confraternities and 60 000 residents.

[46] In sixteenth-century Florence, 75 confraternities in a population of 59 000; in Lyon, 68 in a population which varied between 45 000 and 65 000 in the sixteenth century; Flynn, *Sacred Charity*, p. 17. Bologna's confraternities joined possibly 20 per cent of the adults in a city of 55 000; Nicholas Terpstra, *Lay Confraternities and Civic Religion in Renaissance Bologna* (Cambridge, 1995), p. 132.

[47] Le Bras, 'Les confréries chrétiennes', p. 325; the population estimate for the year 1513 is made by Helmar Junghans, *Wittenberg als Lutherstadt* (Berlin, 1979), p. 73.

[48] Monika Zmyslony, 'Die geistlichen Bruderschaften in Lübeck bis zur Reformation' (Ph.D. diss., Kiel, 1974), p. 28; and Edith Ennen, *Die europäische Stadt des Mittelalters* (Göttingen, 1972), pp. 202, 215. (Le Bras, 'Les confréries chrétiennes', p. 325, says that Hamburg had 'more than a hundred'.) Ennen's population estimates are from 1400 for Lübeck and from the middle of the fifteenth century for Hamburg.

[49] On Emden's lay confraternities at the end of the Middle Ages and the early sixteenth century, see Timothy Fehler, 'Social Welfare in Early Modern Emden: The Evolution of Poor Relief in the Age of the Reformation and Confessionalization' (University of Wisconsin-Madison, Ph.D. thesis, 1995), pp. 84–134, and Johannes Stracke, 'Geistliche Laienbruderschaften im ausgehenden Mittelalter', *EJb*, 51/52 (1971–72), pp. 35–53. In his article, pp. 39ff, Stracke included a transcription of the foundation ordinance from the Confraternity of Our Lady. As an appendix to his article, Stracke published a transcription of the account book and membership list from the Confraternity of Our Lady: 'Unser lever vrouwen register (1486–1523)', *EJb*, 51/52 (1971–72), pp. 53–64. This is the sole remaining source of its kind for any of Emden's confraternities.

[50] 19 February 1497; StaE no. 846 (Emder Protokollbuch), p. 19; printed in *OUB* no. 1526.

active in Emden during the late Middle Ages. For instance, if we compare Lübeck's ratio of confraternities to population, we might expect
Emden to have had seven to nine confraternities.

Each of the confraternities was organised around an altar to its
patron saint. The Clement-Altar and the Antonius-Altar were in Emden's
parish church, the Grosse Kirche; the altars to Our Lady and to St Ann
were in the church of the Franciscan monastery.[51] We have the foundation ordinances for Our Lady and St Clement's, and an account book
with a membership list survives for Our Lady.[52] These sources describe
that a group of shippers and merchants joined together in 1481 to form
Our Lady's Confraternity, although the confraternity refused to exclude
those not associated with the sea trade, admitting up to four other
'pious people' per year. This confraternity's activities were centred around
the monastery's altar to the Virgin, and the earliest membership list
from 1486 begins with the names of four friars and six priests, suggesting the important role played by the Franciscan friars in the initiation of
Our Lady's.[53] By contrast, St Clement's Confraternity was founded by
shippers alienated by a predominance of influential, wealthy merchants
and other non-shippers in Our Lady's. St Clement's therefore was determined to be an exclusive shippers' confraternity that would 'accept no
one into this brotherhood, unless he is [a] shipper or boatsman who
sails out to sea and will dispense charity to the brotherhood'.[54] St
Clement's also chose to organise around an altar in the parish church,
refusing the connections with the monastery. Whatever the combination
of initiatives in their foundations, the confraternities clearly show the

---

[51] Although there were altars to Our Lady in both the Grosse Kirche and the Franciscan
church, they should not be confused since the Confraternity of Our Lady was organised
out of the Franciscan monastery; Kappelhoff, 'Reformation in Emden', I, 99. An altar to
St Jurgen has not been identified in either church, but Stracke points out that of the 12 to
16 altars which were in the Grosse Kirche, only 8 are known with certainty; Stracke,
'Geistliche Laienbruderschaften', p. 50.

[52] Our Lady's 1486 Ordinance: printed in Stracke, 'Geistliche Laienbruderschaften',
pp. 39ff; St Clement's Ordinance: StaE, I. Reg., no. 425; printed OUB no. 1421 and
Loesing, Geschichte der Stadt Emden, pp. 81ff; Our Lady's account book: 'Unser lever
vrouwen register (1486–1523)', EJb, 51/52 (1971–72), pp. 53–64.

[53] Stracke, 'Geistliche Laienbruderschaften', p. 39; 'Unser lever vrouwen Register', p.
58 (fol. 43 in manuscript). The monastery was being heavily criticised by the Countess
Theda for its misbehaviour, inspiring correspondence between countess, pope and bishop,
calling for reform; Reginenses Vat. 683, fol. 425; cited and described in 'Geistliche
Laienbruderschaften', pp. 37–8. Given the complaints about their lifestyle and a papal
demand for reform hanging over their heads, it is not surprising that some friars attempted to display their piety and prove the critics wrong by taking part in the creation
of a confraternity.

[54] OUB no. 1421.

trends in piety as its members attempted to establish spiritual brotherhoods to ensure corporate salvation through prayers, masses, charity
and feasts. Scattered references to the confraternities in contracts and
testaments reveal a bit of their business activities: providing loans (many
of the borrowers were members of the confraternity), buying and selling
property, and receiving bequests and donations.

Ardent piety and religious zeal drove enrolment in confraternities, so
there was a good deal of overlap among the total membership of the
other confraternities as people tried to ensure their salvation by joining
more than one confraternity.[55] Certainly, a majority of those who rose
to leadership in other confraternal organisations were also members of
Our Lady (the one Emden confraternity for which a membership roll
survives). Uko Goltsmyt, a wealthy and influential goldsmith in town,
displayed an almost frantic leadership in civic, religious and confraternal
affairs. This well-situated Emden citizen served as administrator of St
Gertrude's Gasthaus in 1505 and became a churchwarden in 1510, a
position he held until at least 1524. In 1520, he was a member of the
city council before becoming Burgermeister. Uko joined Our Lady's
Confraternity in 1521, and then showed up as an administrator of St
Ann's Confraternity between 1522 and 1525.[56] Such multiple memberships can similarly be found among Emden's other confraternities'
administrators. Three of five identified administrators of St Anthony's
Confraternity were also members of Our Lady's, while at least three of
St Ann's known administrators were also in Our Lady's. St Anthony's
administrator Herman Kleensmyth had earlier been an administrator of
St Gertrude's Gasthaus.

Wills provide additional testimony about such involvement with multiple confraternities as spiritual resources in the quest for salvation.
Along these lines, the shipper Hermannus Sywerts, an administrator of
Our Lady's Confraternity, and his wife Styne indicated in their 1515
testament that all their goods should be divided evenly between the
'two brotherhoods in Emden, as Our Lady's and of St Clement's Brotherhoods, to the salvation of both of their souls and to perpetual memory'
if they died without surviving children.[57] In a similar vein, Our Lady's

---

[55] See Zmyslony, 'Bruderschaften in Lübeck', pp. 88, 127; Flynn, *Sacred Charity*, p. 17.

[56] EKP 1/192, 1/252; 'Unser lever vrouwen register', no. 379; Lamschus, *Herrschaft der Cirksena*, pp. 115, 444; ArchGK no. 81. Stracke, 'St.-Gertruden-Gasthaus in Emden', *EJb*, 51/52 (1971–72), p. 128, claims that Uko died in 1526, but he is still mentioned in contracts after 1527.

[57] EKP 1/79. Of course, if their children survived them, the testament stipulated that they be cared for with food and clothing until they reached their 'bescheydeliken jaren', at which time, after the advice of their guardians about the extent of the remaining goods, they would be 'given to marriage or cloister'.

Confraternity was to give both St Clement's and St Ann's a portion of
the bequest of Burgermeister Edde Uffen, a former administrator of Our
Lady's.[58] Another example involves mere members (rather than
confraternity administrators). When Gobeke Block and his wife Hille
(members of Our Lady's since 1519 or 1520) wrote their testament in
1525, they specified that after both of them had died, one-third of their
goods be divided between 'the three brotherhoods, as Our Lady, St
Ann, and St Clement, each an equal amount of the alms which are being
given for God's sake and to their honour'.[59] Finally, when the brothers
Wycher and Berndt Kremer wrote their testament in 1512, they left
nothing to Our Lady's despite the fact that their parents had joined in
the 1490s.[60] Instead they donated 15 gulden 'to the alms of the brothers
in the glory of St Ann'. The Kremer brothers then supplemented this gift
of alms to an organisation which practised charity with another charitable act by bequeathing 4 gulden to each of the four 'begging', or
mendicant, orders in East Frisia who made their regular rounds through
Emden.[61] These testaments illustrate that even through the mid-1520s
the religious zeal and piety which led people to join confraternities –
sometimes multiple confraternities – was still very much alive. By
donating alms to the confraternity of St Clement or to others, they were
performing an act of charity which would help ensure their salvation.
Through their attempts to ensure the spiritual welfare of their members,
the confraternities also became important institutions for handling
social welfare.

Naturally, in the course of meeting the confraternity's spiritual aspirations, members of the confraternity practised charity in a somewhat
organised fashion. The typical pattern involved providing alms to those
who would pray for and take care of the dead of the brotherhood.
Though specific charitable practices of Our Lady's and Emden's other
confraternities are not thoroughly described in the statutes nor in the

---

[58] 'Unser lever vrouwen register', p. 24.

[59] 'Unser lever vrouwen register', no. 368; EKP 1/244v.

[60] Ibid. 1/46v–7 (12 August 1512); 'Unser lever vrouwen register', no. 129. The
brothers left their house to the parish church 'to the glory of God'. Their gift to
embellish the altars of Our Lady and St Catharine 'for the salvation of both [our] souls'
doubtless had nothing to do with that confraternity. As Catharine's altar was in Emden's
parish church, the reference to Our Lady's altar was probably to the one in the parish
church and not to the altar in the monastery associated with the confraternity; ibid. 1/
46v.

[61] At this time, the four mendicant orders each had houses in western East Frisia: the
Franciscans in Faldern/Emden, the Dominicans in Norden and Dykhusen (convent), the
Carmelites in Appingen, and several Augustinian cloisters had been consolidated into
three independent houses in Sielmönken, Coldinne and Marienkamp; see Smid,
Kirchengeschichte, pp. 104–14. EKP 1/46v–7.

account book and contracts, confraternities generally made payments to the poor or provided them with food and clothing for this service, since they believed in the greater efficacy of the prayers of the poor.[62] They also practised charity in connection with their yearly banquet. Confraternities usually invited a certain number of poor people to participate in the banquet; another common confraternal practice was to provide food to the poor following the banquet. Our Lady's Confraternity probably followed these common practices and provided a fairly regular distribution of alms to the poor. Both St Clement's and Our Lady's paid the funeral expenses of the poorer brothers and sisters of the brotherhood, and they gave a small payment to those who participated in the masses at the confraternity's memorial services.[63] Confraternal charity was not haphazard, but instead it was tied to the calendar with charitable expenditures taking place largely around the time of the banquets and celebrations in honour of the confraternity's patron saint.[64] Yet except for the poor living in housing, which a couple of Emden's confraternities maintained, the poor could not count on regular confraternal support *throughout* the entire year.

Surviving wills and testaments clearly demonstrate the interest in pious bequests to support the confraternities' provision of the poor, whether made out of concern for their own salvation or compassion for the poor. On 1 July 1517, Lambert van Groningen and his wife Luthgart, recent members of Our Lady's Confraternity, made their testament.[65] They stipulated that, following both of their deaths, a donation be made 'to the glory of God and the poor for God's sake, where there is use and distress'. Namely, they wanted a heavy silver bowl 'or something better' to be given to the administrators of Our Lady's Brotherhood in the cloister of the Franciscan Observants. They intended this donation to provide 'improvement in the alms' that the administrators of Our Lady's could distribute to the poor.

By 1523, if it had not previously done so, Our Lady's Confraternity began to offer housing for the poor. An alderman of the confraternity, Johan Deweren, announced that he was constructing a Gotteskammer by the Gasthaus' which he would give to Our Lady's Confraternity. Johan said that he was building the apartment 'according to the distress needs

---

[62] See Flynn, *Sacred Charity*, pp. 76f.

[63] Fehler, 'Social Welfare', pp. 107f, 116.

[64] See Flynn, *Sacred Charity*, 71ff; Zmyslony, 'Bruderschaften in Lübeck', pp. 129–32, shows that some confraternities in Lübeck provided weekly food provisions to the poor; Mollat, *Poor in the Middle Ages*, pp. 142f.

[65] EKP 1/112v. They joined the confraternity in 1516, 'Unser lever vrouwen register', no. 351.

of the poor', and claimed that he 'will be finished with this apartment within 1½ years'.[66] It is unclear which Gasthaus this Gotteskammer was near; at this time in Emden there were two Gasthäuser, St Gertrude's on the outskirts of town by the new marketplace and St Anthony's on Pelzerstrasse near the Ems River. Our Lady's Confraternity would pay the small yearly property tax for the land on which the Gotteskammer was built, but the confraternity's account book makes no reference as to who would administer the apartment. Neither this nor any other Gotteskammer appears again in any documents of Our Lady's Brotherhood. The location of the Gotteskammer was probably chosen for its proximity to the Gasthaus. The administrators of the confraternity would, therefore, be able to take advantage of the expertise of the Gasthaus administrators in providing housing for the poor. Indeed, Our Lady's Gotteskammer, though owned and paid for by the confraternity, might have been administrated with some co-operation with the Gasthaus.

Beyond any formal poor provision given by the confraternities, they also supported their members with loans and other less specific 'welfare' practices. For instance, a contract from the summer of 1522 between Taelke Menckenn and St Ann's administrators looks less like a business transaction than assistance to someone in major financial need.[67] Perhaps Taelke was a member of St Ann's, although no mention of that is made in the contract. According to the records, Taelke 'sold' the administrators of St Ann's her 'collapsed house ... to the service of St Ann and her brotherhood'. She had previously borrowed 50 gulden from someone and used her house as collateral. Now that her house had collapsed, she was left without housing and with no way to pay her mortgage. At this point the confraternity stepped in and 'bought' her collapsed house for the principal of 50 gulden and 'a sum of money'. It is not clear what they did with the property; no record of a subsequent sale by the confraternity is extant. The confraternity was there, however, to help out a (possible) member when her creditors would not accept the damaged or destroyed house.

Of course, confraternities were not the only corporate organisations formed to benefit their members; trade guilds make up a previously unmentioned group of poor relief providers who were concerned especially with their fellow members. By 1504 masters of at least five trades in Emden had organised themselves and drafted ordinances.[68] To this point the focus has been upon the lay confraternities, which were

[66] 'Unser lever vrouwen register', p. 15.

[67] EKP 1/192.

[68] Kappelhoff, 'Reformation in Emden', I, 86: Goldsmiths (1491), Shoemakers (1491), Shopkeepers (1500), Weavers (1504), and Bakers (1504).

primarily institutional expressions of religious motivation. Analysis of the four surviving guild ordinance rolls reveals indeed that the goal of their creation was not inherently religious but to regulate and organise their particular trade.[69] The ordinances established an array of rules governing acceptance into the trade and acceptable business practices, as well as standards regulating the allowable raw materials and quality of the finished product. Yet, in spite of the secular intentions of the guilds, the ordinances demonstrate a definite religious character, similar in some respects to the confraternities.

The surviving guild ordinances refer to their organisations as brotherhoods and describe their religious activities alongside the rules governing the practice of their trade. For instance, 'the community of masters of the Shoemaker trade' gathered together 'in the glory of God and the patron Saint Crispin ... to establish an honourable brotherhood' which would 'hold masses and other worship services every year'.[70] Such spiritual activities were cited as being what 'is traditional in the trade'. The Goldsmith Brotherhood similarly opened its ordinances by describing the 'masses and other services' which it held to the glory of God and its patron saint Eligius.[71] Indeed, the Goldsmith Brotherhood even endowed its own altar in the parish church to St Eligius, where its religious activities would be centred – much like a confraternity.[72] Most of the penalties for misconduct in the guild were to be paid in wax for the candles, thus demonstrating the importance of religious services in the trade brotherhoods.[73]

Of the surviving ordinances, only those of the Shoemakers' Guild mentions assistance for members in need. The ordinance ended with the mandate that 'each master in the trade shall give into the purse ½ krumstert on each religious festival day in such a way that if we in the guild become poor, then the money should be used to prove the work of compassion and come to his aid'.[74] The money was also to be 'brought

---

[69] The Guild Rolls of the Goldsmiths (renewed in 1491), Shoemakers (1491), and Shopkeepers (1500) are printed in the *OUB*, nos 1299, 1298, and 1652, respectively. The Weaver Roll from 1504 is found in StaE (Handschriften) 433.

[70] *OUB* no. 1298, pp. 333f.

[71] Ibid. no. 1299, pp. 335.

[72] Johannes Stracke, 'Das Emder Goldschmiedeamt im Mittelalter', *EJb*, 36 (1956), pp. 134f, 139f; Kappelhoff, 'Reformation in Emden', I, 98f.

[73] *OUB* no. 1298, p. 334. Moreover, when a master joined the guild he was to pay money, provide for a meal of the brotherhood, and give 'twe punt wasses to der kerssen'; see also *OUB* nos 1299 and 1652.

[74] A krumstert was a small unit of currency. The value of the currency fluctuated around the beginning of the sixteenth century with 1 rheinische gulden in 1491 worth 36 krumstert and in 1512 one was worth 40 krumstert; the 'enkelde' gulden was worth 47.5 krumstert in 1520; Lamschus, *Herrschaft der Cirksena*, p. 161, note 384.

to the church, in order to receive the reward from almighty God'.[75] Thus, in these late fifteenth-century guild regulations, we find some of the same corporate religious and charitable motivations that we discovered in the confraternities. However, while such religious energy drove the establishment of the lay confraternities, the trade brotherhoods focused on regulating their craft. Nevertheless, as indicated by the Shoemakers' Ordinance, the craft brotherhoods probably maintained funds to provide for their members who fell into poverty.

St Ann's, Our Lady's and St Clement's Confraternities each had their own small spheres in which they practised poor relief. Providing for members and their families in need ranked first in priority. The statutes of Our Lady's and St Clement's describe paying the expenses of a poor member's funeral, and in practice St Ann's Brotherhood also helped with financial problems (for instance, 'buying' a collapsed house). The question remains as to how much of the confraternity's alms were given to the poor outside the confraternity. Moreover, it is important to remember that the charity practised by these confraternities was only one part – though an important part – of their total activities, all of which were done to ensure the salvation of their members.

In the first decades of the sixteenth century, records detailing the business activities of the confraternities seldom referred directly to poor relief. Gifts to and loan agreements with the confraternities were generally made 'to the service of the brotherhood' and 'for the salvation of [the donor's] soul'. Only a few explicit references to the charitable activities or alms of the confraternities have been discovered from the period before 1520. The language of contracts changed during the 1520s to include new and recurrent references to the poor served by the confraternities. Thus by the 1520s the confraternities became much more open about their charitable activities in the surviving public documents: donors still made gifts 'for the salvation of their souls' but they explicitly focused on the charitable purpose of their bequest with a greater frequency. Although the trend's shift began before the Protestant Reformation, the pace of the shift in specific references to the confraternities' poor relief clearly increased through the mid-1520s. Of course, Protestant theologians thought the only justifiable confraternal practice was charity, so their criticisms no doubt accelerated the trend of the confraternities to publicise their charity more overtly in comparison to their other activities.

---

[75] OUB no. 1298, p. 334.

The situation with St Anthony's Confraternity and St Gertrude's Gasthaus was slightly different from the other confraternities because charitable provision was from the outset the most important of their spiritual activities. Although confraternities supported some poor members, distributed alms on special occasions and even maintained some limited housing for the poor in Gotteskammern, the charity of the Gasthaus was much more extensive and regular. Many cities throughout Europe established hospitals to house the poor, the sick and travelling pilgrims during the twelfth and thirteenth centuries.[76] Along the Frisian coast and in the northern Netherlands, such institutions were called *Gasthäuser* (literally, 'guest houses') when they began appearing around the end of the fourteenth and especially in the fifteenth century.[77] In East Frisia, Gasthäuser appeared later. Given the large number of monasteries and apparently small number of transient poor in this remote corner of Europe, the monasteries were probably able to meet the needs of travellers and the poor for temporary shelter. Evidence of individual, long-term housing for the poor in Emden goes back to the 1460s with the creation of Herr Engelke's Gotteskammern.[78]

Scanty medieval documentation shrouds the origins of Emden's earliest Gasthaus, but the first mention of an Emden Gasthaus indicates that it was already operating in 1484. Herman Kystemaker's death left his widow Tamme in control of all their property. In her subsequent testament, drawn up in 1484, she first divided a portion of the property among her relatives. Tamme then paid the chief priest and the vicar 'for the salvation of Herman's soul and her own' and went on to endow a number of masses.[79] The priests and sacristans at the Altar of Our Lady in the Franciscan monastery and in the parish church in Emden were 'to hold for perpetual memorial with vigils and requiems yearly in the

---

[76] See Mollat, *Poor in Middle Ages*, pp. 146–53; Jesko von Steynitz, *Mittelalterliche Hospitäler der Orden und Städte als Einrichtung der sozialen Sicherung* (Berlin, 1970); Dieter Jetter, *Grundzüge der Hospitalgeschichte* (Darmstadt, 1973).

[77] On St Gertrude's Gasthaus in Groningen, see P. J. van Herwerden, 'Geschiedenis van het Sint Geertruids- of Pepergasthuis te Groningen', *Economisch–Historisch Jaarboek*, 28 (1961), pp. 149–217.

[78] On Gotteskammern in Hamburg see Peter Gabrielsson, *Von den Gottesbuden zum Wohnstift. Die Geschichte der hamburgischen Stiftung 'Dirck Koster Testament' 1537– 1977* (Hamburg, 1980). References to Gasthäuser in the other larger East Frisian towns of Norden and Aurich appear first from the period of the Reformation. For Aurich see Heinrich Reimers, 'Das Auricher Gasthaus im 16. und 17. Jahrhundert', in *Beiträge zur Geschichte ostfriesischer Städte*, pp. 30–33; and G. D. Ohling, 'Das Auricher Gasthaus', in *Heimatkunde und Heimatgeschichte* (Beilage der Ostfriesischen Nachrichten), no. 1 (Aurich, 1932), pp. 4–6. For Norden, see Uffke Cremer, *Norden im Wandel der Zeiten* (Norden, 1955), p. 21.

[79] ArchGK no. 29; *OUB* no. 1142.

parish church in Emden, to pray faithfully for Herman's and Tamme's souls'. Along with this endowment, Tamme directed that 1½ gulden be given 'yearly to the Gasthaus on behalf of the poor'. Moreover, she remembered the poor not only in the vigils for their souls; she also specified that if the yearly income from her property should exceed the amounts of the endowments, any excess money should go to the poor. Despite various bequests to the monastery and to the church in Emden, it was the activities of the Gasthaus that Tamme chose to support when she claimed to be practising charity to the poor.[80]

Whether this 'Gasthaus in Emden' was that of St Gertrude's is not certain, but St Gertrude's Gasthaus was in existence by 1490.[81] Throughout the 1490s, a Gasthaus was in operation in the oldest section of Emden, Pelzerstrasse, on the edge of the river and in the vicinity of the parish church. We can deduce from the Gasthaus's neighbours mentioned in contracts – the two Burgermeisters Hompo Hayen (probably Emden's wealthiest citizen) and Ghert van Gheldern – that this was a wealthy and prestigious section of town.[82] Yet in 1505, the 'administrators and procurators' of St Gertrude's Gasthaus reached an agreement with the Emden church administrators which would move the Gasthaus from its central location on Pelzerstrasse to the town's periphery.[83] In exchange for the Gasthaus's chapel, apartments, and other properties near the church, the parish church provided the Gasthaus with five parcels of land outside the 'Northern Gate' of the city, in the area which would in future decades become the 'New Marketplace' (*Neuer Markt*), and a house (with the adjacent land) in the old section of town to use as a transitional residence, as well as a cash payment.

This exchange of property discloses the realities of poor relief experienced in the growing town and imparts some insights into the operations of the Gasthaus. The restricted availability of choice real-estate space in the old section of town motivated the administrators of St Gertrude's to move 'outside the northern gates'. Their former location at the western end of Pelzerstrasse on the river indicates that the Gasthaus had been there for some time because this was the oldest settled area of town. The population of the town began increasing slowly around 1500, and with increased social stratification – especially at society's lower levels –

---

[80] Tamme's final distribution of resources in her testament also involved large, one-time payments to the Faldern monastery and to the parish church in Emden for a new addition to the high altar.

[81] *OUB* no. 1260 (1 January 1490); *OUB* no. 1631 (21 July 1499). Fehler, 'Social Welfare', pp. 135–48; Stracke, 'St.-Gertruden-Gasthaus', pp. 126–31.

[82] See Maps 2.1 and 2.3. Pelzerstrasse is the oldest street in Emden; the church was built on the river at the western end of Pelzerstrasse.

[83] ArchGK no. 81; printed in Harkenroht's edition of Beninga's *Chronik*, pp. 494ff.

among Emden's inhabitants the Gasthaus needed to expand its facilities.[84] Yet the old area of town was already completely built up, and any expansion here would have been quite expensive. The large amount of property offered by the church in exchange indicates that St Gertrude's complex had a tremendous value. By moving outside the settled portion of the town, the Gasthaus now had the opportunity to expand its operations with more property and at lower costs.[85]

The Gasthaus's charitable activities certainly had the support of Emden's citizenry. Within eleven days of the contract ordering the move of St Gertrude's, the notary registered a contract which included a gift to 'the Gasthaus in Emden ... to help [with] their construction'.[86] The building project lasted at least four years. In August 1509 the administrators of St Gertrude's Gasthaus were forced to take out a loan of 100 gulden for the 'construction of the Gasthaus'.[87] A great deal of building had already been completed by this time as the administrators mentioned as collateral a 'Gasthaus house' which had been built on the north side of the new 'Gasthaus church'. Interestingly, the Gasthaus administrators were able to finance the loan at half the prevailing interest rate of 6 per cent, further demonstrating the esteem in which their relief activities were held in Emden.[88]

At the same time the Gasthaus also received a large gift from former city council member and church administrator Boelhardus van Jemgum, one of the wealthiest men in Emden.[89] He had privately built two Gotteskammern 'by St Gertrude's Gasthaus outside the Northern Gates, on the north side of the chapel of the Gasthaus'. Boelhardus does not

---

[84] Lamschus, *Herrschaft der Cirksena*, p. 423.

[85] Naturally, the church also had interests in making this exchange. A note on the back of the contract indicates that the church soon began using the old chapel of the Gasthaus to expand their school. They also used some portions of the old Gasthaus to house the church organist. See notation from 29 October 1613 on ArchGK no. 81; Harkenroht (ed.), Beninga's, *Chronyk*, p. 495; Stracke, 'St.-Gertruden-Gasthaus', p. 127.

[86] StaE, I. Reg., no. 846 (Emder Protokollbuch), pp. 88–90. On 24 July 1505, Hayge Bagbandt and his wife stipulated in their testament that enough money be given so that 'one reads 10 times 30 masses to the salvation of their souls (five in the glory of the holy five wounds, and the other five in the glory of Our Lady)'. Moreover, each of the four mendicant orders was given a sum of money, and the poor were to receive cloth from Osnabrück. Finally, the Gasthaus was given money to help with its construction, and the Franciscan monastery in Faldern was given additional money for construction or any other needs.

[87] EKP 1/3v.

[88] The administrators of the Gasthaus agreed to pay 3 gulden yearly interest on their 100-gulden loan. Virtually every other surviving loan contract from the late fifteenth and early sixteenth centuries was financed at 6 per cent interest.

[89] 13 September 1509, EKP 1/1; Stracke, 'St.-Gertruden-Gasthaus', p. 129; Lamschus, *Herrschaft der Cirksena*, pp. 116, 443, 456.

2.1 Priest Herman Wessels (d. 1507), detail from his gravestone in the Grosse Kirche (Johannes a Lasco Bibliothek Grosse Kirche Emden)

state whose land these apartments were built upon: he may have financed their construction on the Gasthaus's new property or perhaps he built them on his own property immediately adjacent to the Gasthaus. At any rate, he gave full authority in their governance to the administrators of the Gasthaus. He additionally endowed almost three hectares of land 'to the glory of God to the poor living in the two Gotteskammern', who were to receive and divide equally the yearly rents from these lands. With the stipulation that whatever goods the poor brought into the Gotteskammern should become the property of the Gasthaus on their death, Boelhardus turned the administration over to St Gertrude's Gasthaus. The Gasthaus administrators were to maintain the Gotteskammern in good condition 'and hold them in honour … for ever and ever'. They should also manage the land which Boelhardus was donating. Boelhardus's bequest retained its own identity long after its creation. When the Gasthaus administrators sold off a number of their older properties in 1565 following their relocation into the former Franciscan monastery, they mentioned 'Boelhardtz Goetskamere' as still being in existence; this bequest had not simply become consolidated into the Gasthaus's properties.[90]

Boelhardus ended his donation contract with specifications that illustrate the important connection between charity and familial obligations in late medieval and early modern society. He specified conditions in which his donation, though intended to help the poor, should also provide important security for his own family. For instance, if one of his next of kin or relatives faced poverty and requested a room 'for God's sake', then he or she should enjoy a residence in the Gasthaus 'before another [person], in the [case] that the room is free'.[91] Boelhardus's relatives should always be given first preference when they were in poverty's wake – which was hardly likely, given Boelhardus's wealth. Boelhardus made clear, though, that his relatives should receive a room only if a 'room is free': the administrators would not have to oust anyone from the Gasthaus to accommodate one of Boelhardus's kin!

Despite no clear descriptions of the Gasthaus's organisation and administration, it was evidently organised independently of church and civic control, and its administrators were all laymen. In the first decades of the sixteenth century, three administrators represented the Gasthaus in business contracts (after 1540, almost all contracts list four administrators).[92] The men who held this post were committed to communal

---

[90] EKP 10/244 (23 June 1565).

[91] EKP 1/1.

[92] E.g. EKP 1/26, 1/202v, 2/8v, 2/13v; 2/546, 3/53, 3/83v. Of course, there could have been additional administrators since all of them did not necessarily have to represent the Gasthaus in every contract.

piety and charity as practised by confraternities. All of the first seven identifiable administrators of the Gasthaus were members of Our Lady's Confraternity, although some had not yet joined Our Lady's at the time they began serving as Gasthaus administrators.[93] Two of the seven also served as administrators of other confraternities; for instance, Herman Kleensmyth's experience with Gertrude's Gasthaus probably helped him later as administrator of St Anthony's when they were trying to establish a Gasthaus of their own. The earliest known administrators of St Gertrude's included both a current city councilman and a future councilman and Burgermeister. In addition to drawing men of some prominence, the administration of the Gasthaus also drew men from a variety of occupations: merchant, goldsmith, tailor and smith.

While the administrators handled the financial and business affairs of the Gasthaus, a resident overseer managed the daily operations involving care of the poor residents. This overseer probably lived in the Gasthaus with his wife, as was the practice in later years. His (or their) responsibilities were to procure the daily necessities to run the Gasthaus and to take care of the sick residents. The overseer was apparently authorised to provide medical care, such as binding wounds, an activity normally restricted to the members of the Barber Guild.[94] The extent to which the administrators involved themselves with the daily operations of the Gasthaus is not obvious, but their wives apparently helped out in that regard. Gasthaus administrators' wives visited the poor and provided direct care.[95] Therefore, being married could certainly be an important asset to an administrator of the Gasthaus, and all seven of the earliest identified administrators were, in fact, married.[96]

Gertrude's administrators continued to expand their building complex which lay 'outside the northern gates'. They purchased a small single-room house which expanded the Gasthaus complex one building westward.[97] Still, the use as late as 1523 of the phrase 'outside the northern gates' to describe the location of this purchase illustrates once again that this new part of the city had not yet been fully integrated. Gertrude's Gasthaus had the advantage of being better able to develop its facilities with a location outside the older, more densely populated, section of town.

---

[93] Fehler, 'Social Welfare', pp. 143–6.

[94] In 1516, the 'Gastmeystersche Peter' bound the wounded arm of a boy injured in a fight 'outside the new gates', Quer., fol. 41. It is not clear if the injured boy, Dyle Heeren's son, or Dyle the father had any association with the Gasthaus.

[95] See the example of Hinrich Kerstgens's wife Haseke, p. 66 below; Quer., fol. 37.

[96] Fehler, 'Social Welfare', p. 145 (Table 6).

[97] (4 March 1523) EKP 1/202v.

Unlike Gertrude's Gasthaus, St Anthony's had its origins as a confraternity organised around an altar in the Grosse Kirche.[98] St Anthony's was also the only one of the confraternities to have a cleric as one of its administrators: Johan van Duthen, St Anthony's Altar's beneficient and vicar of the Grosse Kirche, worked with laymen in the confraternity's administration for at least a decade (c. 1516–27). The administrators of the confraternity were already involved in the care of the poor, when they received the gift of a one-room house (Kammer) in 1516.[99] However, St Anthony's did not already provide Gotteskammern for the poor: the donor, Gertrude Wevester, had to stipulate explicitly that she was giving her Kammer 'neither to the priests nor to the altar, but rather to the poor, who will be governed and sent there by the priests and administrators' of St Anthony's Confraternity. Wevester made her gift to St Anthony's on the condition that 'free housing for the rest of her life' be provided 'from the goods of St Anthony'. The administrators also agreed to give her a one-time present of 10 gulden to help her in her current distressing situation. Thus, she gave up her apartment in Schulstrasse (near the church) in exchange for the promise of a residence provided by St Anthony's.

Wevester's contract with St Anthony's administrators ends with a fascinating and unique provision.[100] Emden's Burgermeister and city council – 'in God's will and the sake of the holy confessor St Anthony' – authorised a lifetime exemption for Gertrude from the standard duties, services, and taxes 'to which she and everyone within Emden are obliged for the good of the town', such as 'watch, work, defence, and travel duties, as well as those of the count'. No similar arrangement, offering exemption from all municipal duties and taxes, was made with anyone in Emden. St Anthony's administrators obviously wanted this apartment and were willing to go to great lengths to get it.

A surviving notation on a scrap of paper four years later reveals a possible explanation for the interest shown in obtaining Gertrude Wevester's room. In this 1520 note, the administrators 'of the newly established Gasthaus by Pelzerstrasse, belonging to St Anthony's altar' acknowledged the receipt of Beene Tyaerts's house 'to the use of St Anthony and the poor permanently'.[101] The indication here that

---

[98] Stracke, 'Geistliche Laienbruderschaften', p. 51; Kappelhoff, 'Reformation in Emden', I, 98.

[99] ArchGK no. 46 (18 January 1516), copy included in EKP 1/88v. The date of this donation to the confraternity – the day following the holiday of St Anthony (17 January 17) – could indicate a tie to the annual banquet and celebration of the confraternity.

[100] ArchGK no. 46; EKP 1/88v.

[101] EKP 1/170a (a loose scrap of paper).

St Anthony's had recently established a Gasthaus by Pelzerstrasse is important. St Anthony's real estate was traditionally located on Pelzerstrasse.[102] Apparently the late 1510s saw St Anthony's administrators consolidating the confraternity's property-holdings to create a Gasthaus. Perhaps the annexation of Gertrude Wevester's house was necessary to enable St Anthony's to bring together their various properties into a rough complex centred around the corner of Pelzerstrasse and Schulstrasse.[103] By establishing St Anthony's Gasthaus in the old section of town near the church, they were replacing the presence of St Gertrude's Gasthaus, which had moved from that location to the outskirts of town some 15 years earlier.

The designation *Gasthaus* did not take root to describe St Anthony's charitable provision. Most references to St Anthony's holdings continue to call them *Gotteskammern*, indicating that their housing provision remained long-term rather than short-term. In 1521, for instance, Johan Scroder and his wife Aelheyt bequeathed one of their houses to St Anthony's Gotteskammern: 'to the glory of God and the holy father St Anthony, respectively to the erected Kammern, to the use of the poor placed in the St Anthony's Kammern'.[104] Wyltheth Boels, in 1522, transferred the house which he had just inherited from his uncle (it was located on the corner of Schulstrasse, bordering the St Anthony's Gotteskammern) to the 'administrators of St Anthony's Kammern on Pelzerstrasse', 'for the use of the aforementioned Kammern, erected to the glory of God and St Anthony the confessor'.[105] An exception to the tendency to continue referring to St Anthony's properties as Gotteskammern is found in a 1522 testament that left 'a good cow (the best)' to St Anthony's Gasthaus.[106]

The work of St Anthony's Brotherhood was never again referred to as a Gasthaus.[107] The assistance they provided to the poor was in the form of a number of Gotteskammern in the old area of town near the church on Pelzerstrasse and Schulstrasse. By labelling their dwellings for the

---

[102] As early as 1472, *OUB* no. 907.

[103] There was an official 'St Anthony-Kammer' at this location in 1518; it is not clear if this was Gertrude's apartment or an additional possession of St Anthony's, EKP 1/137.

[104] The bequest was given with the condition that the administrators allow the couple Johann and Wybbekenn Lodewychs to live in one 'good' room of the house for the rest of their lives 'free, without rent'. EKP 1/177v (18 May 1521). The priest Johan van Duthen, one of St Anthony's administrators, was one of the witnesses to the testament.

[105] For transferring the property, Wylteth received 'a small gift' from the administrators, but he returned it 'to the glory of God and the holy father St. Anthony, into the same *Gotteskammern*'. ArchGK no. 86 (6 May 1522); a copy can be found in EKP 1/189.

[106] ArchGK no. 48 (23 June 1522); a copy can be found in EKP 1/193.

[107] Actually, in a loan contract from 1525, the notary originally identified the lender as 'the advocates and administrators of St. Anthony's *Gasthaus*' but then crossed out the word '*Gasthaus*' and wrote '*armen*' (poor) above it; EKP 1/247v (28 September 1525).

poor as *Gotteskammern*, they indicate that St Anthony's provided primarily long-term residences for the needy. While a Gasthaus would offer a good deal of its assistance as short-term lodging for the poor, sick and travellers, Gotteskammern were intended to provide individual housing for the poor. (Recall that St Gertrude's Gasthaus consisted of both a Gasthaus building complex and Gotteskammern.) Therefore, St Anthony's Gotteskammern, located in the inner portion of the town, did not deal as frequently with the transient poor as did St Gertrude's Gasthaus on Emden's outskirts.

Yet poor provision through Gotteskammern was not limited to the confraternities and Gasthaus. Of course, most people who wanted to establish a Gotteskammer for the poor donated or bequeathed their house or room to one of the existing poor relief institutions. Johan Deweren's Gotteskammern with Our Lady's Confraternity and Boelhardus van Jemgum's with St Gertrude's Gasthaus illustrate this tendency. In this way, the dwelling-place could be incorporated into an already operating administrative structure, and the supervisors of the confraternity or of the Gasthaus would handle the affairs of the new Gotteskammer along with their regular poor relief activities. Certainly individuals making a small bequest of one or two rooms to the poor did not have the means with which to create a supervisory board to administer their legacy as an independent institution. Hermen Wessels, however, bucked the trend and provides the most prominent example of a free-standing, independent Gotteskammern foundation in sixteenth-century Emden.

The priest Hermen Wessels held a benefice at the Altar of the Holy Sacrament in the Grosse Kirche in Emden since at least 1487. From 1485 until about 1496, he served as *commissarius* of the episcopal office in Münster, and from 1494 until his death in 1507 he was the main preacher (Kirchherr) of the Grosse Kirche.[108] We have no indication of Hermen's income as Emden's preacher, but he was certainly financially well off.[109] There is no evidence of his membership in any of Emden's confraternities, but this should not suggest a lack of piety. Indeed, his charitable endowments are the largest found in Emden before the Reformation. Shortly before 1507, he endowed a new communion painting for the Altar of the Holy Sacrament.[110] He was most

---

[108] Lamschus, *Herrschaft der Cirksena*, pp. 487f; Kappelhoff, 'Reformation in Emden', I, 100, 102.

[109] Lamschus, *Herrschaft der Cirksena*, pp. 488f, has investigated the property holdings of Hermen Wessels and found seven personal loan contracts with Hermen's capital investment at 374 rheinische gulden, as well as records of Hermen's possession of at least five *Grassen* land (not a large amount), two houses and five *Warfen* (real estate lots) in town.

[110] Kappelhoff, 'Reformation in Emden', I, 97, 100.

generous, however, in his provision for the poor. In his testament, Hermen Wessels established a new, private social welfare foundation, which through the next century bore his name as the 'Hermen Wessels Gotteskammern' or sometimes the 'Hermen Wessels Foundation' (*Spende*). His endowment, which was given 'to the glory of the Holy Sacrament', consisted of five Gotteskammern in which the poor could live. Undoubtedly, the endowment also included land and capital which would provide an income to maintain these Gotteskammern, but Hermen's testament does not survive to indicate the size of this endowment. Unlike Boelhardus van Jemgum's endowment for new Gotteskammern to be administered by St Gertrude's Gasthaus, Hermen Wessels created an independent administration for Gotteskammern.

This foundation first appeared in the sources in 1513 when Ulffert Taltken and his wife Galcke made their testament. In it they bequeathed their entire properties – 'for the salvation of both their souls' – to Hermen Wessels's five Gotteskammern. Ulffert and his wife directed that their goods be imparted 'to the use of the poor in these Kammern' in order to 'improve their rent' incomes by augmenting the foundation's endowment.[111] Following Ulffert's death in 1526, the executors of Hermen's testament sold this house and obtained additional capital 'for the use of the poor'.[112]

Hermen Wessels did not turn to one of the established institutions in order to administer these Gotteskammern. Instead, he appointed two men as administrators. In the earliest surviving documents, these men were referred to simply as the executors of Hermen's testament.[113] Since Hermen Wessels intended his endowment to be a perpetual foundation, he must have specified the method by which new administrators were to be chosen or elected. Unfortunately, because his testament is not extant, it is impossible to determine what Hermen's plan was.

The responsibilities of the administrators of Hermen Wessels's Gotteskammern were similar to those of the other contemporary institutions. They selected the poor people to live in the Gotteskammern; they handled the finances of the foundation and maintained the Gotteskammern with the yearly revenues from the endowment fund; and to enrich the endowment fund they sold property which had been donated to the Gotteskammern. The administrators also invested any available capital by making loans to individuals in Emden.[114]

---

[111] EKP 1/68 (10 November 1513).

[112] Ibid. 1/259 (7 May 1526).

[113] Hyndrick Putnam and Hermen Wolkinn served as the initial administrators; ibid. 1/76; Putnam functioned in this capacity until at least 1526; ibid. 1/259.

[114] For instance, ibid. 1/76 (27 October 1514) and 1/187 (28 September 1522).

The final piece of Emden's late medieval social welfare puzzle, the Lazarus-House, was the oldest of all the known institutions in the city, though none of its records survive. The Lazarus-House was a house intended to care for, or rather confine, the sick, specifically victims of leprosy and the plague. It existed by the beginning of the fifteenth century and was located on the far eastern fringe of town, on the outskirts of the later suburb of Emden, 'Kleine [Small] Faldern'.[115] We know nothing of its actual operation or administration, only that it possessed an adjacent 'garden'.[116] By 1580, the *haussitzenden* deacons of Emden's church owned the Lazarus-House, and the terms *Lazarus-Huus* and *Lazarus-Gang* (alleyway) continue to appear in the sources well into the seventeenth century.[117]

Thus, in analysing the institutionalised forms of charity in late medieval Emden, it becomes apparent that most recorded giving to the poor was done outside the official hierarchy of the church. Lay confraternities and poor-houses administered almost all the organised charity in the town, with little or no organised poor relief provided by the church itself, with the exception of the alms which should have been distributed outside of the Franciscan monastery in neighbouring Faldern (see Map 2.3 and Figure 2.2). To be sure, acts of piety were common in late medieval Emden: endowments to the church and its altars and alms to the poor. Both types of donations were usually given 'to the glory of God' and to the 'salvation of [the donor's] soul'. Yet, interestingly, none of the known bequests of alms to the poor were given directly to the church hierarchy for distribution; donors funnelled almost all charitable bequests to poor relief institutions through the confraternities, hospitals and Gotteskammern. An additional source, pre-Reformation law codes, can help to supplement the picture of Emden's poor relief institutions, by offering a few particular insights into the legal perceptions and expectations surrounding poor relief and poverty.

While the fifteenth and early sixteenth-century territorial law codes allude to the religious connections between the church and the poor, the East Frisian law made no clear references to ecclesiastical poor relief in

---

[115] See Map 2.3. The location of the Lazarus-House is only approximate. EKP 10/720 (18 October 1567); Harkenroht's edition of Beninga's *Chronyk*, p. 354; Loesing, *Geschichte der Stadt Emden*, p. 24; *EJb*, 14 (1902), pp. 479ff.

[116] EKP 4/153v (23 December 1551).

[117] By the end of the sixteenth century, the deacons distributed money and supplies to those in the Lazarus-House: ArchGK no. 1118, p. 29v (1574); no. 3194, 170 (1581), 233 (1582). Harkenroht, p. 354; ArchGK no. 3001, at end of book, after the Testament section, on page dealing with the 'sose und lettse klufft'. The local *haussitzenden* deacons will be discussed in Chapter 4 below.

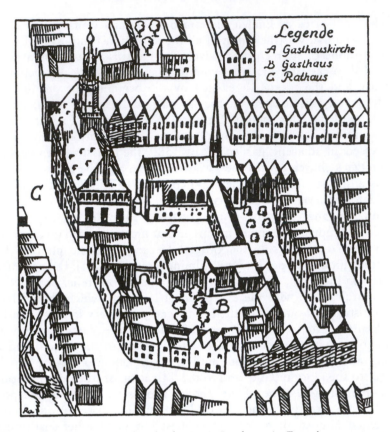

2.2   Seventeenth-century detail of 'New' Gasthaus (a Franciscan monastery until 1557)

the area. The legal protections given by East Frisian law to both the 'administrators of the poor' and the poor-houses paralleled the traditional protections granted to the clergy and may even have stimulated the creation of a number of lay institutions which practised poor relief in late medieval Emden. Although the law codes do not detail the status of the poor and poor relief in late medieval East Frisia, they reveal that a legal distinction was already being made between the deserving and the unworthy poor.

The legal groundwork for medieval life in East Frisia came from the Frisian Law, which took an independent form in each of the East Frisian local territories. The common law of the Emsigerland, the Emsiger Recht, is of the most interest because the jurisdiction of the Emsiger Recht included Emden and the surrounding countryside of the Emsigerland. Moreover, the Emsiger Recht ultimately became the local law that formed the basis for the East Frisian common law, the Ostfriesisches Landrecht, compiled by the Cirksena Count Edzard I in 1509.[118] Frisian law especially emphasised property rights and fines for personal injuries. The surviving fourteenth-century and mid-fifteenth-century manuscripts of the Emsiger Recht dealt with many of the same issues as the Ostfriesisches Landrecht. Count Edzard took the basic principles of the earlier Emsiger Recht and expanded upon them for his new East Frisian law in the early sixteenth century.

One legal principle alludes to the connection between the poor and the church. If a bequest was left with no qualified heir, the goods were to be divided into three parts: 'the judge should take the first portion; the church and poor people should have the second part; with the last third, one should repair the dams and dikes which the whole locality is responsible to maintain'.[119] But surviving manuscripts of the Emsiger Recht contain no specific descriptions of the provision of poor relief.

Nevertheless, the law codes mention the legal status of the poor several times. Since money fines remedied most crimes in Frisian law, most references to poor people in the Emsiger Recht dealt with their ability to pay fines levied on them. The basic principle applied in the law was that if a man were too poor to pay the appropriate fine, his family became responsible. With certain crimes (manslaughter or robbery, for instance), the family's inability to pay would result in a death sentence.[120] Poverty – or the inability to obtain the necessary money to pay the fines – could also determine one's guilt of a crime. The Emsiger Recht called for the ordeal of judicial combat to settle all cases involving the robbery of a woman. If the accused should be too poor to hire a soldier and have no relative to step in for him, he would be considered guilty. If, on the other hand, the female accuser proved to be too poor to hire a fighter, the accused had the opportunity to bring in six men

---

[118] An important reason for the expansion of the Emsiger Recht to cover all of East Frisia may stem from the fact Edzard and the Cirksena family, the first ruling house in East Frisia, originated from the Emsigerland before becoming counts of East Frisia during the second half of the fifteenth century. Wybren Jan Buma and Wilhelm Ebel (eds), *Das Emsiger Recht* (Göttingen, 1967), p. 8. Matthias von Wicht used a manuscript which probably dates from 1527 in his edition (and the only printed copy) of the Ostfriesisches Landrecht: *Das Ostfriesische Land-Recht nebst dem Deich- und Syhlrechte, mit verschiedenen der ältesten Handschrifften zusammen gehalten und von vielen Schreibfehlern gesäubert* (Aurich, 1746). See also Walter Schulz, 'Studien zur Genese und Überlieferung des Ostfriesischen Landrechts', *EJb*, 72 (1992), pp. 81–169.

[119] Buma and Ebel, *Emsiger Recht*, p. 227 no. 75. Compare with the similar rules expressed in the *Ostfriesischen Landrecht*; Wicht, *Ostfriesische Land-Recht*, Lib. I, Cap. 127 (pp. 266–8), Lib. II, Cap. 153 (pp. 452–3).

[120] For example, Buma and Ebel, *Emsiger Recht*, pp. 27 no. 15, 139 no. 3, 159 no. 29, 163 no. 47, 205 no. 3, 217 nos 29–30.

from his family as witnesses; he would then swear twelve oaths that he was completely innocent.[121]

The Emsiger Recht can offer a few other examples of attitudes toward the poor, at least with respect to their status before the law. Certain types of poor people had inherently higher protections under the law: fines for attacking a widow, orphan or pilgrim were to be doubled because these poor 'stand under the king's guardianship'.[122] A man without property was not admitted as a witness in complaints which dealt with property, and the Frisian ecclesiastical law (in a fifteenth-century manuscript) reveals a distinction between worthy and unworthy poor in late medieval society: 'This is ecclesiastical law: A poor man may not be a witness because the opinion prevails that he will do it for the money; this should be understood about the shameless and greedy poor and not about all of the poor.'[123] Thus the law depicts a growing apprehension by the end of the fifteenth century about some poor who were not worthy of the legal rights and protections accorded others.

The Ostfriesisches Landrecht provided no explicit regulation of poor relief, but several of its legal clarifications and descriptions enhance the somewhat hazy picture of poor relief and of the legal status and rights of the poor in East Frisia at the beginning of the sixteenth century. The law codes demonstrate the important religious understanding which forged people's perceptions of poverty and the poor. Alluding to the biblical injunction of Exodus 22 for protection of widows and orphans, the Ostfriesisches Recht imposed greater punishments on those guilty of robbing 'widows, orphans, and all those who are defenceless, such as pilgrims, beggars, those who do public penance and all ecclesiastical messengers'.[124] Likewise, the law accorded the privilege of the general territorial peace both to 'houses of God' (Gotteshäusern) and to 'men of God' (Gottesmännern) in order to protect them against violence.[125]

> In order to understand this other decree correctly according to the opinion of our ancestors, it is to be noted that by Gottes-Häuser, here is understood, churches, hermitages, monasteries, Gasthäuser [poor-houses], in which the poor are being supported, as well as pastors' and priests' houses.[126]

---

[121] Ibid., p. 157 no. 157.

[122] Ibid., p. 37 no. 13. This basic principle made up an earlier decree as well, which included all homeless people, penitents and messengers of the church in this special legal category; p. 25 no. 11.

[123] Ibid., pp. 159 no. 30, 217 no. 32, 235 no. 5b.

[124] Wicht, Ostfriesische Land-Recht, Lib. I, Cap. 54, Cap. 55 and Cap. 96 (pp. 101–6, 197–8).

[125] Ibid., Lib. I, Cap. 21, Cap. 22 (pp. 39–42).

[126] Ibid., Lib. I, Cap. 21 (pp. 39–40).

> By *Gottes-Männer* one understands here all godly and spiritual
> people in cloisters, Beguines or priests, deacons, sub-deacons, wid-
> ows, orphans, as well as poor people, who may not feed themselves
> from their own goods, and shame themselves to beg for bread, and
> anyone who without fraud must seek alms by the streets and
> houses and can earn nothing.[127]

Thus the traditional East Frisian law considered houses to aid the poor
in the same legal category as churches and monasteries. It also placed
the 'deserving poor' – widows, orphans, and those who 'shame themselves' and seek alms 'without fraud' – in the same classification as
clergymen and members of religious orders. This legal status implies a
view of the poor which elevated their religious significance, as was
common in the Middle Ages.

A noteworthy example from later in the Ostfriesischen Landrecht
shows an aspect of the legal application of this privilege of 'general
peace'. If someone were to strike a priest, deacon or sub-deacon, the
amount of the fine would depend on the location of the attack. If the
clergyman were attacked while in a place that was not forbidden to
him, the fine would be tripled. When, however, he were struck while in
a place where he should not have been, such as a public inn or a
dishonourable house, then the penalty was the simple fine for an attack.[128] The law recognised that 'administrators of the poor' would not
have a specific place to which they could be limited, and thus, any
attack on them while they were 'in the service of the poor in order to
sustain them', regardless of where it occurred, would result in a doubled penalty.[129] Unfortunately, there are no sources that document what
the functions of these late medieval 'administrators of the poor' were or
how they were organised.

Clearly, though, the emphasis was placed first on private care by
relatives and friends, rather than on organised relief efforts. When
people became too old or sick to care for themselves, the law made the
next heir responsible to take them in, along with their goods, and to
care for them for the rest of their lives.[130] Another example of legally
mandated familial relief is the Ostfriesisches Landrecht's case of two
brothers, one rich and the other poor. The rich brother had a duty to
provide the poor brother with any necessary support, but the rich
brother was 'not responsible to support him for nothing': if the poor

---

[127] Ibid., Lib. I, Cap. 22 (pp. 40–41).

[128] Ibid., Lib. III, Cap. 29 (p. 686). If the priest could show that he was performing an
honourable task at this place, then the penalty could also be tripled.

[129] Ibid., Lib. III, Cap. 30 (p. 689).

[130] Ibid., Lib. I, Cap. 129 (p. 272).

man could support himself with a craft or other work, then he should not be the responsibility of his wealthy brother.[131]

Such examples of private relief further demonstrate that a legal category of the 'deserving poor' existed. The givers of the relief were not expected to provide support 'for nothing', and those who received support were expected to help themselves as fully as possible before obtaining the legally mandated relief, with whatever goods they still possessed or by working at their craft as much as possible. The Ostfriesisches Landrecht further recognised the need for legal protection in cases of poverty caused by unforeseeable circumstances.

> The fifteenth common law is to be [so] understood: if anyone had given something to a man in his distress, as [he was in] prison, [or] he was burned out of his house or goods, or in other circumstances, and the same man to whom it was given dies with a surviving wife and children, then this widow, with the children, is not accountable to those friends who request [her] to give back this gift.[132]

The law thus granted a small benefit to those who became needy through no fault of their own and recognised the reality that an already impoverished widow with children, deprived of the income of her husband, could easily become forced into poverty if required to repay all of her debts. Hence, East Frisian law treated loans and gifts given in times of distress almost as alms and saw them as necessary to keep people from becoming permanently poor.

The law codes therefore provide insight into attitudes toward the poor at the time when Emden's institutional social welfare just begins to come into view. During the fifteenth century and by the beginning of the sixteenth century, a distinction had clearly developed in East Frisia between the 'deserving' and the fraudulent poor. In most of the references, the poor are defined as those who cannot support themselves, often with emphasis placed on the fact that if they are able to support themselves in any way, they must do so before obtaining aid. The late medieval and pre-Reformation East Frisian law attests to the existence of poor-houses and 'administrators of the poor' and implies an ecclesiastical administration, but provides no insight as to the specific organisation of late medieval poor relief. The legal definitions of 'houses of God' and 'men of God' reveal that the poor (at least the 'shamefaced' poor) and the houses which had been established to aid the poor had a religious significance which placed them on an equal legal footing with church institutions and personnel.

---

[131] Ibid., Lib. II, Cap. 46 (p. 362–3).
[132] Ibid., Lib. I, Cap. 98 (pp. 201–6).

The law code's apparent lack of interest in the regulation of poor relief institutions or practices results largely from a contemporary understanding of poverty as the 'personal fate of the individual'.[133] Despite a scattered variety of small institutions providing poor relief, the poor in Emden could not necessarily count on regular institutional relief as the sixteenth century opened. Beyond any sustenance provided by begging and supportive family and friends, some poor might receive the benefit of charitable activities performed by confraternities. However, if one did not have his or her own shelter or was unable to pay rent, the Gasthaus or the Gotteskammern offered the best, and perhaps only, solution.

We have seen that the institutions of Gertrude's Gasthaus and St Anthony's administered numerous Gotteskammern; even Our Lady's Confraternity decided to establish at least one of its own. Although most donations of property and houses to the poor were bequeathed to one of these communal institutions, there were occasional private foundations outside of these institutional structures. The two foundations for which evidence survives were by Vicar Herr Engelke and Pastor Hermen Wessels, priests who established Gotteskammern which functioned independently for many years. Indeed, Hermen Wessels's donation became a new relief institution with its own endowment and administrative board. In both cases, however, the church hierarchy was not involved. Although both men were priests, they established independent foundations without any official church institutional involvement in their poor relief. These two also did not turn to the confraternity. In the early nineteenth century, Emden still had about twenty Gotteskammern; this estimate would not be far off for pre-Reformation Emden.[134]

Obtaining residence in a Gotteskammern was no mean feat. Several obvious factors increased the difficulty. The limited number of facilities combined with the fact that they provided long-term housing, meant that there probably were not many empty Gotteskammern available. Moreover, many of the donors placed stipulations on their bequests requiring that the administrators provide a room for a specific person or family. Others, such as Boelhardus, indicated that any of his relatives in need were to have precedence whenever there was an opening in 'his' Gotteskammern. Obviously, the poor relief recipient needed to have good connections with either the donor or the administrators in order to obtain approval to live in a Gotteskammer.

---

[133] Uta Lindgren, 'Europas Armut. Probleme, Methoden, Ergebnisse einer Untersuchungsserie', *Saeculum*, 28 (1977), p. 401.

[134] Friedrich Arends, *Ostfriesland und Jever in geographischer, statistischer und besonders landwirtschaftlicher Hinsicht*, vol. I (Emden, 1818), p. 259.

Emden had one fully functioning Gasthaus – St Gertrude's – before the Reformation, while St Anthony's 'Gasthaus' does not appear to have been in existence very long and in fact provided most of its assistance through its Gotteskammern. Although Gertrude's Gasthaus administered Gotteskammern as well, its primary relief was offered through residence in its Gasthaus. Unlike in-house care provided in the Gotteskammern, the purpose of the Gasthaus was to provide short-term maintenance and residence, chiefly for the sick and the travelling. Hence a large proportion of the Gasthaus's recipients were transient. When Gertrude's Gasthaus needed additional space to expand its facilities in 1505, it moved 'outside the northern gates' to a still relatively uninhabited section of Emden. This move had two benefits: first, it put the Gasthaus in closer proximity to the poorer sections of the expanding town, and second, it took the Gasthaus and its poor out of the wealthier part of town. A concern about institutional care of the transient poor in the old (prestigious) part of town probably contributed to the failure of St Anthony's Gasthaus to endure very long after 1520.

The Recipients of Poor Relief

The picture of Emden's poor relief as it functioned before the Protestant Reformation can be made as clear as possible with the available evidence by adding one more component: the poor themselves. The nature of the evidence before the mid-sixteenth century – scattered wills, contracts, the town's 'complaint book' – makes difficult a complete reconstruction of the daily practice of charity and portrayal of the poor relief recipients. In fact, one rarely encounters those who actually received poor relief. Yet a careful analysis of the scanty sources furnishes some indications of the ways in which poor relief was carried out. By going beyond the descriptions of institutions, such a search for the poor recipients themselves can thus provide a better understanding of the institutions, approaches and conflicts that were involved in charity during the early sixteenth century.

Throughout the pre-Reformation period, poverty was largely understood as the personal fate of the individual.[135] The first line of defence against poverty was to receive assistance from a network of family and friends, when available. Take, for example, the case of husbands and wives who provided for their surviving spouse's maintenance, particularly older couples: virtually all of the surviving wills from the early

---

[135] Lindgren, 'Europas Armut', p. 401.

sixteenth century in Emden are joint agreements between a husband and his wife.[136] These contracts indicate that following a death the surviving spouse would have access to all of the couple's combined goods.[137] Testaments frequently specified the surviving spouse's rights to live in their house for life, with food and clothing. Moreover, should emergency situations arise in which the surviving spouse faced poverty, he or she could, without reproach from any heirs, sell any property as necessary. Thus Johan Thonys and his wife Gheseke compacted with each other that the surviving spouse remain 'owner of their combined goods ... including housing with the other goods ... in order to prevent his distress and to make use of [them] if he becomes [burdened] by need'. This couple went even further than this common spousal exchange and stipulated that Gheseke's sister Swaneke also be allowed to live in their house 'for life' and be provided with board and clothing 'according to all her needs'.[138]

Parents, too, specified the way in which surviving children should be cared for, often naming guardians for their children. The previously mentioned Johan and Gheseke stipulated that if they were to have any children, then the surviving spouse 'and no one else [would have] guardianship' of the children. The still-living parent would 'advise and support [the children] in expenses, clothing and all their needs' until the children entered into a 'marriage or cloister'.[139] Other testaments include placement of the child or children into an apprenticeship along with the phrase 'marriage or cloister'.[140] These duties followed the surviving spouse if he or she remarried. When Gheseke, the widow of Lutkenn Hansze, remarried, she and her new husband Gerydt Kuper recognised their duty to provide for Gheseke and Lutkenn's children 'in clothing and board until the time that each is 14 years old and can earn their [sic] own board'.[141]

---

[136] Lamschus, *Herrschaft der Cirksena*, p. 16.

[137] In childless marriages these compacts were generally valid without limits. However, when children survived as heirs, East Frisian law placed a number of restrictions upon bequests (see Wicht, *Ostfriesische Land-Recht*, especially Book II). For instance, the surviving spouse could receive possession of only a portion equal to that of each of the children, plus usufruct to a small additional portion as *Leibzucht* (Wicht, Lib. II, Cap. 182); and according to the Landrecht this could only be broken in the case that the children died before the longest-surviving spouse (Cap. 180). For a discussion of special gifts to spouses and children in East Frisian testaments, see Harm Buss, *Letztwillige Verfügungen nach ostfriesischem Recht* (Aurich, 1966), especially pp. 80–81.

[138] 14 August 1513, EKP 1/67. For other examples of *Leibzuchte*, see EKP 1/44 (1512), 1/68 (1513), 1/92 (1516), 1/111v (1517), 1/174v (1521), among many others.

[139] Ibid. 1/67.

[140] For instance, ibid. 1/202.

[141] Ibid. 1/200 (1523).

Of course, in the case of orphans, guardianships were necessary to maintain the children and oversee the children's inheritance. The duties of the guardian also extended to arranging for the support of an orphan when that child's properties were gone. In order to stave off poverty for the orphaned children of Lutke Hayen, their guardians Hermen Maeler and Johan Pelzer van Ossenbrugge had to sell the children's house. That move, however, proved insufficient to meet the immediate needs of the children for the coming year. So in addition to the sale price of the house the guardians further arranged with the buyer that one of the children, the daughter, be provided with free clothing and board for a year.[142]

In spite of these kinship 'safety nets' which existed in both law and practice, a great many people in pre-Reformation Emden lived on the edge of poverty. Testaments often stipulated that the poor or 'shame-faced' relatives of the testator be provided for from the bequest.[143] The '*haussitzenden* poor' (literally, 'house-sitting') was the local term used to describe those 'shame-faced' local, or non-transient, poor who had housing of their own, yet were in need of additional support.[144] Moreover, there was no clear line of demarcation between those on the edge of poverty and the *haussitzenden* poor. In 1513, for example, Harmen Haetenkerle and Erne Platen were finally able to pay the church the back-rent that they owed on the half-house in which they lived. Yet the church needed to ensure that it received a regular income from the house, and in a newly drafted rental agreement, the church stipulated that Harmen and Erne could live in the house only 'so long as they were able to pay their rent'.[145] Such actions demonstrate that even the church became strict from time to time in enforcing rent payments; if a person could not pay rent, he or she could fall back on the family or, for those in more difficult straits, the possibilities of the Gasthaus or Gotteskammern were available.

Many of those people in, or on the verge of, poverty lived in the 'new town', or the section of the city to the north of Grossestrasse (see Map 2.3). Unlike the older settled area of the city, Emden's 'new town' was particularly open to renters. Some of the wealthier merchants built houses and apartments there to be rented out, especially as the city began expanding at the end of the fifteenth century.[146] One would

---

[142] Ibid. 1/183v (1522).

[143] For example, 'tor eeren godes den armen' (ibid. 1/67, 92), 'tor eeren godes tot salicheit synre sielen der begavynge synenn armenn vrunden' (1/167v, 174v, 183), 'synen scamelenn vrunden' (1/197v).

[144] The term first appears in a testament from 1512: 'in godes eer unnd umme godes wyllen den armen huessyttenden und daer dat best van noeden is'; ibid. 1/44.

[145] ArchGK no. 358, p. 215.

[146] Kappelhoff, 'Reformation in Emden', I, 91. For instance, Johan Kumpeneye, a

furthermore expect the rents there to be lower since the other properties in this part of town cost much less. Hence those without houses of their own could find quarters more easily in the 'new town'.

Only a few of pre-Reformation Emden's *haussitzenden* poor have been identified, and those with identifiable places of residences lived in the 'new town'. Eede, 'a shame-faced woman', lived in 'the new city behind the Gasthaus' with her husband and child and was involved in a criminal complaint in 1515. Eede's complaint reveals that she and her family carried out some type of activity at the marketplace near their house (the nature of the activity is not described, perhaps some type of trading or even begging). This is where Hans Olyslagher ran over Eede and her child with his wagon, forcing them into the mud.[147] Such indignities were not lightly accepted by this poor woman, and she pressed her complaint before the authorities.

While poverty was a fact of life for many people, those who had some housing of their own were in a much better situation than less fortunate poor. Another *haussitzenden* poor person was able, despite his poverty, to maintain some independence from relief institutions by working for the city. 'Shame-faced' Evert worked for the city from 1509 to 1514 as a street-cleaner, and frequent payments to him from the city treasury indicate that he held this as a regular job.[148]

Of course, any poor folks without lodging of their own found themselves in a much more difficult position. For them, the charitable institutions of the confraternities, the Gasthaus and the Gotteskammern were crucial. The administrators of these institutions had to co-ordinate the idiosyncratic wishes of their private donors with the needs of the poor. Often, therefore, close connections to either a donor or an administrator could facilitate the receipt of services since the administrators were responsible for selecting which poor received the charity.[149] One need only remember Boelhardus van Jemgum's stipulation that his poor relatives or friends be given first chance at any free room in his Gotteskammern.[150] Johan Schroder and his wife Aelheyt bequeathed

---

member of one of Emden's rich merchant families, owned apartments by the Neue Müntze which he rented to a number of people in 1510; Quer., p. 7.

[147] Quer., p. 36. Other 'shame-faced' poor who show up in the 'Emden Complaint Book' are 'Meynste eyn schamel vrowken' (1511, Quer., p. 15) and 'scamele Yke' (1512, Quer., p. 18).

[148] Lamschus, *Herrschaft der Cirksena*, p. 185; StaE, AK 2/2, pp. 3, 5, 71, 77, 80, 83, 92, 99, 115.

[149] For example, it was the priest and administrators of St Anthony's Confraternity who selected the poor and sent them to live in the confraternity's Gotteskammern, EKP 1/88v.

[150] Ibid. 1/1.

their house to St Anthony's Confraternity in 1521 as Gotteskammern for the poor. Although they made this gift to expand the confraternity's services to the poor, the donors attached some strings. Specifically they insisted that their friends Johan Lodewychs and his wife Wybbekenn be allowed to live 'for [the rest of] their lives without rent in one good room in the house'.[151]

Because no account books from the Gotteskammern or Gasthäuser survive (if any were kept at this time), very little information is available about the recipients of this sort of assistance. It is certainly possible that some of the aforementioned 'shame-faced' poor received free lodging in a Gotteskammer. 'Shame-faced' Eede and her family may have lived in one of the many Gotteskammern associated with and around St Gertrude's Gasthaus; the notation identified her as living 'behind' the Gasthaus. The only other identified resident of a Gotteskammer was a poor cobbler, whose trade placed him among society's lowest-paid occupations. This unnamed man lived 'in the consecrated house next to Herr Johan van Duten', the priest and an administrator of St Anthony's Confraternity. The confraternity obviously had a Gotteskammer next to the house of their priest, which allowed for daily oversight of the recipient of poor relief by an administrator. In 1520, this cobbler was charged with fighting and injuring a tailor's apprentice.[152] The evidence, however, provides no indication of whether this misbehaviour affected the cobbler's status as an occupant of a Gotteskammer.

Likewise, only one resident of the St Gertrude's Gasthaus has been clearly identified in the period before the Reformation. The soldier Hans van Bakemoer, who was probably only temporarily in Emden, was in the Gasthaus in 1515, where he 'was lying on the bed in his sickness'. Particularly interesting is the complaint that Hans made, and what it reveals about his care in the Gasthaus. Part of Hans's care involved treatment with consecrated oil. Hans complained that when Haseke, wife of the merchant and Gasthaus administrator Hinrick Kerstgens, came into the Gasthaus with the oil as he lay in bed, she began verbally to abuse him and the others in the Gasthaus.[153] According to Hans, Haseke 'maliciously' called them 'lame thieves and lame traitors. Since you have nowhere to go, you come here into the Gasthaus, where someone must provide you with board.'[154]

Although only men served as administrators of the Gasthaus, women – specifically the wives of the administrators – also played an important

---

[151] EKP 1/177v.

[152] Quer., p. 56.

[153] For information on Hinrick Kerstgens, see Fehler, 'Social Welfare', p. 145.

[154] Quer., p. 37.

role in the actual provision of poor relief. In the instance of Hans the soldier, a Gasthaus administrator's wife was the one who came into the Gasthaus bringing treatment for the sick residents. Poor relief extended not only to room and board, but included medical care as well; they tried to cure the sick in the Gasthaus. According to Hans's complaint, a number of sick or disabled people resided in the Gasthaus at the time. It seems fantastic that the wife of an administrator should make such a wild statement while in the process of providing relief to the poor. Haseke might have been upset that her husband's position as a Gasthaus administrator required her to perform such personal care for the sick. Another possible explanation, although it requires quite an extrapolation from the evidence, could be tied to Haseke's opinion of the plundering activities of Count Edzard's troops throughout 1515 in the northern portions of East Frisia.[155] Should personal, family or business associations within East Frisia have upset Haseke about these plundering expeditions, and if the soldier Hans along with some of the other Gasthaus residents were involved in these operations, that might explain the insults of 'lame thieves and lame traitors'. Whatever the full truth of the allegation, this conflict shows that the poor were not always satisfied with the relief they received. Certainly something made Hans dissatisfied with his care in the Gasthaus. Whether Haseke uttered those words or not, Hans's reaction illustrates the existence of some negative feeling toward those perceived as undeserving poor, at least in the minds of the poor themselves.

Pre-Reformation charity did not always result in good will between benefactor and recipient. Another complaint, registered in the town's complaint book in 1520, illustrates further dissatisfaction with poor relief. Styne, the wife of Frederick Kremer, alleged that Lyubbe, Johan Deweren's wife, had not distributed alms properly. Once again the wife of an administrator (this time of Our Lady's Confraternity) is shown to be active in the distribution of poor relief.[156] A dispute arose as to the disbursement of 30 gulden in alms that had been bequeathed 'for God's sake'.[157] The feud and its verbal insults quickly spread to include friends and relatives, even Lyubbe's brother Thomas. Frederick Kremer and Styne 'spitefully spoke to [Thomas] and called him [a] calf and [a] donkey', and they offered 'to prove to him that he is a donkey and a calf'.[158] Occasionally, the conflicts increased from name-calling to

---

[155] Schmidt, *Politische Geschichte Ostfrieslands*, pp. 140f.

[156] Johan Deweren was especially involved in poor relief as he built the confraternity's Gotteskammer in 1523; see above, pp. 41–2, and Fehler, 'Social Welfare', p. 103.

[157] Quer., p. 55.

[158] Ibid.

physical violence. Even the priest of St Gertrude's Gasthaus, the spiritual adviser to the poor, was not safe from attacks or abuse. In 1519, Hermen van Groningen attacked Herr Eyllert, the Gasthaus priest, and beat him about his left arm.[159] This attack took place even while Herr Eyllert was in the churchyard in the Gasthaus, a place explicitly protected by law from violence.

The churchyard of the Gasthaus was certainly no safe haven from acts of violence. Taelke, the wife of the barber Hermen Segheboden, accused a women named Tyade of robbery ('she had stolen a shirt') and chased her into the Gasthaus churchyard where Taelke hit her three times on her left arm with a bedpost. Tyade complained that her arm was 'black and blue and [she] will prove that', indicating eyewitnesses to the attack around the Gasthaus.[160] In another act of violence perpetrated in the churchyard of the Gasthaus, Hermen Segheboden allegedly hit Modeke Haghedoirn four times in the face, causing her nose and mouth to bleed. Hermen Segheboden also allegedly 'pronounced judgement against her' and said to her, 'You feeble whore, you ought not go in there', referring either to the Gasthaus or the Gasthaus church which would both have been adjacent to the churchyard.[161]

Apart from the issue of violence around and on the Gasthaus property, these examples also raise the question of the identity of Hermen and Taelke Segheboden, and of what they were doing at the Gasthaus. They apparently considered themselves some sort of supervisors of order, a self-styled police force. There had been earlier complaints against Taelke for accusing people of theft.[162] Hermen was a respected barber who occasionally could be found binding the wounds of those injured in fights.[163] His assault on Modeke Haghedoirn included a charge of immoral behaviour and an implication that she should therefore not be allowed into the Gasthaus facilities. In another instance, Herman, together with one of the Gasthaus priests, Herr Boele, witnessed a fight that took place in Hermen's house; thus the Gasthaus priest had been present at Hermen Segheboden's house.[164] The fact that

---

[159] Ibid., p. 54. Hermen van Groningen was accused of causing injury to someone else earlier in the year; ibid., p. 53. Herr Eyllert was the priest of St Gertrude's Gasthaus between at least 1512 and 1522; EKP 1/55, 1/199v. He joined Our Lady's Confraternity around 1512 or 1513, 'Unser lever vrouwen register', no. 326. For some time, there were two priests in the Gasthaus: 'Herr Boele mede preester in Sunte Ghertrudenn gasthues' was mentioned between 1519 and 1525; EKP 1/167v, 1/247; Quer., p. 49.

[160] 1519, Quer., p. 47.

[161] 1519, ibid., p. 51.

[162] 1510, ibid., p. 7.

[163] For instance, 1511, ibid., p. 14.

[164] 1519, ibid., p. 49.

each of these incidents involving the Seghebodens and the Gasthaus took place in 1519 raises the possibility of a correlation between them. What official role the Seghebodens had, if any, is entirely a matter of speculation. They might have served as 'Gasthaus father and mother', providing daily supervision of the poor in the Gasthaus.[165] If so, that would suggest that life in the Gasthaus was not always a pleasant experience, and that misbehaviour or perceived disobedience by the recipients of poor relief could be punished violently.[166]

The few references to actual recipients of poor relief in pre-Reformation Emden survive almost solely in the town's complaint book. While this handful of examples should in no way be taken as normative for the period, they clearly demonstrate that Christian charity did not always function smoothly. Harsh words and even violence could erupt within an activity which carried with it great religious significance. Even before the Protestant Reformation, poor relief administrators discriminated against those they perceived as undeserving poor. For their part, the poor sometimes seem to have perceived that wealthy benefactors were involved in charity for their own salvation rather than out of genuine concern for the less fortunate. As the city grew and developed during the first quarter of the sixteenth century, there was a certain amount of discontent among poor relief benefactors and recipients who did not always see eye to eye.

Family relationships were the most expected source of relief when someone fell into poverty. Emden's law codes required family members to provide for each other, and the surviving testaments bear out that it was common practice. When one became poor without adequate kinship support, however, the only means of assistance were from the Franciscan monastery, through the brotherhoods, Gasthäuser, or Gotteskammern, or to support oneself by begging. References to begging and beggars do not appear in any of the contracts, testaments, account books or complaints from pre-Reformation Emden. Begging, however, was certainly the common and expected method for individuals to attempt to stave off dire poverty. When Count Enno composed his Church Ordinance in 1529, he invariably used the word 'beggars' instead of 'the poor' in discussions of poor relief, as will be seen in the following chapter.

---

[165] A 'Gasthaus master' supervised the poor at this time, as the above example of 'Gastmeystersche Peter' demonstrates, although the first actual references to 'Gasthaus parents' (Gasthauseltern) living in the Gasthaus come from the second half of the sixteenth century.

[166] If the complainants in these cases were recipients of poor relief (which, once again, is speculation), it should be noted that they were nevertheless able to bring their charges of injuries before the judge.

Early in the century, the Gasthaus moved from the city centre to the outskirts of town. This relocation moved care of the transient poor and beggars who needed short-term shelter away from the wealthier sections of town and from the immediate proximity of the church. In addition to becoming the locus for care of the transient poor, the newer, developing areas on Emden's periphery also became home to many of those in the lower economic strata; the 'new town' probably had a much higher proportion of people renting their residences than did the older areas of town.

The end of this period presents a picture of a moderately settled world in which the poor could turn to a varied mix of institutions where personal or familial resources were inadequate. In addition to many of the typical relief institutions found in European cities (monasteries, confraternities, hospitals), Emden counted some of a local character (Gotteskammern). Although the Protestant Reformation is often seen as a stimulus for the 'laicising' of hospitals, most of Emden's institutional charity, including the administration of the Gasthaus, was in lay hands, though not under the direct authority of the city government, before the Reformation.

As we depict this world around 1520, however, we know that an approaching storm will soon call many of this settled world of charity into question. Social and economic dislocation will stretch charity provision to its limits, and Luther and Protestant theologians across northern Europe will criticise the theological justifications of monasteries and confraternities; institutions which provided vital help for the poor will be undermined and ultimately destroyed. New theological precepts will produce new principles of charitable giving. Emden's institutions *will* undergo dramatic changes during the sixteenth century. Was it therefore the impact of the Reformation that transformed charitable provision in Emden? The next chapters will turn to this question and its implications.

CHAPTER THREE

Social Welfare after the Reformation
(*c.* 1525–50)

> We have shown that the Reformation created neither the commu-
> nal nor the governmental system of poor relief, since both had
> their counterparts in Catholic countries.
>
> Robert Jütte (1994)[1]

> Without the Reformation the centralisation and increased account-
> ability of poor relief which took place in the sixteenth and
> seventeenth centuries would have been unimaginable.
>
> Ole Peter Grell (1997)[2]

What *were* the effects of the Reformation on poor relief reforms of the
sixteenth century? After the confessionally based interpretations of the
last century, for the past three decades historians have emphasised
socio-economic causes. Ole Peter Grell has recently made an urgent call
for a revisionist interpretation of the socio-economic explanation (offered by Jütte and others) which will 're-insert' the Reformation into
the story.[3] The development of Protestantism certainly affected the story
of Emden's social welfare legislation and institutions, but the new Reformation ideology was not sufficient to bring real practical innovations
in Emden's poor relief. Without a doubt, a mix between the two catalysts helped modify Emden's social welfare system. In fact, the seeming
polar extremes of the controversy in the above quotations dissipate to
some degree if we but read on. Jütte continued his paragraph:

> But there can be no doubt that the discussion of Luther's principles
> of relief and their effects in the sixteenth century shaped the cen-
> tralized poor relief system not only in modern Germany but
> elsewhere in Europe. The Reformation paved the way for the de-
> velopment of a new social policy which favoured secular systems
> of poor relief.[4]

---

[1] Jütte, *Poverty and Deviance in Early Modern Europe* (Cambridge, 1994), p. 108.
[2] Grell, 'The Protestant imperative of Christian care and neighbourly love', in *Health Care and Poor Relief in Protestant Europe 1500–1700*, eds O. Grell and Andrew Cunningham (London, 1997), p. 51.
[3] Grell, 'The religious duty of care and the social need for control in early modern Europe', *The Historical Journal*, 39, 1 (1996), p. 263; compare 'Protestant imperative', pp. 43–60.
[4] Jütte, *Poverty and Deviance*, p. 108.

Even Grell concludes his essay:

> by emphasising that by seeking to re-insert the Reformation into the story about early modern innovations in poor relief and health care provision, I am not arguing that Protestantism alone brought about these changes, or that social and economic factors were of little or no consequence, but only that the Reformation was responsible for the speed and to some extent for the nature of these changes.[5]

As Jütte's and Grell's quotations imply, our investigation of Emden will also demonstrate that the question of the Reformation's role in poor relief provision yields few easy answers. Institutional poor relief change came relatively slowly. Even the institutions to which Luther's doctrines of 'justification by faith alone' and 'priesthood of all believers' were so inimical, Emden's confraternities and monastery, survived for three decades after the Reformation. But when real institutional innovation came (largely under the pressure of immigration after 1550), the transformations were swift and the Reformation clearly affected the nature of the changes. The earliest impact of the Reformation can be seen most clearly in East Frisia's Lutheran Church Ordinances. Yet even here, caution must be exercised. There is often a dramatic disconnection between the worlds of ordinances and of practical charitable provision. The church ordinances of Johannes Bugenhagen, Luther's friend and collaborator, provide an important demonstration of the need for restraint. For instance, his Ordinance for Lübeck (1531) called for the consolidation of the assets of all religious brotherhoods and hospitals into a common chest (*Hauptkasten*) to be administered by the fifteen oldest deacons of the city. Yet these reforms never actually took place in Lübeck.[6] We will begin our investigation with Emden's Reformation-era ordinances, but as we search for the intersection between them and practical poor relief provision, the difficulties of bringing practice into line with ideology become apparent.

---

[5] Grell, 'Protestant imperative', p. 60.

[6] Monika Zmyslony, 'Die geistlichen Bruderschaften in Lübeck bis zur Reformation' (Ph.D. thesis, Univ. Kiel, 1974), p. 153. For Grell's discussion of Bugenhagen's importance to the Protestant ideology of poor relief and health care provision, see 'Protestant imperative', pp. 52–9. See also Frank P. Lane, 'Poverty and Poor Relief in the German Church Orders of Johann Bugenhagen 1485–1558' (Ph.D. thesis, Ohio State University, 1973), pp. 141–224.

The Reformation in Emden

Piety and intellectual activity in Emden before the Reformation offer striking contrasts to the city's seemingly backward communal development. The clergy in Emden's Grosse Kirche were generally well educated; of the thirteen priests named in 1520, three held the title of Doctor, and five Magister.[7] The town's intellectual connections with the Netherlands, and especially with Dutch humanism, were also strong during the decades preceding the Reformation.[8] Emden's Latin school, which was administered in part by the churchwardens, was designed on the model of the schools of the 'Brethren of the Common Life' and the *Devotio Moderna*. Although the school was formally a church school, the teachers were probably not clergy of the Grosse Kirche. The Latin school, moreover, attracted large numbers of students: in 1505 the church had to purchase the buildings of the neighbouring *Gasthaus* (hospital) in order to enlarge the school.[9]

The first Protestant teaching took place in Emden between 1520 and 1524.[10] The first Protestant preacher, Georg Aportanus, arrived in Emden around 1518 from the house of the 'Brethren of the Common Life' in Zwolle, Holland, and served as tutor to the three sons of Count Edzard I.[11] After receiving a benefice from an altar in the Grosse Kirche, Aportanus began preaching. Because of his Protestant theological leanings, his sermons created controversy among his clerical colleagues, to such an extent that his fellow priests attempted to exclude him from his benefice and the pulpit. Nevertheless, he continued his preaching in an open field outside town, and his sermons resonated among some of the town's influential citizens who rallied to his cause. Count Edzard soon ordered Aportanus to be allowed back into the Grosse Kirche, and for a time Protestant and Catholic services took place side by side in this building.

Edzard's reinstatement of Aportanus should not necessarily be read as support for, or even tolerance of, Protestantism. Throughout the last

---

[7] Heinz Schilling, 'Reformation und Bürgerfreiheit: Emdens Weg zur calvinistischen Stadtrepublik', in Bernd Moeller (ed.), *Stadt und Kirche im 16. Jahrhundert* (Gütersloh, 1978), p. 135, note 28.

[8] Menno Smid, *Ostfriesische Kirchengeschichte* (Pewsum, 1974), pp. 115f.

[9] Bernd Kappelhoff, 'Die Reformation in Emden', part I, *EJb*, 57 (1977), p. 113f. On the church's transaction with St Gertrude's Gasthaus, see Chapter 2 above.

[10] Smid, *Kirchengeschichte*, pp. 116–21; Kappelhoff, 'Die Reformation in Emden', part II, *EJb*, 58 (1978), pp. 23f, suggests 1520 as the more probable beginning date.

[11] Friedrich Ritter, 'Zur Geschichte des ostfriesischen Reformators Georg Aportanus', *EJb*, 18 (1913), pp. 142–56; Smid, *Kirchengeschichte*, p. 118f; Kappelhoff, 'Reformation in Emden', II, pp. 23ff.

decade of his life – after the beginnings of the Protestant Reformation in Europe – Count Edzard maintained a certain restraint, bordering on lack of interest, in religious affairs. To be sure, his reinstatement of Aportanus probably had more to do with his concern that Aportanus be allowed to exercise the right to his legal benefice. Just as Count Edzard had not allowed priests to act 'unlawfully' in prohibiting Aportanus's new teachings, nor did he side with those citizens who favoured prohibiting the old. In 1527 Edzard appointed as Emden's provost the priest Poppo Manninga, who was, along with the humanist vicar Jacobus Canter, one of the strongest supporters of the old faith and fiercest critics of Aportanus and his supporters; Manninga held the office of Emden's provost until his death in 1540.[12]

Edzard's *de facto* policy of religious tolerance throughout the last years of his reign and the early years of the Reformation resulted in the arrival of a number of Protestant teachers and sects in East Frisia in addition to the strong survival of Catholic practices. Despite the count's dominance in civic and political affairs, Edzard allowed Protestantism to develop relatively freely within the city and territory. The religious fracturing which occurred within Emden's citizenry as a result of the Reformation was one more setback to the gradual communal developments of the previous decades.

Count Edzard's death on 16 February 1528 allowed his 23–year-old son Count Enno II to impose a religious settlement whose goal was to create a unified territorial church after the fragmentation of the Reformation. Enno entered straight away into negotiations with the Lutheran ministers of Bremen to create a territorial church ordinance which was based on Lutheran theology as expressed in Luther's 'German Mass' of 1526 and Johannes Bugenhagen's Lutheran Church Ordinances for the cities of Braunschweig and Hamburg. The new count brought two Bremen ministers to preach in the three major East Frisian cities of Emden, Aurich and Norden, but they faced great opposition, especially from local ministers who had accepted a Reformation along more Zwinglian lines. On 13 December 1529, Count Enno approved a church ordinance for East Frisia which organised the territory along Lutheran lines.[13] But a number of ministers responded by telling the count to stay out of the 'communion question'; they would follow him on the organisation of church ceremonies but could not go along with him on the

---

[12] Smid, *Kirchengeschichte*, pp. 115f, maintains some distance between the evidence of Humanism and the path toward the Reformation. Canter was from an important Groningen humanist family and was named Poet Laureate in 1494.

[13] The East Frisian Church Ordinances are edited in Emil Sehling's *Die evangelischen Kirchenordnungen des XVI. Jahrhunderts*, VII/2/i (Tübingen, 1963).

implementation of a Lutheran theology of the sacraments. Indeed, due to the intellectual connections with the Netherlands, the form of Protestantism which found most active support among the clergy and populace of East Frisia was closer to Zwingli than to Luther in its view of the sacrament of communion.[14] In order to arm themselves against the attacks of Lutherans, the East Frisian Zwinglians drew up a confession of faith in 1528 which rejected the Lutheran view of communion.

Count Enno had begun the secularisation of the monasteries in May 1529 by seizing the goods and properties of a number of East Frisian cloisters and his 1529 Church Ordinance banned the Catholic Mass in the territory – with the exception of Emden's Franciscan monastery.[15] Enno's most immediate religious concern, however, was not the Catholics but the existence in the territory of a number of Protestant sects which brought criticism upon Enno from all sides. Enno complained to the Landgraf Philip of Hesse that he had found it necessary to dismiss several intransigent (largely Zwinglian) ministers from their posts.[16] And on 19 January 1530, Enno issued a sharp directive against the Anabaptists in the territory, ordering them to leave East Frisia on threats of confiscation of property and execution. This mandate forced the radical Andreas Bodenstein von Karlstadt to leave East Frisia for Zürich. In East Frisia he had been receiving asylum from a leading local Protestant nobleman, the Junker Ulrich van Dornum in Oldersum, who had been one of the most influential of Count Edzard's advisers.[17] The Anabaptist leader Melchior Hoffman had also been in East Frisia, probably accompanying Karlstadt and staying at Dornum's residence, where he gave assistance to the local 'sacramentarians' in their battle against Count Enno's Lutheran state church.[18] Dornum had mobilised

---

[14] For instance, Hinne Rode, the Dutch priest whose communion teachings were quite similar to those of Zwingli (actually developed from the theology of Johann Wessel Gansfort), became the minister in Norden in East Frisia for several years after around 1526 when he fled from Deventer; Smid, *Kirchengeschichte*, pp. 115, 119.

[15] Ibid., p. 137; Heinrich Reimers, *Die Säkularisation der Klöster in Ostfriesland* (Aurich, 1906); Hemmo Suur, *Geschichte der ehemaligen Klöster in der Provinz Ostfriesland* (Emden, 1838).

[16] (25 March 1530) Staatsarchiv Marburg: Politisches Archiv des Landgrafen Philipp Nr. 2377. Cited by Sprengler-Ruppenthal in note 51, Sehling (ed.), *Kirchenordnungen*, pp. 317–18.

[17] Zwingli had called Dornum his 'alter ego'; Klaus Deppermann, *Melchior Hoffman*, trans. Malcolm Wren (Edinburgh, 1987), p. 155.

[18] Deppermann, *Hoffman*, pp. 152–9; Smid, *Kirchengeschichte*, pp. 138ff. Hoffmann returned to East Frisia in 1530, despite the edict against Anabaptists, and allegedly baptised 300 converts, 'both burgher and peasant, lord and servant', at one ceremony in the sacristy of Emden's Grosse Kirche; Deppermann, *Hoffman*, pp. 312–20; Ernst Kochs, 'Die Anfänge der ostfriesischen Reformation', Part III, *EJb*, 20 (1920), p. 74, note 5.

support to pressure Enno into lack of enforcement, and Enno's efforts at implementing a Lutheran church regulation proved ineffective in the early years. Philip of Hesse, Zwingli, and the Strasbourg reformers all wrote to Enno urging clemency for his opponents. Luther, who had supported the 1529 Ordinance, decried Enno's acquiescence to pressure and the 'victorious trickery of the Sacramentarians', complaining in a letter in 1531 that in Friesland the faithlessness of the sacramentarians 'predominates without restraint and that the Count is now allowing everyone to teach what he wants'.[19] A later church ordinance blamed 'rotten Anabaptists and similar wicked people' for the religious fragmentation and lack of respect given to pastors.[20]

Despite Count Enno's strict Lutheranism and the more radical Protestantism which also existed in Emden and East Frisia, a significant number of Emden citizens continued to champion Catholicism. As provost, Poppo Manninga served as the rallying point for adherents of the old faith in Emden. During the first years of the Reformation, the Catholics and the Protestants seem to have shared the Grosse Kirche for their services. Shortly thereafter, however, a new solution most probably resulted in the use of the Franciscan church by the Catholic party and the use of the Grosse Kirche by the evangelical citizens. With Count Enno's 1529 prohibition of the Catholic Mass everywhere but in the Franciscan monastery, this arrangement became more formal. Nevertheless, the old altars remained in the Grosse Kirche, and one wonders if, in fact, masses at the side altars completely disappeared.[21]

Following some military setbacks in 1533, Enno signed a treaty pledging to regulate ecclesiastical affairs in East Frisia according to the 'manner of the Saxon elector' and other evangelical territories in the Empire. Since the 1529 Church Ordinance was largely ineffectual, Enno's Catholic opponents hoped that the creation of a firmly controlled territorial church would make the step toward re-catholicisation that much closer. The Duke of Lüneburg, who had been able to implement an absolute territorial church with a conservative Lutheran character, offered Enno advice on meeting the terms of the treaty and avoiding further sanctions or military defeats. In a process parallel to that of the 1529 Church Ordinance, two orthodox Lutheran ministers came to East Frisia from Lüneburg to preach and help construct a new church

---

[19] Martin Luther, Briefwechsel VI, 16, Weimar Ausgabe.

[20] Sehling (ed.), *Kirchenordnungen*, p. 386.

[21] Heinz Schilling points out that only one of the twelve priests in 1520 supported Aportanus and the Reformation: *Civic Calvinism* (Kirksville, MO, 1991), p. 20f; compare his 'Reformation und Bürgerfreiheit', p. 140, note 47; Kappelhoff, 'Reformation in Emden', II, 27f.

ordinance. The East Frisian Church Ordinance from 1535, the so-called 'Lüneburger Church Ordinance', followed closely the Lutheran formula of the 1529 Ordinance.

This second attempt to create a Lutheran orthodoxy in East Frisia was also largely unsuccessful in practice. Anabaptist activity continued throughout the 1530s. Following the siege and defeat of Münster's Anabaptist kingdom (1535), new waves of sectarian refugees migrated to East Frisia. The radical Protestant leaders Dirk Philips, Menno Simons and David Joris all lived in or visited East Frisia between 1536 and 1544. Hendrick Niclaes, the founder of the 'Family of Love', stayed in Emden from 1540 until his expulsion in 1560. Simons and Joris each had a large number of disciples and adherents in East Frisia. Thus it can be seen that Count Edzard's policy of relaxed religious supervision had created a religious scene comprised of Catholics, Lutherans, Zwinglians and Anabaptists by the late 1520s.

East Frisian Church Ordinances (1529 and 1535) and Police Ordinance (1545)

Despite the inefficacy of the 1529 and 1535 Church Ordinances in ending the religious fragmentation in East Frisia, they, together with the 1545 territorial Police Ordinance, illustrate some of the rulers' goals and intentions for dealing with the poor. Enno issued his first church ordinance on 13 December 1529 after consultation with Johannes Bugenhagen and the Bremen ministers Johann Timann and Johann Pelt.[22] The character of the ordinance, especially with respect to its teachings on communion, was Lutheran, representing the preference of Count Enno. Bugenhagen, who was in Hamburg at the time, sent letters to Wittenberg for advice. Both Timann and Pelt had been Lutheran representatives at the recent Marburg Colloquy. Despite some resistance of the ministers in the largest East Frisian towns of Emden, Aurich and Norden, Enno and his advisers assembled the 'Church Ordinance of 1529', which used the Articles of the Marburg Colloquy (1529) as well as Bugenhagen's Church Ordinances for the cities of Braunschweig (1528) and Hamburg (1529). In discussing the celebration of communion, the East Frisian Church Ordinance refers to Luther's German Mass (1526) as the standard of measure: 'that it thus [be celebrated] according to the Ordinance which is used in the Electorate of Saxony'.[23]

---

[22] Sehling (ed.), *Kirchenordnungen*, pp. 360–72.

[23] Ibid., p. 364; see also the introduction by Anneliese Sprengler-Ruppenthal on pp. 316–18.

His experience of resisting strong attempts at re-Catholicisation by outside forces in the early 1530s encouraged Count Enno to try once again to bring order to his religiously fragmented territory. In 1534 he requested conservative Lutheran ministers from Lüneburg to help bring order to the church institutions in East Frisia and hence reduce Catholic claims of religious disorder.[24] As models for this new East Frisian Church Ordinance (the so-called 'Lüneburger Church Ordinance of 1535'), the Lüneburger ministers used the Church Ordinance of Brandenburg–Nuremberg (1533) as well as two works by Luther: the 'Little Book on Baptism' (1526) and the German Mass (1526).[25] The goal of the 1535 Church Ordinance was to call once again for a pure, Lutheran reform in church teachings.[26] Count Enno's 20 mandates, which directed the implementation of the 1535 Church Ordinance, corresponded largely to the 1529 Church Ordinance, but the supporting documents of the Church Ordinance and the opinions of the Lüneburger ministers went much further than those of 1529 in establishing a set of explicit guidelines for religious services and church administration in East Frisia.[27]

Despite the venomous attacks of Protestant reformers, including Luther with his 1519 'Sermon on the Blessed Sacrament of the Body of Christ and the Brotherhoods', these Lutheran church ordinances made no references to the confraternities or Gasthäuser, and no centralised poor relief institutions were established.[28] Protestant theology based on faith and grace also led to a rejection of the voluntary poverty practised by the mendicant orders. To this end, Enno banned East Frisia's mendicant orders from their traditional activities. Very early in his reign, Count Enno had begun a dissolution of the East Frisian monasteries, with the confiscated properties and church goods entering his coffers. The 1529

---

[24] Smid, *Kirchengeschichte*, p. 146; Sprengler-Ruppenthal, in Sehling (ed.), *Kirchenordnungen*, pp. 318f; Heinrich Schmidt, *Politische Geschichte Ostfrieslands* (Leer, 1975), pp. 174ff.

[25] Smid, *Kirchengeschichte*, p. 147; Sehling (ed.), *Kirchenordnungen*, p. 319.

[26] Just as the 1529 Church Ordinance aimed to prevent the further preaching of 'the false opinions, namely on the words of Christ, baptism and the Last Supper of Christ ... in our land', the 1535 Church Ordinance contained the more explicit condemnation 'that no one in our land any longer preaches the dubious opinions of Karlstadt, Zwingli, Oecolampadius and their followers about the sacraments of the baptism and the Last Supper of Christ': Sehling (ed.), *Kirchenordnungen*, pp. 361, 376.

[27] In contrast to the brevity of the 1529 Church Ordinance, the 1535 Church Ordinance began by presenting complete liturgical formulae for baptism, communion, and the general worship services and went on to include specific instructions for performing the ceremonies of vespers, matins, weddings, communion for the bed-ridden, and burials. The three sets of documents which made up the 1535 Ordinance are in Sehling (ed.), *Kirchenordnungen*, pp. 373–97.

[28] *Luthers Werke* (Weimar Ausgabe, 1884), vol. 2, pp. 754f.

Church Ordinances made the dissolutions official, but granted an exemption to the Faldern Franciscans. Due to reforms of the Franciscan monastery in Faldern/Emden during the last two decades of the fifteenth century and the introduction of the very strict rule of the Franciscan Observants in 1498 (including the ban on the ownership of earthly goods), Count Edzard I received all ownership rights for the Faldern monastery.[29] That the ruling house already possessed the Faldern monastic properties can help to explain why the 'Observanten toe Embden' were granted an exemption in the 1529 Church Ordinance and allowed to continue a private existence.

In addition to the many theological and ceremonial discussions contained in the territorial church regulations, the 1529 Church Ordinance also presented the first general instructions for the financing of a system of poor relief in East Frisia. The 1535 Ordinance offers no further instructions for poor relief, but it supplements some of the 1529 descriptions. 'On the Beggars', the ninth topic of the 1529 Church Ordinance, began the short discussion on the support of the poor in East Frisia.[30] It opened with a rejection of support for foreign beggars in the territory, except for those 'who have been a long time in the parish or because of age or because of sickness cannot wander'.[31] The 1529 Church Ordinance went on to describe the manner in which each parish should support its own beggars. First, each parish should elect two 'upright' men who 'should concern themselves with the suitability and ways through which the registered beggars may be maintained in their dwellings and not in front of the gates or on the streets'.[32] The count did not prescribe one particular set of guidelines for caring for the poor throughout the territory, but rather charged the two elected overseers in each parish with the responsibility of thinking about appropriate ways to care for their own beggars and poor.

---

[29] Smid, *Kirchengeschichte*, pp. 105, 137; Sehling (ed.), *Kirchenordnungen*, pp. 367, 370f.

[30] Sehling (ed.), *Kirchenordnungen*, pp. 366–8.

[31] Ibid., p. 366. The Bible citation 'Deute. 15', which deals with the cancelling of debts of fellow Israelites, is written in the margin. See, for example, Deuteronomy 15:3–4,7,11: 'You must require payment from a foreigner, but you must cancel any debt your brother owes you. However, there should be no poor among you ... for God will richly bless you, if only you fully obey the Lord your God ... If there is a poor man among your brothers in any of the towns of the land that the Lord your God is giving you, do not be hardhearted or tightfisted toward your poor brother ... There will always be poor people in the land. Therefore I command you to be openhanded toward your brothers and toward the poor and needy in your land.'

[32] Sehling (ed.), *Kirchenordnungen*, p. 366. The Bible citation 'Acto. 6' in the margin at this point relates to the election by the Jerusalem church of the first seven deacons to care for the poor widows of the community.

The first post-Reformation church ordinances reflected the traditional East Frisian manner of self-administration through the individual communities which had developed in the medieval church polity.[33] Each parish was responsible for the care of its own poor, both in determining need and in financing relief. To carry out these duties, each parish was instructed to elect its own supervisors of the poor – the 1529 Ordinance specified two men; the 1535 Ordinance was indefinite as to number:

> It shall also be ordered that some fine, clever, god-fearing and reputable persons, pious men, in all cities, country-towns and villages, who are responsible for the poor, that these [men] as advocates request alms, privately and publicly, in the community as occasion offers, and distribute [the alms] according to distress irrespective of the standing of the person.[34]

Although this 1535 description followed a discussion of the duties and moral requirements of superintendents, pastors and churchwardens, the 'supervisors of the poor' were never included in the category of 'church officers' (*kerckendener*) whose list always designated 'pastors, chaplains, schoolmasters, and sextons'.[35] By implication, therefore, the supervisors of the poor came from outside the traditional positions of leadership in the church.[36]

Contrary to typical post-Reformation changes, Count Enno established no 'common chest', normally considered a 'Lutheran' hallmark of social welfare reform, into which some proceeds from his secularisation of church properties would return to cover parish expenses.[37] Indeed, no such financing system was ever established in Emden.[38] Of course the

---

[33] On the development of communal self-administration in the medieval East Frisian churches, see Smid, *Kirchengeschichte*, 25–81; Smid, 'Zur Geschichte und Bedeutung des Ostfriesischen Interessentenwahlrechts', *Jahrbuch der Gesellschaft für niedersächsische Kirchengeschichte*, 68 (1970), pp. 39–58; G. Krüger, *Der münsterische Archidiakonat Friesland in seinem Ursprung und seiner rechtsgeschichtlichen Entwicklung bis zum Ausgang des Mittelalters* (Hildesheim: Borgmeyer, 1925); D. Kurze, *Pfarrwahlen im Mittelalter* (Köln: Böhlau, 1966), p. 319.

[34] Sehling (ed.), *Kirchenordnungen*, p. 391. Article 18 of the 1535 Ordinance's 20 published decrees mandated, 'One shall also appoint a few God-fearing men, who understand and take care of the poor and [who] procure and distribute the alms': Sehling (ed.), *Kirchenordnungen*, pp. 396f.

[35] This list occurs, for example, several times in Sehling (ed.), *Kirchenordnungen*, p. 389.

[36] The first reference to the actual existence of these 'supervisors of the poor' in Emden is in a contract from 9 March 1532; EDP 2/179v.

[37] On Philip of Hesse's use of monastic properties, see Richard Cahill, 'The sequestration of the Hessian monasteries', in *Reformations Old and New*, ed. Beat Kümin (Aldershot, 1996), pp. 73–91.

[38] Jütte is incorrect in his assertion that 'all Protestant systems of poor relief' were

count's elimination of traditional sources of income for the parishes after the Reformation created some major financial problems for the parishes, which saw many of the church properties secularised into the count's hands. A fascinating contemporary account was noted by the same church bookkeeper whom we saw lamenting church finances in Chapter 1. On 14 October 1593, the 80–year-old widow Tobe Buttels soliloquised in the sacristy on how the count, during the Reformation two-thirds of a century earlier – 'in the time when the changes of the papacy and Gospel occurred' – had taken from Emden's parish church all the ecclesiastical incomes which had belonged to the priests and kept them for himself. Although the count had much later allowed the church, after many requests, to have control again over some of the goods, 'in the meantime the preachers of the Gospel suffered great poverty' and were for 'long years fed and supported by the citizens who were fond of the Gospel'.[39]

Since Enno seems to have pocketed the ecclesiastical revenues, how did he propose that the new supervisors' activities be financed? The fund-raising method ordered by Count Enno was based on the traditional medieval Frisian practice of supporting the priests and worship services of the community, the so-called *huusdelinge*. According to the region's traditional regulations, in the *huusdelinge* 'the people, [both] poor and rich, according to their means' provided donations to their priests at regular intervals.[40] Under the 1529 Church Ordinance, however, the two newly elected supervisors were diligently to collect the *huusdelinge* along with the pastor.[41] The pastor took half and kept it for himself, but the other half now went to the two elected men for the poor. A 10-gulden fine was imposed on anyone who refused to participate in the *huusdelinge* as it was ordered. The church ordinance further instructed that no parish should refuse their 'duty' to the pastors and included the assurance that with the proposed funding system, poverty would be reduced.[42]

---

based upon the idea of a common chest which contained the funds from, among other sources, the monastic properties; *Poverty and Deviance*, pp. 105f.

[39] *Liber Expensarum*, 1572–95; ArchGK no. 364, p. 4.

[40] Section 5 of the late medieval Emsgauer Sendrecht, in Conrad Borchling (ed.), *Die niederdeutschen Rechtsquellen Ostfrieslands*, vol. 1 (Aurich, 1908), pp. 134f; see also K. van Richthofen, *Friesische Rechtsquellen* (1840), pp. 406ff, 484. Smid, *Kirchengeschichte*, pp. 44–51.

[41] Sehling (ed.), *Kirchenordnungen*, p. 366. The Bible citation '1. Tim. 5' in the margin after this section makes reference to the financial compensation due to the ministers of the church. See, for instance, 1 Timothy 5:17–18.

[42] Sehling (ed.), *Kirchenordnungen*, p. 367. The 1535 Ordinance decreed that 'all our subjects' continue to give their pastors everything that they are 'from old times and custom responsible to give' so that the pastors might have their livelihood: Sehling (ed.), *Kirchenordnungen*, p. 396.

As the widow's recollections imply, the traditional, tax-like *huusdelinge* with its mandatory payments to support both pastor and parish poor would not fully finance every parish's poor relief needs. The Church Ordinance of 1529 included several additional suggestions to underwrite the relief of the poor. Of course, since the practices of mendicant friars in East Frisia had recently been forbidden, alms that had been 'wasted' on them could now go to the 'true' poor. Moreover, the friar's alms-collection methods illustrated how to further support the poor. Just as the mendicants had their *terminei* or districts where they possessed the right to collect alms (especially bread, cheese, wurst, etc.), the two newly elected men were now to circulate through the parish 'as often in the year as they think it to be useful' in order to collect 'bread and other sustenance' for the poor.[43] The ordinance related the count's hope that Protestant obligation to charity ('love your neighbour as yourself', Matthew 22:39) would bridge any financial gaps (many left by his seizure of the ecclesiastical properties): 'We are without doubt that our people, out of Christian love, will indeed know their duty and, each according to their ability, will not deny their help to the poor.' Yet, if the number of beggars in the parish was large and the mandatory and voluntary contributions proved insufficient to their maintenance, the two men should approach the churchwardens, and if anything at all was left over from the church goods, it should be bestowed on the poor.[44]

Finally, the liturgy ordered by the 1535 Church Ordinance offers a brief glimpse into the practice of alms collection during worship services in East Frisia after the Reformation.[45] In particular, it outlined the prescribed duties of the 'supervisors of the poor'.[46] Either 'during or

---

[43] For definitions of *terminei* see Grimm, *Deutsches Wörterbuch*, vol. 11, 1, 1 (1935), pp. 259–60.

[44] Sehling (ed.), *Kirchenordnungen*, p. 367.

[45] Debates have occurred among historians and theologians over the place of alms collections in the Protestant worship service. Although the practice of almsgiving was varied, the traditional interpretation among historians is that Lutherans usually collected their alms during the sermon while Reformed made their collections at the door afterwards. The debates, as well as the relevant church ordinances which serve as evidence, are discussed in detail by Elsie McKee, *John Calvin. On the Diaconate and Liturgical Almsgiving* (Geneva: Droz, 1984), esp. pp. 30–65. The implications of the concluding exhortation to charity by the minister have also come under debate. Here, the question arises whether the exhortations to charity at the end of the service, by themselves, are implicit references to a collection of alms at the church door. After investigating many church ordinances which make an explicit connection between the exhortation and a collection, McKee adjudges that this interpretation is 'extremely probable', though she points out that any conclusive proof linking this liturgical occurrence to a specific almsgiving practice is missing.

[46] McKee, *Diaconate*, does not mention the 1535 Church Ordinance anywhere in her discussions. She does, though, refer in a note to Emden's Poor Relief Ordinance of 1576

after the sermon', preachers were to exhort the community to remember the poor, 'and the supervisors of the poor should request and collect the alms after the custom of the city before or after the sermon'.[47] Here, then, ecclesiastical legislation explicitly linked the preacher's exhortation to charity to a collection of alms during the regular worship service, although each parish could decide the specific place in the service for the collection.[48] The supervisors therefore ultimately depended upon 'Christian love' to finance their efforts, requesting alms 'privately and publicly' whenever they had the opportunity. Thus it was crucial that most people should condone the plans and activities of the supervisors. But when people did not approve of the social or religious situation, they were frequently unwilling to make even mandatory contributions, much less any voluntary gifts.

Such attitudes toward charitable giving in the first decades of the Reformation can be gleaned from the 1535 Church Ordinance. The ordinance noted a problem involving the payment of the salaries for the pastors: many people, especially farmers, were not contributing to the support of their pastor. Interestingly, it can be inferred from the ordinance that farmers were discriminating in their support of the poor, and that they viewed sustenance of the pastors only as a special case of poor relief.[49] In this instance, apparently, the farmers did not judge the pastors to be worthy of support:

> and when the farmer sees one so poor and miserable, he is easily moved not to recognise his poor pastor by his learning because he does not see the pastor studying and thinks that [the pastor] had simply composed such things out of his head [while] behind the plough or the canals.[50]

The ordinance blamed the religious turmoil and diversity of teachings during the first decades of the Reformation in East Frisia for the lack of respect given to the work of the preachers: 'And unfortunately this is

---

(p. 35, note 23) and makes references to Lasco's and Micronius's Ordinance for the London Refugee community (and the latter in East Frisia) published in the 1550s and 1560s (e.g. pp. 37, note 30, 39f).

[47] Sehling (ed.), *Kirchenordnungen*, p. 380.

[48] Unfortunately, no evidence survives which explicitly describes the practice in Emden until 1576 with the Emden Poor Relief Ordinance: Sehling (ed.), *Kirchenordnungen*, pp. 457–8. For Johannes a Lasco's proposed practice *after* he left Emden, see his church ordinance for the London congregation: Sehling (ed.), *Kirchenordnungen*, esp. pp. 605, 638.

[49] 'Wo kan he gastfry wesen jegen denen, so to onhe kamen, gelerde luide und armen, welcke alle ohre toflucht plegen to hebben to den bisscupen und pastoren als den sundergen vorsorgeren der armen?' Sehling (ed.), *Kirchenordnungen*, p. 386.

[50] Ibid.

the only thing that the farmers have learned out of all the sermons which have occurred in the last 12 years: to give no one anything.' They had heard so many different propositions that they no longer took any pastor seriously. 'We have no one to thank but the foolish and un-learned preachers' who had been going around since the early 1520s, especially the 'rotten Anabaptists and similar wicked people'. The ordi-nance went on to describe how the farmers paid no attention to the punishments for withholding their mandatory payments.[51] Should this differentiating attitude – deciding that certain people, in this case poor preachers, were not worthy of support – be widespread among the population, then the supervisors of the poor would have the burden of making certain that potential contributors perceived that the poor were working appropriately for their upkeep.

The 1529 deliberations on poor relief ended with instructions regard-ing the importance of work by the poor. The two overseers were also instructed to maintain 'a diligent inspection' to ensure that all beggars worked according to their abilities – for instance, each as 'a cobbler or something else that he can do'.[52] Moreover, children who are able and of an age to work should in no way be directed toward begging, but should instead be taken care of, fed and guided toward a trade 'so that no one has cause to take to wickedness or idleness'.[53] Even before the

---

[51] The farmers did not consider it appropriate 'that they should be punished by such a pitiful preacher, who is poorer than he': ibid.

[52] Ibid., p. 367. The Bible citations of 'Gene. 3; Iob. 5', written on the margin after this passage, each demonstrate that man was born to toil and labour. Genesis 3:17–19 involves God's curse of difficult toil on Adam for disobedience: 'Cursed is the ground because of you; through painful toil you will eat of it all the days of your life ... By the sweat of your brow you will eat your food.' Job 5:6–7 refers to the origins of hardship or trouble: 'Yet man is born to trouble.'

[53] Sehling (ed.), *Kirchenordnungen*, pp. 367f. The Bible citations 'Ezec. 16; 1. Tessa. 5; 2. Tessa. 3', written in the margin, all contain admonitions against idleness and wicked-ness. Thus 1 Thessalonians 5:12–14: 'Now we ask you, brothers, to respect those who work hard among you ... And we urge you, brothers, warn those who are idle,' and 2 Thessalonians 3:6–13 is a warning against idleness: 'we command you, brothers, to keep away from every brother who is idle and does not live according to the teaching you received from us ... For even when we were with you, we gave you this rule: 'If a man will not work, he shall not eat'. We hear that some among you are idle. They are not busy; they are busybodies. Such people we command and urge in the Lord Jesus Christ to settle down and earn the bread they eat.' The sixteenth chapter of Ezekiel is an extended allegory of an unfaithful Jerusalem, in which God describes Jerusalem as an abandoned infant whom he rescued, sustained and richly clothed. But, instead of living uprightly in accordance with the gifts and blessings which had been bestowed to her, Jerusalem became a prostitute and offered her body 'with increasing promiscuity to anyone who passed by' (vss 15, 25–6). The choice of this particular example as the illustration of wickedness is interesting and may imply an otherwise unspoken concern with prostitution among the poor.

Reformation, East Frisian law distinguished between worthy and undeserving poor. Yet, especially prominent in Protestant poor relief
legislation, this emphasis on supervision and work was prominent in
many of the poor relief theorists of the period, including Vives and
Bugenhagen. These new elements of social control in the governance of
poor relief made the church ordinances an important component in the
development of Emden's early modern social welfare system.

Unlike Bugenhagen's Church Ordinances for Braunschweig and for
Hamburg, which served as models for East Frisia's Church Ordinance,
Enno's regulations lacked detail both in outlining the system of relief as
well as in providing theological discourses elucidating the changes.[54]
Both Braunschweig and Hamburg established a Common Chest for the
care of their poor and provided thorough descriptions specifying which
poor should be supported, why they should be supported, and how the
Common Chest should be administered. Enno, however, simply encouraged the continued use of the Frisian practice of supporting the pastor,
but now with half of the proceeds going to the poor. Count Enno
delegated the implementation of relief administration to the elected men
in each parish and admonished them to use creativity in providing
support to the poor. Bugenhagen's Ordinances for these two northern
cities, especially those of Hamburg, also regulated the local hospitals
and confraternities in their care of the poor, but the East Frisian Ordinance made no mention of the Gasthäuser or confraternities in the
territory. Thus, despite Enno's utilisation of the distinctly Lutheran
Church Ordinances of Braunschweig and Hamburg as models for the
theological matters in the East Frisian Church Ordinance, these Protestant prototypes seem not to have influenced Count Enno's poor relief
strategies in East Frisia.

Despite the lack of detail in delineating a system for financing and
administrating poor relief, the Church Ordinances of 1529 and 1535
did furnish general guidelines which were to be observed by the East
Frisian churches. One difference among early modern approaches to
poor relief reform was that Catholics generally sought to regulate and
control begging while Protestants prohibited begging of any kind. Although these earliest church ordinances did not ban begging, a primary
goal of the 1529 Church Ordinance (with respect to social welfare) was
clearly the ultimate elimination of the need to beg among the poor. First

---

[54] The Braunschweig Church Ordinance of 1528 is in Sehling (ed.), *Die evangelischen
Kirchenordnungen des XVI. Jahrhunderts*, vol. VI, 1 (Tübingen, 1955), 348–555 (dealing with poor relief, 445–55); the Hamburg Church Ordinance of 1529 is in Sehling, vol.
V (Leipzig, 1913), 488–540 (dealing with poor relief, 531–40). Unless specifically mentioned, all other references to Sehling are to the East Frisian Ordinances (vol. VII/2/1).

of all, foreign beggars were to receive no support from the East Frisian communities. This prohibition limited poor relief to the 'local beggars', but new initiatives were still needed to reduce begging generally. As a replacement for the now discouraged indiscriminate almsgiving to beggars, the first post-Reformation church ordinance in East Frisia directed the creation of a church-administered organisation to serve as an intermediary between those giving alms and the poor. The church ordinance expected that the supervisors of the poor would deal creatively with the local beggars and devise new methods, appropriate to the situation in the parish, for taking poor relief off 'the streets' and from 'in front of the gates' and bringing it into domiciles. Moreover, the poor relief supervisors were given the task of maintaining 'social discipline' by keeping a diligent surveillance to ensure that the poor worked at any job for which they might have an ability. This 'social disciplining' became even more important in aiming to eliminate future begging; poor children should be directed toward a trade in order to prevent the begging (and the ensuing wickedness and idleness) that resulted from poverty.

Just as the ruler sought an end to territorial religious disorder with the church ordinances, the 1540s witnessed another attempt to bring order to East Frisia, this time emphasising social order, with the issuance of a territorial police ordinance. Enno's widow, the Countess Anna, and her advisers inaugurated 'to the common welfare' a new police ordinance, which was 'inclined to bring anew an orderly government control' to East Frisia, with these words:

> Since all governments are ordained by almighty God to protect the pious and to punish the malefactor, so that their subjects are taught in the fear of the Lord and brought up in good discipline ... [and] in order that blasphemy, the shedding of blood, adultery, usury, excess, and all other depravity (of which the world is now unfortunately full) are not tolerated, then [the powers that be] are responsible, as much as is possible for each government, to preserve their land and people in rest, peace, and unity.[55]

More than any of the earlier East Frisian territorial ordinances, the Police Ordinance of 1545 called for general supervision, cutting across secular and religious domains, of the local residents by authorities. On matters of theology, church teaching and ceremonies, people were instructed to conduct themselves 'henceforth according to the ordinances

---

[55] Sehling (ed.), *Kirchenordnungen*, p. 398. A portion of the text of the 'Polizeiordnung der Gräfin Anna 1545', which was issued on 15 February 1545, is edited in Sehling, pp. 398–413; a full version is printed in E. R. Brenneysen, *Ost-Friesische Historie und Landes-Verfassung* (Aurich, 1720), vol. II, pp. 181–211.

of the Christian Religion' issued by Count Enno in 1535.[56] Despite this deference to the church ordinances on topics dealing with teaching and confession, the Police Ordinance sought to maintain social order in the religious domain as well. For example, the Police Ordinance specified the procedure for disciplining blasphemers and made attendance at the sermons mandatory under penalty of punishment and fine.[57]

Although it is unclear if Johannes a Lasco worked personally on the preparations for the Police Ordinance, the emphasis which the ordinance placed on discipline and orderly life paralleled his own views and efforts. Since becoming superintendent of the East Frisian churches in the spring of 1543, the Polish reformer Lasco had endeavoured to set strategies in motion which would unify the East Frisian churches and implement greater church discipline.[58] Lasco's efforts included discourses with Menno Simons and David Joris, the removal of images from the churches in September 1543, and the introduction of a process of 'belief investigations' to root out sectarianism from orthodox beliefs. Through his writings, Lasco also made several attempts to provide a Confession for East Frisia: for instance, his *Epitome doctrinae ecclesiarum Frisiae Orientalis* (1543), which was rejected by Melanchthon and the ministers in Zürich, and a second, toned-down attempt, *Moderatio doctrinae* (1544).[59] The most influential of these efforts involved Lasco's two organisational innovations within the East Frisian church in 1544, namely the *Coetus* of East Frisian ministers and the Emden church consistory. Lasco particularly augmented the effectiveness of enforcing church discipline by his creation of the Emden consistory, with the participation of the most respectable lay members of the community alongside the pastors. The emphasis on an orderly life and discipline prescribed by the Police Ordinance of 1545 complemented parallel attempts to achieve greater church discipline being promoted by the countess's superintendent of churches.

The Police Ordinance's very first topic involved poor relief and begging. Here the purpose was not to establish a regulated system of social welfare, but to lay down the guiding principles and strategies for the

---

[56] Sehling (ed.), *Kirchenordnungen*, p. 398. The purpose of this admonition was also stated: 'Although God's word has not been preached for a long time in our County East Friesland and proclaimed to everyone, we fear, nevertheless, that the seeds have unfortunately in many places fallen upon a hard boulder or rock, from which no roots are acquired. Thus, one sees [this] daily through manifold abuses before his eyes.'

[57] For instance, ibid., pp. 412f.

[58] See Smid, *Kirchengeschichte*, pp. 158–72; and Smid's article 'Jan Laski' in *TRE*, vol. XX, pp. 448–51.

[59] These writings are printed in A. Kuyper (ed.), *Johannes a Lasco opera tam edita quam inedita* (Amsterdam, 1866), vol. I, pp. 481–557 and 465–79 respectively.

towns to use in caring for the poor. The most important beneficiaries of the proposed social welfare policies were the *rechten hussyttenden gadesarmen*, or those genuine godly poor who did not beg but instead 'felt ashamed to ask for their bread with their small children'.[60] A further identifying characteristic of these 'genuine poor' was that they either 'through old age or sickness in their limbs cannot earn' their keep. The Police Ordinance admonished pastors and church officers to supervise diligently those poor who were born and lived in their town so that these same poor 'with scanty clothing, hunger, and thirst' might be cared for.[61] Thus, by 1545, specific policies were being spelled out which limited poor relief to those local, 'shame-faced' poor who were unable to support themselves due to a specific disability.

The stated goal of the Police Ordinance was to reintroduce order to society. Thus the begging associated with vagabondage and wandering was bluntly prohibited. Foreign beggars were not to be tolerated; moreover, those beggars who were not born in East Frisia or did not live there were to be driven out of the land. Importantly, the Police Ordinance cited the new evangelical teachings as the inspiration for the ban on foreign begging:

> Since in all principalities, territories, and cities, where God's word is being proclaimed, no foreign beggars are allowed the privilege of begging, and each [territory] is maintaining their own *haussitzenden* poor (as is also ordained here), therefore we want to ask everyone earnestly, that they do not allow the foreign beggars in this land ... to beg, and to drive out those [beggars] not born in this land or resident here.[62]

The 'new' preaching of God's word which followed the Reformation, then, provided one impetus for the elimination of begging. The lure of order in the territory furnished another: the countess wanted to stop roaming beggars since 'it is mostly murderers and other evil rogues, who [during] the days beg together and in the evenings encourage good-for-nothing activities'.[63]

The prohibition on begging was then widened to encompass all beggars, not just foreign vagabonds. The reason for this broader prohibition was practical, going beyond new Protestant teachings relating to 'good works' and 'charity', and emphasising the financial burdens which begging placed on the poor relief system. The writers of the Police Ordinance saw only a finite reservoir of money available for use in caring for the

---

[60] Sehling (ed.), *Kirchenordnungen*, p. 399.
[61] Ibid., p. 400.
[62] Ibid., pp. 400f.
[63] 'One has found [this fact] in truth both here and in other places'; ibid., p. 401.

poor. The amount of resources procurable for the 'shame-faced' *haussitzenden* poor thus needed to be conserved and not given out to those 'who brazenly walk around before everyone's door' – *even* 'if they are sincere beggars'. Begging of any kind would be 'a detriment to the genuine *haussitzenden* poor' and must, therefore, be banned.[64]

The Police Ordinance does not explicitly address the issue of financing poor relief. It does, however, specify an additional source of income which does not seem to have been previously used for poor relief: fines. Whereas Countess Anna's Police Ordinance followed the earlier territorial ordinances, such as Edzard's Landrecht of 1508, in specifying money fines as punishments for almost all offences, it broadened the scope of how revenues from fines were to be used. Now, fines collected for disobedience to the ordinance were to be divided, half going to the government, half going to the godly poor.[65] Interestingly, fines were levied not only on those who broke the ordinance, but also on pastors, preachers and church officers if they were found to be dilatory or negligent in their supervisory responsibilities, and on anyone else who knew of an offence but remained quiet.[66] The ordinance was beginning to place great emphasis on supervision as a means of improving order.

Whether or not this new arrangement of financing poor relief through fines linking civil punishment and poor relief had any effect on societal attitudes toward the poor cannot be determined from any surviving sources. Apparently, the utilisation of fines in financing social welfare was intended to keep citizens mindful of the poor in the community. For instance, drunkenness was an obvious problem in East Frisia, and most of the rules for maintaining orderliness in the Police Ordinance regulated celebrations in the hope of limiting the amount of drunkenness and disorder. Even the *Weinkauf*, the customary drink which sealed the completion of a legal transaction (e.g. sale of a house, land or animals),

---

[64] Ibid. This was a common complaint against able-bodied beggars. In Delft, Holland, for instance, municipal ordinances against begging frequently began with a statement that 'such beggars do damage to the upright poor'; Charles H. Parker, 'Moral Supervision and Poor Relief in the Reformed Church of Delft, 1579–1609', *ARG*, 87 (1996), p. 350.

[65] In some cases, blasphemy for instance, the whole sum was to be turned over to the church officials for the '*haussitzenden*' poor (Sehling, ed., *Kirchenordnungen*, p. 413). The principle of using the fines for the '*rechten hussyttenden gadesarmen*' is first cited in the introduction of the Police Ordinance; ibid., p. 399. See p. 405 for the fines involving improper drinking following the conclusion of contracts, p. 409 regarding unseemly wedding celebrations, p. 410 for the fines relating to improper celebrations following the birth and baptism of a child, pp. 411f for the fines for serving beer in taverns before or during sermons or too late in the evening, p. 413 for the fines for blasphemy, for inattendance of church services, and for improper drinking.

[66] Ibid., p. 413.

got out of hand in East Frisia, and it happened that 'daily the great waste occurs with the *wynkopen*, where some are induced into drunkenness'. Furthermore, by 'old malpractice in pre-fast celebrations, on holidays, on church masses, in the guilds, in engagement celebrations, in the wedding celebrations, when the children are born, when children are baptised, when the dead are given to the earth, and when great excess occurs daily in the inns', people end up drinking so much 'that they do not hold themselves as Christian people but rather as beasts'.[67] In order, therefore, to prevent such disarray, the ordinance attempted to link punishments for disorderliness, especially the rowdiness associated with excessive drinking and eating, with an evocation of the poor, namely those who could benefit from a proper utilisation of the resources being used to excess by the offenders. The Police Ordinance made this association most clearly in the section entitled, 'Order and Police in the city Emden and in the other market-towns'.[68] Here the shippers and all other trades and guilds were commanded to revise and correct their regulations 'so that especially the godly poor' were not forgotten and 'so that also the unnecessary expenses as with the excessive eating and drinking' at their gatherings be abandoned and instead be 'laid in their collection boxes on the behalf of the poor and distributed through the eldermen' of the guild. Likewise, following the conclusion of a legal transaction in East Frisia, when the participants customarily drank to seal the contract, the Police Ordinance required that the participants in the transaction give a small token gift to the poor, 'of whom one should at all times be especially mindful'.[69] The punishments thus had a dual purpose: to bring an end to excessive alcohol consumption (and the concomitant disorder) in East Frisia and, at the same time, to keep people aware of those in need.

One mandated alteration in guild activities clearly demonstrates the results of the Reformation. People who wanted to become merchants or cloth-handlers should now direct their entrance fees to the 'magistrates of the city and the genuine godly poor, instead of the monks and priests'. The Police Ordinance further ordered the guild rolls to reflect this change.[70] Once again we see the authorities' attempts to shift some of the traditional perceptions of almsgiving.

The countess and her advisers recognised that fines would not sufficiently support the *haussitzenden* poor, and thus asked the communities

---

[67] Ibid., pp. 405, 413.

[68] Ibid., pp. 406f.

[69] Ibid., p. 405. The churchwardens were also to give a 'good exhortation to the buyer and seller, that they will be mindful of the poor', p. 413.

[70] Brenneysen, *Ost-Friesische Historie*, II, p. 197.

to exhort frequently from the pulpit for alms 'according to common Christian ordinances'.[71] But beyond fines and reminders from the pulpit encouraging Christian love, the Police Ordinance provided no particular details as to how each community should raise money for the poor. Nevertheless, the Ordinance required those who distributed poor relief to keep track of the amount of alms raised from the pulpit or the revenue from the fines and to provide accounts of how the moneys had been dispersed.[72] This new accounting requirement demonstrates the authorities' increasing interest in rationalisation as the poor relief system evolved in the mid-sixteenth century.

Beyond the outright ban on begging and these brief guidelines, the 1545 Ordinance was most clear in establishing detailed policies governing the poor in ways some have referred to as 'social disciplining'.[73] It specifically spelled out the requirements of schooling and work for the poor. If the poor were burdened with children, who were at least five or six years old, then the children should be placed in the schools in order to learn the Confession of Faith (a catechism for Emden had not yet been written), the Ten Commandments, and the Lord's Prayer. Since the parents would not be well off, the local officials would need to provide them with 'school-money'.[74] In this matter, the Police Ordinance gave little choice to the parents, for if they struggled against this mandate, then they should 'be persuaded' by the Burgermeister and guild officials.

Mandatory schooling for the poor was primarily intended to provide the fundamentals of the faith and basic beliefs which would train people to live in an orderly fashion. Thus, once the poor children ('both boys and girls') had learned the Lord's Prayer, the Ten Commandments and the Confession of Faith, and were 'so old and strong that they can

---

[71] Sehling (ed.), *Kirchenordnungen*, p. 400.

[72] After describing the order to be maintained at wedding celebrations and the fines for disorder, the Police Ordinance stated that 'the elders in the guilds and church officials in all other places should receive the violation for the poor and make account of it'. In the regulation of the guild ordinances, the guild elders were instructed to account yearly for the money given on 'behalf of the poor in their collection box ... what was taken in and why it was given out'; ibid., pp. 409, 407.

[73] For example, Robert Jütte, 'Poor Relief and Social Discipline in Sixteenth-Century Europe', *European Studies Review*, 11 (1981), pp. 25–52.

[74] Sehling (ed.), *Kirchenordnungen*, p. 400. The goal that 'everyone send his children to school' was already stated in the 1529 Church Ordinance. It mandated the establishment of Latin schools 'so that the youth will not be so deplorably corrupted and the noble Latin art will not be scorned'. In this process, however, the ordinance made it clear that the traditional German schools, both for the boys and the girls, should not be destroyed. The 1529 Church Ordinance was especially interested in the Latin schools and mentioned no provision for getting poor children to school; ibid., *Kirchenordnungen*, p. 368.

earn their board', they were to be brought into a trade. By requiring basic education and training in a trade, the authorities tried to bring order to the poorer communities, and bring an end to the need 'to beg by the houses' in the future.[75] Once again, the Police Ordinance made obedience to this provision obligatory for the parents of the poor children, making parents responsible for the actions of their children. Consequently, if the parents did not persuade their children, and 'the children do not want to let themselves be drawn into a service, they shall be denounced to the government so that the parents are therefore punished'. Moreover, training children in a trade became a precondition for the parents' poor relief. 'One shall also give no assistance to such parents [until] they have brought their children into a service, each according to his strength and opportunity.'[76] In this respect, the authorities intended to use poor relief and the withholding of alms to implement social discipline.

The Police Ordinance included a special provision that allowed some poor children to continue their studies beyond just the basic education previously described. If the pastor or church officials found among the poor children 'one, two, or three who were endowed by the Almighty with an exceptional intellect', then 'with the help of the community' they should be allowed to remain in school 'according to the opportunity in the city, town, or village'. Thus poor children from Emden, which had its own Latin schools, would be able to continue their education in the city. We would expect that occasionally some of the 'exceptionally intelligent' poor children from neighbouring villages with no Latin school of their own might be sent to Emden. In this latter case the home community of the poor children would continue to provide the school-money from their local poor relief funds, and the children would not become the responsibility of the Emden relief system.

Selection of the few brightest children from among the poor for additional schooling had the practical intention of training them for the job of schoolteacher. The 'exceptional' poor children should be held in the school 'until the time that they are old enough and have achieved a foundation to teach'.[77] But the writers of the East Frisian Police Ordinance recognised that being a schoolteacher would not ensure that one could earn a living. Hence they instructed the East Frisian communities that when one of their poor students was sent into other schools out of the territory as a teacher, the local authorities there should be notified

---

[75] Ibid., p. 400.

[76] Ibid. This was, in fact, the policy maintained by the deacons over the next several decades, for example, KRP, pp. 124, 133 (27 January and 13 October 1561).

[77] Sehling (ed.), *Kirchenordnungen*, p. 400.

of the situation so that if the poor teacher fell into 'distress again, he will be provided for'.[78]

While the 1529 Church Ordinance laid down some basic requirements regarding the supervision of the poor and work assignments, the 1545 Police Ordinance delineated detailed policies regarding begging as well as the education and training of the poor. We cannot be sure how quickly the moral tone of the ordinances, with the increased emphasis on social control, had a tangible effect. Early attempts at increasing discipline often met with resistance, but evidence later in the century illustrates that these precepts were not entirely disconnected from practice. The outright ban on begging and the emphasis on placing poor children in a trade remained explicit strategies of the Emden poor relief administrators throughout the rest of the century. Furthermore, providing a basic education for poor children was also an important objective of Emden's relief administrators, as evidenced by the frequent distribution of 'school-money' by the church deacons in their account books later in the century. Thus the Police Ordinance provided the first explicit description of some of the essential principles that would govern poor relief in Emden during the second half of the sixteenth century.

Institutional Developments after the Reformation

Despite the interest in certain aspects of poor relief shown by the ordinances, there is an apparent disparity between these new ordinances and Emden's practical provisions depicted in the last chapter. Neither confraternities, Gasthäuser, nor Gotteskammern, which were the primary administrators of poor relief in pre-Reformation Emden, were mentioned in the post-Reformation ordinances. Protestant theology clearly attacked the spiritual purpose of the confraternities, yet Emden's confraternities declined only gradually in the decades after the introduction of Protestantism. St Gertrude's Gasthaus, which was already in lay hands by the time of the Reformation, changed very little until the 1550s. The dissolution of the East Frisian monasteries would have reduced the sources of assistance available to the territory's poor, and the failure of Count Enno to use the funds from ecclesiastical properties for charitable or educational ends meant that the removal of monastic charity was not directly counterbalanced. Still, we must remember that the prohibitions exempted Emden's Franciscans. The urban poverty of the growing town (in the midst of a largely rural territory)

---

[78] Ibid.

and the need or desire to maintain Emden's successful relief institutions probably contributed to the Franciscan monastery's survival. Their continued existence also facilitated the survival of the confraternities. Although no records survive from the friars, we know that their inability to handle adequately the growing numbers of poor was cited as a reason for their ultimate dissolution almost forty years after the Reformation.

Beyond the gradual development of legislation aimed to prohibit begging, the East Frisian ordinances basically refrained from attempting to reorganise any of the traditional aspects of charitable provision. The church ordinances which came on the heels of the Reformation in East Frisia mandated the creation of a system administered by lay overseers to provide relief to the parish poor. While the mere existence of ordinances does not prove practice, hard evidence of the implementation of portions of the ordinances does exist. Since institutional changes beyond the limited scope of the Reformation-era ordinances also occurred, it is worth investigating the extent to which the legal, religious and social changes of the 1520s and 1530s affected the already existing institutions of social welfare in Emden.

Although Count Enno realised limited success in implementing the religious programme advocated in his 1529 Church Ordinance, the new ideas regarding the selection of parish poor relief administrators found some acceptance. The first evidence of these 'administrators of the poor within Emden' appears in March 1532. In this instance, they oversaw the allocation of a woman's bequest to her brother, who lived outside Emden.[79] Overseers next appeared in the surviving sources a decade later. By this time they were called 'advocates and supervisors of the *haussitzenden* poor in Emden'. It is here that some of the administrators are named for the first time: two 'advocates' represented their 'fellow administrators' as proxies in a contract for a house sale. One of them had previous experience as an administrator for Our Lady's Confraternity, and the other was possibly a churchwarden.[80] There is no indication of the actual number of administrators of the *haussitzenden* poor at this time. These two plus their 'fellow administrators' obviously signify that a town the size of Emden needed more than the two administrators called for in the 1529 Church Ordinance, but we have no means by which to reconstruct their early organisation.

---

[79] EKP 2/179v (9 March 1532).

[80] Ibid. 2/620 (29 April 1542). On the early administrators of the *haussitzenden* poor, see Timothy Fehler, 'Social Welfare in Early Modern Emden: the Evolution of Poor Relief in the Age of the Reformation and Confessionalization' (Ph.D. thesis, University of Wisconsin-Madison, 1995), pp. 213–18 (esp. Table 7).

In the 1542 source, these administrators are shown building their endowment for the '*haussitzenden* poor'. Hinrick Scroder bequeathed his house (with an 'apartment out back') to the '*haussitzenden* poor'. Shortly after his death, the administrators chose to sell the house in order to increase their endowment to the poor.[81] By definition, '*haussitzenden* poor' were the local, residential poor. Thus, at this time, providing housing would not have been a normal responsibility of an administrator of the *haussitzenden* poor, so the house itself was less important to them than the money it could bring to their endowment. They therefore sold the house for 300 Emden gulden, accepting a 100 gulden payment and providing 'on behalf of the poor' a 6 per cent mortgage for the remaining 200 gulden.[82]

Emden's church would come to be administered by pastors, elders and deacons, as it began implementing a Reformed model of church organisation. By the second half of the century, the administration of relief to the *haussitzenden* poor was in the hands of deacons in Emden's Reformed church. How did this institutional change occur? Were the so-called 'deacons of the *haussitzenden* poor' a new creation of Emden's Reformed church or was there a connection with the earlier 'administrators'? Johannes a Lasco created the Emden consistory in the summer of 1544.[83] Lasco's consistory was made up of the pastors and four lay 'elders'. In a letter from that summer, Lasco identified four Emden burghers who were 'earnest men, filled with pious zeal', and who were working with him and the ministers to help implement church discipline guidelines.[84] The 'administrators of the *haussitzenden* poor' were already in existence by the time of the consistory's establishment. There is no evidence to indicate that Lasco created in 1544 the church office of 'deacon' out of these poor relief administrators, along with his creation of the consistory. There can be no question, however, about the early connection between those poor relief administrators and the consistory. Notably, three of the five men identified in loan contracts from 1548 as 'administrators of the common *haussitzenden* poor in Emden' also belonged to Lasco's initial group of four elders in 1544.[85] Thus, in its

---

[81] EKP 2/620.

[82] Ibid. 2/620v (1 May 1542).

[83] See Chapter 4 below. Unfortunately, records from the meetings of the consistory survive only after 1557, so many of the questions regarding its earliest work and composition require conjecture; cf. Heinz Schilling, *Die Kirchenratsprotokolle der reformierten Gemeinde Emden 1557–1620* (2 vols, Cologne, 1989–92).

[84] Jan Weerda, 'Der Emder Kirchenrat und seine Gemeinde' (Habilitationsschrift, Münster, 1948), p. 123; Kuyper (ed.), *Lasco opera*, II, 575. On the question about the conclusion that these four were the first (and only) elders, see Fehler, 'Social Welfare', p. 216, note 81.

[85] EKP 4/12v (15 May 1548); 4/27v (December 1548).

early years, a significant connection existed between the consistory and the administrators of the *haussitzenden* poor.

Had these earnest men been 'administrators of the poor' and thus caught Lasco's eye as he chose them as elders when he created the consistory, or did the work of the elders appropriate the charitable activities of the early 'administrators of the poor'? Menno Smid has suggested that these four elders, as 'the best and most respected members of the congregation', were simply the churchwardens (*Kirchgeschworenen*), which all East Frisian parishes already had in the Middle Ages for the purposes of administration of the church properties, and whose functions were simply expanded by Lasco.[86] It seems no coincidence that at least three of the first four elders also served as administrators of the *haussitzenden* poor in Emden.[87] One plausible answer to this question might be discovered in part from a clue regarding a fourth of the five named poor relief administrators in 1548: Gerdt van Gelder, as 'administrator of the *haussitzenden* poor', also served as churchwarden for the Emden congregation.[88]

The traditional 'office' of churchwarden serves as a clue in teasing out the otherwise tangled origins of Emden's Reformed diaconate and eldership. One construction of events would perhaps have the Emden congregation turn first to their traditional lay administrators in the church, the churchwardens, when establishing the lay positions of 'overseer of the poor' which were called for in the 1529 Church Ordinance. Indeed, the church ordinance even acknowledged the important knowledge and experience of the parish churchwardens, suggesting that the new 'overseers of the poor' approach the churchwardens for help from the properties of the church when short of funds.[89] Exceptional financial acumen can also be found among the early 'administrators of the *haussitzenden* poor': for instance, Johan Goltsmit served over 25 years as the count's revenue collector; Meynert Kremer oversaw the operation of Emden's mint.[90] The churchwardens, as administrators of the church's properties, would have been the logical choice to handle the administration of Emden's poor relief funds. A 1539 testament offers further demonstration of the

---

[86] Smid, *Kirchengeschichte*, p. 166.

[87] On Weerda's partially mistaken reading of the evidence on the origins of the elders ('Kirchenrat', pp. 71f and especially 122f), see Fehler, 'Social Welfare', p. 217, note 84.

[88] Fehler, 'Social Welfare', p. 218, note 85; KRP, p. 335, note 1; Weerda, 'Kirchenrat', p. 123, note 1.

[89] Sehling (ed.), *Kirchenordnungen*, p. 367. Evidence indicates that churchwardens in England became more actively involved in the provision of assistance in the late fifteenth and early sixteenth centuries. M. K. McIntosh, 'Local responses to the poor in late medieval and Tudor England', *Continuity and Change*, 3, 2 (1988), p. 220.

[90] Fehler, 'Social Welfare', p. 215 (Table 7).

connection between the administrators of the *haussitzenden* poor and those who oversaw the affairs of the church: a couple left half of their goods to the 'administrators in the parish church, because of and on behalf of the *haussitzenden* poor'.[91] Smid's hypothesis regarding the office of elder initially as a renamed churchwarden could also explain the significant overlap between the 'administrators of the *haussitzenden* poor' and the earliest elders. Both of Lasco's 'new' Reformed church offices of elder and deacon, therefore, probably emerged out of the medieval Frisian lay position of 'churchwarden'.

Similarly, institutional continuity is evident when we turn our attention to the confraternities after the Reformation. In this instance, however, traditional continuity is surprising at first glance, especially in the light of the Protestant condemnation of confraternities. 'If a sow were made the patron saint of such a brotherhood,' Luther wrote in his 1519 sermon on brotherhoods, 'he would not consent. Why then do they afflict the dear saints so miserably by taking their names in vain in such shameful practices and sins, and by dishonouring and blaspheming with such evil practices the brotherhoods named after these saints?'[92] One 'shameful practice' was the brotherhoods' gluttony and drunkenness: 'The brotherhood is also supposed to be a special convocation of good works; instead it has become a collecting of money for beer.'[93] Luther identified a second 'evil practice' as the confraternities' 'spiritual nature' that stemmed from a theology of works: 'This is the false opinion they have that their brotherhood is to be a benefit to no one but themselves, those who are members on the roll or who contribute'. Luther considered this 'damnably wicked opinion' to be 'an even worse evil than the first' because the results of the religious practices of the confraternities were harmful to the members' souls. For him and other Protestant reformers, the communal fellowship and the religious or spiritual aspects of the confraternities should be ended. Only the charitable activities, when taken seriously, were worthy of continuance.

> If men desire to maintain a brotherhood, they should gather provisions and feed and serve a tableful or two of poor people, for the sake of God. The day before they should fast, and on the feast day remain sober, passing the time in prayer and other good works.

With these activities, they would finally truly honour 'God and his saints'. The proper goals of the charitable activities were to honour God

---

[91] The other half was to go to the administrators of the Gasthaus poor; EKP 2/451.

[92] From Martin Luther's 1519 'Sermon on the Blessed Sacrament of the Body of Christ and the Brotherhoods', in *Luthers Werke* (Weimar Ausgabe, 1884), II, 755; translation taken from *Luther's Works* (Philadelphia, 1960), vol. 35, p. 68.

[93] *Luthers Werke*, II, p. 754; translation from *Luther's Works*, vol. 35, p. 67.

and to set a good example for others to follow, not to receive spiritual benefit for good works.[94] The 'divine' brotherhood in which all Christians are 'brothers and sisters' was the most important and strongest of the brotherhoods. Luther stressed that any other brotherhood 'should be so conducted as to keep this first and noblest brotherhood constantly before their eyes and regard it alone as great'.[95] Their emphasis should be on the Christian duty of love and compassion rather than on selfish interests.

Protestant polemics aside, the introduction of the Reformation did not necessarily result in immediate large-scale changes in Emden's confraternities. Although the 1529 and 1535 Church Ordinances did not mention the confraternities in East Frisia, the 1545 Police Ordinance instructed 'the shippers and all other trades and guilds' in Emden to 'correct' their regulations so that the poor (*gotzarmen*) were not forgotten. In particular, all the 'useless expenses' were to be eliminated and the money given instead 'on behalf of the poor'.[96] Though none of the confraternities left individual records from the period after the 1520s, we can trace some of their activities through the surviving contracts and testaments, noting both changes and continuity in their manner of operations following the Reformation.

The function of the confraternities as loan-banks continued long after the Reformation, reflecting the size of their capital and resources. One of the most visible changes was the increase throughout the 1520s of the use of phrases in notarial records that emphasised the confraternities' charitable activities. Before the 1520s, contracts seldom referred directly to the confraternities' poor relief work. Early loan agreements – especially those made by the three confraternities of Our Lady's, St Clement's and St Ann's – universally indicated that the interest was to be collected 'to the use of the brotherhood'. The phrase 'to the utility of the brotherhood' continued in most loan contracts into the middle of the 1520s.[97] Occasional pre-Reformation testaments, however, explicitly referred to poor provision with bequests to the poor dealt with by the confraternities.[98]

---

[94] *Luthers Werke*, II, p. 755; translation from *Luther's Works*, vol. 35, p. 69.

[95] 'With all their works they should be seeking nothing for themselves; they should rather do them for God's sake,' *Luthers Werke*, II, p. 756; translation from *Luther's Works*, vol. 35, pp. 70f.

[96] Sehling (ed.), *Kirchenordnungen*, pp. 406f.

[97] For instance, EKP 1/208v (1522, 1523, St Clement's), 1/192 (1522, St Ann's), 1/232v (1525, Our Lady's).

[98] For instance, in Lambert van Groningen and Luthgart's 1517 testament, they left their money to the poor where the most 'use and distress is', especially to Our Lady's Confraternity 'in order to improve their alms'; EKP 1/112v.

By the mid-1520s, the language of the contracts had changed: 'the poor of the brotherhood' were always mentioned. The first such surviving contracts date from 1525, when the 'advocates and administrators of St Ann's Brotherhood' agreed to sell a house in their possession for 80 gulden 'to the use of the brotherhood and of the poor, who for a time have their alms out of the brotherhood'. Two weeks later they financed the unpaid portion of the principle with the yearly interest designated 'to the use of the brotherhood and of the poor who may be improved by it'.[99] By the late 1520s, such phrases were commonplace, as the loan made by Our Lady's Confraternity, 'to the use of the common poor who for the time receive the alms from [the confraternity] according to God's will'.[100]

Although terminology that highlighted the charitable activities became dominant in Emden after the beginnings of the Reformation, it should not be assumed that the confraternities immediately abandoned the spiritual activities that motivated their foundations. Donors typically used the phrase 'to the salvation of their souls' in testaments that bequeathed goods to the poor. An Emden citizen and his wife drew up their testament in 1523 to provide for their children until they could enter a trade, a cloister or be married, and they concluded their testament with a gift of 20 gulden to St Ann's Brotherhood. Ten gulden should go to 'the holy mother St Ann for her use' and to improve the endowment of her altar; the other 10 gulden were to be used 'for the salvation of both of their souls' to care for the 'common poor' of the confraternity. In a 1525 example, a husband and wife donated all their remaining goods after both of their deaths as 'alms, distributed according to the will of God and to their honour'. These alms were to be divided into equal thirds: 'to the three brotherhoods, Our Lady's, St Ann's, and St Clement's'.[101]

Count Enno banned the Catholic Mass in East Frisia in January 1530, but the Mass was allowed in the Franciscan monastery until the 1550s. The fact that the confraternities of St Ann and Our Lady were centred in the monastery suggests that their religious endeavours continued for two to three decades after the Reformation. In the mid-1540s, Lasco railed against the activities of the friars, claiming that they still had a great influence among many of Emden's citizens.[102] Among other things, Lasco wanted the friars to stop their writing of testaments. The

---

[99] Ibid. 1/252–2v.

[100] Ibid. 2/4v (8 April 1528); the same phrase was used in 2/9 (21 May 1528); the simple phrase 'to nutticheyt der Armen' was used in 2/63 (26 November 1529).

[101] Ibid. 1/214 (4 February 1523); 1/244v (28 August 1525).

[102] See Chapter 4 below.

installation of a Protestant notary by the city compelled those who wanted a traditional testament – that is, with bequests made 'to the salvation of their soul' and like terminology – to approach the friars to write their wills. Because none of the testaments drawn up by the friars made it into the surviving corpus of contracts and testaments from the city's notaries, there is no clue as to the number of citizens who used the friar's testament-writing services.

That the Franciscan friars continued writing testaments helps to explain the total disappearance of the confraternities from the surviving testaments of the 1530s. Although we know that the confraternities of St Clement, St Ann and Our Lady continued to exist throughout this period, not one surviving testament written in the 1530s or the early 1540s mentions them. Instead, the many testaments which made charitable donations left goods 'according to God's will' their 'poor [or shame-faced or suffering] relatives' or the 'poor of Christ'. This phrase, or one similar, although not absent from the pre-Reformation testaments, became the standard form for a charitable bequest in the 1530s.[103] Such vague phrases rarely specified a charitable institution or even an amount to be donated. But other similar bequests to the 'proper house-poor' (*huesarmen*), 'God's poor' (*Gaedes armen*) and the *haussitzenden* made it clear that the new administrators of the *haussitzenden* poor were to distribute the goods, and these testaments were usually specific about the amount of money, food or clothing bequeathed.[104]

The loss of any testaments written in the monastery hampers investigation into the survival of the confraternities' traditional spiritual activities. Traditional notions of charity as a good work leading to salvation did not pass away completely with the Reformation. As late as 1541, Reiner van Klewert specified that if he should die before his wife Tibe, the money he had brought into the marriage should be given 'into the hands of the poor for the salvation of his soul'. Specifically, the

---

[103] For example, 'synen schamelen frunden eder aermen Christi', this phrase was used among other places in EKP 2/256v, 259, 263v, 265, 265v, 269, 276, 276v, 278, 281, 283, 288v, 289, 296v, 301, 301v, 306, 313v, 318, 325, 349, 351v, 352, 363, 375, 375v, 384v, 389v, 395, 405, 408v, 411, 413v, 418v, 419v, 420v, 421v, 423, 424, 425v, 428v, 429, 435v, 450, 450v, 454, 454v, 475v, 535, 539v, 550v; 'dem elendigen Aermen unnd Christen', 2/446v; 'synen vrunden offte thor erenn gaedes, wes wolde denn armen gheven', 2/79v; 'synen scamelen frunden ader armen kristen wolde gheven', 2/175; 'den Aermen ... und offt oick jemand van syne schamelen frunden na queme oick ... thor ene milde gave', 2/231; see also 2/112v, 133v, 193v, 216, 218v, 340v, 468.

[104] Ibid. 2/43, 122v, 192v, 443, 482, 486. While the phrase 'synen frunden ader aermen Christi' did not usually specify an amount to be donated (see exception 2/231), these more specific terms did generally specify an amount of money, food or clothing – for instance, '40 Embder gulden unnd 2 grawe laken', 2/103; 'de elendigen Aermen 1/2 tunne botter', 2/445.

money was to be divided, 'half to the *Gasthaus* and the other half to the *haussitzenden* poor'.[105] Both Reiner's 1541 charitable bequest for the 'salvation of his soul' and Lasco's complaints against the friars' influence confirm that such traditional notions of piety did not disappear after the prohibition of the Catholic Mass in Emden. That almost all records of the friars have been lost conceals other such testaments as well as the spiritual activities of the confraternities (at least the confraternities centred around altars in the monastery).

Of all the confraternities, St Anthony's was probably the first to have many of its traditional activities 'reformed'. One of this brotherhood's administrators was a priest in the Grosse Kirche, so the ban on the Catholic Mass and clergy had a significant impact on its administration. The priest Johan van Duten last appears in the sources as one of St Anthony's administrators in 1527.[106] Two of St Anthony's other administrators continued in their positions within the brotherhood well into the 1530s.[107] By this time, though, we see them approving the distribution of their alms in a decidedly Protestant manner. On 14 April 1535, St Anthony's administrators agreed to give 20 gulden to a woman in need. Anna, the woman receiving the gift, was not simply a poor woman. She was a nun who had decided to leave the Cistercian monastery of Meerhusen, near Aurich, and needed the money to re-establish herself at home. She turned to St Anthony's for help because her father, Folkert van Noertdorp, a former bailiff in Emden, had bequeathed 6 *Grassen* of land to the 'suffering poor of St Anthony's Brotherhood' before his death in 1516.[108] This was the last surviving reference to the Brotherhood of St Anthony's or even to administrators of their properties. By this point, the confraternity seems to have embraced Protestantism. Curiously, these two who continued were the only two of St Anthony's administrators not to have been members of Our Lady's Confraternity. Perhaps on the conversion of St Anthony's from a spiritual brotherhood, the others left in order to meet their spiritual needs in Our Lady's.

Given that many of the documents regarding St Anthony's Confraternity found their way into the church archives (unlike the other confraternities), it seems likely that the church quickly took over the activities of this lay confraternity, one of whose administrators had been a priest in the Grosse Kirche. These activities included providing

---

[105] Ibid. 2/569.
[106] Ibid. 1/286 (14 November).
[107] Fehler, 'Social Welfare', p. 130.
[108] EKP 2/303v; Joseph König, *Verwaltungsgeschichte Ostfrieslands bis zum Aussterben seines Fürstenhauses* (Göttingen, 1955), p. 536.

housing to the poor in 'Anthony's Gotteskammern' on Pelzerstrasse, and continued well into this century.[109] Although these Gotteskammern later focused their relief on old women and widows, in the 1530s they were still open to both sexes. For instance, in 1537 Clawes Bemelt 'currently lived' in a 'St Anthonius Kammer'.[110] These Gotteskammern also housed married couples. In 1527, the confraternity's administrators had still been busily acquiring new Gotteskammern when they established a contract 'in friendship toward peace' with the daughter and son-in-law of the donor, allowing them to live in one of the Gotteskammern 'for free for the rest of [the daughter's] life'.[111]

Relief provided in Gotteskammern was not limited merely to free housing. Modifications of a previous contract between the administrators of St Anthony's and Gertrude Weversche provide the evidence. Gertrude, remember, was the woman who in the last chapter received some special compensation – exemptions from civic duties such as watch – as well as housing from the administrators in exchange for her well-situated house in 1516.[112] In 1529, the administrators praised Gertrude and modified their previous contract in order to allow her to move into a different Gotteskammer which had just been vacated. They also specified that she should receive a yearly allowance of 'red butter', along with a small amount of bread every week.[113] Daily provisions of food were a basic feature of the care provided to the poor in the Gasthaus, but we have less evidence to confirm whether regular food allowances were normally given to the poor in all the Gotteskammern across town.[114]

When the confraternities disappeared from the surviving testaments during the 1530s, most of the charitable bequests were made simply to 'the poor of Christ', but many were made to the *haussitzenden* poor, to St Gertrude's Gasthaus, or to both institutions. Beginning in 1539, most testaments which bequeathed goods to the poor left them to be divided between the Gasthaus poor and the *haussitzenden* poor. Interestingly, in

---

[109] Six 'Antonii-Gottes-Kammern' remained in existence near the church on Pelzerstrasse until World War II, providing housing for six old women; Heinrich Siebern, *Die Kunstdenkmale der Stadt Emden* (Hannover, 1927), p. 89; Johannes Stracke, 'Geistliche Laienbruderschaften im ausgehenden Mittelalter', *EJb*, 51/52 (1971–72), pp. 52f.

[110] EKP 2/379.

[111] Ibid. 1/286 (14 November 1527).

[112] ArchGK no. 46; copy in EKP 1/88v.

[113] ArchGK no. 47; copy in EKP 2/29v (16 April 1529).

[114] For instance, a donation to 'sunte gheertrudes gasthuse in Embden … tho nuttycheydt der armen de dair van daghelycks gespysiget unde in denn gasthuse gheherberget werdenn', EKP 2/41 (1 May 1529). Some donors stipulated their bequest in the form of food rather than in an amount of money. For instance Rodolff van Cunne and Bawe bequeathed to the suffering poor half a ton of butter to be purchased out of their remaining goods, EKP 2/445 (9 February 1539).

the first such testament, the combination seems to have been an after-thought. Lubbert Backer had left 15 gulden to the *haussitzenden* poor; later, he changed the '15' to a '10' and wrote into the bottom margin: 'the Gasthaus poor – 5 gulden'.[115] On the same day before the notary, another testament divided 20 gulden evenly between the *haussitzenden* and the Gasthaus poor.[116] One wonders if, after witnessing the second testament being written, Lubbert Backer decided to modify his testament. As this type of bequest became increasingly frequent, equal donations were generally made to the two institutions.[117] Yet, on occasion, equal divisions of property would be difficult. Peter van Enckhusen bequeathed his portion of a multi-family house to the *haussitzenden* poor, and to the Gasthaus he gave 10 gulden and a bed.[118]

Confraternities continued to function despite their disappearance from the records during the 1530s. Again, the parish church probably took over the operations of St Anthony's charitable activities during the mid-1530s. St Clement's Shippers' Brotherhood survived the changes of the sixteenth century and is still in existence today. Perhaps due to their connections with the Franciscan monastery, the Confraternities of Our Lady and St Ann were able to survive at least 25 and 35 years, respectively, after the introduction of the Reformation. They continued their activities as loan banks and contributors to the feeding of the poor. In 1538, the 'administrators of St Ann's poor' made a loan of 50 gulden out of their capital.[119] In 1541, the 'administrators of Our Lady's Brotherhood by the Observant brothers' made loans in order to receive yearly interest payments 'to the use of and on behalf of the poor who are being fed there'.[120] This period also marked the re-emergence in the records of St Clement's Brotherhood, which had last appeared in 1523 and whose last surviving loan contract dated from 1512.[121] When 'the advocates and administrators of St Clement's Brotherhood' loaned out 50 gulden in March 1540, it marked the first of increasingly frequent appearances of the confraternities as a source of capital for loans. The loan-making activities of St Clement's blossomed fully in the late 1550s.[122]

Evidence suggests that Our Lady's and St Ann's Confraternities merged into St Clement's Brotherhood, although it is difficult to establish the

---

[115] Ibid. 2/463 (20 May 1539).
[116] Ibid. 2/464 (20 May 1539).
[117] For examples through 1542, see ibid. 2/559v, 569, 576v, 604; 3/34, 37v.
[118] Ibid. 2/548v (21 February 1541).
[119] Ibid. 2/434 (8 November 1538).
[120] Ibid. 2/559 (5 May 1541); 2/581 (8 August 1541).
[121] 'Unser lever vrouwen register', fol. 24; EKP 1/41.
[122] For instance, EKP 5/199v, 265, 265v, 281v; 6/59, 60, 82; 8/192, 193, 323, 385, 417, 418, 498, 635 for references through 1555–59.

date of the final disappearance of Our Lady's and St Ann's. The final record of Our Lady's Confraternity is a testament from 1547 in which a man modified an earlier will (from 1539) to include his children. He also expanded his description of his charitable bequest. In the earlier testament he used the simple phrase 'to the suffering poor and Christians'.[123] In the amended testament from 1547, he offered more explicit stipulations. Any remaining goods should first go to any of his 'shame-faced' (*schamele*) relatives who needed them, but if there should be 'no shame-faced relatives who need them according to God's will', then his goods were to be given 'to Our Lady's Brotherhood and St Clement's poor'.[124] Our Lady's Confraternity, identified as being 'by the Observant brothers', still existed as an entity separate from St Clement's. Yet earlier loan contracts suggest that the two brotherhoods had merged their administrations as early as 1541: the four administrators of 'Our Lady's Brotherhood by the Observant Brothers' identified in May 1541 are the same four named as administrators of St Clement's Brotherhood in March 1540.[125]

A similar situation can be observed with respect to St Ann's Confraternity. In the summer of 1557, the 'advocates of the Brotherhood of St Clement's guild', along with one of the churchwardens, had to settle a dispute with an heir over a testament.[126] The dispute involved the 1522 testament of Tyge and Dedde Harenn in which they left their goods to be divided between Emden's parish church and St Ann's Confraternity in the Faldern monastery.[127] It seems that one Hayo Pelser had been 'for some time improperly occupying' the house of Tyge and Dedde following their deaths. The dispute was settled by ruling that Hayo could continue to live in the house for the rest of his life, but he had no authority to sell it, borrow against it or the like. Upon his death, the house would return to the full possession of the church and St Clement's guild.[128] This dispute is significant because it brings to light the merger of St Ann's into St Clement's and demonstrates the complete legal authority that St Clement's had over all previous assets and properties of St Ann's, even property collected from a 35–year-old testament. Indeed, the two advocates of the brotherhood were identified as administrators of St Clement's in the original and as advocates of St

---

[123] Ibid. 2/446v.

[124] Ibid. 2/233v (18 March 1547).

[125] Compare Fehler, 'Social Welfare', pp. 103 and 118; EKP 2/499v (2 March 1540), 2/559 (5 May 1541).

[126] On the participants in this dispute: ArchGK no. 89 (2 July 1557); EKP 6/105; 6/59; Fehler, 'Social Welfare', p. 118; KRP, pp. 12ff, 17.

[127] ArchGK no. 48; EKP 1/193; see p. 52, n. 106 above.

[128] ArchGK no. 89.

Ann's in the notarial copy. Unfortunately, we cannot pinpoint the dissolution of St Ann's more accurately than between November 1538 and July 1557. The aforementioned 50-gulden loan made by St Ann's administrators on 8 November 1538 was their last recorded action. A note at the bottom of this loan agreement indicates that when the loan was paid off in 1559 the payment was received by the 'administrators of St Clement's brotherhood'.[129] The traditional spiritual activities of Our Lady's and St Ann's which were organised around the Franciscan monastery definitely continued to prosper even when the financial administrations merged with St Clement's, perhaps as early as the 1540s for both confraternities. Certainly at least as late as 1547, people perceived Our Lady's and St Clement's as separate institutions despite their shared administration for at least six years.

Though the confraternities continued for a couple of decades after the Reformation, it is difficult to ascertain changes in their composition. In Protestant Lübeck, for example, some of the wealthier brotherhoods survived, but only to distribute alms to the poor. They stopped taking new members, and only a board of directors remained to administer their assets.[130] At what point this happened in Emden, or even if it happened, is not clear. St Ann's and Our Lady's Confraternity probably continued receiving new members for a time, given that they were able to continue their spiritual activities under the auspices of the monastery's exemption from the prohibition of the Mass. The only surviving membership list from one of Emden's confraternities, that of Our Lady's, ends with the membership class of 1523.[131] Although 'evangelical' teachings were taking place throughout East Frisia, there was absolutely no religious consensus by 1523 and there would not yet have been any external pressure on the confraternity to end its traditional religious activities. Moreover, among the final entries in the confraternity's accounting portion of the register is a record of their payment to a painter to better adorn the altar of Our Lady.[132] The confraternity's account book also ends in 1523, despite external evidence of many later financial activities. Thus no apparent significance

---

[129] EKP 2/434.

[130] The consolidation of the assets of the confraternities into a *Hauptkasten* did not occur, as called for in Bugenhagen's 1531 Lübeck Church Ordinance. The former confraternities continued as 'private relief institutions under civic oversight' until 1846; Zmyslony, *Bruderschaften in Lübeck*, p. 153; Max Hasse, 'Maria und die Heiligen im protestantischen Lübeck', *Nordelbingen*, 34 (1965), pp. 72–81.

[131] 'Unser lever vrouwen register'.

[132] Ibid., fol. 16. This 'register' of Our Lady's contains both an account book and the membership list.

regarding the growth of the confraternity can be placed on the end of the membership list in 1523.

More evidence survives about the confraternities' administrators than the members. Among identified names of confraternal administrators, including the administrators of St Gertrude's Gasthaus, are those who began their service before the Reformation and continued for many years after. There were also new administrators who began their service after the Reformation.[133] Thus the Reformation did not cause a break in the continuity of the confraternities' leadership; nor did it lock into place the 'old boys' who had been in charge.

The gradual decline of the confraternities paralleled an increase in the activities of Emden's trade guilds, but the religious changes in the town contributed little to any guild's institutional changes. By 1536, there were at least nine craft guilds in Emden.[134] For the first quarter of the sixteenth century, the sources are silent on the activity of the guilds. But in 1529 evidence from the Shoemakers' Guild begins to emerge. Like many of the confraternal and other contracts discussed previously, the Shoemakers' Guild loaned some of its capital so that the 6 per cent annual interest would go 'to the use and profit of the common poor, who for the time have their alms from' the guild.[135] Similar loans made 'to the use of the poor whom the Shoemakers' Guild maintains' can be found in 1537 and 1538 (34 and 100 gulden).[136] In the last two cases, the recipients of the loans were, in fact, shoemakers; the first example is unclear. Hence the guild reinvested its funds primarily among its members. Moreover, these loans demonstrate that the guilds (the Shoemakers, at least) not only maintained a fund to provide for poor members and relatives, but also that they had enough assets in this fund to invest large amounts of capital in the form of loans. One wonders if the size of the relief fund was large enough to provide for all the guild's members, and, if so, whether any extra funds were directed to external (non-guild) poor in the city. In the 1538 example, the loan's interest was to return to 'their guild and to the *haussitzenden* poor'. From this phrase it is unclear whether the contract referred simply to the residential poor guild members or if the Shoemakers' Guild also provided some donations to the 'administrators of the *haussitzenden* poor' in Emden.

---

[133] For example, Fehler, 'Social Welfare', pp. 103, 124, 131, 145.

[134] Kappelhoff, 'Reformation in Emden', I, 86f. Those whose existence can be proven with a Guild Roll: Goldsmiths (renewed in 1491), Shoemakers (1491), Shopkeepers (1500), Weavers (1504), and Bakers (reference to the old Roll of 1504). Additional guilds mentioned in the sources: Tailors (1517), Carpenters (*c.* 1520), Barber–Surgeons (1527), Painters and Glaziers (1536).

[135] EKP 2/26v (6 May 1529).

[136] Ibid. 2/391v (11 November 1537); 2/434v (12 November 1538).

In the 1545 Police Ordinance, the craft guilds were admonished, along with the Shippers' Brotherhood, to revise and correct their ordinances. They were to eliminate excessive eating and drunkenness and utilise the money in remembrance of the poor. But as the evidence from the Shoemakers' 1491 Ordinance reveals, the obligations to provide for the guild's own poor existed long before the Reformation or the Police Ordinance.[137] Although the evidence is in no way conclusive, there might have been an expansion of the guild's charitable activities – 'works of compassion' in the 1491 Ordinance – to include some non-guild-members as well. As the activities of the confraternities began to decline in the 1530s, the guilds began to serve as loan banks, although these loans were probably made to members of the trade.

The Protestant Reformation came early to East Frisia but took a long time to be effectively organised into a uniform religious settlement in Emden. In the realm of poor relief the Reformation brought even slower changes: the traditional methods and institutions of social welfare continued, with only gradual modifications, for several decades. Confraternities continued their activities at least until the 1540s, albeit after the mid-1520s with a more explicit and visible role in poor relief. Their traditional activities, especially those of a spiritual nature, were probably facilitated by the Franciscan monastery's exemption from the ban on the Catholic Mass. Given the continuation of the confraternities of St Ann and Our Lady, as well as the Franciscan monastery, a new 'Protestant' view of poor relief could not have quickly replaced the traditional late medieval view of piety and good works, a view that constituted one of the founding principles of Emden's confraternities. Unfortunately, the writing of testaments by the Franciscan friars, whose records do not survive, probably obscures the survival of most such beliefs from any investigation. As late as 1541, among the wills drawn up by the Protestant notary, a testament can be found that still considered its donor's charitable donation as an aid 'to the salvation of his soul'.[138] The traditional views of charity and piety which had governed the establishment of the confraternities continued.

By the 1540s, changes in Emden's poor relief became more pronounced. The confraternities were stripped of their religious functions. St Anthony's Brotherhood had already been taken over by Emden's parish church. St Ann's and Our Lady's Brotherhoods were merged into the Shippers' Brotherhood of St Clement's. The survival of St Clement's

---

[137] *OUB* no. 1298.
[138] EKP 2/569.

can probably be related to the fact that it was the one confraternity that provided relief to a specifically defined group of poor, those involved in shipping, for whom there was no other designated relief institution.

Other poor relief institutions also demonstrated gradual developments after the Reformation. The Gasthaus and Gotteskammern apparently continued their work with no significant institutional changes. The Church Ordinance of 1529 did not mark an abrupt break with past relief methods: the traditional *huusdelinge* tax was still to be assessed but now a portion would be earmarked for the *haussitzenden* poor, and no common chest was established for poor relief. Even the duties of the new 'administrators of the poor' mandated by the ordinance were probably assigned to the traditional lay churchwardens in Emden. By the early 1540s, as these 'administrators' became a familiar feature of Emden's welfare system, Emden residents came to see the 'poor in Emden' (as recorded in the contracts and testaments) ever more exclusively as either those in the Gasthaus or those provided relief by the *haussitzenden* administrators.

Through the 1540s and early 1550s, these poor relief institutions sufficiently addressed the modest social welfare problems in the still small town of Emden. The muted prohibition of begging and proscription of relief to foreign poor mandated by the 1545 Police Ordinance might even successfully have regulated vagrancy in Emden and East Frisia, had not a number of social and economic factors changed during the 1550s. One of the greatest single catalysts of change was the arrival of Dutch refugees. The population exploded, housing and food shortages occurred, shipping boomed, and increased numbers of foreign and transient workers and poor arrived: the poor of Emden were no longer simply the *haussitzenden*. Indeed, the institutional structures of social welfare which had gradually evolved throughout the first half of the sixteenth century were suddenly weighed and found wanting. While the Reformation brought some tinkering with the institutions of poor relief, the decade of the 1550s would see a massive overhaul of Emden's social welfare system.

CHAPTER FOUR

The Evolution of
New Social Welfare Institutions

> Within a couple of decades, mainly between 1540 and 1580, Emden, the provincial town without proper urban constitution, social diversity, and transregional economic significance, developed into a metropolis with intellectual, economic, and political connections reaching over the continent and the seas.
>
> Heinz Schilling, *Civic Calvinism*[1]

While the main impetus for this transformation began in the 1550s with the arrival of the refugees from the Dutch Revolt, the pace of change began to increase earlier, around 1540. Countess Anna, Enno's wife, assumed the regency for her three sons – Edzard, Johan, and Christoph – shortly after Enno's death in 1540.[2] The year 1540 also marked the arrival of the Polish nobleman and cleric Johannes a Lasco in East Frisia.[3] Lasco was a widely travelled, humanist-trained friend of Erasmus of Rotterdam, and many of the developments in Emden during the second half of the sixteenth century can be traced back to seeds which Lasco sowed in Emden's ecclesiastical constitution. The previous chapter hinted at Lasco's creation of elders in Emden.

Lasco guided the East Frisian church during the mid-1540s after Countess Anna persuaded him in the spring of 1543 to fill the post of superintendent of the East Frisian church. Both the 1529 and 1535 Church Ordinances had called for the creation of the office, but it was filled for the first time by Lasco. He quickly began trying to unify the Church in East Frisia, making attempts to define the church clearly from within and without. He spoke with the friars in the Franciscan monastery – the centre of Catholic activity in Emden – and attempted to narrow the scope of their influence. Lasco also held disputations in order to force the Anabaptist leaders in East Frisia to defend their beliefs, with hopes of persuading them to abandon their beliefs. He met

---

[1] Heinz Schilling, *Civic Calvinism* (Kirksville, MO, 1991), p. 21.

[2] Enno's brother Johann von Falkenburg was regent until 1542, when Anna was able to negotiate for the role. Johann had earlier returned to Catholicism.

[3] For biographical information on Lasco, see Hermann Dalton, *Johannes a Lasco* (Gotha, 1881); Menno Smid, 'Jan Laski', in *TRE*, vol. XX, pp. 448–51; Smid, 'Johannes Laski', in *Neue Deutsche Biographie*, 13, pp. 657f. Lasco's writings have been edited by Abraham Kuyper, *Joannis a Lasco opera*, 2 vols (Amsterdam, 1866).

the followers of David Joris in 1543 and held a public debate in Emden with Menno Simons in 1544. Lasco also worked toward having the altars and images removed from the East Frisian churches. Many of these activities met with stern resistance.[4] Yet his organisational changes in the church, especially the Emden consistory and the *Coetus* of East Frisian ministers, shaped the institutional make-up of the church from that time forward. Moreover, Lasco was especially interested in church discipline, and he attempted throughout his service in Emden (and later in London as superintendent of the refugee churches) to bring about reform in the church which emphasised it.

Lasco's most influential innovation for the Emden church was the creation of the Emden consistory in 1544.[5] In an attempt to increase discipline within the church community, he established an institution which, together with the pastors, consisted of elders chosen from amongst the most honourable lay members of the parish.[6] Their duties were first and foremost to oversee the discipline in the church on matters of belief and morals, and they also administered the church's properties. The consistory was also heavily involved with questions regarding the administration of poor relief. In the consistory meeting of 16 July 1557, the earliest meeting for which records exist, the 'deacons of the city of Emden, both the old and the newly elected supervisors', met the members of the consistory (preachers and elders) to discuss several issues regarding poor relief in Emden. The minutes of the meeting deal entirely with questions about poor relief and the deacons.[7] With this first entry in the consistory minutes, it is clear that a complete organisation of the diaconate in Emden existed by 1557.

As early as the 1540s, another civic committee (*Bürgerausschuß*) was formed. It granted appointed citizens some supervision of the town's financial revenues. This citizens' committee organised the 1546 collection of customs duties on wine and beer to pay for enlarged defences for the city. Although little is known about the size of this temporary committee, its creation demonstrates the growing participation by Emden's citizenry despite the lack of autonomy of the town's magistrate. Emden's Burgermeisters and city councillors still remained fully

---

[4] Menno Smid, *Ostfriesische Kirchengeschichte* (Pewsum, 1974), pp. 158–65.

[5] The actions of the consistory during the first 13 years of its existence are unknown; records of the minutes of the meetings begin only on 16 July 1557. The manuscript minutes are in the ArchGK no. 329. Heinz Schilling has recently edited the minutes through the year 1620: *Die Kirchenratsprotokolle der Reformierten Gemeinde Emden 1557–1620*, 2 vols (Cologne, 1989–92).

[6] Smid, *Kirchengeschichte*, p. 166. Originally consisting of four lay members, the consistory soon expanded the number to 12 due to the enlarged set of duties given them.

[7] KRP, pp. 1f (16 July 1557).

dependent upon the countess for their appointments, a dependence which lasted until the Emden Revolution in 1595. The creation of these new civic committees was contemporaneous with the creation of new lay church offices by Lasco. Complementing Lasco's attempt to bring religious order to the church, the aforementioned 1545 Police Ordinance of Countess Anna was issued to bring political and social order to the territory.

With the emperor's victory over the Protestant forces in the Schmalkaldic War of 1546–48 came the imposition of his religious settlement, the Augsburg Interim. Fearful of losing Emden's imperially granted right to collect customs duties on passing ships (*Vorbeifahrtsrecht*), the Countess Anna was forced to accept the Interim. Lasco resigned his post as superintendent and accepted Archbishop Cranmer's invitation to visit England, where he ultimately became superintendent of the exile churches in London. Nevertheless, the Interim's religious settlement did not take place in Emden without significant popular resistance. All of Emden's remaining ministers refused to accept the provisions mandating restoration of the Catholic Mass. They had popular support for their decision, and the Grosse Kirche was closed. No worship services were held, and the church was opened only three times per week for baptisms and marriages. The resolve of Emden's ministers and congregation held out until the political atmosphere in Germany had so changed by 1552 that the Interim settlement was no longer meaningful, and the Emden church recommenced its normal church activities.[8]

By 1550, Emden's population was probably about 5 000.[9] Settlement of the town expanded eastward to take in Middle Faldern, the suburb which included the Franciscan monastery, although the suburb was not yet included within the city walls. The town's economic activities had increased in the first half of the century largely as a result of the rising demand for grain imports in the German hinterland (Westphalia was especially important for Emden), which was met by grain from the Baltic transported through Emden. But Emden's slow growth during the first half of the sixteenth century was soon dwarfed by the changes that were spurred on by the immigration of thousands of Dutch refugees.

During the reign of the English King Edward VI, many Protestants from the continent had fled to England and established large exile

---

[8] Jan Weerda, 'Die grosse Probe: Die Emder Gemeinde und das Interim, 1549–50', *Sontagsblatt für ev.-ref. Gemeinden*, 54 (1954), pp. 372, 378ff; Smid, *Kirchengeschichte*, pp. 173ff; Bernd Kappelhoff, 'Die Reformation in Emden', part II, *EJb*, 58 (1978), pp. 61–4.

[9] Hermann de Buhr, *Die Entwicklung Emdens in der zweiten Hälfte des 16. Jahrhunderts* (Ph.D. diss., Hamburg, 1967), p. 53.

communities. However, when Mary came to the throne in 1553, the foreign Protestants, along with several thousand English Protestants, were forced to leave for the continent. Many of them came to Emden. Lasco's London refugee congregation ultimately made its way to Emden and was admitted into the town by Countess Anna in 1554. Because most of the refugees from the London congregation were fleeing persecution in the Spanish-controlled Netherlands, and because of the similarity between Dutch and the East Frisian dialects, these exiles assimilated easily into the Emden church congregation. French Protestant refugees, however, were granted the right to form their own congregation with their own minister and church organisation.[10] Among these early Dutch refugees were a number of influential merchant families, particularly from the commercial centre of Antwerp, who left the Netherlands as much for business as for religious reasons. They sensed the growing unrest and instability in the Netherlands, and brought their businesses and ships with them to Emden.

Over the next 20 years an enormous number of Dutch refugees entered Emden's city gates.[11] Emden's population increased to at least 10 000, and at the height of the immigration in 1572 might have been as high as 20 000.[12] About one-third of Emden's population in the 1560s were Dutch refugees; the proportion climbed to no less than half by the 1570s.[13]

The importance of the grain trade between the German hinterland and the Baltic continued to grow for Emden, but the appearance in the city of international merchants, bringing their entire fleets, marked a dramatic shift in Emden's commercial development. Political turbulence in the Netherlands resulting from the outbreak of the Revolt in 1565 and Emden's neutrality in the war elevated Emden's commercial position to new heights. Suddenly, Emden transcended its regional significance to become a centre of the trade between England and the continent as well as between the Baltic and the Atlantic ports of Europe. In 1570, the tonnage capacity of Emden's fleet was larger than that of the entire

---

[10] The English Marian exiles also formed a separate church in Emden, although there is no surviving evidence of an official authorisation for them. For the only published study of this group, see Andrew Pettegree, 'The English Church at Emden', in *Marian Protestantism. Six Studies* (Aldershot, 1996), pp. 10–38.

[11] On the Dutch refugees in the sixteenth century, especially in Emden, see Andrew Pettegree, *Emden and the Dutch Revolt. Exile and the Development of Reformed Protestantism* (Oxford, 1992); Heinz Schilling, *Niederländische Exulanten im 16. Jahrhundert* (Gütersloh, 1972); Aart Arnout van Schelven, *De Nederduitsche Vluchtelingenkerken der XVIe Eeuw in Engeland en Duitschland in Hunne Beteekenis voor de Reformatie in de Nederlanden* (The Hague, 1908).

[12] Schilling, *Civic Calvinism*, p. 21.

[13] Schilling, *Niederländische Exulanten*, p. 66.

kingdom of England.[14] Many merchants from across Europe, not just from the Netherlands, took advantage even temporarily of Emden's neutrality and moved their base of operations to Emden to sail under the city's banner.

During the 20-year flood of Dutch refugees (1554–c. 1575), a number of key events and developments help to illustrate the general demographic and commercial expansion and ecclesiastical development in Emden. Even the modest numbers of refugees after 1554 quickly stretched Emden to the limit of available housing. Housing shortages led to sharply rising prices, and a development project was started to build new streets and houses in the Faldern suburbs.[15] The growing population, coupled with two bad harvests in 1556 and 1557, provoked grain shortages and concomitant sky-rocketing grain prices, and the poor relief institutions in Emden were stretched to their limits. The combination of continuous immigration, housing shortages, over-extended relief agencies, and the growing Protestant identity in the city served as the motivation behind the expulsion of the last remaining Franciscan friars in 1557–58. Not only were the Catholic friars no longer wanted on religious grounds; more practical concerns, such as the need for additional housing for the poor, propelled the negotiations between Countess Anna and the monks for the control of the monastery properties.

The religious impact of the Dutch refugees upon Emden's church should not be overlooked. Before the arrival of the Dutch, Lasco had been trying to move Emden's church towards a Reformed style of organisation with a consistory, elders, and an emphasis on church discipline. While still in its infancy, however, the church polity soon faced decay from Emden's experience with the Augsburg Interim which required an end to most Protestant ecclesiastical innovations. The earliest Dutch refugees after the effective end of the Interim brought with them to Emden a keen sense of church discipline which had been enthusiastically fostered in the London congregation under Lasco. Their church ordinance, written by Lasco, had been put into practice during their brief experience in London.[16] The theological and organisational energy of the Dutch refugees, as well as their disciplined faith, left its mark on Emden's church. This was illustrated most clearly by the renovation of Emden's consistory in the second half of the 1550s.[17] The existence of

---

[14] Bernhard Hagedorn, *Ostfrieslands Handel und Schiffahrt im 16. Jahrhundert*, vol. i, (Berlin, 1910), p. 251.

[15] See p. 132 below.

[16] *Forma ac Ratio tota ecclesiastici Ministerii* (London, 1550), in Kuyper (ed.), *Lasco opera*, vol. II.

[17] See Schilling, 'Einleitung', KRP, p. xx.

consistory records after 1557 suggests that the renovation may have taken place around that time. The consistorial model brought to Emden by the London church deployed a Reformed church constitution with real congregational participation in the administration of the church. Because the London church was a free church, the ministers and elders were representatives of the congregation and not of the civic authorities. This London model truly affected Emden's consistory, and over subsequent decades this church council became increasingly independent of the count. From the 1550s onward, the Dutch exiles played an important role in the consistory: in 1571, the consistory even had to protect the influence of Emden's 'old burghers' in the consistory by stipulating that in an upcoming election to replace dead elders only half should be Dutch, the other half 'old burghers'.[18]

The emigration from cities in the Netherlands spread Dutch cultural and social influence across northern Europe in the early modern period, and the Dutch refugees probably also affected the communal mentality of the town and the drive for civic participation by Emden's citizens.[19] Many of the refugees brought with them civic experiences from their home cities in the Netherlands (cities such as Bruges, Antwerp, Brussels and Amsterdam) which differed greatly from the limited civic constitutional development in Emden.

The direct role of Johannes a Lasco in Emden was rather limited following his return with much of his London congregation. He did not return to his post as superintendent (indeed, that position remained unfilled), but he did work to establish the position of the Dutch refugees within Emden's congregation. His role as their pastor allowed him to appoint the deacons who would administer the poor relief for the refugee community (*fremdlingen* deacons). He also played an important role in the production of the Emden Catechism of 1554.[20] Lasco, however, did not stay long in Emden this time. In the spring of 1555, he left for the refugee community in Frankfurt-am-Main and then went on to Poland where he died in 1560.

The Dutch Revolt against Spanish rule in the Netherlands began with great hope and promise in 1565. Yet, by the end of 1566 or early 1567,

---

[18] KRP, p. 426 (9 November 1571). See Schilling's comment on p. xxi.

[19] Compare Jonathan Israel, 'Dutch influence on urban planning, health care and poor relief: the North Sea and Baltic regions of Europe, 1567–1720', in *Health Care and Poor Relief in Protestant Europe 1500–1700*, eds O. P. Grell and A. Cunningham (London, 1997), pp. 66–83.

[20] The authors of the catechism intended it to be the instructional basis for a unified East Frisian church, but its theology went too much in a non-Lutheran direction to be acceptable to the Lutheran party, which had been growing especially in the northern regions of East Frisia; Smid, *Kirchengeschichte*, pp. 177ff.

setbacks by rebel forces led to widespread emigration before the advancing Spanish Catholic troops. Exiles from the Dutch Revolt flooded into refugee communities across western Germany (especially Wesel, Aachen, Duisberg, Frankenthal, Cologne, Heidelberg and Frankfurt) and into England. No fewer than 4 000 sought refuge in Emden at this time. An immigration of this size put massive pressure on the economic resources and housing of the small town, and the exiles ended up primarily in the Faldern suburbs, frequently finding accommodation in the houses of earlier residents of the town. During much of the next decade, Emden came to serve as a 'mother church' for the Dutch churches 'under the cross'. The Reformed churches in the Netherlands turned frequently to the Emden consistory for advice on questions of church organisation and discipline. Emden also became a missionary centre, providing pastors to fledgling Reformed congregations in the Netherlands as well as large amounts of Dutch Protestant literature which was frequently smuggled into the Netherlands. Many Reformed ministers sought exile in Emden while they waited for the way to clear for their return to their home congregations.[21]

Throughout the period of the Dutch Revolt, the city of Emden and the counts of East Frisia sought to maintain their neutrality. Despite their official neutrality it was clear, even to many contemporaries, that Emden favoured the Dutch rebels. The count tried to discourage direct aid to the rebel forces, but Emden's role for a time as headquarters for the Sea Beggars (as well as its position as a refuge for the Dutch Protestants and a centre for missionary and propaganda activities into the Netherlands) frequently raised the ire of the Spanish rulers fighting against the Dutch.

The potential aftermath of the Battle of Jemgum on 21 July 1568 horrified Emden and the East Frisian counts and forced them to be a bit more circumspect in their support. The Duke of Alva had pursued the Dutch rebel forces, after defeating them near Groningen, all the way to the village of Jemgum – on East Frisian soil. After delivering a crushing blow to the Dutch troops at Jemgum, it seemed likely that Alva would then continue his march northward to Emden, which the Spanish rulers felt (not without some justification) was aiding the rebel cause. Alva, however, did not proceed against Emden, but instead returned to the

---

[21] The authoritative treatment of all the intricate relationships – religious, political, economic, commercial, even printing – between Emden and the Dutch refugees during this period is Pettegree's *Emden and the Dutch Revolt*. For a more general comparative analysis of the impact of Dutch exiles in the chief cities of refuge (Wesel, London, Emden, Frankfurt, Cologne, Hamburg and Aachen), see Schilling's *Niederländische Exulanten im 16. Jahrhundert*.

Netherlands. The fear of Alva's possible advance inspired a building project to expand the fortifications of the city, bringing the suburbs of Middle Faldern within the city walls.

Those in Emden realised that they would probably have been at Alva's mercy had he chosen to exact retribution from the city. From this point in 1568 onward, Emden's political involvement in the Nether-lands became much more cautious. Even the religious leaders were more circumspect in their relationship with the Netherlands. A case in point is the Emden Synod of 1571. Although the synod, which was held in Emden from 4 to 13 October, was one of the single most important events in the organisational development of the Dutch Reformed church, the officials of the 'Mother Church' played no visible role either in its planning or in the synod itself which took place within its city. Even the consistory records of the time of the synod are silent about the impor-tant meeting taking place in Emden. The only representatives to the synod from any East Frisian congregation were the minister and two elders of Emden's French refugee church. Emden apparently wanted to avoid the appearance of a close connection with affairs of the Dutch church.

The height of Dutch immigration into Emden occurred in 1572. Dutch victories in the Netherlands in 1574–75 motivated a great number of refugees to return to the Netherlands. One contemporary account claimed that in April 1574, 3 000 people with families moved from Emden and the surrounding East Frisian countryside back to the Neth-erlands (to Holland, the Maas region and Zeeland) and in May an additional 300 set sail for Holland.[22] By the end of 1575 a majority of the Dutch exiles had left Emden for the Netherlands, establishing in their home country much of what Emden had provided as 'Mother Church' and taking with them their ships and commercial experience. Nevertheless, a significant number of Dutch continued to reside in Emden throughout the rest of the century.

Although large-scale migrations ended about 1575, the period around 1570 was the high point in the social and economic development of Emden. The demographic explosion and the resulting settlement of the easternmost Faldern suburbs led Emden to officially incorporate Gross-Faldern and Klein-Faldern into the city itself. Emden began one of its largest building projects of the century in 1574, the construction of a new city hall (Emden Rathaus, see Figure 4.1). Located just across the

---

[22] Portions of the so-called 'Emder Chronyk' from the sixteenth century were tran-scribed and published by Hemmo Suur as 'Zur Geschichte der Stadt Emden', in *Jahrbüchlein zur Unterhaltung und zum Nutzen zunächst für Ostfriesland und Harlingerland auf das Jahr 1837*, ed. G. W. Bueren (Emden, 1836), p. 102.

4.1 Emden Rathaus. The Town Hall was built between 1574 and 1576.

bridge from the old Rathaus and next to the former Franciscan monastery (now a poor house), this large and expensive project of civic pride took two years to complete and clearly demonstrates that money was not exactly short in Emden. The city fathers chose a design for their new Rathaus based unashamedly upon that of the Antwerp Rathaus. Emden seems, therefore, to have been making a statement about its own perceived commercial significance by drawing a parallel with the great commercial centre of Antwerp.

Thus, during the 1550s several events came together to spur significant innovations and modifications of Emden's social welfare system. As we saw in the previous chapter, specific individual modifications to the office of poor relief administrator in its first decades are difficult to trace, but by 1557 the 'advocates and supervisors of the poor' had become the 'deacons' of the Emden church with a relatively complete organisational structure. Lasco's 1554 arrival, with his London church of Dutch refugees, led to institutional and social changes in the Emden church. Most prominent among the refugees' influences on Emden's poor relief system was the establishment of the special *fremdlingen* (foreign) deacons, in 1558. Additionally, the attempts which began in 1557 to organise an exclusive diaconate for the 'poor of the Household of Faith' can most certainly be traced to ideals, which had developed in the refugees' exile church, of a pure community of faith and discipline.

The mid-1550s saw, too, the expulsion of the last Franciscan friars from the monastery in Emden/Faldern, and in 1557 the citizenry of Emden gained control of the monastery buildings. The properties and functions of the previously existing Gasthäuser were centralised into one foundation. The economic experience of extremely high grain prices in 1557 was a further factor in the creation of new poor relief institutions; a group of Emden citizens formed the Grain Reserve (*Kornvorrat*) as a private initiative to provide grain to the needy at low prices during periods of high grain prices. The origins of these new poor relief institutions will become clearer by tracing the developments of the 1550s.

The lay church administrators of the poor appeared in Emden shortly after they were called for in Count Enno's Church Ordinance of 1529. These supervisors later took on the title of 'deacons of the *haussitzenden* poor'. The phrase *haussitzenden* to describe the local, non-transient poor was used in Countess Anna's Police Ordinance of 1545, but its roots go back even further. This was the traditional term used to describe the local poor in Emden and can be found in testaments dating back to 1512.[23] These supervisors (*Vorsteher*) of the *haussitzenden* poor

---

[23] EKP 2/44, refers to the 'armen hussittenden' in Emden.

appear frequently in the Emden notarial records in the 1540s and 1550s. Gradually, perhaps under the Reformed influence of Lasco, these supervisors began to be referred to as 'deacons'.

The earliest surviving Emden Church Council records, the consistory records of 16 July 1557, reveal several characteristics of the deacons of the *haussitzenden* poor in Emden. First, unlike deacons in other Reformed cities such as Groningen, Emden's deacons did not belong to the consistory. The 'deacons of the city of Emden ... both the old as well as the newly elected supervisors' appeared before the consistory, which was 'the assembly of the preachers and elders of the congregation within Emden', in order to deliberate on matters concerning the poor. Although the deacons were not members of the consistory, it is clear from the number of poor relief issues handled during this meeting that the deacons looked to the consistory for advice in working out social welfare questions.[24]

The minutes of this meeting used the term 'deacon' for the first time in any surviving source, though they still refer to the poor relief officers intermittently as 'supervisors' as well. The first issue attended to by the consistory was the length of service of the deacons of the *haussitzenden* poor. An election of new deacons had recently occurred, for 'newly elected' deacons appeared before the consistory with the older deacons. At this time, the consistory appears to have established a two-year term of office for the deacons. The time limit was not intended to be strictly enforced, however; after the two years, the older deacons should remain in office, provided that neither they nor the congregation had reasonable grounds to elect someone else in their place.

This rule governing the length of office of the deacons remained largely unchanged until the extensive poor relief ordinance from 1576.[25] On 4 February 1566, the consistory was notified that three deacons of the *haussitzenden* poor were missing from service. The consistory considered it best that the preachers and elders, with the 'advice and consent' of the current deacons, elect replacement deacons in order to ease the burden. In addition, they inaugurated the rule that every year in each administrative district (*Kluft*) the two oldest deacons should retire and be replaced by two new deacons.[26]

---

[24] KRP, pp. 1f.

[25] The text of this ordinance and the supplementary orders through 1579 are printed in Timothy Fehler, 'Social Welfare in Early Modern Emden' (University of Wisconsin-Madison, Ph.D. thesis, 1995), pp. 505–17. The surviving copy is in ArchGK no. 3001, pp. 1–32. Sehling (ed.), *Kirchenordnungen*, pp. 455–63 reproduces most of the provisions.

[26] KRP, p. 232.

In the July 1557 meeting of the consistory, the deacons had complained that they did not have enough resources to care adequately for all the poor of the city. The deacons attempted to establish policies to reduce the deficiency, and subsequent consistory records shed some light on their practice of collecting alms for the poor. The 'deacons of the city' appeared before the consistory two weeks later, and the decision was made in favour of added measures to make up for the shortage in the weekly alms collections. First, the deacons were to make two pouches and then take them around on Sundays to collect supplementary alms. A second innovation came in the form of a dish placed at weddings: 'when one gives to the bride and groom', they also 'give into [the dish]' for the poor.[27] These additional methods of gathering alms were to be used when the regular weekly alms given in the church service did not suffice to meet the expenses of the deacons.

None of the *haussitzenden* deacons appear to have held simultaneously a position as elder. On 13 December 1557 the consistory nominated Hyndrick van Loningen for election as elder.[28] The following week, the pastors spoke (or attempted to speak) with the nominees, but virtually all of them declined the position. Hyndrick was no different, but his excuse was not that he did not feel qualified. Rather, he said that 'what he could do, he would gladly do'. However, 'he must also frequently withdraw, [and] he could not well serve the office because he also has the office of the diaconate'.[29] He did say, though, that 'he will do what the consistory advises him'.[30] Despite his willingness to serve in both offices, Hyndrick was not asked again to serve as elder, thus maintaining a separation between the elders and the deacons of the *haussitzenden* poor.[31]

Some of Emden's congregation, however, were not satisfied with the relief of the *haussitzenden* deacons. Arguments for a new, exclusive diaconate of the 'household of faith' apparently had their origins in Lasco's ideal conception of the pure church congregation. As

---

[27] Ibid., p. 7 (3 August).

[28] Ibid., p. 15.

[29] Hyndrick van Loningen appears as 'Voerstander' of the *haussitzenden* poor in the first surviving account book of the *haussitzenden* deacons (1561–73), ArchGK no. 1117; for instance, pp. 2 (9 April 1561), 154 (23 April 1564), 170 (8 July 1562). There are, unfortunately, no earlier references to his service as deacon so we are unable to determine when he began.

[30] KRP, p. 17.

[31] The final list of new elders was presented to the congregation about 13 March 1558; KRP, p. 39. Hyndrick was not chosen to be an elder, while much arm-twisting was used to persuade other elder nominees who were more reluctant than Hyndrick. For instance, see ibid., pp. 17, 20f; the example of Evert Kuper is discussed in the following section on the 'Deacons of the *Becken*'.

superintendent of the refugee churches in London during the reign of
Edward VI, Lasco was able to set in motion many of his ideas regarding
church discipline, which had failed to achieve widespread support during the time he was in Emden and East Frisia. The refugees' successful
implementation of church discipline was due largely of course to its
existence as an exile church, one whose membership was formed substantially of religious refugees who had fled the Netherlands and come
together in London because of their religious beliefs. With a well-
defined membership requirement, they were especially concerned to
maintain strict church discipline within their ranks.

The aspiration to maintain a pure congregation extended even to the
refugees' distribution of poor relief. Lasco's church ordinances for the
London congregation (1550) instructed the deacons to distribute the
alms conscientiously and wisely to the poor, 'especially to the members
of the household of faith'.[32] The exclusive distribution scheme, combin-
ing the dual activities of poor relief and discipline, displays the reformers'
'social concern and social control'.[33] There is even vague evidence which
suggests that Lasco had tried to introduce the distinction of the poor of
the 'household of faith' during his earlier tenure in Emden.[34] We can

---

[32] Lasco's *Forma ac Ratio tota ecclesiastici Ministerii* (London, 1550), in Kuyper (ed.),
Lasco opera, II, 78: 'imprimis vero domesticis fidei'; cites Gal. 6 [:10], Acts 4 [:32–5].
For the terminology in the Dutch and German translations: see Marten Micron's translation *De christlicke Ordinancien der nederlantscher Ghemeinten te Londen* (London,
1554, p. 34), ed. W. F. Dankbaar, p. 56: 'in sonderheit den huysghenooten des gheloefs';
cites Gal. 6. Micron's German translation *Kirchenordnung ... in der statt Londen in der
niderlendischen gemeine Christi* (Heidelberg, 1565), Sehling (ed.), *Kirchenordnungen*,
p. 597: 'insonderheit den haußgenossen des glaubens'.
The Strasbourg reformer Martin Bucer used the term 'hausgnossen des glaubens' in
November 1547 with reference to the members of the narrow congregation: 'was [Gott]
befohlen: einander lieben, wie uns Christus der herr liebet, eins seien, wie er und der
vater eins sind, und einander dienen und helfen wie glider an einem leib. Es sind ja ernste
wort, das alle die, so ware christliche liebe nit zu allen menschen und besonders zu den
hausgnossen des glaubens, iren brüderen in gott und mitgliederen Christi, haben, vor gott
nichts sind, weder kinder gots, noch glider Christi, sonder entfrembdet von gott und
Christo und ewiger verdamnüß verpflichtet sind'; Martin Bucer, 'Mehrung götlicher
gnaden und geists ... ' fol. 91v; printed in Werner Bellardi, *Die Geschichte der 'Christlichen
Gemeinschaft' in Straßburg (1546/1550). Der Versuch einer 'zweiten Reformation'* (Leipzig, 1934), p. 130.
[33] Such is Pettegree's conclusion in *Foreign Protestant Communities in Sixteenth-
Century London* (Oxford, 1986), pp. 198–214.
[34] In a letter to Countess Anna's secretary, Herman Lenthius, in September 1545,
Lasco complained about the lack of church discipline and piety in East Frisia. He
threatened to resign unless he received more support from the countess. In his extensive
list of complaints, Lasco also included the vague grievance, 'Annon est pudendum, me
hoc non posse impetrare, ut iusta habeatur egenorum ratio?'; Kuyper (ed.), *Lasco opera*,
II, 596f.

only speculate, however, whether Lasco, while in Emden, was already considering the restrictions of poor relief to the 'household of faith' which he would later implement in the London congregation.

This undertaking finally came to fruition at Emden in 1557, perhaps due to the influence of Dutch refugees who came from London to Emden in 1554. Their experience in London in a narrow congregation with strict church discipline was tested as they merged with the local church in Emden. By 1557 the Emden consistory was pondering a special arrangement by which to care for the poor of the 'household of faith', identified as those who were admitted to partake in communion. The economic situation in Emden was apparently such that the deacons of the *haussitzenden* poor no longer had funds and materials to care for all the house-poor of the city. The mid-1550s saw increasing housing problems as Emden's population grew, and 1556–57 was a period of rapidly increasing grain prices. Deacons appeared before the consistory on 16 July 1557 and raised the following question: can we exculpate ourselves before God for our practice of withholding support from some of the poor from outside the communion-congregation because we 'have no more with which to support the members of the household'? The consistory responded, 'Yes, you are doing correctly; however, you should make use of all [the] diligence which you can, so that one also helps those on the outside' of the congregation. The consistory went further and instructed them to curtail relief even to the poor of the congregation if the poor would not work, hold themselves piously, and be assiduous in God's work.[35] In this way, the general funds for the poor could be stretched a little further, and here at this July meeting appeared the first indication of thoughts about a separate source of funding for the poor of the communion-congregation.

The consistory furthermore decided to set up a *Becken* (literally, 'dish') in the choir of the church during communion for a special collection of alms on behalf of the 'members of the household of faith'.[36] By so doing, they would separate the care of poor members of the 'household of faith' from the general poor relief offered by the *haussitzenden* deacons. This decision was not to take effect immediately, however; the consistory decided to place the *Becken* for the first time in an upcoming communion service, either on Michaelis (29 September) or Martini (11 November). In the meantime they would be able to deliberate and prescribe more specifically 'how one should provide for the members of the household'. At the agreed-upon communion

---

[35] KRP, pp. 1f.

[36] The location is corroborated by a supplemental Poor Ordinance from 1578; ArchGK no. 3001, p. 25; Sehling (ed.), *Kirchenordnungen*, p. 461.

service, all communicants were to be exhorted to give alms generously, and the council also suggested that communion be held more frequently, perhaps every four weeks. In addition, to help provide for a short-term need, the consistory designated the next communion service for a collection of clothing, and ordered that the congregation be exhorted beforehand to give richly.[37]

The first recorded use of this special fund to assist someone of the 'household of faith' actually occurred before the official placement of the *Becken*. On 16 August 1557, the shopkeeper Luetke Schroer appeared before the consistory and asked for a loan of 1, 2 or 3 gulden to help with his business. In response to this request, the elder Joest Roße loaned him 1½ gulden on behalf of the congregation 'out of the *Becken*, which one will establish'.[38] Luetke agreed to repay the loan on the following Easter.[39]

We can only speculate as to when the first *Becken* communion service was held,[40] but on 15 November 1557 there was once again a general concern about questions of poor relief before the consistory. The consistory decided that each of the preachers should walk about and visit the poor in his own *Kluft* (neighbourhood). The point of this special visitation of the poor was apparently to question the poor of the congregation, as occasion offered, about how their needs could be met. According to the minutes of the meeting, the pastors would report their findings to the consistory at a future meeting.[41] Perhaps the implementation of the *Becken* at the previous communion service had motivated the consistory to follow up and visit the poor to see how effective the new funding was and what still needed to be done.

Armed with the reports of the pastors' visitations of the poor, the consistory took up the issue of relief of the 'household of faith' in their following meeting on 22 November. The preachers related that they had been around the town and had noted the members of the congregation, identifying those 'who need more and who do not need more'.[42] At this time, the consistory decided indeed to elect 'three supervisors to

---

[37] KRP, pp. 1f.

[38] Ibid., p. 8.

[39] That he did not repay the loan until 7 January 1566 (ibid., p. 226) was largely a result of his excommunication from the congregation in July 1558 and his decision not to be reconciled with the congregation until 1566 due to what he saw as the hypocrisy of the Emden church; see ibid., pp. 52 and 58 (20 June and 25 July 1558).

[40] Minutes of the meetings between 16 August and 2 November are missing (with the exceptions of 13 September and 4 October) because the transcriber of the consistory minutes, Gerd thom Camp, was out of town.

[41] KRP, p. 11.

[42] Ibid., p. 12.

the members of the household of the faith'. To this end, three names
were suggested for election: Siabbe Focken, who was already an elder,
Sipko Mennens and Hermen Sporenmaker. The consistory also issued
instructions that each officer should consider the nominations and when
an election should be held. They also gave the following rules governing
the new diaconate: 'Moreover, he that serves one office, shall not serve
the other. Also, if they are able, the three deacons should come here
every Monday [to the weekly consistory meetings].'[43] It seems very clear
from these initial deliberations on the nature of the new diaconate that
the consistory hoped that the functions of these new deacons would be
separate from those of the elders, but that, unlike the deacons of the
haussitzenden poor, the new deacons would become a part of the
consistory along with the pastors and the elders.

The issue of a deacon election arose at each of the next two consistory
meetings before a full-scale discussion of possible nominations to the
diaconate occurred on 13 December. The minutes of the 29 November
consistory meeting included, among several matters that still needed to
be considered at future meetings, the note to remember to take care 'to
elect the deacons'.[44] On 3 December, the matter arose again, and the
consistory decided that 'now on a future Monday [the issue] should be
handled: which men should be elected as elders and deacons for the
congregation's poor'. Each member of the consistory was to bring in
names for nomination, and on 13 December the consistory held its
deliberations on nominations to the eldership and diaconate.[45] The
consistory nominated seven men to be elders and then three to be
'deacons for the poor of the congregation'. The three deacon nominees
included the previously mentioned (on 22 November) Sipko Mennens
and Siabbe Focken as well as Evert Kuper. Evert had been nominated
on the elder list, but was also nominated to be a *Becken* deacon 'in case
he does not want to be an elder'.

What transpired with respect to the diaconate over the next three
months illustrates the difficulty of implementing ideal goals. The
consistory obviously wanted to separate the duties of the new deacons
from the responsibilities of the elders.[46] Yet by March 1558, the
consistory had at least temporarily given up its attempt to form a new
diaconate, and the duties of these proposed deacons had fallen to the

---

[43] Ibid., pp. 12f.

[44] Ibid., p. 13.

[45] The congregation was also to be exhorted in the coming communion service to pray
to the Lord about the election of the elders; ibid., p. 15.

[46] See also Jan Weerda, 'Der Emder Kirchenrat und seine Gemeinde' (Habilitationsschrift,
Münster, 1948), II, 123, for his partial misreading of the connection between the offices of
elder and deacon in Emden, see Fehler, 'Social Welfare', p. 217f.

pastors and the elders. What happened to the nominations of the three men to the diaconate of the poor of the 'household of faith' sheds light on the evolution of the new diaconate and on the conflicting conceptions of parish poor relief which existed within Emden's church.

The election of Siabbe Focken as a deacon of the *Becken* was never realised. The consistory had put forward his name from the first deliberations on the diaconate on 22 November, although he was currently an elder. They made it clear, however, immediately after proposing his name, that 'those who serve one office, shall not serve the other'. He would thus need to give up the office of elder if he became one of the new deacons. Siabbe died some time between his official nomination on 13 December and the presentation of new elders to the congregation on 13 March. Unfortunately, Siabbe does not appear in the consistory minutes between his nomination and the 13 March reference to his death.[47] His nomination to the diaconate was never again discussed in the records so it is unclear whether his death precluded his selection as deacon or if other reasons prevented his switch from elder to deacon before he died.

In the week following the nomination to both elder and deacon ('if he does not want to be an elder') of Evert Kuper, both a pastor (Hermannus Brass) and an elder (Henderick Wilting) talked to Evert about the nomination as elder. 'Evert would not like to accept it', was the report of the pastor, but the elder requested that Evert at least come to the next consistory meeting.[48] On 27 December, despite Evert's protestations that he was not qualified or properly prepared to be an elder, the consistory finally persuaded him to devote his gifts to God and the congregation and to accept an eldership. 'Although with difficulty, after that he accepted the office and offered [Pastor] Hermannus his hand.'[49] Therefore, Evert was the second of the three official nominees to the new diaconate not to become a deacon.

Consequently, Sipko Mennens found himself the only remaining official nominee for the position of deacon of the *Becken*. After most of the

---

[47] The new elders were presented to the congregation during communion on 13 March, and the minutes supply the text of the presentation address. The address stated that the election of new elders was necessitated by the departure of several of the older elders, including Siabbe Focken, who had died; KRP, p. 39f.

[48] The visiting elder 'spoke so much with [Evert], that he could not say anything against' the request (21 December 1557); ibid., p. 17.

[49] One of Evert's reasons related to his occupation as carpenter, 'that he must now build and thus cannot devote himself as much as the office truly requires'. However, the consistory responded that 'carpentry is not unchristian for an elder' and that it would offer him opportunities 'to better the people' with whom he comes into contact; ibid., p. 20f.

elder nominees had accepted their positions in the 27 December meeting, the consistory introduced Sipko, 'that the brothers desire him to [be] deacon for the members of Christ and the members of the household of faith, and that he would come constantly to the assembly'.[50] Sipko said that he 'gives himself willingly over to the service of the poor', and he shook pastor Hermannus's hand in acceptance of the position. It was furthermore agreed that each member of the consistory should bring to the next meeting appropriate names of those who would 'be helpers with Sipko in the office of the diaconate'.[51]

The consistory was thus able to fill at least one of the three proposed positions as deacon of the *Becken*. By the end of 1557, the consistory had succeeded in forming the diaconate which would administer the alms collected in the *Becken* during the communion services. The first such service with the special collection for the poor of the 'household of faith' probably occurred in mid-November, and now the actual election of a deacon happened just in time for the next communion service, which would be held in early January.[52] For some reason, however, the consistory was slow in finding 'helpers' to work with Sipko. The issue of the remaining diaconal positions did not come up in the minutes of the next several consistory meetings. Finally, on 24 January, Sipko vented his frustration to the consistory, complaining 'that one should of course make a completion of the diaconate: [decide] how one should entrust it with the burden of the poor of the congregation'.[53]

Although the consistory had not yet chosen deacons for the poor of the *Becken*, the records show that the church had separated moneys for the poor 'members of the household of faith' from the resources administered by the deacons of the *haussitzenden* poor. At the same time that Sipko had complained that the positions of the diaconate had not yet been filled, the consistory bookkeeper recorded that two unidentified 'brothers' of the congregation had been to the house of a man named Jurgen and reported to the consistory that 'someone should come to [his] aid' in order that Jurgen 'might progress from poverty with [his] children'.[54] The consistory, however, saw the matter differently and decided that Jurgen had no right to the alms of the members of the household of the faith because 'he is not a member of the household

---

[50] The remaining new elders accepted on 1 January and 24 February; ibid., pp. 22, 30f.

[51] Ibid., p. 21.

[52] Ibid.

[53] Ibid., p. 27.

[54] Ibid., p. 28. The two men were not identified by name or church office. Jurgen was also not identified, except to note that he lived in the Faldern suburbs.

and also not godly'. Exclusion from these alms, though, did not mean that he should not be helped. The consistory's decision ended with the argument: 'Nevertheless, as much as one can really undertake it, they should help him, since he suffers affliction.' Because this decision prevented the new diaconate from helping Jurgen, the matter fell to the jurisdiction of the deacons of the *haussitzenden* poor.

While the special funds from the *Becken* remained strictly earmarked for the 'household of faith', the consistory was not able to maintain the earlier proposed separation of the elders and the deacons in poor relief matters since the consistory had not filled all the new deacon positions for the *Becken* poor. For instance, on 26 January, Sipko and the new elder Evert Kuper were assigned to provide for the sister-in-law of the pastor Gellius Faber in her need.[55] A month later, Evert was once again given poor relief responsibilities: to help find a shopkeeper with whom to apprentice the son of a man who could not afford to pay for the entire apprenticeship himself.[56] This mingling of duties probably resulted from the consistory's failure fully to staff the new diaconal offices.

During their 28 February 1558 meeting, the consistory finally decided how to structure the new organisation for the 'poor of the congregation'. Yet, contrary to all earlier attempts to separate the duties of elders and deacons, at this point the functions of relief of the poor of the congregation were officially assigned to both pastors and elders – not to new deacons. Emden's three preachers, Gellius Faber, Hermannus Brass and Arnoldus Veltman, were to see that the poor did not have any need:

> and Sipko shall assist Gellius in [these duties]; Hermannus shall have Evert Kuper to help [him], and when Evert can not watch over [then] Frans Smit will look after his task for him. Harmen van Loppersum or, when he can not take care of it, Hinderick in den Gulden Voet shall assist Arnoldo in his *Kluft* [neighbourhood].[57]

Of the five 'helpers' for the pastors in the care of the poor of the congregation, four were current or newly elected elders.[58] Only Sipko had been chosen as a deacon. In the meantime, though, even his election seems to have been reconsidered, for Sipko Mennens was included among the newly elected *elders* presented to the congregation on 13 March![59] The consistory, it seems, had given up on the plan to create a

---

[55] KRP, p. 29.

[56] Ibid., p. 33 (28 February 1558).

[57] Ibid., p. 34.

[58] Harmen thom Camp van Loppersum and Hinderick Wilting in den Gulden Voet were already elders. Evert Kuper, who had already been given some poor relief-like duties, and Frans Smit became elders in late December.

[59] KRP, p. 39.

diaconate to administer the new source of funds for this special category of the poor and instead had delegated the responsibilities to the elders.

The 28 February consistory entry elaborated further on the reasons for the change in the poor relief apparatus to care for the 'household of faith': 'This arrangement is therefore made, so that no disturbance occurs amongst the other deacons, who do not like to see that one should have special deacons to the poor of the congregation.'[60] The deacons of the *haussitzenden* poor did not want to see the creation of a separate diaconate to care for a group of the poor under their supervision, 'even though', as the consistory complained, the poor of the congregation 'are not adequately provided for by [the *haussitzenden* deacons] and cannot be'.[61] Because of deficiency in care for the poor of the household of faith, however, the consistory felt it necessary to create some special provision for these more 'deserving' poor, including, of course, a separate source of alms as well. Although no records of previous discussions with or about the *haussitzenden* deacons were written in the consistory minutes between the end of December and the end of February, we can assume that it was this concern which had caused the delays (and the complaint of Sipko) in the naming of new deacons.

Despite their decision not to sanction a new diaconate to administer the funds for the *Becken* poor, the church council was compelled to set up guidelines for the use of the alms which were collected in the communion *Becken*. One such guideline was established on 28 February 1558, when the pastor Hermannus posed a hypothetical question to the consistory.[62] He presented the situation involving a woman who was a member of the congregation, but whose husband was not. The man, moreover, 'could or would not provide for the house'. Should one 'feed the whole house as a member of the congregation or not; or how should one handle' the situation? All members of the consistory felt that the woman with her children should not be allowed to suffer. Regarding her husband, the concern seemed to be especially with his attitude: so long as the husband could not provide for his family but no doubt *would* if he were able, one may give him the alms 'along with the message'. The consistory was apparently willing to mingle their alms with a non-member of the congregation under these specific conditions,

---

[60] Ibid., pp. 34f.

[61] Ibid., p. 35. As discussed in the following section, the 'deacons of the foreign poor' were officially formed in December 1557–January 1558, during the same time therefore as attempts were being made to form the 'deacons of the *Becken*'.

[62] KRP, p. 34.

arguably with the intention of encouraging the husband to join his wife in the congregation of those who partook in communion. The consistory went on to make it clear, however, that the alms should not be given to someone who can work but will not. The supervisors 'and the wife also' were to try to prevent idle behaviour as much as possible. 'If he does not work, [he] shall not eat.'[63]

Although the initial attempts to create a separate diaconate foundered on the misgivings of the deacons of the *haussitzenden* poor, the Emden church nevertheless succeeded in establishing a separate fund for the poor of the 'household of faith' by the end of 1557 and early 1558. Godliness, a good work ethic, and being a member of the communion-congregation were all prerequisites for accessibility to these funds, although the consistory (as evidenced in the previous example) was willing to distribute the *Becken* alms under certain circumstances as an act of evangelism. By 1565, however, a separate diaconate of the *Becken* had been formed, and poor relief duties had been removed from the elders.[64] Unfortunately, no surviving sources exist which allow for a more precise dating of this diaconate's official establishment. An interesting, but ambiguous, consistory entry from 1560 made reference to the selection of Johan van Knypens as a new elder. He accepted the offer, and 'the consistory has promised Johan that one should relieve him of the distribution to the poor'. Without corroborating evidence this statement is open to two possible interpretations. The first – that Johan was a deacon and would be relieved of that office's duties when he became an elder – is unlikely since such action was apparently common practice and would hardly seem to merit special attention in the consistory minutes. The second, therefore, seems more likely, namely, that the poor relief for the 'household of faith' was still the responsibility of the elders at this time and that the consistory had granted Johan a special exemption.[65]

Approximately twenty years after the initial attempts to establish a two-fold diaconate, one for the 'common, wild poor' and one for the poor members of the communion-congregation, the experiment was brought to an end, and the diaconate of the *Becken* was merged back into the *haussitzenden* diaconate.[66] In a 1578 mandate issued to

---

[63] Here was a restatement of the biblical principle (2 Thessalonians 3:10) alluded to in the first entry of the consistory records (16 July 1557, KRP, p. 1): 'men voer de van der gemene nicht holden sal, de nicht arbeyden wyllen'.

[64] The consistory decided that 'six new deacons' should be chosen to take care of the poor members of the congregation. Whether or not the word 'new' refers to a pre-existing diaconate is not clear; KRP, p. 208 (8 June 1565). Schilling's transcription of this entry reads '5 nye diaconen', but the original minutes read '6'.

[65] (26 August 1560) KRP, p. 118.

[66] See Chapter 5 for a discussion of these developments.

supplement the Emden poor relief ordinance of 1576, the merger was announced along with reasons for the termination of the *Becken* deacons.[67] Here the records identify one of the motivations guiding the diaconate's formation: 'one had previously instituted the *Becken* so that the poor members of the congregation of Christ may be prevented from begging according to the command of God's word and the nature of love'.[68] Thus the goal of the establishment of a special *Becken* diaconate was to eliminate the need for begging among the most pious poor of the congregation (those admitted to partake in communion), and to eliminate criticism from outside the church that the church did not take care of its own members. Clearly this diaconate, confined to the congregation, demonstrates the desire among church leaders to reinforce discipline by social provision. That the elders performed the poor relief duties until the diaconate was formed further confirms that purpose. Of course, the Dutch refugees not only brought with them the emphasis on discipline and the 'household of faith'; the arrival of so many new refugees contributed to the economic problems and no doubt created tensions with the local inhabitants. As in Geneva, where the French refugees founded the deacons of the Bourse française (French fund) by 1550 to reinforce discipline and relieve tensions with the local inhabitants, Emden's Dutch refugees founded a diaconate of the *fremdlingen* (foreign) poor.[69]

In 1560, Jan Utenhove from Ghent, an elder in the Dutch church in London during the reign of Edward VI, recounted the turbulent winter journey of the London Dutch refugees, after the accession to the throne of Queen Mary.[70] Beginning in September 1553 when they were forced out of England, this group of 179 travelled from London through

---

[67] 10 February 1578, ArchGK no. 3001, pp. 23–7.

[68] Ibid. (Reason no. 2). On this point, the claim of Marion Weber, 'Emden – Kirche und Gesellschaft in einer Stadt der Frühneuzeit', part I, *EJb*, 68 (1988), p. 92, note 90, that the *Becken* poor formed a special group of 'pious beggars' in the medieval tradition of a connection between 'religiosity and poverty', is incorrect. This statement in the ordinance is very clear in pointing out that the motivation behind setting up the *Becken* – even if unsuccessful – was to *eliminate*, not facilitate, begging among the more pious poor. Compare Carter Lindberg, '"There Should Be No Beggars Among Christians": Karlstadt, Luther, and the Origins of Protestant Poor Relief', *Church History*, 46 (1977), pp. 313–34; also Ole Peter Grell, 'The Protestant imperative of Christian care and neighbourly love', in *Health Care and Poor Relief in Protestant Europe 1500–1700*, eds O. P. Grell and A. Cunningham (London, 1997), pp. 47–9.

[69] See, for instance, Jeannine Olson, *Calvin and Social Welfare. Deacons and the Bourse française* (London, 1989).

[70] Jan Utenhove, *Simplex et fidelis narratio de instituta ac demum dissipata Belgarum, aliquorumque peregrinorum in Anglia ecclesia* (Basel, 1560), in *Bibliotheca Reformatoria Neerlandica* (hereafter cited as *BRN*), eds S. Cramer and F. Pijper, IX, 29–186.

Norway, Denmark and north-east Germany, were driven out of at least six refuge sites, and finally arrived in Emden in the spring of 1554.[71]

> After our difficult wanderings the Lord God ... gave us places with the illustrious dowager, the countess of East Frisia; both the ministers and citizens of Emden lavished on us every courtesy of humane hospitality. And thus, for the sake of his fatherly goodness, God is accustomed to give peace to the church after fierce and stormy trials.[72]

So began Emden's role as a refuge centre for those Dutch Protestants fleeing religious persecution, and later revolt, in the Netherlands.

The importance of adequate poor relief for the exile community was apparent from the start. The Countess Anna, Utenhove's 'illustrious dowager', required as a condition of her admission grant to the refugees, among whom were included 'many poor and common handworkers', an assurance that the local poor would not be overburdened by the maintenance of 'these newly arriving foreign poor'.[73] Given the well-developed organisational structure of the London church in Lasco's Church Ordinance, with its characteristically Reformed arrangement of preachers, elders and deacons, and the fact that four of the London deacons accompanied the refugees to Emden, these refugees no doubt maintained the administrative functioning of the London church, and under the administration of Johannes a Lasco were able to keep a relatively close watch on the economic needs of the community.[74]

The arrival of Lasco with much of his community in the spring of 1554 was merely the beginning of the influx of refugees into Emden. With England now closed to Dutch refugees, Protestant exiles from the Netherlands chose Emden as their primary destination. With assurances that the refugee community would take care of its own poor, the countess encouraged this practice of settlement, gaining in the process many wealthy Dutch merchants. This policy had prompt economic

---

[71] This journey is also described by Mülder, *Die Diakonie der Fremdlingen-Armen 1558–1858*, (Emden, 1858), esp. pp. 1–5, and Frederick Norwood, 'The London Dutch Refugees in Search of a Home, 1553–1554', *American Historical Review*, 58 (1952–53), pp. 64–72.

[72] *BRN*, IX, 148. Translation in Pettegree, *Emden*, p. 26.

[73] J. J. van Toorenenbergen in his edition *Stukken betreffende de Diaconie der Vreemdelingen te Emden 1560–1576* [actually 1569–75], (Utrecht, 1876), p. 2; compare STAA Rep. 241, Msc. A190, pp. 581–3.

[74] Jan van de Ryvere, Jacob Michielson, Willem de Visscher, and Paulus van Winghen; Pettegree, *Emden*, p. 37, note 40. Van de Ryvere and Michielson became *fremdlingen* deacons at least by the first records of the diaconate in 1558, van Wingen in 1565; de Visscher served as an elder in the Emden church, but we have no record of any service as a *fremdlingen* deacon.

benefits for Emden: its trade increased and its tax rolls blossomed. Concerned by this new competition, the Amsterdam city council commissioned two travellers to report on activities in Emden in 1555. Among the many details in their long account, they reported that the Faldern suburbs to the east of town, 'in which mostly the foreign nations live, which have recently come here', were now being developed with the construction of some 200 houses and newly laid-out streets. They also recounted to the Amsterdam city council that the houses now cost 'half again as much as they had cost five or six years ago' and further related specific examples of houses which were recently purchased for almost 300 per cent of their price only two and three years before.[75]

The difficulties brought about by such a large influx of refugees, combined with the immediate effects of housing shortages and high prices, must have strained the informal organisation of poor relief within the refugee community. The organisation was finally formalised in late 1557 or early 1558 with the naming of eight relief administrators who had the official title 'deacons of the poor foreigners in Emden' (*Diaconen der aermen fremdelyngen binnen Embden*) to stand in contrast to the deacons of the local poor (*haussitzenden*).[76]

The Dutch refugees in Emden did not establish a separate church. Due to similarities between the language spoken in Emden and that of the neighbouring Netherlands, the refugees did not have the linguistic problems which occurred in the other German cities of exile, such as Wesel or Frankfurt. The refugees who came to Emden joined the pre-existing local church structure and placed themselves under the authority of the Emden consistory, which actually came to represent the opinions of the Dutch exiles as increasing numbers of refugees served as elders.[77] This integration stands in contrast to the French Walloon and English

---

[75] Their letter to the Amsterdam city council was published in *Niederländische Akten und Urkunden zur Geschichte der Hanse und zur deutschen Seegeschichte*, ed. Rudolf Häpke, vol. I (Munich, 1913), pp. 576–8.

[76] The traditional foundation date given for the *fremdlingen* diaconate is 1558. Indeed, the diaconate celebrated its 300th anniversary in 1858 and its 400th in 1958; see Mülder, *Diakonie der Fremdlingen*. On the evidence that the diaconate was active before 1558, see Fehler, 'Social Welfare', pp. 282, 285–6.

[77] The effect of the Dutch refugees on the Emden church leadership can be seen especially through their roles as elders in the consistory. In September 1564 the consistory resolved that of the two elders responsible for the present examinations before communion, one should be a citizen and one a '*fremdeling*'; KRP, p. 187. Another example of parity within the consistory is detected in November 1571 in the decision to elect six new elders, three from 'all the fremdelingen' and three from the 'old citizens'; ibid., p. 426. Schilling argues that this decision was based less on a desire to guarantee the Dutch representation as to protect a declining local influence in the consistory; ibid., I, p. xxi.

exiles in Emden who, for reasons of language, needed to and were allowed to create their own churches. The only separate institution created by the Dutch refugees was the 'diaconate of the foreign poor', which was to be funded and administered by the Dutch refugee community.

Before the formalisation of the institution around 1558, we have virtually no records. The financial principle from the beginning of their Emden exile was that the wealthier Dutch refugees were to care for their poorer companions in Emden, and Countess Anna apparently allowed occasional collections to be made from among the citizens of Emden on behalf of the refugees.[78] No other organisational details from the years before the formalisation can be distinguished. The four deacons who came with the original London refugees certainly would have played a role in continuing to support the community and probably served in positions of leadership. In fact, two of them, Jan van de Ryvere and Jacob Michelsen, became deacons of the *fremdlingen* poor by 1558.[79] Records indicate that Lasco himself appointed deacons to work with the Dutch refugee community in Emden, as with Lauwrens de Vos, who had served as a deacon with Lasco 'from the beginning' (that is, 1554). Another of the initial eight 'founding' deacons from 1558, Bartolomeus Huysman, had accompanied Lasco from London in 1553. Huysman had helped procure money for the refugees during their voyage, and he was still working in July 1557 to procure supplies and clothing for the Dutch exiles.[80]

The first surviving account book of the Dutch exiles dates from December 1557.[81] The early pages of the book do not demonstrate a great concern on the part of the bookkeeper for organised recordkeeping. In the period from 1558 into 1564, the accounting reveals no systematic approach. Records of donations to the deacons from 1559 are, for instance, listed on the same page with expenditures from 1563, and there is little concern with itemisation of accounts, especially of

---

[78] Toorenenbergen, *Diaconie der Vreemdelingen*, p. 3; Mülder, *Diakonie der Fremdlingen*, p. 6.

[79] Michielson joined the refugees first when they were in Helsingor in Denmark, and at a time of great poverty he brought with him a large sum of money from England and Belgium for the poor; Utenhove, *Simplex et fidelis narratio*, in *BRN*, IX, 88.

[80] Ibid., p. 77. On 16 July 1557, the consistory accepted Bartolomeus's request for a special collection in the church for clothing for the refugees on a certain Sunday; KRP, p. 2.

[81] The earliest surviving account book of the 'fremdelingen' deacons from December 1557 to 1568 has been badly damaged and burned (hereafter cited as *Fremdlingen I*); many corners and portions of the brittle pages have been lost. Although it is still the property of the deacons of the *fremdlingen* poor in Emden, the book and the microfilm are currently being housed in ArchGK.

expenditures. Very few records indicate exactly who was getting the money, and it difficult to reconstruct the diaconate's standard revenues and expenses.[82] Although the account book has been badly damaged, it is possible to reconstruct in a surprising amount of detail the record of the diaconate's early years. This results, in part, from the deacons' lack of organisation in their bookkeeping. That is, since the accounts of the first several years are scattered throughout the first half of the book, when a page is missing or damaged, one can still often find corroborating evidence for that period on another page of the book. It is actually harder (in some cases impossible) to reconstruct the accounts from the years 1564–68 because they were kept in such an organised manner that, when pages were destroyed, there is no corroborating information anywhere else. The book does contain evidence, though, that it was not the first account book kept by the *fremdlingen* deacons. In the records of the deacons' 1558 expenditures and income, there is a reference to the accounts from the earlier years in another *bouck*.[83] In fact, late in 1557 the *fremdlingen* diaconate was deep in debt. The deacons had needed to use their own personal funds to support the poor as their expenditures rose above their income from donations. The debt owed to five of the deacons alone had risen to over 227 gulden.[84] Facing such a financial crisis, the diaconate was apparently able to obtain permission to make a special 'voluntary assessment' (*goetwillinghe schattinghe*) of the brothers in exile in December 1557. The term *Schattinghe* implies that this collection was a tax based on the property or assessed value of the refugees, but the word *goetwillinghe* means that it was voluntary. Thus the exact nature of this collection remains murky. It appears from descriptions of the collection that the wealthier refugees were expected to donate an amount of money in proportion to their assets (which their exile in Emden had enabled them to keep), but what if they refused? There is no indication that any of 'the brothers' did not participate in the 'voluntary assessment'.

---

[82] Mülder, *Diakonie der Fremdlingen*, p. 7, complained in 1858 of the lack of organisation and the faint ink of the account book when he jumped to the year 1567 and said, 'It is impossible to reconstruct anything more precise from the still available papers.' Indeed, the numbers that he cites are not accurate; see Fehler, 'Social Welfare', pp. 285, 524.

[83] *Fremdlingen I*, fol. 9v refers to the pre-1558 debt of the diaconate as had been recorded in the deacon Jacob Michielson's *bouck*. Other references imply that Jacob Michielson had served as bookkeeper for the diaconate at least until the beginning of 1558; for instance, on 4 January 1558 (fol. 2), the deacon Jasper Celosse reimbursed the deacons for their debts 'which Jacop Michels[on] has substantiated to him from his accounts'.

[84] Compare the first 20 pages of *Fremdlingen I*; the list provided on fol. 9v includes an incorrect amount for Laurens de Vos (compare fol. 3).

In any case, this 'voluntary assessment' collection yielded over 254 gulden, and when it was combined with a special gift of 24 gulden from the French Walloon congregation in December 1557, the deacons were able to pay off their debts and make a fresh start on the new year of expenditures.[85] The existence of such a large debt indicates that the deacons had been busy for at least several months providing relief to the poor of the refugee community.[86] The crisis of 1557 must have forced the refugee community's overseers to overextend themselves and give out more aid to the poor than they had collected. The crisis played an important role in the reorganisation of the Gasthaus and in the foundations of both the Grain Reserve and the *Becken* diaconate which were also formed at this time.[87] Perhaps the financial crisis faced by the leaders of the refugee community led to the formalisation of the Dutch poor relief activities into an official diaconate. Seen in this light, the 'voluntary assessment' of December 1557 might indeed mark the foundation of a formal diaconate, as the refugee community established a formal organisation to deal with such financial problems.

Any crisis faced by the community in 1557 did not, however, seem to burden the deacons in subsequent years. In general, for the next several years, the amounts collected each month in the alms-box were enough to support the expenses of the diaconate when occasionally supplemented by small gifts or bequests. The *fremdlingen* deacons were able to avoid great budget deficits without holding another large-scale 'voluntary assessment' at least until the beginning of the Dutch Revolt in the late 1560s.[88] In fact, the influx of refugees from the Dutch Revolt in 1567 during a period of plague in the city forced the *fremdlingen* deacons to make two 'voluntary assessments' that year.[89]

By reconstructing the accounts of the deacons, we can see that typically eight deacons were active. On a monthly basis the deacons rotated the responsibilities of collecting donations from the alms-box and distributing aid to the poor.[90] The deacon in charge maintained the 'regular'

---

[85] Ibid., fols 1v and 10.

[86] The amount which was reimbursed to the five deacons (227 gulden 9 schap 10 witten) in January 1558 was equal to almost half of the *fremdlingen* diaconate's expenditures for 1558 (497 gulden 2 schap 19 witten); for a breakdown of their income and expenditures (1558–66), see Fehler, 'Social Welfare', pp. 524–32.

[87] See pp. 122ff. above and pp. 148ff. below.

[88] For a financial analysis of their 'voluntary assessments', see Fehler, 'Social Welfare', p. 362.

[89] Mülder, *Diakonie der Fremdlingen*, p. 7. Corroborating evidence for the two 1567 *Schattinghe* is absent due to missing pages from the account book *Fremdlingen I*.

[90] Each of the eight deacons took his turn as 'presiding deacon' for a month, although they followed no strict pattern in making the monthly assignments. In the years 1562 and 1563 only seven deacons took part in the monthly service rotations.

relief roll, or list, of those frequently receiving relief from the refugee community. From all appearances, aid was given to these 'regular' poor in the form of a monthly stipend.[91] The deacon in charge was also responsible for handling requests for extraordinary relief, though decisions on extraordinary requests could also be made by an assembly of the deacons.[92] In most of the early years of the diaconate, the 'regular' or 'ordinary' relief rolls made up about 75–80 per cent of their expenditures. Thus it appears that the *fremdlingen* deacons were able to concentrate their efforts predominantly on a relatively stable group of poor refugees who made up their 'regular' relief rolls. A number of refugees, mostly widows, received long-term, regular relief consistently through much of the period from 1558 to 1575.

The manner by which deacons were chosen remains unclear for the first decade of the *fremdlingen* diaconate's existence. At the beginning, Johannes a Lasco appointed some helpers, such as Lauwrens de Vos, to handle the charitable activities of the refugees.[93] The first recorded election of new *fremdlingen* deacons took place about 21 December 1564 when three new deacons were chosen and asked to report before the consistory.[94] On two separate, earlier occasions new *fremdlingen* deacons began appearing in the account books shortly after an equal number of deacons disappeared from the records, suggesting elections for replacement deacons. In both of these instances (1558–59, two deacons; 1560–61, three deacons), the temporal proximity of two or three new deacons' appearances in the account book leads to the inference that the groups of deacons were selected together, rather than being merely individual appointments to the diaconate.

Yet what was the nature of the selection process in these early instances? It is unclear whether the new deacons were chosen by the diaconate themselves, by the consistory, or a combination of both bodies. Perhaps the refugee congregation had already been electing their new deacons even before the first identified election in 1564. In any case, these events seem to have arisen out of the urgency of the situation, with a shortage of deacons. No policy had yet been instituted to

---

[91] This method becomes clear in the 'regular' roll of 1560 where the monthly stipends are listed individually under each recipient's name; *Fremdlingen I*, fols 18v–44v. Supplements to the monthly stipends were generally listed separately: see, for example, Willem de Vos, whose roll shows for January 1561 his monthly stipend of 1.5 gulden followed by an extraordinary supplement of 1.25 schap for rye; fol. 24v.

[92] References in the second, more organised account book (*Fremdlingen II*; 1569–75) indicate that decisions were frequently made by 'the brothers' and not just by the deacon in charge.

[93] KRP, p. 202.

[94] Ibid., pp. 190, 192.

schedule regular elections or establish the length of a term in office. For example, Jasper Celosse served for at least eight years, Lauwrens de Vos for 12 years, and Jacop Payen for 13 years.

By the mid-1560s, however, the selection process had evolved from appointment by the pastor to election by the refugee community. This change is illustrated by the dispute involving Lauwrens de Vos toward the end of his service in 1565. Within a few months of the December 1564 *fremdlingen* deacon election, the deacons appeared before the consistory with a question about the status of Lauwrens's appointment. He had been appointed by Lasco 'from the beginning' of the refugee community in Emden, but his appointment had been 'without the consent of the pastors or of the congregation'. Some deacons felt that this made his position tenuous and that 'his appointment should be viewed [as] weaker' than that of those who had been elected by the congregation.[95] Obviously, at least by 1565, many had come to feel that the *fremdlingen* diaconate should be an elective church office, representing the consent of the refugee congregation. This idea would be refined even further after the tremendous influx of refugees in 1567 as the principle was voiced that the refugees representing each 'nation', or province, in the Netherlands (rather than the refugee community as a whole) should elect their own deacons.[96]

Despite the foreign deacons' apparent success in taking care of their own community, the town experienced a significant increase in refugees and transients as Emden's reputation as a refuge centre spread. Of course, the Gasthaus was the local relief institution entrusted particularly with provision for the transient poor. By the mid-1550s, St Gertrude's Gasthaus had consolidated its large complex of buildings and houses on the north side of the town's marketplace. Throughout the 1530s and 1540s, this area of town (formerly called the 'new town ... outside the northern gates') became fully inhabited. Around mid-century, when the phrase 'the new town' appeared in the sources, it now denoted the area of Middle Faldern, where the Franciscan monastery was located. The massive social and economic surges of the 1550s, which greatly affected social welfare institutions of the diaconates, did not leave the Gasthaus unaffected either.

The newly arrived, large numbers of poor in Emden overburdened the organisation of the Gasthaus greatly. Thus, by 1555, even the local institutions had problems providing adequate space to care for the increased numbers of poor. At the end of April 1555, the countess sent

---

[95] (2 April 1565) ibid., pp. 201f; the issue was first drawn to the consistory's attention on 19 March 1565.

[96] See discussion of *fremdlingen* deacons in Chapter 5.

her secretary and adviser, Wilhelm Gnapheus, to meet the friars in the Franciscan monastery in an attempt to buy a portion of their convent to use for the poor of the town. The number of resident friars had been declining since the Reformation, and they apparently had unused space available in their monastery.

Gnapheus reported to Anna that his conversations with the guardian of the monastery had not gone well.[97] After discussing the countess's desire 'to purchase from them a certain place on behalf of the poor', the guardian told Gnapheus, after consultation with 'his co-brothers', that without the approval of his supervisor in the order, he could not do anything.[98] His supervisor would arrive to visit the Faldern monastery in a few days, and he would put the proposition to the supervisor at that time.[99]

An additional conversation with one of the other friars made Gnapheus a little doubtful of the friars' straightforwardness in negotiating. This friar confided to Gnapheus that he felt it would be unfortunate to sell a portion of their monastery. If the friars should concede too much to the countess, 'perhaps [she] would want to take the entire cloister'.[100] Gnapheus's confidence that the friars would genuinely consider the countess's request was further shaken when he visited the monastery the following week to carry out the order of the countess's chancellor, Friedrich ter Westen, to view the original foundation document of the cloister and make a copy of it to bring back to the court.[101] The Franciscan guardian told Gnapheus that he could not answer the request: 'all the letters are not here at hand'. He would, with all possible diligence, attempt to get the letter. None the less, he gave Gnapheus his own account of 'how the foundation of the cloister had been' and described which letters were at hand.[102]

The guardian of the monastery once again provided assurances that he stood ready to negotiate when he had the consent of his supervisor. The supervisor was to visit Groningen within a few days, but now 'believed that he would have difficulties in coming to East Frisia'. Gnapheus now advised the countess to write the supervisor a short letter requesting that he 'immediately come over here' to resolve the issue.[103]

---

[97] A copy of his letter from 30 April 1555 can be found in the STAA, Rep. 135 (files of the Konsistorium Aurich), no. 12, pp. 1–2.

[98] Ibid., p. 1.

[99] Ibid., pp. 1–1v.

[100] Ibid., p. 1v.

[101] Gnapheus's second report back to Anna on 6 May 1555 is in ibid., pp. 5–6.

[102] Ibid., p. 5.

[103] Ibid., pp. 5–5v.

Whereas Gnapheus continued to carry out his orders from the countess, he did not fail to inform Anna of his interpretation of her legal
position. If the friars were not willing to negotiate, he felt that the
countess could still act justly. In his first report, Gnapheus advised that
the countess had enough authority simply to take the portion of the
monastery in question in the presence of a notary and witnesses for the
purpose of poor administration and offer the friars an appropriate
compensation.[104] The pressure of the enormous emergency and the
manifold poor who were entering the town justified such a seizure. It
need not be a total seizure, either. Gnapheus argued further that the
countess should allow a wall to be constructed which would separate
the convent from the section which she would take.[105] Under this plan
the friars would be allowed to remain in a portion of the monastery.

One friar's admitted fears that they might concede too much to the
countess and lose the whole cloister were not without foundation.
During Lasco's tenure as superintendent of the East Frisian churches
in the mid-1540s, he had wanted to expel the Franciscans. Lasco was
sorely disappointed with the level of church discipline in the city when
he arrived. In addition to the foothold that the Anabaptists had in
Emden, Lasco was concerned that too many citizens and 'most of the
city council' were still entangled in 'the old superstitions'.[106] He placed
much of the blame for this on the 'wicked practices of the friars in the
Franciscan cloister' and wanted to put an end to their influence in the
town. That the friars were still officially tolerated in the city, even
after the Reformation, infuriated Lasco. Although he could apparently
not get the countess's approval for their expulsion, Lasco did get
permission to order the friars to stop their public activities in the
town. These activities included baptising children, visiting the sick
and writing testaments.[107] The friars protested against Lasco's order
on the following grounds: they first made reference to the new Speyer
decrees for the Holy Roman Empire; further, they argued that their
rules allowed them to administer sacraments and make testaments
when given permission by a pastor of the church. Here, they harked
back to the memory of Dr Poppo Manninga, who had been Provost
and an adviser during the reign of Count Enno, to whom they had

---

[104] Ibid., pp. 1v–2.

[105] Ibid., p. 2.

[106] Ubbo Emmius, *Rerum Frisicarum Historia* (Leiden, 1616) LIX, 916–7; this passage
was cited in and translated by Joachim Christian Ihering, *Ausführliche Kirchen-Historie
von Ostfriesland* (*c.* 1710), vol. 2, p. 220v (Ihering's manuscript is in STAA, Rep. 135,
no. 147); here see pp. 219v–21.

[107] Emmius LIX, 917; Ihering, II, 221v–5.

sworn an oath. He had permitted these activities, and since his death they were not aware of any pastor in the town who had the authority to judge the matter. And certainly not Lasco, who 'is a foreign, unknown person, about whom no one knows where he is from; he also wears a beard, with which [he] can in no way be recognised as a rightful pastor'.

The Augsburg Interim and the subsequent departure of Lasco reinforced the tolerated position of the Franciscans in Emden. Now, in the mid-1550s, the friars recognised a growing opposition to their presence in the town. With the arrival of countless Dutch Protestant refugees, the religious tenor of the city was finally swinging in the direction which Lasco had desired. The changing social situation necessitated additional facilities to care for the poor, and the Franciscan monastery was sitting partially empty due to the ever-dwindling number of friars. The friars were now as fearful as ever of being expelled from the city. It is no wonder that they attempted to stall the countess's request for part of their cloister.

By 1556, the friars had lost their fight. Countess Anna composed an 'open letter' explaining why she was taking over the monastery.[108] Despite her decision against the friars, she felt it necessary to give 'testimony to the truth' and emphasise that the friars had lived completely according to their Rule and were not driven out for any misbehaviour. Rather, Anna seized the cloister 'to the advancement of the glory of God and according to the opportunity of the common use and emergency needs of this city' and asked that the friars 'depart from here with honour and good will'.[109] The countess did not cite religious or confessional grounds. The primary publicised reason for the appropriation of the Franciscan convent was the town's dramatic social evolution, tremendous population explosion and shortage of adequate housing – because 'our town Emden daily multiplies and takes in to itself, both rich and poor out of other and foreign lands'.[110] The properties of the Franciscan monastery were now to be used as a new parish church and cemetery, and also as a school, hospital and orphanage. Thus the friars, 'who are not more than six or seven' in number, were not to remain there any longer.

Evidently, the number of friars had continued to shrink in the decades immediately after the Reformation. Although their presence was tolerated in Emden, they apparently took few, or perhaps were prohibited from taking any, new novices. As the last five friars prepared to leave

---

[108] STAA, Rep. 135, no. 12, pp. 3–4.
[109] Ibid., pp. 3–3v.
[110] Ibid., p. 3.

the monastery in 1557, they complained of old age and poverty.[111] This substantiated Anna's argument that a handful of elderly men were no longer able to take care of the monastic properties. 'Indeed,' Anna wrote in her letter, 'the structure of the [monastery's] church and of the other buildings cannot be preserved for long without the help of the community at the present opportunity.'[112]

In the open letter of 1556, the countess claimed to have offered the friars residence in another East Frisian monastery, but they refused.[113] None the less, should the withdrawing friars desire support from the countess in the future, she and her children as territorial rulers would be willing to provide it.[114] The friars wanted to stay in the Faldern monastery, and they attempted to remain for a while. By the summer of 1557, however, the situation had worsened so much because of refugees and inflation that the administrators of the poor needed the whole monastery. In August 1557, the five friars wrote to Anna and acknowledged that they would be leaving the monastery. The friars could no longer share their ever-shrinking residence with the poor: 'We poor brothers have still supported ourselves here to this time, and now from this point on because of the multitude of poor – through which our garden and other nourishments and quarters have been reduced – we can no longer include ourselves here because otherwise the poverty will become too great.' They wrote that their convent had in practice already been converted to a Gasthaus 'through the manifold emergency and the multiplication of the people and poverty of the city ... (and we hope that it did not occur out of our fault or crime, but is rather out of emergency as stated), but now there was simply not enough room for them to live in their greatly reduced quarters.[115]

The friars now took Countess Anna up on her earlier offer of support. They asked her for 300 gulden to settle their debts and help them get settled as they travelled from Emden, 'in our old age and poverty, as we are naked and bare in all defence'. Since they were going to join 'other convents', the friars requested that they be allowed to take 'our books which would surely be of use to no one'. Although they recognised that they were going to have to leave their cloister, they closed their letter by stating that 'we do not believe that you [Countess Anna] know everything that has happened to us'.

---

[111] The five remaining friars signed a letter to Countess Anna on 26 August 1557; StaE, I. Reg., no. 423; the text of the letter is reprinted in Fehler, 'Social Welfare', p. 518.

[112] STAA, Rep. 135, no. 12, p. 3.

[113] Ibid.

[114] Ibid., p. 3v.

[115] StaE, I. Reg., no. 423, fol. 2.

In response to the friars' request, Countess Anna sent a letter in October 1557 to the Burgermeisters and city council of Emden.[116] The letter orders the city administration to get busy refurbishing the monastery as a Gasthaus. Negotiations between the countess and the friars had already taken place several times prior to this letter. Now that the friars had signalled their willingness to leave, Anna ordered the council to procure the necessary money to meet the friars' request so that 'we are completely relieved with the [matter of the] aforesaid friars, and the poor [can] make use of the place in their necessity'. Furthermore, the council should speak with the administrators of the Gasthaus to discuss how this conversion could best be achieved 'with the smallest damage' financially and 'how the arrangements [may] finally be handled to the utility and profit of the poor and to the common best of our city Emden'.

Many, including the German 'Regulierungs-Kommission' of 1872, view this letter as a 'deed of gift' from the countess to the city, that Anna gave the property (and hence control of the Gasthaus) solely to the city.[117] But viewed in the context of the deliberations taking place at the time, such an opinion fails to pass muster. Countess Anna clearly did not give the Gasthaus to the city; indeed, the city councillors at the time were fully under her authority. Rather, the countess's letter ordered the city council to begin deliberations on the specific elements of the conversion from monastery to Gasthaus. She had negotiated with the friars to obtain use of the monastery; now the city government should consult with the Gasthaus administrators who knew the precise needs of the poor. Moreover, the monastery had already been used in part as a Gasthaus for the previous year or two. The departure of the friars would now leave the entire properties free for the use of the poor. The countess's letter of 1556 had already indicated that the structures of the monastery were badly in need of repair, and now that the Gasthaus administrators would have complete control of the properties, they needed to consider the best way to go about the renovation.

Now began the slow conversion of the monastery into a Gasthaus. Unfortunately, we cannot be sure when the friars finally left. Although the aforesaid correspondence of 1557 implies that the friars were on the verge of leaving, the final settlement of their departure was only finished early in 1561. In January of that year the countess sent her adviser Tido von In- und Knyphusen and the Emden Burgermeister Herman

---

[116] The letter can be found in StaE, I. Reg., no. 423, fols 1–1v; the text is printed in Fehler, 'Social Welfare', p. 519.

[117] For example, see Pastor J. Conrad, 'Gedenkschrift zur Gasthaus- und Gasthauskirchefrage' [Emden, 1919], p. 5; his manuscript is in ArchGK no. 120.

Lent to inventory the items in the Franciscan monastery.[118] Their commission sent back word that they had come to an agreement with the
friars and the administrators of the Gasthaus. The friars would be
allowed to take the 'songbooks in the choir and their own books and
clothing which they had brought in with them'. The friars would leave
behind for the poor in the '*Gasthaus* and orphan-houses' all the household furniture and utensils and church ornamentation. It thus appears
that at least some of the few remaining friars were allowed to live in
their monastery until the end of 1560 or early 1561.

Nevertheless, the administrators of the Gasthaus had clearly begun
converting the old Gasthaus on the marketplace (where St Gertrude's
had moved in 1505) even as the negotiations were going on with the
friars. As early as December 1556, the Gasthaus administrators had
sold part of the old Gasthaus's properties to an Emden citizen.[119] Thomas Kremer purchased the house just to the north of the 'old Gasthaus'
at the far eastern end of the Gasthaus. The position of this house behind
one of the taller buildings in the city, namely the chapel of the Gasthaus
(see Map 2.3), meant that certain building restrictions had to be placed
on the neighbour who lived to the north, Lubbert Grone, in order to
protect Kremer's 'right to light in the north from Luberth Gronen's back
wall and from the wall in the west, which must always remain
unconstructed'.[120] The fact that the Gasthaus administrators could regulate the construction enterprises of their neighbour Lubbert Grone
suggests a wide regulatory role over the adjacent properties.[121] Perhaps
the selling-off of the buildings of the old Gasthaus complex had begun
even earlier.

In December 1557, there are records of three additional sales by the
Gasthaus administrators of properties within their marketplace complex.[122] By 1559, there is evidence that portions of the actual Gasthaus

---

[118] Their report of 4 February 1561 is printed in Enno Rudolph Brenneysen's *Ost-
Friesische Historie und Landes-Verfassung*, vol. I, lib. V, no. 50, pp. 238–9. The countess
made her request on 25 January. The bailiff of Emden, Johann Braemsche, declined her
request to participate.

[119] EKP, 5/342 (19 December 1556).

[120] Ibid., 10/846–7. These building restrictions were included in the final contract
from the administrators of the Gasthaus, when Kremer's heirs completed the financing of
this expensive house in 1568.

[121] The contract from 13 July 1505, which established the Gertrude Gasthaus's move
from the old location by the church on the waterfront to the marketplace, stipulated
Lubbert Grone's house as the northern boundary of St Gertrude's Gasthaus's properties;
ArchGK no. 81 (see also EKP 1/3v).

[122] EKP 7/15, 7/21 (12 and 23 December 1557); one of these sold again in 1562, EKP
9/387.

were being sold off.[123] In fact, the contract reveals that the buyer of this house, Herman van Asschendorp, who would later be a Gasthaus administrator, had already been living in the house for a while. Between 1555 and 1557, the administrators of the Gasthaus poor were scrambling for space to house their clients. By 1559, they must have been able to take over enough of the old monastery that portions of the old Gasthaus building were dispensable.

In 1561, the way was clear to begin the building of the new Gasthaus. The friars were now gone, the furnishings of the monastery inventoried, and the new construction could take place. In the only example found of this type of fund-raising in sixteenth-century Emden, the administrators and the city council launched a lottery to finance the conversion of the old monastic properties into a Gasthaus for the poor. Some external repairs to the building had already been performed. On 11 January 1561, the city accounts record that the city had paid more than 50 daler for the repair of the spire of the 'new Gasthaus'. The city had advanced the money with the consent of the countess after the administrators of the poor had complained about their lack of funds and because the 'tower is a community decoration'.[124]

On 14 April 1562, the city account books announced a lottery 'on behalf of the Gasthaus and the improvement of its structure'. Once again, as with most of the actions concerning the Gasthaus conversion, the lottery was established with the 'consent of our Grace the countess'. Initially, the lottery failed to raise enough money so 'that the poor could remain without injury in all respects'. Therefore, Emden's Burgermeisters and city council, 'in consideration of this opportunity for the poor and the necessity of the construction on the Gasthaus', decided to increase their contribution to the lottery by 500 gulden.[125] They boosted their donation on the condition that they, too, now be eligible for the prizes. The lottery drawing was evidently held in October 1562. On 30 October, we find record of a small payment of 12 schap for the construction of the little stand in front of the city hall where the lottery results would be announced.[126] Unfortunately, we have no records which show how much money was raised by the lottery for the administration of the Gasthaus. The city did,

---

[123] Ibid. 8/508–9 (12 December); this house was next to the portion of the old Gasthaus which served as the 'sick house'; compare ibid. 8/433–5 (12 July 1559).

[124] StaE, AK 2/10, p. 240.

[125] The city had previously spent 39 gulden helping to get the lottery established and publicised; ibid., p. 295.

[126] Ibid., p. 336.

however, get back 175 gulden of its investment by winning the first, third, and fourth prizes in the lottery.[127]

The Gasthaus continued to receive the revenues from its old endowments even as it relocated into the Franciscan monastery, but the yearly interest from these funds could not sustain this massive project. As soon as portions of the renovations were completed, the Gasthaus supervisors could sell off additional sections of the 'old Gasthaus' on the marketplace.[128] Meanwhile, some of the poor continued to live in the unsold areas of the 'old Gasthaus'.[129] The transfer of facilities from the old to the new Gasthaus occurred gradually as the renovations of the monastic properties progressed. The gradual pace of the transfer had a financial reason as well. By moving out of portions of the old Gasthaus as soon as possible, the supervisors freed up those portions for sale and could infuse their project with additional shots of capital.

Despite these property sales, the supervisors of the Gasthaus remained dependent upon the goodwill of the citizenry to finance the project. Additional information regarding the construction of the new Gasthaus in the old Franciscan monastery is not available in any of the account books. There exists, however, an anonymous poem from the end of the sixteenth century which supplements our knowledge of the construction of the new Gasthaus.[130] The writer composed the poem as 'A remembrance of the cloisters in Friesland' to ensure that 'child and child's child' know the history of the monasteries in East Frisia, which 'their forefathers gave to the glory of God'.[131] The first third of the poem simply mentions the names of all the monasteries which were dissolved by the count and is critical of his seizure of the properties. The poem then pronounces that 'Only from the monastic properties in Emden and in Norden/was a just use made./In Norden, one has

---

[127] Each of the prizes was a gold-plated chalice: first prize was worth 100 gulden, third prize 50 gulden, and fourth prize 25 gulden; ibid., 2/11, p. 55v.

[128] See, for example, EKP 9/109 (14 May 1561) and 9/128 (16 June 1561) for sales of the old Gasthaus properties.

[129] Ibid. 9/387, 14 October 1562, a financing contact for an apartment, which had been part of the old Gasthaus on the marketplace, stated that 'Gasthaus poor' were still living in the adjacent buildings.

[130] The poem 'Memorialis Designation der Praelaturen, Clostern, Conventi und andern Kerckleven in Ostfrießlandt', can be found in STAA, Rep. 135, no. 12, pp. 44–5. The poem was printed as an appendix by Hemmo Suur, *Geschichte der ehemaligen Klöster in der Provinz Ostfriesland* (Emden, 1838), pp. 182f. Based on internal evidence from the poem itself (lines 59 and 75), I would date the poem between 1571 and 1590.

[131] Ibid., lines 1–6, 'Eyn denckzedell der Kloster in Vreßlandt/Wil ick ut orsacke onß scryven tor Handt/Weiln alst lopt under und over, up und neder,/Sol sunst Kindt, und Kindes Kindt, niet weten, weder,/Wat, wovöle der Kloster, und war sie gebleven,/Die ehre vorvadern, tot ehren Gades gegeven.'

established a school/in Emden [they] founded a poor Gasthaus'.[132] The
remainder of the poem describes the role of Emden's citizens in building
the Gasthaus and the attempts later in the century to recover the monastic properties and church goods from the ruling house to put them to
the 'common use'.[133]

According to this poem, the Emden citizens bore the brunt of the
costs for the renovations, to make 'a Gasthaus from the collapsed
cloister'.

> The one gave money, the other the stones, the third the caulking;
> The nobleman Tydo van Kniphausen gave the wooden beams.
> They brought [goods] into reserve and yearly pension,
> Solely to the service of the poor for God's reward
> With great costs and difficulties to the citizenry.[134]

The city council had needed to increase its contribution to the lottery
because the lottery had not raised enough funds for the renovations.
Once the construction got under way, many local residents apparently
donated building supplies, and the countess's adviser Tydo made a large
individual donation. His earlier inventories of the properties of the monastery reveal a high level of interest in this project. Emden's citizenry also
showed its commitment by bringing in supplies to build up the Gasthaus's
reserves as well as making new endowments toward its further operation.
The use of this poem as evidence can certainly be problematic. Yet it
corroborates our picture of the Gasthaus supervisors scrambling to finance this huge project: they had to sell off many of the older properties
and even resort to a lottery to get the necessary funds. In the view of this
poem's writer, the residents of Emden came together 'with great costs and
difficulties ... solely to the service of the poor', showing a strong communal commitment and a sense of obligation to the poor.

The period of renovation lasted until 1563 or 1564. By 1563, the
construction in the Franciscan church was completed and Sunday

---

[132] Ibid., lines 37–40: 'Allein die Klöster gebawe to Embden und to Norden,/dar is ein
rechter gebruck utt worden./To Norden hefft men ein schole gericht,/Tho Embden ein
armen gasthauß gestifft'.

[133] Ibid., lines 84–9: 'Man shol der armen shatte so nit vorternn mit pracht,/Und tot
seinem [the count's] eignen nutte alle Clöstere und Kerckguttere to sick rieten/Alß ein
roff met Perden, Hunden, und Jegers vernieten/die doch nit gestifft seindt von den
Graven,/dan sein der gemeynen und armen underthanen gaven,/die sie ock pillix wederumb
thom gemeinen nutz t'gnieten.'

[134] Ibid., lines 47–53: 'Dieselb die burgere dan tletzten kofften darauß/Und mackten
also vant verfallen Closter ein Gasthauß./Der eine gaff gelt, d'andern den Stein, der dritte
die Calcken,/Der Edel Tydo van Kniphausen gaff die balcken/Bröchtens also in vorrat
und Jarlicher pension,/Allein tom dienst der armen umb Gottes lohn,/Met groten unkosten
und burgerlichen beshwerden.'

worship services were being held in the new 'Gasthaus church', and on 12 July the consistory decided to hold its gatherings there.[135] On 24 April of the next year, the consistory decided that the most affluent citizens of the town should be asked to come to the 'Gasthaus chamber' later that week to collect alms for the poor.[136] The full-scale operation of the new Gasthaus is further implied by the sales in 1565 and 1566 of most of the remaining portions of the old Gasthaus.[137] In February 1566, the Gasthaus supervisors even sold part of the building which had been the 'sick-house' of the old Gasthaus.[138] Thus, by this time the new Gasthaus must have been fully operational in all its functions for caring for the poor, even for the sick who would be isolated from the rest.

From this period, the Gasthaus began establishing contracts specifying their maintenance of mentally ill people who could no longer be cared for by their relatives.[139] The first such contract was made on 25 March 1561, as the renovations were getting under way. The brothers Peter and Johan Stapelmoer tho Aurich initiated a contract with the Gasthaus to care for their mentally ill brother, Hinrich. Hinrich Stapelmoer had an 'extraordinary sickness, given from God', and his brothers did not have the means to care for him. The Gasthaus agreed to care for Hinrich for the rest of his life. In return, it would be given all Hinrich's goods and inheritance. In this case, the Gasthaus recognised the costs incurred by the family in their support and allowed Peter and Johan to keep 100 gulden from Hinrich's goods to compensate them for the care they had provided for their brother.[140] After the conversion of the large monastic properties into a new Gasthaus complex, the Gasthaus apparently now had new facilities in which to look after those who needed special care which could not be provided by their families. Of course, if those for whom the Gasthaus provided were not poor, then they (or their families) were expected to finance their care by giving their goods to the Gasthaus administrators.

As we have seen, the turmoil and increased poverty stimulated by the 'difficult, expensive time' (*dusse svare duire tyt*) in the years 1556 and 1557 corresponded to some wide-scale innovations in Emden's major poor relief institutions: the creation of the *Becken* diaconate (to reinforce discipline with social provision and to ensure the care of the most

---

[135] KRP, p. 164 (12 July 1563).

[136] Ibid., p. 183 (24 April 1564). Meiners, *Oostvrieschlandts Kerkelyke Geschiedenis*, I, 394, provides a slight misreading of KRP.

[137] EKP, 10/244, 342, 347 (23 June 1565, 18 and 19 February 1566).

[138] Ibid., 10/347 (19 February 1566).

[139] For an additional discussion of the Gasthaus's care for the mentally ill, see Chapter 5.

[140] EKP 9/65.

pious poor since the poor funds could not reach all the poor), the formalisation of the *fremdlingen* diaconate (to relieve the tension caused by the arrival of so many new refugees), and the relocation of the Gasthaus into the large Franciscan monastery. Yet the earliest of the 1557 poor relief innovations had occurred in February when a group of Emden citizens created a civic Grain Reserve (*Kornvorrat*) 'to the welfare of the poor of this city'. Indeed, the formation of the citizen's Grain Reserve has been cited by Schilling as one of the earliest indications of the 'rise of corporate institutions and communal mentality' in mid-century Emden when 'urban development had reached a stage when a burgher movement in favour of corporate institutions of government and of civic participation became almost inevitable'.[141]

No original sources from the sixteenth century survive for the Grain Reserve. Only two published copies of documents exist. First, a nineteenth-century history of Emden contains a copy of the institution's 1566 foundation statutes.[142] Although it was initially formed in 1557, the Grain Reserve received official ratification of its governing statutes on 10 January 1566. The only other surviving source is a copy of the accounting of the first collection which formed the Grain Reserve in 1557 and which lists each donor alongside the amount of his or her gift. The list was published as a note to an eighteenth-century edition of Eggerik Beninga's sixteenth-century chronicle of East Frisian history.[143]

As winter had exacerbated the already sky-rocketing grain prices, a large number of 'good-hearted citizens' gathered together on 5 February 1557 in the Gasthaus church to consider a plan to make grain affordable for the middle and lower classes in the city.[144] The meeting,

---

[141] Schilling, *Civic Calvinism*, p. 27. In the original German version of this article ('Reformation und Bürgerfreiheit. Emdens Weg zur calvinistischen Stadtrepublik', pp. 147f), Schilling made this statement – which was not included in the revised translation – about the Grain Reserve: 'Unabhängig von und zeitlich vor der Einrichtung der reformierten Diakonie war also in Emden eine bürgerliche Institution.' (Independent from and temporally before the establishment of the Reformed diaconate, it was an institution of the citizenry in Emden.) While it is true that the Grain Reserve preceded the *Becken* diaconate, the Reformed *haussitzenden* diaconate was certainly already established.

[142] Helias Loesing, *Geschichte der Stadt Emden bis zum Vertrage von Delfsyhl 1595* (Emden, 1843; reprinted Leer, 1974), pp. 123–6. These statutes are reprinted in Fehler, 'Social Welfare', pp. 520–22.

[143] Eggerik Beninga, *Chronyk van Oostfrieslant*, ed. Eilhardus Follardus Harkenroht (Emden, 1723), pp. 861–5.

[144] (Preface), Loesing, *Stadt Emden*, p. 123. This would be the new Gasthaus church, formerly the Franciscan monastery (rather than the old Gertrude's Gasthaus on the 'neuen Markt' which was the only Gasthaus until at least late 1557). Harkenroht (ed.), Beninga's *Chronyk*, p. 862, states explicitly that this was the 'Broer Kerke' of the

'in consideration of the great distress of the common folk', took place 'not without the consent and knowledge' of the Countess Anna and the city council. Although the extent of the authorities' influence is not exactly clear, this phrase suggests a largely passive role of the authorities in organising the gathering.

In earlier times of emergency, the poor had been taken advantage of or received 'shoddy rye' for their money.[145] Since this also 'unfortunately occurred at the present' moment of distress, those at the special gathering decided to create 'a reserve of rye' so that in the future the poor 'might have refuge and consolation ... at a tolerable price'. To this 'Christian and praiseworthy' end, the gathering chose six 'eminent and pious citizens' to make a circuit through the city and collect from everyone a generous donation toward the establishment of a Grain Reserve.[146] Only one of these, Johan Kuell, had direct connections with the church leadership as churchwarden, but his selection here was probably due more to the financial competence demanded by his job than to any connections with the church.[147] Another, Johan van Amsterdam Jr, would soon be elected to the city council, and later as Burgermeister. The third identifiable man from this group was the rich merchant Johan Boeltzen, who was an alleged disciple of David Joris.[148]

Significantly, the first donor to the Grain Reserve was Countess Anna herself. She gave a Last of rye, worth between 120 and 135 gulden in 1557.[149] In all, 282 donors contributed about 935 gulden to the formation of a civic Grain Reserve; the average contribution was approximately

---

Franciscan monastery. Only after the relocation of the Gasthaus to the Franciscan monastery (between late 1557 and 1561) was the former Franciscan complex referred to as the Gasthaus and the Gasthaus church. But this ambiguity is caused by the fact that the foundation statutes of the Grain Reserve were not drawn up until 1566. Although the meeting place would not have been called the Gasthaus church at the time of the meeting, by the time of the foundation statutes, the Gasthaus had been relocated there. Indeed, when discussing the storage of the grain, the statutes refer to 'des olden Gasthuses Kerchchen bohne' (Article 5).

[145] The typical sequence of events in cases of crop failures and grain shortages is outlined in Robert Jütte, *Poverty and Deviance in Early Modern Europe* (Cambridge, 1994), pp. 31–2; on nutrition during grain crises, see pp. 72–3.

[146] The six elected to perform the city-wide collection were Johan Boeltzen, Johan Gerdes, Johan Kuell, Johan van Amsterdam der junge, Antonius Prickher (Tonjes Prikker?) and Gerdt Mestekmaker.

[147] This is the opinion of Weber, 'Kirche und Gesellschaft', I, 99.

[148] On Boeltzen, see H. Reimers, 'Eine Landesbeschreibung von Ostfriesland aus der Zeit um 1600', *EJb*, 17 (1910), pp. 317, 322ff. Each of the 6 men themselves donated at least six gulden in the collection; Tonjes Prikker contributed the largest individual (excepting Countess Anna) amount (18 gulden) in the entire collection; only the Smiths' Guild gave more (30 gulden); Harkenroht (ed.), Beninga's *Chronyk*, p. 862.

[149] Loesing, *Stadt Emden*, p. 126.

3.3 gulden.[150] Almost all of the donors made their contribution in money, though some donations were in kind: grain or valuables such as jewellery.[151] Over half of the donations were less than one gulden and almost 85 per cent donated less than 5 gulden, while less than 4 per cent of the donors contributed sums greater than 10 gulden.[152] While these figures do not provide solid evidence regarding the wealth of the initial founders, they do suggest a broad level of support that went beyond the wealthiest of Emden's citizens.

The purpose of the Grain Reserve was, of course, to facilitate the purchase of large amounts of grain more inexpensively than any individual could buy. We can estimate that with the 935 gulden in donations, the Grain Reserve began operation with between seven and ten Lasten of rye.[153] The Reserve did not distribute grain without cost to those in the middle and lower classes. Instead, it served as a buffer against massive increases in the price of grain during times of shortage. In the one instance for which we have a record, the Grain Reserve provided grain at about half the regular price: in 1565, during the next major economic and social crisis in Emden (caused in part by the beginning of the Dutch Revolt), the Grain Reserve was able to sell units of rye for 12 schap when 'the common price' was 22 schap.[154]

The Grain Reserve functioned without formal regulations until the mid-1560s. Finally, in response to growing concerns in 1565, those involved with the temporary Grain Reserve found it necessary that 'a good ordinance be conceived and instituted' to regulate the use of the Reserve's money. Minimum quantities of fluid assets were established to ensure that the Grain Reserve would not be taken off guard in a sudden shortage. A fixed set of statutes also provided for regular elections and rotation of those in the administration of the Grain Reserve. Thus they set about creating formal statutes to be officially ratified by Emden's city council and Burgermeisters on 10 January 1566.

---

[150] Weber's general breakdown of all donations (*EJb*, 69, p. 61) is accurate, but her analysis of the donations to the *Kornvorrat* by elders and deacons (p. 62) was not complete because it was based on incomplete lists of deacons.

[151] Countess Anna gave a *Last* of rye; Harkenroht (ed.), Beninga's *Chronyk*, p. 862; Andres Grote gave a *Tun* of rye (p. 864); the Emden elder Gert van Camp donated a silver goblet in addition to his 2.1 gulden in cash (p. 864); Gepke Amelling gave two *Tunnen* rye (p. 864).

[152] Fehler, 'Social Welfare', p. 315.

[153] This is based on the cost of a *Last* of rye in 1557, estimated at between 120 and 135 gulden. Probably by purchasing several *Lasten* (or wagonloads) at once the Reserve was able to get a better price.

[154] KRP, p. 221 (26 November 1565).

While the Reserve had an administrative board which oversaw its collection of donations, grain purchases and sales of grain, the duties did not extend to regular care and inspection of the poor. Because so few records survive describing the activities of the Grain Reserve and because it did not provide regular maintenance of the poor, the Grain Reserve has typically been de-emphasised in descriptions of Emden's social welfare institutions. Nevertheless, its importance in providing a safety net for Emden's residents with little means in times of grain shortage can be illustrated by a comparison of the size of the Grain Reserve's initial foundation with the expenditures of Emden's church deacons. The Grain Reserve was able to procure 935 gulden in donations from Emden's citizenry in early 1557; a number of deacons contributed as well. Putting that amount in perspective, the total income of the *fremdlingen* deacons in 1558 (the first year for which we have complete totals) was less than 430 gulden.[155] Even more surprisingly, the recorded revenues of the *haussitzenden* deacons in the early 1560s were generally between 340 and 400 gulden.[156] Thus the assistance provided by the *Kornvorrat* made up a significant portion of Emden's total social welfare programme.

When making their initial round of collections through the city, the six administrators 'orderly noted every name and donation which was given' in a book which they kept for some time with the Reserve's account book. The purpose of the list of 'founders', according to the later statutes, was

> so in future times, not only that the charity of each of the good-hearted citizens be praised, instead that it may be seen and emulated by their successors, what a civic charitable assistance [institution] to the use and best of the poor fellow citizens of the city – God Almighty be thanked – was once procured by the common citizenry.

Pride in civic participation was clearly evident in the foundation of the Grain Reserve.

References to the immoral business practices of some grain merchants demonstrate the potential usefulness of the Grain Reserve. In 1563 the consistory accused a number of merchants of selling tainted grain (and

---

[155] This total does not include the revenues from December 1557 in which the first major *Schattinghe* collection was held (to pay off a previous deficit). Yet, even when one includes the totals from December 1557 with the 1558 revenues (they are all added together in the account book), the total for the 13 months was only 725 gulden; Fehler, 'Social Welfare', p. 524.

[156] These totals come from the sums of the weekly collections in the church, the rent incomes, and the collections from the alms-boxes placed around the town; they do not include revenues from the capital investments of the *haussitzenden* deacons; Fehler, Social Welfare, p. 317, note 184, and pp. 554–61.

mixing it with good grain) and of seeking undue profit during a time of scarcity.[157] The church leaders felt the need to intervene (the merchants were ordered to provide restitution and an additional penalty to the poor) in order to maintain social order. The concern with social order was widespread, and the visceral fear among the well-off of food riots among the lower orders was common during times of grain short-ages.[158] Such fears perhaps explain the fascinating popularity of this form of provision among the well-off in Emden, who provided the Grain Reserve (at least at its foundation) with greater resources than the other relief institutions in town received annually. Although crea-tions of grain reserves occasionally occurred in other towns, these were almost always radical, short-term reactions to severe crises financed by municipal funds or by pre-existing institutions (such as hospitals); when the crisis was over, the reserves (or the city funds to subsidise grain prices) would cease their separate existence.[159] Yet in Emden the Grain Reserve was a popular, private institution which became a permanent feature of Emden's system of provision and a source of civic pride.

The latter years of the 1550s witnessed the rapid reorganisation of poor relief in Emden. The pace of changes brought about by the arrival of the foreign refugees and the economic crises of 1557–58 reached a fever pitch: no more gradual evolution as in previous decades. The religious changes in the Emden church affected the shape of many of these changes. The 'administrators of the *haussitzenden* poor', probably the sole institutional innovation in matters of charity resulting from the 1529 Church Ordinance, as a body continued its activities and saw its structure modified to fit into the Reformed church office of 'deacon'. Moreover, growing interest in church discipline in the Emden commu-nity inspired the creation of a specialised diaconate to care solely for the members of the 'household of faith'. Even the Dutch refugees created their own diaconate to provide for members of their community; the Dutch belonged to the Emden parish church and played an active role in the consistory as elders, but their separate *fremdlingen* deacons worked

---

[157] EKP, p. 160–61 (29 March).

[158] On food riots, see Jütte, *Poverty and Deviance*, p. 188; on the possible correlation between theft and poverty/hunger (especially in contemporaries' perceptions), see ibid., pp. 151–2 and Kathryn Norberg, *Rich and Poor in Grenoble 1600–1814* (Berkeley, 1985), pp. 237, 258.

[159] In late eighteenth-century Grenoble, the city government experimented with public subsidies to provide a multi-tiered price structure for grain provision only after all other expedients had been exhausted; Norberg, *Rich and Poor*, p. 282.

to ensure that the local relief institutions were not overburdened by the refugees.[160]

The dramatic social, economic and religious upheaval of the mid-century also affected the non-church relief institutions. The independent Gotteskammern and St Clement's Shippers' Brotherhood continued their activities into the mid-century, but their work was soon outstripped by the new and revitalised institutions of the 1550s. St Gertrude's Gasthaus took advantage of the expulsion of the Franciscan friars to centralise its holdings in a much larger complex (the name 'St Gertrude's' gradually disappeared from the sources by mid-century). As it had done half a century earlier, the Gasthaus moved again to the suburbs of the growing town, it required tremendous expansion to keep up with the influx of massive numbers into the town. Finally, the economic crisis of 1557 reveals a growing civic consciousness in Emden as the leading citizens formed the Grain Reserve. Indeed, what was in many towns a radical, temporary response to grain shortages became a permanent fixture of the Emden social welfare landscape.

---

[160] This function was also successfully performed by Geneva's Bourse française; Olson, *Social Welfare*, p. 183.

CHAPTER FIVE

The Administration of Poor Relief in the Second Half of the Sixteenth Century

> During that time the numbers of poor increased dramatically, strain-
> ing, and sometimes breaking, the systems of relief that governments
> and churches had established and challenging the principles by
> which people had chosen which poor to aid.
> 'Social Welfare', *The Oxford Encyclopedia of the Reformation*[1]

All across Europe, in both Protestant and Catholic lands, new modes of poor relief were severely tested in the second half of the sixteenth century. As the previous chapter demonstrated, Emden's settled world of poor relief that had gradually evolved by the early sixteenth century was suddenly thrown into confusion by the severe social and economic turbulence of the late 1550s. Emden's city and church fathers reshaped many of their traditional institutions (consolidating the Clementiner Shippers, renovating the Gasthaus) and even created several new institutions (the Grain Reserve, the *fremdlingen* and *Becken* diaconates) to deal with the crisis. But could these new efforts work in a town such as Emden with so little experience of coping with many of these problems?

The effectiveness of the reorganisations of the 1550s is demonstrated by the survival of most of the institutions through the sixteenth century and even well into the modern period. Yet the 1550s were just the beginning of the refugee arrivals. The crisis caused by continued immigrant influx triggered further institutional developments as Emden's city fathers and leading residents developed practical responses to meet the continuing practical problems. The city's poor relief authorities exhibited remarkable insights as they adjusted their activities to accommodate continued difficult issues and particular cases, yet institutional continuity after the dramatic shake-up of the 1550s proves that the new creations were flexible enough to respond effectively without additional major institutional changes. An analysis of the administration of these new social welfare institutions will reveal the impressive effort of provision in the light of difficult circumstances.

---

[1] Lee Palmer Wandel, 'Social Welfare', *Oxford Encyclopedia of the Reformation* (Oxford, 1995), p. 82.

The administration of social welfare in Emden in the second half of the century was divided into both indoor and outdoor relief. Indoor relief was provided primarily by administrators of the Gasthaus. Although housing was sometimes provided by another institution such as a Gotteskammer, the relief recipient of such housing was also generally served with outdoor relief from the deacons or the Shippers' Brotherhood. The primary administrators of outdoor relief in Emden were the groups of deacons. Taken as a whole, the jurisdiction of the deacons covered virtually the entire town, with the exception of the minority confessional groups. Each diaconate maintained a separate organisational structure which provided contrasting methods of distributing aid to the poor. The types of outdoor relief were diverse and based on the needs of individuals. This investigation into the institutional organisation of the deacons will be followed by a brief examination of the types of aid they offered.

The oldest of the diaconates, the 'deacons of the *haussitzenden* poor', maintained a two-tier hierarchy in their administration of poor relief. The earliest evidence of this organisational structure survives in a list of deacons from the late 1560s.[2] From the list we discover that the town was divided into three geographic districts (*Klufts*) for the distribution of relief to the poor by the deacons (see Map 5.1). The partitions paralleled the historical development of Emden, with one sector encompassing the oldest settlement area ('*de kluft by denn boom*'), a second area to the north around the marketplace in what *had* been called the 'new town' at the turn of the century (*de kluft up die nie marckt*), and finally the newly assimilated village of Middle Faldern to the west, representing the town's expansion and now referred to as the 'new town' (*de kluft up de nie stadth*). The division of the town into three *Klufts* probably facilitated the supervision of each by one of Emden's three pastors. The pastors were from time to time explicitly connected with the *haussitzenden* deacons, as in 1563 when the consistory decided that each deacon should take a pastor along with him in his *Kluft* and 'comfort, teach, exhort, and punish the poor as the occasion arises'.[3]

Eight deacons were assigned to each of the three *Klufts*. At the end of the list, an additional four deacons were then distinguished as those 'who go around in the church' to collect alms. There existed, then, a division of duties within the diaconate of the *haussitzenden* poor. Four deacons handled the financial administration of the diaconate while 24 deacons were responsible for the actual distribution of funds and materials to the poor. The reorganisation of Emden's *Klufts* in February

---

[2] ArchGK no. 1117, p. 1.
[3] KRP, p. 167 (26 July 1563). Emden's first 'fourth minister' was called in 1569.

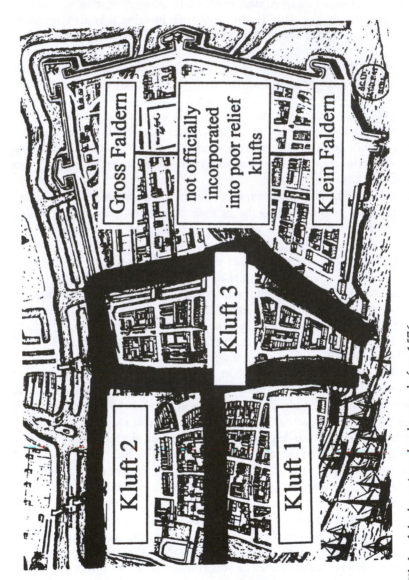

Map 5.1 *Klufts* of the *haussitzenden* deacons before 1576

1576 included the naming of these diaconal positions as 'head-deacons' and 'under-deacons' respectively.[4] These names 'head' and 'under' indicate a hierarchy within the diaconate, perhaps with the more experienced deacons chosen as supervisors and administrators.

The diaconal duties were divided between the two positions within the hierarchy, although there was some overlap of responsibilities. In general, the head-deacons handled the collection of funds and the recordkeeping in account books. The head-deacons were also sometimes referred to as 'supervisors' (*Vorsteher*) of the *haussitzenden* poor, and it was they who represented the entire diaconate in loan contracts, negotiations and disputes.[5] The characterisation given to these deacons in the list of names – 'those who go around in the church' – further describes their duties, for they collected the alms which were given weekly in the church after the sermon.[6] The head-deacons recorded the additional revenues from gifts and testaments and then disbursed the funds as necessary to under-deacons for distribution and on occasion to the poor who came directly to them for consideration of extraordinary cases. They also transacted the business of the diaconate: buying supplies, such as cloth, food and peat, which were to be distributed to the poor.

The *haussitzenden* deacons also maintained a number of collection boxes throughout the town in which people could make donations to the poor. At one point, in the mid-1560s, at least seven collection pouches were hung in various houses (probably inns or hostels) across Emden.[7] We are not sure how frequently the head-deacons actually made rounds in the city. It seems most probable that the money collected in these pouches would have been regularly gathered by the 'under-deacons' during their work in the *Klufts* (neighbourhoods). Yet these alms-boxes in the inns were probably locked in order to provide some protection for the donations, so perhaps one of the 'head-deacons' with the keys made occasional trips to empty them. Of course, just

---

[4] 'Hoefft-diaconen' and 'onder-diaconen' are the most common terms. The phrase 'over- und underdiakenen' (over- and under-deacons) appears once; KRP, pp. 596f.

[5] E.g. EKP 8/129, 8/849, 9/25, 9/108, 10/22, 12/2, 13/22, 15/158v; ArchGK no. 1117, p. 2.

[6] ArchGK no. 1117, pp. 2–34, contains a list of the amount of each weekly collection between 11 April 1561 and 24 October 1567; the list is printed in Timothy Fehler, 'The Evolution of Social Welfare in Early Modern Emden', (Ph.D. thesis, University of Wisconsin-Madison, 1995), pp. 554–61.

[7] No other lists of this sort exist. Two locations on the list were definitely taverns, both on Faldernstrasse: 'The Boat' and 'The Emperor'. The others were all identified as individuals' houses, but unless the houses were frequently visited by others, it would seem unprofitable to hang an alms-pouch there. ArchGK no. 1117, p. 179.

because an alms-box was locked does not mean that its contents were secure. On 29 October 1581, the deacons' accountkeeper recorded that 'a dishonest hand' broke into the general alms-chest of the *haussitzenden* deacons 'by night, with great violence' and stole over 232 gulden. The thief also took 'some non-converted foreign money' so the deacons told the city council and the entire citizenry to be on the lookout for the foreign coins. Fortunately for the *haussitzenden* poor, the deacons were able to operate with a surplus throughout most of the last quarter of the sixteenth century, so the loss probably had no direct effect on their aid (indeed, the diaconate ended 1581 with a 399-gulden surplus despite this loss).[8]

The under-deacons had the most direct contact with the poor. They visited the poor in their *Klufts* (neighbourhoods) and were to keep records of the recipients of the relief distributions. That the under-deacons were supposed to keep accounts of their individual disbursements is evidenced by the purchase on 17 January 1580 of '5 books which the under-deacons have received, and [in which they] should write their service'. Unfortunately, none of the books of the under-deacons of the *haussitzenden* poor survive. Whether they have been lost or were never kept in the manner that they were supposed to be kept is uncertain. The only account books that we have for the *haussitzenden* deacons are the general records for the whole diaconate kept by the head-deacons which do not contain the records of individual disbursements for each *Kluft*.[9] As the closest mediators between the poor and poverty, the under-deacons sometimes had to distribute more money than had been disbursed to them by the head-deacons. In such cases, the under-deacons used their own personal resources to come up with the needed money and had to appear before the 'head-deacons' in subsequent weeks to receive reimbursements.[10] From time to time, the deacons of the *haussitzenden* poor were called upon by the consistory to use their poor relief visitation rounds in the *Klufts* to increase church discipline and proper behaviour.[11]

The reorganisation of the *haussitzenden* diaconate in 1576 (including the Poor Ordinances of 1576) ratified and put into writing the distribution methods which had developed over the previous decades. The hierarchical organisation was validated with the official naming of the head and under-deacons. Emden's incorporation of the Faldern suburbs

---

[8] Fehler, 'Social Welfare', p. 562; ArchGK no. 3194, p. 185. Compare with Part II of ArchGK no. 3001, on the page with the yearly accounts from 2 January 1582.

[9] ArchGK no. 3194, p. 60.

[10] For two examples of many, ibid., no. 1117, pp. 42, 47 (1570, 1572).

[11] For example, 16 January 1576 (KRP, p. 592); 24 October 1580 (KRP, p. 748).

in 1573 necessitated an adjustment of the city's *Kluft* organisation, and this geographic modification finally occurred with the general diaconal reforms of 1576.

The consistory met on 17 February 1576 to discuss the new *Kluft* organisation and to record the *Kluft* assignments of the *haussitzenden* deacons. The city, including Faldern, would now be divided into five *Klufts*, and the consistory discussed the precise streets and houses which would mark the boundaries of the *Klufts* (see Map 5.2). Each *Kluft* was also assigned to one of Emden's four pastors; without a fifth pastor, the extra *Kluft* would be served by the 'visitator' (in this case, an elder), who would now receive part of the salary of the fifth pastor.[12] Along with the pastors, three elders were assigned to each *Kluft* to oversee church discipline. The secretary of the church council then recorded the names of the 'over- and underdeacons alongside their division of the *Klufts*'.

With six deacons per *Kluft*, the size of the diaconate had now increased to 30 deacons; it is here that we have a clear indication that each *Kluft* was overseen by a head-deacon. The references to the supervising deacons (*Vorsteher*) before the 1576 reorganisation revealed only a board of supervisors; at the time of the reorganisation, each head-deacon was assigned to serve a particular *Kluft* alongside 'his' under-deacons.[13] Such a characterisation is evidence not only of a division of labour within the diaconate, but also a hierarchy between the deacons.

The hierarchy signifies that each head-deacon was responsible for the fiscal and administrative supervision of the under-deacons in his *Kluft*. Besides presiding over the under-deacons, the primary duties of the head-deacons included the collections of alms and donations in the church on Sundays,[14] the purchase of supplies in bulk (food, cloth, etc.) for disbursement to the poor,[15] and the maintenance of provisions for the poor in wintertime (flax, for instance, to provide the poor with work).[16] Each Sunday, two of the five head-deacons were supposed to collect alms in the church and immediately place them in a box. The account books are full of expenditures for cloth (*Laken*), peat (*Torf* or *Turf*), and other supplies for the poor as the head-deacons handled the

---

[12] KRP, pp. 660ff.

[13] For instance, ibid., p. 596.

[14] '1576 Poor Relief Ordinance', ArchGK no. 3001, p. 7; Emil Sehling (ed.), *Die evangelischen Kirchenordnungen des XVI. Jahrhunderts*, VII/2/1 (Tübingen, 1963), pp. 457f.

[15] ArchGK no. 3194, fols 116–22.

[16] '1576 Poor Ordinance', ArchGK no. 3001, pp. 4f (Sehling (ed.), *Kirchenordnungen*, p. 456).

5.1 'The installation of the deacons according to Acts 6' (by Martin Faber, 1624). The painting portrayed the faces of Emden's current *haussitzenden* head-deacons.

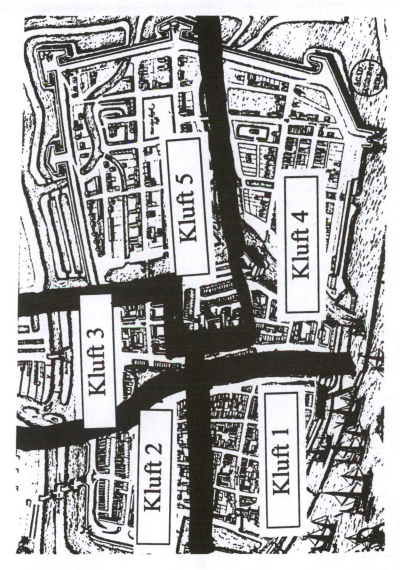

Map 5.2 *Klufts* of the *haussitzenden* deacons after 1576 reorganisation

business transactions of the diaconate. Although examples can be found in virtually every week of expenditures, at some points in the account books the deacons centralised their recordkeeping; on 1 January 1581, for instance, the head-deacons recorded all their expenses on clothing for the poor in 1580 (both cloth purchases and payments to tailors).

The head-deacons apparently rotated monthly in their service of presiding over the administrative functions of the entire diaconate – with the exhortation that they 'should not allow their problems' to fall upon their successors.[17] Two of the head-deacons of the *haussitzenden* poor were to meet every Sunday afternoon at one o'clock in the consistory chamber of the Grosse Kirche. At this meeting, they recorded their weekly disbursements to the under-deacons of each *Kluft* and recorded all extraordinary disbursements to the poor and purchases of supplies. A general account book detailing all the incomes and expenses of the diaconate was kept, and the under-deacons were to keep account books of their expenditures in the *Klufts*. Expounding upon 2 Corinthians 8:21 that 'we have regard for what is honourable, not only in the sight of the Lord, but also in the sight of men', the 1576 Poor Ordinance exhorted the deacons to provide 'good accounting and approach all things honourably'. Therefore, they should 'faithfully receive' the alms and 'orderly record all income in a special book', and after faithfully and diligently distributing the goods 'among those for whom it was given, [the deacons shall] record all expenditures in a special book'.[18] The early account book entries are completely haphazard, and show that the recordkeeping methods were not fully systematised until late 1576, six months after the *Kluft* reorganisation and the Poor Ordinance.

Other participants at these Sunday meetings were the five under-deacons who were at the time handling the primary service for their *Kluft*. By examining the trends in weekly disbursements to the under-deacons, we can see that one under-deacon in each *Kluft* 'presided' (my word) for a period usually of about six months. While presiding, these under-deacons attended the Sunday meetings with the head-deacons and received the weekly disbursement for their *Kluft*. In practice, therefore, a three-level hierarchy functioned within the *haussitzenden* diaconate. At the top, overseeing the administration of the *Kluft*, was

---

[17] See Fehler, 'Social Welfare', pp. 516–17 (Appendix III/H), 'Ordinance Governing Diaconal Meetings', Article 9; original in StaE, I. Reg., no. 424 (pages unnumbered, these Articles follow a letter from 1622); compare Sehling (ed.), *Kirchenordnungen*, pp. 464f; Sprengler-Rupenthal dates this document from 1577/78.

[18] ArchGK no. 3001, p. 3; Sehling (ed.), *Kirchenordnungen*, p. 456; compare bookkeeping methods in ArchGK nos 1117, 1118, and 3194.

5.2   The head-deacons in 1665 (Johannes a Lasco Bibliothek Grosse Kirche Emden)

the head-deacon. In the middle, one of the five under-deacons received money from the head-deacon and accounted for the weekly expenditures within his *Kluft*, usually serving in this function for about six months. At the bottom of the hierarchy, the remaining under-deacons, along with the presiding under-deacon, went through their *Klufts* and made their distributions to the poor each week.

The under-deacons maintained the poor-rolls for their *Klufts* and distributed alms to those on the relief rolls; generally about two-thirds of the diaconate's total expenditures were through the weekly disbursements of the under-deacons in the *Klufts*. The *haussitzenden* poor, therefore, must have kept a close relationship with the under-deacons in their *Kluft* in order to receive regular relief from the diaconate. The under-deacons also provided the means by which special purchases or gifts of peat, clothing or food were distributed to the *haussitzenden* poor of the community. In unusual circumstances, such as sickness or family emergency, people could receive extraordinary relief. Frequently the under-deacons saw to these extraordinary requests themselves, and they would need to request reimbursements from the head-deacons for amounts above their regular disbursement. In many instances, poor persons, especially those passing through from outside the city who needed extraordinary relief, approached the head-deacons directly to make their request. Often, preachers distributed alms to poor people whom they came upon in their pastoral visitations; then, from time to time, they would approach the deacons and ask for reimbursements from the 'poor-box' of the diaconate.[19] While the deacons seem to have been on their own in making their disbursements, the pastors could clearly make their preferences known from time to time – for instance, when the pastors unanimously asked the deacons to provide large gifts to people in distress; to a refugee who 'lost everything because of the gospel'; and to one whose name was to be kept secret 'out of respectability'.[20] The deacons also recorded expenditures made on requests (or orders) of the Burgermeister or the territorial judge.[21]

Respectability – and ensuring that the congregation's poor were cared for separately from the 'common' or 'wild' *haussitzenden* poor – was one of the reasons behind the creation of a special fund for the 'household of faith'. But because no account books or independent records of the deacons of the 'household of faith' exist, their administrative organisation must be inferred from the fragmentary surviving evidence.

---

[19] For instance, ibid., no. 3194, pp. 16, 27, 34, 41, 42, 44, 54, 87, 137, 139, 144, 190, 235.

[20] Ibid., pp. 203, 245.

[21] Ibid., pp. 46, 91.

Fortunately, because of this diaconate's heightened concern with church discipline, references to the work of the *Becken* deacons' work often appears in the minutes of the consistory. It is not clear whether or not these deacons were members of the consistory. In the earliest deliberations about the creation of the *Becken* diaconate, the consistory voiced its desire that the new deacons participate in the weekly church council meetings.[22] Original plans for the *Becken* diaconate conceived of three 'supervisors of the poor of the congregation'. The failure of this earliest attempt to create the diaconate resulted in the elders performing the proposed diaconal duties for a while. From records made after actual *Becken* deacons were chosen, these deacons seem to have not attended consistory meetings regularly. Although *Becken* deacons sometimes approached the consistory with reports or questions about their work, it seems that they were not considered members of the consistory, as were the pastors and elders. Indeed, the consistory occasionally had to send a messenger to summon the deacons of the *Becken* to a consistory meeting.[23]

The word 'deacon' was rarely used in these early years to designate those who cared for the poor of the 'household of faith'. While elders carried out these additional responsibilities, phrases such as 'the administrators of the congregation for the poor' were used.[24] The temporary nature of an arrangement made between pastors and elders in February 1558, which we saw in the last chapter, was questioned the following year. Though no consensus could be reached, the consistory voted to confirm the 'administrators' of the poor of the congregation in their positions. They 'should remain in their office' and if they could show important justification, perhaps their number could be doubled.[25] No figures were given to indicate the number of 'administrators' at the time or if its size was actually doubled.

From all the evidence, the *Becken* fund for the 'household of faith' was administered by elders until 1564/65. The consistory minutes in the early 1560s are full of individual requests for small amounts of relief, help with rent, business loans, or aid in finding an apprenticeship. Sometimes virtually the entire record of a consistory meeting contains a

---

[22] KRP, p. 13 (22 November 1557).

[23] Ibid., p. 210 (9 July 1565) when an elder was sent to summon the *Becken* deacons. At the consistory meeting on 20 January 1578, the minister Johan Petrejus needed to inform the deacons of the *Becken* of an upcoming special meeting and thus summoned two deacons and instructed them to spread the word; ibid., p. 289. Very likely this special meeting involved discussions about the imminent dissolution of the *Becken* diaconate since the ordinances of dissolution were published on 10 February.

[24] That is, 'die voorstanderen des ghemeine van de armen'; ibid., p. 85 (1 May 1559).

[25] Ibid.

list of small relief payments to the poor of the congregation who made requests to the consistory.[26] In most cases, the person making the request is not named. However, when additional action was required outside the consistory meeting, the case was assigned to people whom we can definitely confirm as elders. Henderick Wilting was the elder typically assigned to poor relief cases; after him, Evert Kuper and Sipko Mennens, also elders, took care of a number of relief-related cases; Frans Smit was given responsibility in a couple of cases. These four elders were the same ones originally assigned to 'the service of the poor' in February 1558.[27] The continued recurrence of these particular elders in poor relief cases through 1564 implies that only a core group among the elders served in the 'administration of the poor of the congregation'.

Hints of a change in the make-up of the institution begin to appear about 1564. On 24 April, the consistory considered only two issues. First, it announced that it needed more elders since 'some of the elders have moved, such as Henderick Wilting', who moved to Groningen, and some elders could not continue in their office.[28] Obviously, the loss of Hindrick, who seems to have overseen most of the congregation's poor relief matters, affected not only the eldership but also the administration of the congregation's charity. The second issue was the decision to inform the 'wealthy citizens, that they will come to the Gasthaus chamber in order to collect alms for the poor'.[29] The consistory's concerns this day must have been about the proper care of the congregation's poor.

Henderick Wilting had moved from the city, and Evert Kuper left the eldership at this time in order to become a member of the city council.[30] Losing these two, the consistory needed to modify the arrangement which had handled the vast majority of the recorded relief out of the *Becken* fund for the previous seven years. Perhaps the consistory hoped that three new elders elected in November would continue to help with poor relief responsibilities as had the previous elders.[31] Yet the issue was important enough that, shortly after the election of elders, the consistory held a special Thursday meeting to consider the matter of the replacement 'of a deacon in Evert Kuper's place'. Johan Ameling, one of the recently elected elders, accepted his duties on the condition 'that we free

---

[26] For example, ibid., pp. 66, 67 (19 September and 10 October 1558).

[27] Ibid., p. 34 (28 February 1568).

[28] Ibid., p. 182.

[29] Ibid., p. 183.

[30] Evert was already one of Emden's 'radtzheren' by 27 December 1565; ibid., p. 224.

[31] Ibid., p. 187 (13 November 1564); they were nominated on 11 August; ibid., p. 185.

him of the diaconal duties of the residential poor'.[32] The consistory consented to his request.

It is not clear whether this decision was intended to establish a new policy or if it was only for Johan Ameling's case. Nevertheless, one can imagine how the other elders who had been assigned additional poor relief responsibilities might have reacted to this compromise, especially since they had to compensate for the extra workload.[33] Finally, on 8 June 1565, they decided upon a 'ripe remedy' for the situation and agreed to 'diligently be on the look out for six new deacons' whom they could choose to administer the fund for the poor of the congregation.[34] The consistory elected the new deacons no later than 9 July.[35] With this 'remedy', the consistory effectively removed the duties of charity from the elders' responsibilities and gave them, finally, to a new diaconate.[36]

One of the most fundamental results of the evolution from elders to deacons was the limitation of the direct role of the consistory in poor relief. New methods of distribution also developed. Elders had made rounds throughout the city to monitor church discipline, and those elders assigned to poor relief duties no doubt paid special attention to the poor of the congregation when out supervising morals. Yet the elders had responsibilities which went beyond poor relief and therefore probably limited their effectiveness in matters of charity. With the creation of separate deacons to handle these functions and 'go through the whole city to serve the members of the congregation faithfully', the poor now received increased attention and scrutiny in their requests for relief but were less frequently in contact with the elders when receiving it.

Before 1565, many of the congregation's needy had to approach the consistory with their extraordinary requests. This extended far beyond the occasional complicated cases involving questions of church discipline and poor relief on which the consistory needed to deliberate.[37] The elders probably did not make frequent rounds through the city to check on the poor. (It is not even clear that they maintained a regular relief roll of recipients in these early years, though they probably did.)

---

[32] 30 November 1564; ibid., pp. 188f.

[33] The consistory had made a similar agreement with a nominated elder once in the past. On 26 August 1560 (ibid., p. 118), Hinrick Harberti and Johan van Knypens were asked to serve as elders, however 'the consistory has also promised Johan van Knipens that one should remove from him the [duties of the] distributions to the poor'.

[34] Ibid., p. 208. Schilling's text is a misreading; the original reads '6 nye diaconen'.

[35] 9 July 1565; ibid., p. 210.

[36] At some point during the next decade, the size of the *Becken* diaconate was slightly increased, probably to nine; ibid., p. 590 (9 January 1576).

[37] See the church discipline case studies in Chapter 7.

During this period, the consistory minutes are full of frequent, some-times nondescript, references to small, individual disbursements of aid out of the *Becken* fund.[38] When Jan Stoeldreyer approached the consistory asking for help with his rent, the elders Sipko Mennens and Evert Kuper were instructed to look into his request.[39] When the car-penter Berent was wounded and unable to work, he apparently could not attract the attention of a poor relief administrator without appear-ing before the consistory; his case was a straightforward one, requiring no consistorial discussion of discipline problems or merits. After the administrators of the *Becken* fund had been informed of his circum-stances, the consistory instructed the elder Frans Smit to check up on him every week and give him money when necessary.[40]

While earlier disbursements from the *Becken* fund often involved consistorial deliberation, in later years, after the creation of the *Becken* diaconate, such requests were brought directly to the deacons in the regular course of their poor relief rounds. The deacons consulted the consistory only when tough questions regarding the discipline of a poor relief recipient needed to be answered, and after 1565, the number of references to poor relief disbursements in the consistory minutes fell dramatically. The creation of the diaconate is in some ways unfortunate for the historian because the *Becken* deacons left no independent records, and the poor relief activities of the congregation begin thereafter to disappear from the consistory minutes.

Questions of church discipline played the central role in the work of the *Becken* diaconate, even after the elders were removed from the scene. Since these deacons were to care for the poor members of the 'household of faith' (the pious members who were allowed to attend communion), church discipline on the part of the recipients was a necessary precondition of the alms. The Dutch exile congregations also strove for this ideal of church discipline within their ranks, but the *fremdlingen* deacons faced the practical reality of a fluid, ever-changing refugee community, of whom they could not always maintain strict supervision. The *Becken* deacons, by contrast, dealt with a largely local constituency.

The *Becken* deacons may have maintained a roll of recipients who received assistance on a regular basis, but given the nature of the

---

[38] In such cases, the consistory minutes read very much like an account book; see, for example, 19 September and 9–10 October 1558, KRP, pp. 66, 67.

[39] Ibid., p. 106 (23 February 1560).

[40] Ibid., p. 121 (28 October 1560). Berent's needs were brought before the consistory on later occasions as well, for example; ibid., pp. 125, 129, 260–61. His mother re-quested aid before the consistory 3 May 1563; ibid., p. 162

organisational structures described above and the lack of independent diaconal records, these recipients remain invisible to us.[41] Instead, what we have are records of many extraordinary disbursements and the cases of individuals who faced special scrutiny (and sometimes the loss of alms) due to misbehaviour or false belief. Virtually all these recorded extraordinary requests involved short-term or one-time needs, such as help with a rent payment, in an illness, or in finding an apprenticeship (and the initiation fees) for a child. Frequently relief took the form of a loan. Moreover, the consistory expected the recipient to work and meet as many of the expenses as possible. If the disbursement was not a loan, it was often predicated upon a number of conditions (in addition to maintaining proper discipline, of course). Sometimes a loan recipient himself would write a receipt in the minutes of the consistory: for example, 'I, Jaspar Hermanss, attest with my own hand that I have borrowed from the congregation a bed with a pair of sheets and a blanket and two pillows and a bolster.'[42]

Numerous examples can be drawn upon to illustrate the conditions placed upon disbursements from the *Becken* fund. Jacob Lutkens requested a 6-daler (or 9-gulden) loan to pay for a house which he had just purchased. The consistory said that it could not meet his request, but if he proved himself with work, and did his best to make as much as possible on his own, then 'the congregation would not abandon him'. Two weeks later the *Becken* fund gave him 1 daler.[43] Provision to a family was sometimes limited to the time during which the husband was sick, and relief would end when he was able to work again.[44] When the unemployed Stephan van Ditmer approached the consistory wanting 'to learn a craft of a schoolmaster', the consistory agreed that if he travelled outside Emden to look for a schoolmaster position, the *Becken* fund would provide his wife and child the small amount of 2 or 3 schap (0.2–0.3 gulden) per week 'until he discharges [his training] and returns'.[45]

One of the most common requests was for help in finding an apprenticeship for a child. Since placing a child in an apprenticeship could reduce the daily burdens on a needy family, the consistory and the

---

[41] It is also possible that many of these poor would have been shame-faced poor who did not want to be identified as recipients of charity. Cissie Fairchilds describes the special year-end ceremony of one of Aix's institutions which burned all its records every year to protect its alms recipients; *Poverty and Charity in Aix-en-Provence 1640–1789* (Baltimore, 1976), p. 76.

[42] KRP, p. 111 (16 April 1560).

[43] Ibid., pp. 140, 142 (16 and 31 March 1562).

[44] For instance, ibid., p. 81 (3 April 1559).

[45] Ibid., p. 98 (14 August 1559).

Becken deacons generally considered the apprenticing of qualified children an essential precondition, along with the adult's willingness to
work, for the receipt of relief. In the first recorded example, when a
father announced that he could not support his son properly, the
consistory instructed him first to apprentice out his son, 'and [we]
would gladly help him with what he cannot afford'.[46] The consistory
informed the widow of Wyllum Schoemaker that 'the congregation
would not consider helping her as long as she holds the older daughters
in her house' and does not let them serve 'a good man'. As soon as she
agreed to let her older daughters work for 'a good man', the 'congregation would not desert her in her distress'.[47]

The case of Anne Jeronimus illustrates a combination of imposed
conditions for relief as well as the frustration that such conditions could
create for the recipient. Anne first appeared by name in the consistory
minutes on 27 January 1561. The consistory agreed to give her 6 schap
per week for 'three or four weeks more' on the condition 'that she set
her son by a trade'.[48] The members of the consistory must have helped
her search for an apprenticeship, and on 14 April 1561 they announced
that Anne's son had been placed with the brother of an Emden elder in
the nearby town of Norden. The apprenticeship would last for four
years, and the fee was 25 schap per year: for two years the congregation
would pay the fee, but the other two years could not be guaranteed.
The congregation basically told her that if she did not improve her own
situation within two years, it would be her own fault: 'instead, if she
holds herself in this state, so will she justly find herself there'.[49]

Her financial situation did not improve greatly, and on 21 December
1561 the consistory considered Anne's request that the congregation
pay her rent. The consistory apparently investigated her circumstances
and discovered that her landlord would be willing in this case to 'suffer
until around Easter' a delayed payment. After eliminating the urgency
of Anne's request, the consistory instructed Anne that 'she should diligently employ herself in midwifery or some other work, and that she
shall earn it and pay it herself. If on the other hand she petitions with a
sickness so that she cannot earn anything, then the congregation shall
pay the rent for her.'[50] Anne did not appreciate this response to her
request and apparently responded to the consistory in critical fashion,
so critical that she was twice summoned and admonished for her

---

[46] Ibid., p. 7 (3 August 1557).
[47] Ibid., p. 133 (13 October 1561).
[48] Ibid., p. 124.
[49] Ibid., p. 126.
[50] Ibid., p. 136.

'blasphemous speech'.[51] In addition to an emphasis on church discipline in their provisions for the poor, the *Becken* deacons also stressed the need for work among the recipients. A year and a half later the consistory agreed to help Anne once again with the small sum of 1 gulden. But they stressed that 'such money was loaned to her': in her case the congregation could not give her the money outright, and she was reminded that she would have to repay it. Obviously, they did not feel that she was yet acting responsibly, but nevertheless needed some short-term assistance.[52]

The administrators of the *Becken* fund made their decisions based very much on a case-by-case basis. As late as April 1577, ten months before the dissolution of the *Becken* diaconate, the consistory eschewed establishing prescribed rules for the distribution of relief to the 'household of faith'. In this instance, the *Becken* deacons had asked the consistory for guidelines in providing help with the rent payments of the needy (rent payments made up a significant percentage of the records of the *Becken*'s expenditures). The consistory 'saw it for good' and argued that the deacons 'themselves know quite how to regulate' rent payments by using 'discretion' and recognising the individual 'circumstances of the poor': 'just as all people's character is not the same, so one can also prescribe no fixed rule for them'.[53] As the discussion on church discipline and poor relief in Chapter 7 will illustrate, even in the realm of church discipline the *Becken* deacons did not always follow strict rules. Instead, the deacons allowed some people to receive alms even when banned from communion, while the offender was counselled by a minister or an elder. The circumstances of an individual case were always considered despite attempts to maintain high standards of discipline, and sometimes a charitable spirit would override the enforcement of discipline.

Sources of income for the *Becken* diaconate were limited largely to alms collected at the communion service held every four to six weeks. Only two records of the size of the communion collections survive; if these were typical then we would expect the *Becken* contributions during communion to have been about 50–70 per cent of what the *haussitzenden* deacons collected in a typical month of Sunday services.[54] As a newly created institution, the *Becken* diaconate (like the *fremdlingen* diaconate) had no established endowment based on landed

---

[51] 5 January and 12 January 1562 (ibid., p. 137).
[52] Ibid., p. 162 (3 May 1563).
[53] Ibid., p. 666 (22 April 1577).
[54] Ibid., pp. 66f (11 September and 9 October 1558); ArchGK no. 1117, pp. 2–34; Fehler, 'Social Welfare', pp. 554–61.

or house properties from which it could receive rent payments. For late medieval and early modern charitable institutions, these traditional forms of endowments provided the first basis of financial support and security. In this regard, the older, traditional Emden institutions of the *haussitzenden* deacons, the Gasthaus, and the Shippers' Brotherhood had a stronger base of assured income from old endowments and therefore operated with more financial stability than the newly established institutions.

The *Becken* deacons, therefore, were from the beginning dependent on another source of revenue: voluntary collections and donations.[55] Supplementing the collection in the *Becken*, the diaconate must certainly have encouraged additional donations and bequests to support the poor of the 'household of faith'. We certainly find remarks in the account book of the *haussitzenden* deacons indicating that Pastor Colthunis actively encouraged people to leave money and goods (sometimes quite large sums) to the *haussitzenden* poor; we would expect similar exhortations made on behalf of the *Becken* poor.[56] On occasion, in times of especially great financial distress or even deficit, the consistory authorised special rounds of collections. In one instance, the consistory publicised the 'deficit of the poor of the congregation, which is why a collection round has been ordered'.[57] However, before official deacons were established who could make a house-to-house collection throughout the city, the consistory had to make arrangements to ensure that 'affluent citizens' came to them in a special meeting 'to collect alms for the poor'.[58] On one occasion the *haussitzenden* deacons paid 44 gulden to the *Becken* deacons 'because they complained that they are short of money'.[59]

We would expect these pious and disciplined poor – as opposed to the 'common' poor cared for by the *haussitzenden* deacons – to have been popular among donors. Yet records of only 11 testaments survive which bequeathed anything to the *Becken* poor; and most of them included the

---

[55] The *fremdlingen* deacons, as depicted below, had to go even further to what was, in practice, a tax to support their tremendous size with no endowments.

[56] ArchGK no. 1117, pp. 181–5.

[57] The temporal proximity of the reference to this publicised house-to-house collection for the 'poor of the household of faith' (30 May 1569, KRP, p. 351) with the authorisation of a special collection for the *fremdlingen* poor (16 May 1569, ibid., p. 350) suggests that the two collections were in conjunction with each other; the *fremdlingen*'s *schattinghe* was actually held about 1 July 1569 (*Fremdlingen II*, fol. 8; J. J. van Toorenenbergen (ed.), *Stukken betreffende de Diaconie der Vreemdelingen te Emden 1560–1576* (Utrecht, 1876), p. 14).

[58] KRP, p. 183 (24 April 1564).

[59] ArchGK no. 1117, p. 43 (June 1571).

Becken poor in combination with another relief institution (especially the *haussitzenden* and Gasthaus poor, as well as the Shippers).[60] Not all testaments from Emden survive, but during this same period, dozens of testaments survive which left money to the *haussitzenden* poor or to the Gasthaus. Interestingly, this suggests that most Emden residents who made bequests to the poor favoured the town's traditional poor relief institutions rather than the concept of the 'pure' congregation – even when it supposedly cared for the most worthy poor. Emden's donors clearly responded to dire socio-economic difficulties and were also moved by arguments about their religious duty to help those less fortunate, but they were not convinced about the merits of the new Reformed theological distinction in matters of poor relief.

In addition to the concerns for proper church discipline, fiscal constraints also affected decisions to provide alms. As a result of financial strains, the *Becken* administrators and deacons were forced to be very careful with disbursements. Any help from the congregation was generally to be given as a last resort after the recipient had exhausted his or her own efforts or was incapacitated. Many of the disbursements were loans instead of outright gifts. By often making the disbursements subject to repayment, the consistory seemed to be trying to give the recipient the impression that he or she was fortunate to be getting any kind of help from the *Becken* fund.

Fiscal restrictions also kept the focus of the *Becken* fund primarily on the members of the Emden congregation. In one instance, two members of the congregation proposed a charitable act to the consistory. They knew a blacksmith in another village who had a large debt (for iron used in his work), and they asked if the 'supervisors of the congregation might collect something from some rich citizens toward the payment of his debt'. What the collection failed to raise, the two members would personally pay toward the blacksmith's debt.[61] A pastor responded 'that we would like to help him in that way, but do not find it prudent to do'. First, 'we cannot collect enough in the congregation with which to support our own poor'. Given that fact, the congregation should not then 'collect for the debts of someone who lives in Esens'. The pastor offered to visit the smith, exhort him and give him some advice, including 'at least to wait until ... he is blessed by God in his work so that he can make his payment'. Hence, the *Becken* deacons were expected to expend their resources and influence to facilitate primarily the care of the poor of Emden's 'household of faith'.

---

[60] For a list of all surviving references to bequests made explicitly to the *Becken* poor, see Fehler, 'Social Welfare', p. 387, note 143.

[61] KRP, pp. 172–3 (20 September 1563).

These fiscal concerns and the desire to serve only the local congregation coalesced again in the dispute which arose over the maintenance of fugitive Dutch ministers who had fled to Emden and the surrounding villages.[62] The relief of the ministers raised special issues for the deacons. On the one hand, the *fremdlingen* deacons did not generally consider the ministers as having quite the same needs as the 'common poor refugees'. In fact, they made complaints that the able-bodied ministers frequently did nothing to earn money for themselves while waiting for an opportunity to return to their home congregations in the Netherlands. On the other hand, the *Becken* deacons did not feel that they should have to provide care for foreigners. Cases arose throughout the 1560s and 1570s in which compromises were made between the two diaconates and the maintenance costs were shared, but the complaints and jurisdictional disputes continued none the less.

Financial problems and jurisdictional disputes helped encourage the ultimate dissolution of the *Becken* diaconate on 10 February 1578.[63] The dissolution ordinance was published as one of several statutes issued in subsequent years to supplement 'the current Poor Ordinances' of 1576. It recognised that for some years before the 1576 Poor Ordinances a differentiation had been established between the 'deacons of the common, wild poor' (i.e. *haussitzenden*) and the 'deacons of the poor members of Christ' (i.e. *Becken*). The 'recommendation of the preachers, elders, head-deacons and deacons from the *Becken*' to combine the 'two services' of the poor into a single diaconate was based on four officially published reasons.

The first reason for ending the separation of duties was 'in order that the poor of the *Becken*, since they are the proper and most pious *haussitzenden* poor, also may claim part of the interest payments and bequests of the *haussitzenden* poor'. The *Becken* deacons contended that when people had made bequests in the past to the *haussitzenden* poor, they had in mind 'without doubt the most pious poor'. Yet the *haussitzenden* deacons, who had resisted the formation of a second diaconate from the start, had cut off the *Becken* poor from the endowments of the *haussitzenden* poor: if the congregation was going to form a new diaconate, then it should also provide new funds for it. Thus, without an endowment to provide financial security, the *Becken* poor faced too much fiscal instability and needed to regain access to the traditional endowment of the *haussitzenden*.

---

[62] For discussion of the conflict with the *fremdlingen* deacons over the maintenance of the refugee Dutch ministers, see below pp. 179–81.

[63] The texts of the Poor Ordinance of 1576 and the subsequent decrees, including the dissolution ordinance, are included in Appendix III in Fehler, 'Social Welfare', pp. 505–17; ArchGK no. 3001, pp. 1–32; Sehling (ed.), *Kirchenordnungen*, pp. 455–65.

The second reason cited illustrates a changing definition of the congregation. Church discipline, with attempts to delineate a 'household of faith', was the defining characteristic of the pure congregation. The 1576 Poor Ordinances had stressed, however, that even the *haussitzenden* deacons needed to ensure that their recipients acted in an orderly fashion. This point was emphasised in the accompanying statute to the dissolution ordinance on 10 February 1578:

> that one shall not serve the disorderly poor – these are adulterers, whores, drunks, sluggards and idlers, and the like – even in the most complete, greatest distress. [This is ordered] so that they are not strengthened in their misconduct, but instead through the withdrawal of the alms are drawn toward humility and conversion, as far as possible.[64]

The head-deacons of the *haussitzenden* deacons were also to ensure that the citizenry was not bothered with disorderliness by begging. 'The justification of the differentiation of the services has been removed through the newly installed Poor Ordinance' by extending these elements of what had been largely church discipline to the charity of the *haussitzenden* deacons. The *Becken* had been originally established so 'that the poor members of the congregation of Christ might be kept from begging, according to the command of God's word and the nature of love'. Without the *Becken* fund, this could not have been achieved because the goods of the poor in the late 1550s 'were not enough to maintain all the poor'. But now, the new Poor Ordinance had explicitly banned begging by everyone. Thus the congregation did not need to maintain a separate fund to keep its own poor members from begging since the begging prohibition was to be strictly enforced against everyone. Because the reorganisation of the *haussitzenden* deacons and the Poor Ordinances in 1576 had now made all the poor of the city, not just members of the 'household of faith', legally subject to key behavioural elements of Reformed church discipline, the significance of any distinction between the 'true Christians' and those outside the communion-congregation was de-emphasised.

The third reason for the dissolution of the *Becken* fund was the incessant disputes and argumentation between the two diaconates. The church leaders wanted to 'avoid all divisions and disunity'. Unfortunately, 'as experience has often taught', when it came to testaments to the *haussitzenden* poor, 'great fights and errors originated between the deacons of the *Becken* and the wild *haussitzenden* poor'. With the merger of the two diaconates, the root of the fighting was 'hereby removed'.

---

[64] ArchGK no. 3001, p. 23.

The final reason given for the dissolution and merger was administrative in nature, so that the deacons might have 'better supervision over the poor'. A more efficient, centralised administration with better supervision would enable the deacons to 'more richly serve the pious and withdraw the alms from the whores and adulterers'. Under the previous bipartite diaconal administration, some of the poor had been able to exploit the feuding and lack of communication on the part of the two diaconates, thereby receiving relief from both diaconates. With the new centralisation, now 'one may make known such people and bring such people to order'. To this end, the *Becken* diaconate was not simply dissolved: three of the *Becken* deacons were added to the colloquium of the five head-deacons of the *haussitzenden* diaconate. By deliberating together, they 'may be able to serve and understand *all* the poor'.

The dissolution of the *Becken* diaconate did not signal the sudden end of caring for the poor of the congregation. According to the aforementioned reasons, the consolidation of the diaconates was intended to improve their alms, to 'serve the pious more richly'. Thus it is not surprising that the term '*Becken* poor' did not immediately disappear from the sources with the end of the *Becken* deacons. For instance, in November 1578, six months after the *Becken*'s dissolution, when the diaconate sold a house in their possession, four 'head-deacons of our church' represented the diaconate in making the contract and were also referred to as 'administrators of the *haussitzenden* and *Becken* poor'.[65] The *Becken* poor continued to survive for a while in some people's consciousness. Thus, as late as 1582, a couple left in their testament the large sum of 200 gulden to both the Shipper Poor and 'the poor in the *Becken*'.[66] Despite these later donations to the *Becken* poor after 1578, all the money was administered by the *haussitzenden* diaconate and could not be earmarked only for the 'household of faith'.

The two-decade-long *Becken* experiment, in the end, represents the failure of one model of provision. Nevertheless, this fascinating example demonstrates the growing desire among many in the congregation and church leadership to separate the most worthy members on the basis of this Reformed Protestant theological conception of the 'household of faith'. It failed, however, to capture the hearts and minds of Emden's poor relief donors or, for that matter, of many of the other deacons who opposed the creation of the *Becken* diaconate and apparently quarrelled with them over poor relief administration until their dissolution. Because of the clear economic needs posed by the presence

---

[65] Three of four proxies were from the older head-deacons, and one was a former *Becken* deacon; EKP 15/158v (1 November 1578).

[66] Ibid., 16/453f (21 September 1582); ArchGK no. 3001, part IV, pp. 18v–19.

of so many refugees, the new diaconate created to deal with the foreign population fared better (in terms of survival) than did the deacons of the 'household of faith'.

The organisational methods of the diaconate of the *fremdlingen* poor were strikingly different from those of the *haussitzenden* diaconate. A similar pattern of individual visitations and disbursements by the deacons to the poor on the regular relief rolls was maintained by the refugee deacons. These deacons maintained wonderfully organised account books, usually describing in precise detail each of their sources of income as well as each recipient on their regular relief rolls and each recipient of an extraordinary payment.[67] However, their administrative organisation was different from that of the local deacons and reflects their status as refugees and their recent arrival in the town. Whereas the *haussitzenden* poor were associated with the town and hence their service determined by the neighbourhood in which they lived, the *fremdlingen* poor were exiles in Emden, and their community was defined by membership of the Dutch refugee church rather than by local place of residence. Instead of being assigned to geographic *Klufts*, therefore, the poor of the Dutch community were served by their own deacons regardless of where they lived within Emden.

From its earliest surviving records, the *fremdlingen* diaconate consisted of eight deacons who rotated their service as 'deacon in charge' on a monthly basis. Although occasional turnover among the deacons obviously affected the monthly rotations, patterns of rotation were remarkably stable over the years. During his month of service, the deacon collected the donations placed in the alms-box which was set out for the refugee poor. He also handled the monthly disbursements to the poor. The diaconate at this time did not have an additional bookkeeper; one of the eight deacons performed this function.[68]

The *fremdlingen* deacons' actual method of distribution of resources is a bit less clear. In the first decade of their existence, when they rotated their periods of service monthly, more responsibility seems to have fallen on the deacon in charge than in later years. Making up a financial shortfall was the obligation of this deacon, who would be reimbursed when extra funds became available, that is, at the end of a subsequent month when the 'deacon in charge' held a surplus. In fact, when we follow the money, we see that the *fremdlingen* deacons

---

[67] Two account books survive. The account book 1557–68 will hereafter be cited as *Fremdlingen I*; the account book 1569–75 will be cited as *Fremdlingen II*.

[68] Fehler, 'Social Welfare', p. 346. This changed in 1600 when a bookkeeper for the *fremdlingen* diaconate was chosen in addition to the 12 deacons; J. Mülder, *Die Diakonie der Fremdlingen-Armen 1558–1858* (Emden, 1858), p. 30.

co-ordinated their month-to-month surpluses and deficits in such a way as to keep the individual debts of any one deacon from rising too high.[69]

Various networks of communication within the refugee community must have helped the deacons identify those in need. A great number of refugees settled in the Faldern suburbs of the city. Nevertheless, the refugees were scattered throughout Emden, and the *fremdlingen* deacons had to traverse the entire city and suburbs to distribute their relief, instead of intimately knowing a *Kluft* and its residents as the *haussitzenden* deacons did.

All or most of the deacons were active and visible to the refugee community during the entire year. The deacon in charge for the period would lead the rounds to distribute the alms, but the other deacons could facilitate the process by drawing to the deacon in charge's attention newly arrived poor or those with extraordinary needs, such as women about to give birth or those who were sick. Sometimes the urgency of a situation might compel a deacon to provide extraordinary relief without first consulting the deacon in charge that month. For instance, in March 1562, deacon Willem Bastink, who was not to be deacon in charge until August, came upon a *vremt man* (foreign man) and gave him 3 schap; the current deacon in charge later reimbursed Willem.[70] The distribution of alms was not the sole responsibility of the deacon in charge; he seems mainly to have co-ordinated distribution. Further evidence suggests that deacons would cover for each other from time to time. For instance, Jasper Celosse served for two consecutive months (May and June) in 1561.[71] Another example, from June 1560, shows that deacon in charge Lauwrens de Vos collected the money from the alms-box and distributed the bulk of it to the poor.[72] For some reason, however, Lauwrens was unable to fulfil all his duties for the month, and a number of poor people received extraordinary aid through the services of Jacop Payen, who served the next month as deacon in charge.[73] Yet these two deacons were not alone in distributing alms that month. An elder of Emden's church, Henderick Wilting, also helped Lauwrens make his disbursements to the poor on his regular relief list. Although Lauwrens de Vos apparently needed more help that year (receiving major assistance from Jacop Payen), the elder Henderick Wilting can be seen making additional disbursements

---

[69] Fehler, 'Social Welfare', pp. 346–7.

[70] *Fremdlingen I*, fol. 47v.

[71] The fact that Jasper, who kept the deacons' books at least until 1567, served as deacon in charge more frequently than any other deacon implies that he acted as substitute when the others could not serve.

[72] *Fremdlingen I*, fol. 2v.

[73] Ibid., fol. 3.

to the refugee Pieter van Groningen during two other *fremdlingen* deacons' months of service (in May and November).[74] Such activities indicate that the authority to distribute alms was not limited to the deacon in charge, although he exercised the official supervision of the diaconate's monthly activities.

Henderick Wilting's actions illustrate one of the primary networks of communication within the refugee community: the connections with other refugees from one's home town or region in the Netherlands. In fact, Henderick's connections with Groningen were strong enough that he travelled there fairly regularly.[75] Thus it is very likely that he worked especially closely with other Groningen exiles in Emden, and Henderick was probably in a good position to provide the monthly stipends to the poor refugee Pieter van Groningen in May, June and November. Although Pieter usually received a monthly stipend of 1.2 to 1.5 gulden, in May Jasper Celosse reimbursed Henderick the 10.45 gulden which Henderick had given Pieter – perhaps Pieter needed this much to pay off some debt because he had not received his regular monthly stipend since August 1559. In the following month, Deacon Lauwrens de Vos reimbursed Henderick for a 1.2 gulden payment to Pieter, and in November Henderick gave Pieter 3.9 gulden 'for 3 months'.[76] Since the May and November payments followed periods when Pieter had been absent from the *fremdlingen* deacons' regular rolls, we can see that Henderick Wilting's relationship with the Groningen refugee community kept him informed of distress that for some reason had not been relieved by the deacons, and Henderick was able to intercede on Pieter's behalf when he did not receive aid from them.

By 1563, we can see the beginnings of strain among the separate diaconates in Emden. The rise of violence involving Dutch Protestants in 1562 and 1563, particularly the beginnings of armed preaching, led to a crackdown on many evangelical groups in the Netherlands. As a result, a new group of exiles made their way out of the Netherlands and into Emden; many of these were fugitive ministers. Perhaps the most exposed of these ministers were former religious who had left their orders to join with the Protestants. In September 1563, one of the deacons of the foreign poor, the merchant and bookseller Jacob

---

[74] Ibid., fol. 35v.

[75] Andrew Pettegree, *Emden and the Dutch Revolt* (Oxford, 1992), p. 80, note 100. Pettegree, pp. 80f, describes the deeply rooted economic connections between Emden and Groningen and Friesland. With the economic traffic between Emden and Groningen, 'a number of prominent members of the [Emden] Church were fairly regularly in Groningen, including Gheert tom Camp, Hendrick Wiltinck, and Gerard Mortaigne'.

[76] *Fremdlingen I*, fol. 35v.

Michielson, who had come with the old refugees out of London, asked the consistory if the *fremdlingen* deacons 'might be helped out of the *Becken* fund [in caring] for the monks, who come here steadily'.[77] This was the first of a number of complaints and jurisdictional disputes about the maintenance of the fugitive Dutch ministers in Emden.

The relief of ministers raised special issues for the deacons. The financial connection between poor relief and provision of the pastorate was especially close in Protestant churches cut off from the traditional sources of income. We saw this earlier as the East Frisian Church Ordinances attempted to use the *huusdelinge* to support both the pastor and the poor, and the connections could be particularly close in the Calvinist exile churches. In fact, the French Synod decreed that one-fifth of all money collected for the poor be used for ministerial education.[78] Emden's 'deacons of the foreign poor' did not consider ministers in quite the same category of need as the 'common poor refugees'. The distinction is evident in the earliest reference to the relief of a fugitive minister. In January 1561, the consistory decided that the *fremdlingen* deacons should take care of the wife of the Antwerp minister Adrian Haemstede.[79] In May 1561, it was decided that he too should receive support while he was in exile, but they could not decide 'out of what means'.[80] Meanwhile, the deacons of the local 'household of faith' (*Becken*) did not feel that they should have to care for foreigners. We find cases in which compromises were made and the two institutions split the maintenance costs, but the complaints continued. The deacons appealed to the countess for more funds from the secularised monastic properties to finance the strong influx of foreign preachers, but apparently to no avail.[81] The problems were exacerbated in the late 1560s/ early 1570s as the refugee population in Emden reached its peak and the *fremdlingen* deacons began operating with large deficits. During this time of exile in Emden, many of the refugee ministers refused to accept available preaching posts because of commitments to their churches back home, as they waited for the revolt to be successful. In 1568–69, one of the foreign preachers lost out on his maintenance because, in part, 'he did not work actively enough'.[82] This criticism

---

[77] 20 September 1563, KRP, p. 173.

[78] J. Quick (ed.), *Synodicon in Gallia Reformata* (2 vols, London, 1692), I, 137, 210.

[79] KRP, p. 124 (27 January 1561).

[80] Ibid., p. 127 (19 May 1561).

[81] Ibid., pp. 191, 193 (29 December 1564, 8 and 12 January 1565).

[82] The deacons complained that the Dutch minister Aggeus Hillenzoen 'niet flytichliken genoch arbeitet' (ibid., p. 355). Aggeus was called before the consistory on a number of occasions between 1569 and 1570 and eventually excommunicated; see especially 22 November 1568 and 8 July 1569 (ibid., pp. 329, 355) which deal with his receipt of alms.

was echoed in August 1571 in a general complaint from the deacons before the consistory, demanding that they instruct several refugee ministers 'who have been supported completely with alms now for some years, that they must make some plan in order to earn a living for their own person and wives and children, since people know that with the great difficulties of the congregation they henceforth cannot be so maintained solely [by the community]'.[83] While this exhortation might have affected a few ministers, overall the number of ministers receiving relief from the *fremdlingen* deacons remained relatively constant.[84]

But this problem with a few dozen ministers was in no way the most important one faced by the deacons. In the winter of 1566/67, following the collapse of the Dutch advances made in the 'Wonderyear' (1566) of the Dutch Revolt, Emden, along with several other German cities, was inundated with refugees. This crisis posed particular difficulties for the Emden's *fremdlingen* deacons. While the earliest waves of refugees in the mid-1550s contained numbers of wealthy economic refugees fleeing the Netherlands to protect their investments and properties, a much higher proportion of poorer refugees composed the wave of exiles after 1567. Most of these new refugees fled the Netherlands with little or no notice before advancing troops, frequently bringing very few belongings. Therefore, the refugee community's assets did not increase in proportion to the vast rise in the number of refugees, and the *fremdlingen* diaconate began to face demands for institutional reform. The reforms that they ultimately instituted reflect the importance of the regional communication networks within the refugee community.

The financial burden borne by the *fremdlingen* deacons certainly increased. Between 1566 and 1568 the expenditures of the *fremdlingen* diaconate almost tripled: from 947 gulden in 1566 to 2 825 gulden to the refugee poor in 1568.[85] As the flood of refugees poured into Emden in 1567, the bookkeeper scrambled to keep up. His list of the hundreds of one-time extraordinary expenditures to the poor that year ran to more than 11 pages, when previous years were usually listed on one or two.[86]

The poor relief crisis was exacerbated because it occurred when the diaconate was not at full strength. From 1562 through 1566, only six or

---

[83] 11 August 1571 (ibid., p. 420).

[84] Beginning with the second account book, *Fremdlingen II*, the deacons recorded their expenditures for each year in three categories: 'ordinary' service (routine relief provided on a regular basis), 'extraordinary' (grants for special circumstances), and 'service of the preachers'.

[85] *Fremdlingen I*, fols 59–64, 235v; Mülder, *Diakonie der Fremdlingen*, p. 10.

[86] *Fremdlingen I*, fols 160v–66.

seven deacons were active at any one time. Elections were held only irregularly, and there was apparently no set length of term in office: Pauwels van Mechelen left the diaconate after only a year and a half to become an elder, while Jacop Payen served as a *fremdlingen* deacon for at least 13 years. So the flood of refugees began when the diaconate was short on manpower: at the end of 1566, they may have been down to five deacons.[87] These deacons were barely able to keep up with the individual requests for poor relief, let alone incorporate all the newly arrived poor into the regular relief roll or have time to solicit more contributions.

It is no surprise, therefore, that the year 1567 marks the beginning of significant institutional changes in the *fremdlingen* diaconate. At the 1 May meeting of Emden's consistory, which was attended by 'brothers from various congregations: Antwerp, Ghent, Amsterdam, and all other surrounding lands', the fugitive Antwerp minister Isebrand Balck presented a three-part plan regarding the 'present emergency'.[88] First, he suggested that the diaconate be equipped with eight deacons because of the 'distress from the countless arrivals and exiles'. This time, however, in order to represent the newly arriving refugees, the deacons should be selected based on their 'nation' or province in the Netherlands. Each provincial community should choose its own deacons: two from Flanders, two from Brabant, two from Holland, and two from West Friesland (these provinces were the largest sources of refugees in Emden; note the absence of Groningen, where the conflicts in the Dutch Revolt were less intense at this moment and whose refugees were for the time included with those from West Friesland). This petition suggests that some in the refugee community might have been upset with the previous arrangement, feeling that their region was under-represented or even neglected in matters of poor relief. Such perceptions could create tensions and rivalries, especially when communication networks from home were so important among the exiles. Moreover, Pastor Balck requested that the deacons be instructed to require recipients to present a holy certificate from their home church, to ensure that the deacons assisted no 'hypocrites and rogues through whom the congregation may come into trouble'. This was a common problem experienced by exile churches: since such payments were a drain on the community's limited finances, there were even serious attempts in Reformed synods to ensure that the exile churches were supporting genuinely poor 'brothers' rather than mere vagabonds surviving on their alms.

The problem had recently been stated at the National Synod of Paris in 1565:

---

[87] Fehler, 'Social Welfare', pp. 354, notes 61–2, 524–32.
[88] KRP, pp. 277f (1 May 1567).

that abuses committed by divers Vagrants may be prevented, who wander up and down with Attestations from Ministers whereof they serve themselves at all times and places, shamelessly begging from the Churches and thereby robbing God's true poor of their necessary relief. This assembly adviseth Ministers for time to come, rarely to give such Attestations, and when they do, to none but those who upon their particular knowledge are assured to be Persons of true Godliness, and of an upright Conscience, and groaning under pressing Necessities.

The Emden Synod itself took up this issue in 1571, setting down detailed guidelines and requiring attestations 'to reduce the heavy burdens of the churches, which daily increase from the fickleness of those who move so quickly from place to place and who, on the pretext that they are needy faithful, appropriate necessary alms which are intended for the household of faith'. Like Emden's *fremdlingen* deacons, the Genevan Bourse française also dealt with issue of attestations for recipients.[89]

Balck's second point would require that the deacons make a written list of the wealth and assets of the Dutch refugees – by individual name – so that the *fremdlingen* deacons could collect alms appropriately.[90] Third, he requested that the new deacons meet together weekly with their ministers (that is, the exile ministers like Balck himself) and elders to discuss problems. The Emden consistory cheerfully approved the first two suggestions and praised them, but understandably balked at the third: the creation of a refugee consistory. In addition to concerns about the potential threat to their own authority over religious affairs in the city, the consistory also realised the political implications of giving the Dutch refugees too much influence or recognition during the Dutch Revolt, when Emden and East Frisia had supposedly claimed neutrality: 'the brothers find [this suggestion] troublesome on account of our counts, who indeed greatly fear the Burgundians'. Emden's consistory granted, however, that 'we could certainly suffer it, that the exile brothers come together in the emergency of the poor' to discuss poor relief problems within their community.[91]

Discussions took place with the city magistrates during the following week, and the next consistory meeting, on 8 May, opened with a

---

[89] J. Quick (ed.), *Synodicon in Gallia Reformata*, I, 60, 73, 76, 117, 137, 192, 349; 'Die Akten der Synode der niederländischen Kirchen zu Emden', ed. J. Goeters (Neukirchen, 1971), pp. 44–51; Jeannine Olson, *Calvin and Social Welfare* (Selinsgrove, 1989), p. 139.

[90] Note that there is no record of any such contributors' roll for the local *haussitzenden* deacons as was the practice in the Reformed city of Nîmes; Raymond Mentzer, 'Organisational Endeavour and Charitable Impulse in Sixteenth-Century France: the Case of Protestant Nîmes', *French History*, 5 (1991), p. 17.

[91] KRP, p. 278.

'command from the Burgermeister and Council' that a list be compiled of 'what people with good zeal and conscience, in this great advance from various lands, may come here because of religion'. Such a registration of legitimate refugees would, according to the city council, make it easier to recognise the others and reduce 'danger' to the city. Taking the opportunity of the magistracy's mandate, the consistory instructed the refugee community to carry out what was, in effect, Pastor Balck's first suggestion. In order to better serve the poor, 'two [men] in each nation' were to be chosen to make a register of all the devout refugees, based either on personal knowledge or the presentation of a membership certificate. A copy of the list would be given to the Burgermeisters and city council. Yet, this did not go as far as the leaders of the Dutch community desired. To preserve the integrity of their congregations, they wanted unregistered refugees ordered out of town. The consistory told the exile leaders that that was not the magistrates' purpose in compiling the register; the city leaders wanted to have the list only in case of future unrest, not to carry out expulsions solely upon religious grounds.[92]

The refugee community had in the meantime rounded out their diaconate with two additional deacons, bringing the total back up to eight.[93] The five 'old' deacons continued in their service. Pastor Balck's first proposal contained two concerns regarding the selection of deacons: first, that enough deacons be in service to provide adequate charity and, second, that the principle of 'two from every nation' be maintained in selecting the composition of the diaconate. The issue of congregational election of the deacons had previously been discussed in 1565 regarding Lauwrens de Vos so the suggestion that the congregations themselves should 'choose' was not new.[94] Nor did this reorganisation create a clean slate of new deacons. This is a common misreading of Balck's proposal that 'the new arrivals should themselves elect two deacons from each of the "nations" represented among the new arrivals'. Assuming that the previous deacons were discharged, and eight new deacons selected, Pettegree concludes, 'The reorganisation of the diaconate was the most radical departure from established practices ... prompted by the refugee influx of 1567.'[95] On the contrary, when investigating the continuity of the *fremdlingen* deacons through this period of reorganisation, it becomes clear that the new refugees did not want a total revamping of the diaconate with *new* deacons (they kept

---

[92] Ibid., p. 278 (8 May 1567).
[93] *Fremdlingen I*, fol. 156v.
[94] KRP, p. 202; see Chapter 4 above.
[95] Pettegree, *Emden*, pp. 152–3.

all their old ones). Rather, they were interested in ensuring that when new deacons were selected, each 'nation' would be represented. Moreover, missing from the claim of a 'radical departure from established practices' is any mention of the real administrative changes that *were* instituted at this time: in collection procedures, length of service and training, for instance. The refugee leaders were most interested in an adequate workforce and a fair provincial representation among the deacons.

Yet even with a full complement of deacons, the *fremdlingen* diaconate was probably incapable of collecting donations sufficient for the influx of refugees. Fault could not be placed entirely on the personnel or their inexperience. Indeed, three of the eight deacons had already administered their offices for several years: Jacop Payen since late 1558, and Jan Noorman and Willem Bastink since 1561. None the less, questions about the ability of the *fremdlingen* diaconate to handle the current crisis effectively plagued the consistory for some time.

The consistory's subsequent discussions in the 8 May meeting turned to the practical issue of providing adequate alms for a refugee population bulging with new arrivals. What should be the new manner of administration over the refugee poor? How could enough money be collected? New administrative methods for the *fremdlingen* diaconate needed to be devised and the deacons trained in the practical operation of these methods. The consistory mandated a new method of bookkeeping by the *fremdlingen* deacons. In effect, this decision followed Pastor Balck's second suggestion from the previous week's meeting. Each of the eight men chosen by the 'four nations' was instructed to circulate diligently among his compatriots, making a list of each name and noting their wealth.[96] This scheme portends the implementation of regular *freiwillige schattunghen* (voluntary assessments) among the Dutch refugees living in Emden to support the charitable activities of the *fremdlingen* deacons. In addition to the individual donations in the alms-box and testaments which the deacons continued to receive, the account books reveal bi-yearly collections from the refugees based on their wealth. Although they were called 'voluntary', they amounted to a tax paid by the wealthier refugees to the deacons of their province. From this point on, the deacons of the foreign poor would take a much more organised and aggressive stance toward the collection of alms.

To facilitate a successful new, aggressive alms campaign, the consistory instituted the practical training of the *fremdlingen* deacons. They suggested that four of the eight *fremdlingen* deacons should work with the

---

[96] KRP, pp. 278f (8 May 1567).

local deacons.[97] This 'on-the-job training' for the more inexperienced of the *fremdlingen* deacons would be carried out 'temporarily, in this [time of] distress'. At a special gathering of 'all nations of the foreigners' and the Emden church leaders on 28 May, they determined how 'to serve the poor with the most suitable [methods]'. After consideration of all suggestions, the consistory decided that the local deacons could best help the *fremdlingen* deacons deal with the practical problem of collecting enough alms to support the flood of refugees. For 'the first time' one deacon from each of the Dutch 'nations' should accompany 'our deacons' in their collections. In this way they would learn how best 'to exhort everyone to rich alms'.

These early attempts to assess collections according to 'nation' were intended to increase the efficiency of collections made by the *fremdlingen* deacons. Beginning in mid-1567, the *fremdlingen* deacons started holding *freiwillige schattinghen* approximately every six to eight months.[98] These special contributions from each 'nation' generally made up between 35 and 50 per cent of the deacons' yearly revenues, depending on whether one or two collections were held in a given year. The deacons did little at this time, however, to modify the existing method of distributing charity to the poor refugees.

The new emphasis on recording separate contributions according to the individual provinces did not extend to the distribution of charity. Although the deacons collected a relatively large proportion of their income from exiles identified with specific provinces, the money was then placed in the general fund for the *fremdlingen* poor, and distinctions were not made among the recipients based on their place of origin in the Netherlands. In only about one-quarter of the cases did the bookkeeper even identify the origin of the poor relief recipients. The deacon in charge was still responsible for all the disbursements necessary during his period of service, whether the recipients were from his province or not. Thus the reorganisation according to province was intended to be a method by which the deacons could increase the size of the contributions which they received, not as a method to differentiate between recipients.

This new method of collection, even with the collaborative work of the local deacons in 'exhorting richly to alms', did not immediately resolve the financial crisis facing the *fremdlingen* deacons. If anything, circumstances got worse for the refugee deacons during the next several months. Disputes arose within the refugee community over the

---

[97] 8 and 28 May 1567. For alternative readings of the 8 May consistory text, see Fehler, 'Social Welfare', p. 360, note 76.

[98] Fehler, 'Social Welfare', p. 361, note 78; for a breakdown of recorded *schattinghen* (1568–74), see p. 362; compare pp. 524–32.

collection of alms. The exile ministers of the Antwerp congregation, Isebrand Balck and George Wybo, so angered their congregation during the collection of alms in October 1567 (perhaps regarding the new *freiwillige schattinghen*) that the Emden consistory had to arrange a public reconciliation in which the two ministers were ordered to apologise before a gathering of 'all men of their congregation'. Interestingly, the two elders who brought the incident to the awareness of the consistory and oversaw the reconciliation were former *fremdlingen* deacons turned elders.[99] Turmoil continued among the exiles from Brabant. A number of unspecified complaints from the 'Brabanters' prompted the consistory to consider the election of new deacons: 'two from the Brabanters, two from the Flemish, two from the oldest *fremdlingen*'. The source of the Brabanters' complaints is not recorded, but the consistory felt in this instance that the current service should continue 'without respect to the grievances about which those from Brabant protest'. Neither do we know if the Brabanters were calling for supplemental deacons or for replacement deacons.[100] At least regarding the question of a new election, the consistory apparently thought that the refugees had had their chance of new elections back in May when the church council had suggested them.

And the refugee crisis continued. In spite of the new revenue collection procedures and their third *schattinghe* collection (May 1568) in a year, the *fremdlingen* deacons protested to the consistory in July 1568 about the problems stemming from the daily onslaught of refugees for whom they must provide. They complained about both their workload and their growing deficit: the problems were falling too hard upon the shoulders of the *fremdlingen* deacons, 'the longer, the harder'.[101] Representatives from the refugees agreed to solutions for this two-pronged problem. First, they decided that each 'nation' should elect two new deacons to work alongside the current deacons, thus doubling the workforce. Second, they assented to a short-term advance of money from 'each nation ... in the meantime, until a general collection can occur'.

Over the course of the next two months, each of the four 'nations' offered loans to the *fremdlingen* deacons.[102] These advances from the exile 'nations' helped ease the burden on the deacons until the next *schattinghe* was authorised in November. But this extraordinary measure did not resolve the deficit, and as the deacons distributed charity to the incoming poor refugees, they were still forced to use their own

---

[99] KRP, pp. 289ff (30 October; 6, 13, 20 and 24 November 1567).
[100] Ibid., p. 299 (26 January 1568).
[101] Ibid., p. 318 (19 July 1568).
[102] *Fremdlingen I*, fols 194v, 195v, 197v, 200.

personal resources to make ends meet during their periods of service as deacon in charge. By the time of the November 1568 *schattinghe* collection, the diaconate was almost 700 gulden in the red. Of this deficit, 11 deacons themselves had advanced 62.1 per cent of the funds, 21.4 per cent came from the four 'nations', and four private individuals (one of whom was also a deacon who had earlier personally advanced money) made small loans from their business which financed 16.5 per cent of the *fremdlingen* deacons' debt.[103] While the 650 gulden raised in the November 1568 *schattinghe* – plus a 50-gulden gift from the congregations in England in December – allowed the diaconate to repay most of this 700 gulden debt, it did not leave any surplus funds to finance the subsequent charitable activities of the deacons.[104] On 20 December 1568, the consistory agreed to circulate a letter to the 'godly pastors' in the neighbouring villages asking for a charitable donation to Emden's poor, 'to halt the manifold poverty with which the city is ferociously oppressed'. Emden's church planned to hold a 'day of fasting and prayer' on 9 January, and requested that 'all the godly, true preachers in the territory … exhort their kind-hearted, godly parishioners' for prayers 'for the church's difficult afflictions' on that day. Although the amounts collected were not large (small amounts of money with meat, butter, beans, and even half a goose), this appeal received responses from a number of villages around East Frisia in January and February 1569. The pastor in Osteel wrote a compassionate letter to the consistory stating his intention to hold a collection to help support 'the great distress of the poor, suffering, exiled poor – the sorrow of God' who arrive daily in Emden with nothing or little of their goods. (Unfortunately, no record survives of this collection ever being sent to Emden's *fremdlingen* deacons.)[105] By May 1569 the *fremdlingen* deacons bemoaned a 500-gulden deficit and asked that the three Emden ministers accompany the deacons on their next collection rounds 'in order heartily to exhort the people to charitable alms-giving' and that the minister offer exhortations after the weekly catechism lessons as well.[106] The consistory authorised the collection with the accompaniment of the three ministers and three elders. And a week later the deacons appealed again to the consistory, saying that their deficit had increased another 60 or 70 gulden.[107]

---

[103] Ibid., fol. 200.

[104] Ibid., fol. 200v.

[105] KRP, p. 333 (20 and 27 December); *Fremdlingen II*, fols 3–5; ArchGK, Rep. 320A, no. 78 (printed in Fehler, 'Social Welfare', p. 523).

[106] KRP, p. 348 (9 May 1569).

[107] Ibid., p. 350 (16 May 1569). Publication of an upcoming collection for the poor of the 'household of faith' was ordered on 30 May; ibid., p. 351. It is not clear if the consistory somehow tried to consolidate the two collections which would take place

The decision on 19 July 1568 to elect additional deacons had more lasting effects on the operations of the diaconate than the previous short-term loans. It constitutes the first reorganisation of the distribution apparatus of the *fremdlingen* diaconate of which we have record. Now, for the first time, the number of *fremdlingen* deacons was increased.[108] The size of the diaconate was officially doubled to 16, or four deacons from each of the specified provinces (Holland, Flanders, Brabant and West Friesland). The election of the eight deacons took place on 4 August 1568, though one had to withdraw and be replaced less than three weeks later due to marital problems.[109]

With this increase in size came a number of practical changes in the manner in which the *fremdlingen* diaconate administered and distributed poor relief, changes that were not discussed before the consistory but which show up in the account books of the deacons. At the same time that the diaconate was expanded, the rotation as deacon in charge was modified from monthly to half-monthly. Beginning in August 1568, the deacon in charge oversaw the diaconate's operations for only half a month.[110] From the surviving accounts, the total monthly collections after the change to half-monthly appear to be 20–30 per cent less than before the change. Perhaps more frequent appearances of a deacon with an alms-box caused people to make smaller donations. This reduction in the period of service as deacon in charge corresponded to a reduction in his responsibilities. While he still oversaw the diaconate's finances during his service, extraordinary disbursements by other deacons occurred much more frequently than before. With additional deacons in the field, they could more effectively locate those in need and evaluate their circumstances. The deacon in charge would then reimburse any other deacon who gave out aid to a needy refugee. Of course, the deacon in charge was still responsible for the deficits which accrued during his period of service, including the expenditures of other deacons, so he must have attempted to maintain supervision of the activities of all the deacons. One assumes that when a deacon gave out alms of which the deacon in charge did not approve, he would not be reimbursed.

Undoubtedly, communication networks among refugees from the same homeland continued to play a vital role in bringing the needy to the

---

around the same time. The *fremdlingen* deacons held their *schattinghe* on 1 July 1569; *Fremdlingen II*, fol. 8; Toorenenbergen, *Diaconie der Vreemdelingen*, p. 14.

[108] Fehler, 'Social Welfare', p. 367, notes 90–91.

[109] KRP, p. 319, 321 (2, 3 and 23 August).

[110] For instance, *Fremdlingen I*, fols 233–33v. The rotation was modified slightly in 1572, going from half-monthly (24 periods per year) to bi-weekly (26 periods per year); see *Fremdlingen II*, after fol. 260.

eyes of the deacons. Although accounts of charitable disbursements were never kept on the basis of separate expenditures to different provinces, the deacons must have worked primarily among the exiles of their 'nation'.[111] It was these local networks that they knew best. Unlike the *haussitzenden* deacons, who would become familiar with the residents of a certain neighbourhood of the town, the *fremdlingen* deacons were dependent upon the word of mouth of their compatriots to keep track of the ever-growing, ever-changing and often-transient refugee community in Emden; deaths and turnover among the deacons could strain the established communication networks. The crisis created in 1571 by the deaths of a number of deacons was magnified by the fact that by August there were only ten active *fremdlingen* deacons, none from West Friesland. Moreover, three *fremdlingen* deacons became elders in December.[112] While a deficiency of deacons would pose a problem for the workload of the *fremdlingen* diaconate, a complete absence of deacons representing one province meant that the poor of that 'nation' would have difficulty receiving effective support. Thus, on 10 August 1571, with the deacons' dire need of help, the consistory found it necessary to order an election for replacement deacons.[113]

These major reorganisational steps not only affected the administrative procedures of the *fremdlingen* deacons; they also influenced the manner in which alms were distributed. By disbursing half-monthly stipends to the 'regular' poor relief recipients, the deacons were able to provide a bit more supervision of the poor community. Monthly stipends required the deacons to give the recipient a larger sum of money or other provision. Now, the deacons would see the recipients more frequently and could evaluate their need every two weeks. In practice, however, one wonders if the shorter period of service might have caused the deacons in charge to be less familiar with the particular circumstances of the regular poor. Without the time to make several rounds through the city, the deacon in charge might find it easier simply to repeat the same disbursement amounts provided by the previous deacon in charge in the account book. Indeed, the regular relief rolls – especially those after 1569 – show a remarkably stable level of disbursements from period to period, for a given recipient. The early rolls of the late 1550s and early 1560s, when organisation was more haphazard, seem

---

[111] All expenditures were listed in the account books under the current deacon in charge regardless of the 'nationality' or home town of the recipient.

[112] KRP, p. 427 (3 Dec 1571).

[113] Records of an actual election do not exist. One must have occurred, however, since eight new deacons appear in the sources after February 1572, bringing the total number back up to 16; see *Fremdlingen II*, after fol. 260.

to reveal a much higher level of variation from month to month in the disbursements to an individual recipient.

Although no set length of term in office was established, the increased size of the diaconate brought increased turnover among the deacons. Unlike the first couple of generations of *fremdlingen* deacons who frequently served for extended periods, most of those deacons elected after 1568 served more limited terms. Deaths, elections to serve as elder, and one case of removal from office were the only cited reasons for turnover among the *fremdlingen* deacons. Another plausible explanation for the more frequent disappearance of the later deacons could be the desire to return home to the Netherlands; returning home increased especially after 1572. Nevertheless, with the exception of the disciplinary removal from office of Jooris van Meerbeke due to drunkenness, there is no indication that a *fremdlingen* deacon could not serve in this office as long as he wanted.[114]

The sources provide a fairly full picture of the institutional developments of Emden's relief agencies, but as administrative documents, they are less useful in depicting the poor themselves. Still, however, we can at least get a sense of the types of poor relief offered by Emden's deacons. The deacons – at least the *haussitzenden* and *fremdlingen* for whom detailed expenditure records survive – provided the broadest range of relief services of any of the social welfare institutions in Emden. For those receiving regular relief on a weekly, bi-weekly or monthly basis, their support consisted primarily of a cash stipend. Generally the stipend would be supplemented once or twice a year with a rent payment by the deacons directly to the landlord of the poor person or family. Additionally, both diaconates, *haussitzenden* and *fremdlingen*, frequently acquired through purchase (or sometimes donation) large supplies of cloth, rye, peat moss, even butter. The cloth was used for clothing and for burial shrouds for the poor. The deacons frequently contracted out to specific tailors or bakers who would manufacture finished products for distribution as is indicated in contracts found throughout the deacons' account books.

In addition to provision for the 'regular' poor, the deacons gave necessary aid according to the specific emergency of the individual.

---

[114] Jooris van Meerbeke was involved in numerous disputes with the consistory before his election to *fremdlingen* deacon in 1568; his complaints included criticisms of the diaconate; KRP, pp. 84, 97, 101f, 111f, 120, 180f, 184f, 188f, 203, 448ff, 458f, 469ff (24 April, 31 July, 10 and 18 December 1559; 6 May, 16 September 1560; 28 February, 13 and 27 March, 19 June, 3 and 17 July, 7 August, 27 November, 4 December 1564; 2 April 1565; 2, 6, 16 and 20 June, 15, 22 and 29 September 1572; 10 and 16 February 1573). He was removed from office on 22 February 1573 (ibid., p. 471), and he does not appear in the deacons' account book after September 1572.

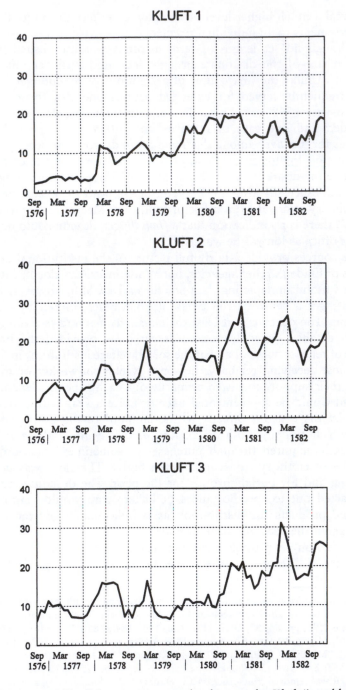

5.3 Average weekly disbursements to under-deacons, by *Kluft* (in gulden)

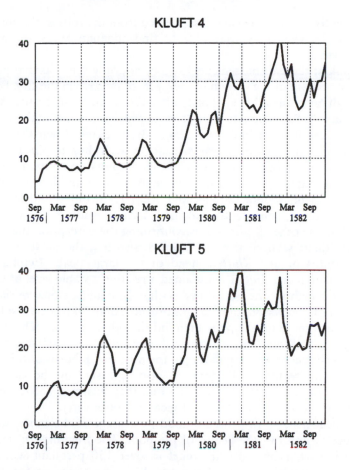

KLUFT 4

KLUFT 5

Shoes, clothing and work tools (for instance, shovels, saws or spinning tools) were given as extraordinary relief to the poor who approached with special requests.[115] In times of sickness or unemployment, many individuals or families not normally in need of assistance, but none the less on the edge of poverty, received temporary assistance or help with rent payments or private loans. As the accompanying graphs illustrate (Figure 5.3), the amounts of relief provided by the deacons generally decreased during the summer months when work opportunities were more plentiful. In the case of the *fremdlingen* poor, whose 'regular' relief rolls still survive, we can see that most single men as well as many of the families with surviving fathers, even those who received relief

---

[115] For instance, work implements: *Fremdlingen II*, fols 50, 228, 235, 328.

consistently for several years, disappeared from the rolls in the summer, presumably when they were able to find adequate work to support themselves.

A look at these disbursements exposes not only this seasonal pattern of provision but also a certain topography of poverty in the city. For the period of September 1576 (shortly after the creation of the five *Klufts*) to January 1583, adequate records exist which allow an analysis of the expenditures in each individual *Kluft*. By breaking down the regular expenditures of the *haussitzenden* deacons according to *Kluft*, we can obtain a glimpse of the approximate topography of poverty in the city, at least noting the parts of town where the highest and lowest percentage of 'residential' poor were located. *Kluft* 1, the oldest and wealthiest section of town, consistently had the lowest expenditures – sometimes far below the other *Klufts* – thus confirming the perception that it was the wealthiest section of town. *Kluft* 1 also had the most consistent expenditures of any *Kluft*; instead of the large peaks (winter) and troughs (summer), *Kluft* 1 maintained a relatively stable level of expenditures throughout the period and with only small seasonal variations. For most of this period, the deacons of *Klufts* 5 and 4 (the new suburbs) spent much more on the poor than did the other deacons. The gradual emergence of *Kluft* 4 at the top of the expenditure chart suggests the later development and populating of the northern suburbs of town after the southern section of Faldern. As also suggested by the Gasthaus's moves to the edge of town in 1505 and then again in 1557, Emden's periphery was home to the highest incidence of poverty.

The deacons also dispensed a good percentage of their expenditures in order to improve the health of the poor. The *fremdlingen* deacons, for their part, provided extra relief to over 150 pregnant women or those in childbirth between 1569 and 1575; for those on the regular relief rolls, an additional child usually brought an accompanying increase in the amount of the monthly stipend. Both sets of deacons apparently contracted out to a doctor and a pharmacist for their services for the sick.[116] In the situation where one of their poor became sick, a deacon would bring the doctor to the sick person and authorise his

---

[116] For a sixteenth-century version of the guild ordinances of the barber–surgeon guild in Emden, see Ernst Friedlaender, 'Eine Ostfriesische Gildenrolle des 16. Jahrhunderts', *EJb*, 1, 2 (1873), pp. 67–75; Friedlaender dated the ordinance from about 1545, but it must have been written toward the end of the century, probably in 1595 when most of Emden's guilds revised their ordinances. On the roll of apothecaries in Emden, see Louis Hahn, *Emdens Apotheken und Apotheker in fünf Jahrhunderten* (Abhandlungen und Vorträge zur Geschichte Ostfrieslands, XXXI, Aurich, 1954); for East Frisia more generally, see Heinrich Buurman, *Die Apotheken Ostfrieslands von den Anfängen bis zur Gründung des Deutschen Reiches 1871* (Aurich, 1990).

treatment. In the account books of each diaconate are expenditures in which a doctor or a pharmacist was reimbursed for his treatment or 'cure' of poor individuals and for the medicines involved.[117] While most of the reimbursements were for individual treatments, one complete 'doctor's bill' survives from about 1578.[118] A variety of treatments was paid for by the *haussitzenden* deacons as they provided poor relief. In each instance, in order to receive reimbursement, the doctor had to identify the deacon who had taken him to the sick person. The *haussitzenden* deacons, moreover, maintained a doctor on salary to care for the poor. The yearly salary paid by the deacons was 31 gulden in 1578, but had risen to 100 gulden in 1582.[119] In addition to the salary, the deacons reimbursed the doctor for many of the expenses he incurred while treating the poor, although the amount of reimbursements decreased with the 1582 rise in salary. The *haussitzenden* diaconate took advantage of having a barber/surgeon among its ranks as deacon (and did not consider it a conflict of interest) and hired Master Gerdt Bartscher to care for 'the poor in their miserable sicknesses'. Thus, while Gerdt was an under-deacon, actively involved in the weekly relief distributions in *Kluft* 1, he also served as the diaconate's salaried doctor, at least between 1578 and 1581, and he received frequent reimbursements for his care of the sick. Supplementing the doctor's care and the visits of the deacons themselves, the deacons sometimes paid poor relief recipients to visit and watch over the sick, thereby, in a small way, creating some work for those on their rolls.[120]

Although the deacons, as the official administrators of the poor, were men, there were opportunities for women to be involved in the organised relief of the poor, generally in the roles of midwife, wet-nurse and foster mother. In cases of pregnancy, the deacons often paid for a midwife to assist a poor woman in giving birth.[121] We saw earlier the case of Anne Jeronimus where the deacons suggested midwifery as a way for a poor woman to support herself. Another important part of the deacons' activities was the support of children without parents. Such support included payments to women to wet-nurse infants who had come into the deacons' care. For instance, in May 1571, the *haussitzenden* deacons paid Marri Kornillis 2.5 gulden per month to provide for a small foundling infant 'by the breast'. In this case, a problem arose when the mother of the infant appeared in Emden to

---

[117] For instance, ArchGK no. 1118, p. 43; no. 3194, pp. 63, 64, 67.
[118] Transcribed in KRP, pp. 698–9.
[119] ArchGK no. 3194, pp. 22, 89, 161, 173, 205, 232.
[120] For instance, ArchGK no. 3194, pp. 170, 176.
[121] Ibid., p. 85.

claim the child; the dispute was heard by the Burgermeister, and when the woman claimed she could provide witnesses that it was her baby, she was given custody. Unfortunately, no record survives regarding any admonition or punishment of the mother because of the abandonment.[122]

Moreover, the deacons tried not to resort to giving orphans over to the Gasthaus for relief, but rather relied on other alternatives and provided care themselves for the children. Numerous members of the congregation – primarily, though not exclusively, women – took in orphans and foundlings as foster parents, and they received a stipend and the necessary supplies from the deacons. Sometimes the deacons provided foster care for the temporary support of a child whose parents were in poverty at the time.[123] Lammert Cornellyson's wife, for example, was paid 20 gulden a year to take care of an orphan who had been in the Lazarus-House.[124] Some women took in several children. Lubbert Harthower's wife received frequent reimbursements and stipends for the support of orphans.[125] Caring for orphans and providing short-term housing for the poor could also be a means of support for the provider: frequently mixed with the deacons' alms stipend to 'Ziwer Assweri's widow', for instance, was reimbursement for the support of orphans and others.[126] The Dutch refugee Willem Maes fell into poverty and was unable to support his children. The *fremdlingen* deacons in this event provided a regular stipend for him and four of his children; his fifth child was maintained by the deacons in a foster home. Whether or not it was Willem's choice to place his child in foster care is not indicated, but his child continued to receive foster care for several years. Finally, the deacons paid for food and freight costs for Willem's travel to England.[127] During this time the *fremdlingen* deacons recorded a number of expenditures to refugees to emigrate, particularly to England, Hamburg, Cologne and Wesel.[128]

Sometimes attempts to provide foster care from within the congregation failed, and children had to be placed in the Gasthaus. The deacons'

---

[122] ArchGK no. 1117, p. 44.

[123] The account books of the *haussitzenden* deacons provide scores of examples, for instance, ArchGK no. 1117, pp. 42–5, 50, 53, 54; no. 1118, pp. 23, 24v, 25, 26, 49, 50; no. 3194, pp. 72, 83, 172.

[124] ArchGK no. 1118, pp. 29v, 30.

[125] E.g. ArchGK no. 1117, pp. 55, 56; no. 1118, pp. 23v, 25, 26v, 27v, 28v, 44, 46.

[126] E.g. ArchGK no. 3194, pp. 6, 27, 37, 52, 95, 100, 110, 132, 152, 167, 171, 178, 191, 200, 238, 258.

[127] *Fremdlingen II*, fols 26, 96, 170.

[128] Compare the activities of the Genevan Bourse française in providing aid to encourage refugees to move on; Olson, *Social Welfare*, pp. 131–2.

accounts record frequent payments to the Gasthaus for the maintenance of those placed there. After paying for foster care initially, the deacons paid to place Kornellis Sackedraeger's child in the Gasthaus, but it is not clear if they maintained him after that.[129] Various agreements between the deacons and the Gasthaus must have existed to regulate the care of orphans and the responsibility for the costs involved, but none survive from the sixteenth century. Did the deacons try to provide for their orphans by means of foster care because it was less expensive than the Gasthaus, or was the Gasthaus unwilling to accept responsibility for orphans who had been in the care of the deacons? There is evidence of some cost sharing between the deacons and the Gasthaus, but the first surviving report of any complete cost-sharing plan dates from the late seventeenth century.[130] By this time, it had been decided that the Gasthaus would provide the full costs of orphans, but children for whom one parent still survived or for whom the whereabouts of their parents was in question were called 'one-third part children' (*derde parts kinderen*). In the case of these children, the costs were to be shared between all the poor relief agencies: one-third by the Gasthaus, one-third by the *haussitzenden* deacons, one-sixth by the *fremdlingen* deacons, and one-sixth by the Shippers' Brotherhood.[131]

Education and training was seen as a vital component of poor relief – as already mandated in the 1529 Church Ordinance, attempts were made to prevent future poverty. Thus the deacons provided not only for the material well-being of the poor, but also sent the children to school or apprenticed them with craft masters. The account books contain frequent expenditures to one schoolmaster or another to provide for the instruction of poor children, as well as occasional 'school-money' paid by the deacons for the continued teaching of a child whose parents were temporarily unable to pay for school. The rector of the Latin school received a regular salary from the deacons for his instruction of poor students.[132] In one instance, the deacons dealt with 49 poor youths who had come from outside Emden without their parents: some were apparently orphans, but most had at least one surviving parent. The deacons sent letters to the youths' home towns to verify their family information. In the meantime, however, they sought a stable residence in Emden

---

[129] ArchGK no. 1118, pp. 44v, 45v. For some of the deacons' payments to the Gasthaus: ArchGK no. 3194, pp. 39, 46, 108, 128, 183, 250.

[130] For example, in 1581, the Gasthaus and the *haussitzenden* deacons each paid half (5 gulden) of the cost of placing an orphan into an apprenticeship; ibid., no. 3194, p. 232.

[131] Ibid., no. 3052.

[132] Ibid., no. 3194, pp. 102, 106.

for each youth, provided many with training in a craft or instruction from a schoolmaster, and placed a few orphans in the Gasthaus.[133]

The deacons' services ranged remarkably from aiding childbirth and wet-nursing to caring for the elderly who could no longer provide for themselves, to burial of the poor who had died. Just how effective the deacons were in providing their relief is another question. Certainly, various restrictions were placed upon the recipients of the relief. The lifestyle of each recipient was open to frequent examination by the deacons, and the standards of proper behaviour – and to a certain extent, proper beliefs – were expected to be met as a precondition for poor relief. Of all Emden's poor relief institutions, the *haussitzenden* deacons provided relief to the broadest range of recipients. Although their relief was intended primarily for the 'residential' poor in Emden, they did provide relief in extraordinary circumstances to foreign poor, travelling students, and the like.[134] It is not clear if the deacons administered any of the old Gotteskammern, but the *haussitzenden* deacons also maintained several apartments in which they could provide housing for the poor. They supported a man who lived 'in the poor apartment (*armen kamer*) behind the *bodelie*' and by the 1580s they owned the Lazarus-House; they spent money both on inhabitants and repairs.[135]

The charitable work of the deacons was eased to some extent by the Clementiner Shippers' Brotherhood, which focused its activities around Emden's harbours. Having survived the Reformation, this former confraternity continued its activities as a fraternal brotherhood of shippers and merchants. The statutes of the 'Clementiner' had been revised, however, according to the Police Ordinance of 1545, so that its activities were now directed to 'the use and profit of God's poor'.[136] The overt religious activities, such as the yearly masses and the requiems for dead members, had been removed from the ordinances, but the Brotherhood still maintained its yearly banquet and mandated attendance at a

---

[133] (January 1575) ibid., no. 1117, pp. 171–6. Unfortunately, neither the responses from the letters nor the ultimate fate of the youth was preserved in any of the surviving sources.

[134] For example, ibid., no. 1118, p. 40; no. 3194, pp. 203, 245. For instance, the *haussitzenden* poor funds provided money for a boy who had been in the Gasthaus to travel to Danzig and for two men 'imprisoned by the Turks', ibid., p. 29; no. 3194, pp. 151, 231.

[135] It is not clear if the deacons administered any of the old Gotteskammern. ibid., no. 1118, pp. 28, 29v; no. 3194, pp. 78, 122, 170, 233; no. 3001, at end of book (after Testament section).

[136] The earliest surviving revised ordinances of the brotherhood are from a printed copy in 1630 (by the printer 'Helwigen Kallenbach tho Emden'), StaE, I. Reg., no. 425; it is reprinted in *OUB* no. 1421, pp. 435f, and in Sehling (ed.), *Kirchenordnungen*, pp. 508f, note 40. From the language and the descriptions of activities, the ordinances were probably relatively unchanged (if at all) from those of the mid-sixteenth century.

member's funeral.[137] If a member did not attend either of these functions, he or she would be fined one 'dalder' to 'the best of the poor' – if a member was not home at the time of the funeral then 'the wife or someone out of the house was bound to go with [the procession] to the grave'. The social functions and activities of the Brotherhood continued, but the mission was primarily that of a poor relief agency.

The administration of the Clementiners remained the same. Two aldermen (*Oldermannen*) were chosen for life, and four additional administrators (*Schaffer*) served four-year terms in office. The Brotherhood's ordinances added an admonishment to those elected to serve as *Schaffer*: they must not be 'stubborn', they should accept the post with good will, because 'forced service is not pleasant to God', and they should serve the poor remembering what Christ said, 'Whatever you have done to the least of mine, you have done it to me.'[138] The lifetime tenure of the aldermen provided the Brotherhood with stability.[139] All of those who became aldermen had previously held the office of *Schaffer*, although they were not always in the current circle of *Schaffer* at the time of their elections to the aldermanic office.

Shippers and merchants in the Brotherhood pledged to remember the poor in all their business dealings. They would continue to turn the 'Gottespfennig' from their business transactions over to the *Schaffer*, and beyond that, 'each according to his resources' would try to earn as much as possible 'to the profit of the poor'. Beyond exhorting the Brotherhood to remember the poor, the financial duties of the *Schaffer* were primarily to receive the yearly rents and interest payments, though as a security measure, none of the *Schaffer* were to receive any money unless in the presence of at least one other *Schaffer*. Although no account books for the sixteenth century survive, the Clementiner shippers must have had a sizeable amount of capital, especially after the consolidation of St Ann's and Our Lady's assets. During the last half of the sixteenth century more than 100 loan agreements between the Shippers' Brotherhood and individuals survive in the collection of Emden's contracts, making the Brotherhood the most active money-lenders of any of Emden's poor relief institutions.[140]

Added to these revenues were the money and goods donated in testaments. While the Shippers' Brotherhood was listed in testaments

---

[137] ArchGK, I. Reg., no. 425, final article.

[138] StaE, I. Reg., no. 425.

[139] For instance, from 1575 to 1613, no more than five men served in the two alderman positions; see list by Harkenroht in Beninga's *Chronyk*, pp. 405–7; STAA, Dep. 1, Msc., no. 41, II, 276–9; StaE, Prot. I, no. 7, p. 172.

[140] Emder Kontraktenprotokolle (EKP) in STAA, Rep. 234.

less frequently than the *haussitzenden* or Gasthaus poor, a number of surviving wills left money or goods such as butter to the Shippers' poor. Yet most of these testaments divided their bequests between the Shippers and either (or both) the Gasthaus or *haussitzenden* agencies; only about half a dozen individuals left the charitable portion of their testament solely to the Shipper poor.[141] When Master Theus Timmermann disinherited his two daughters with 'immensely moving reasons', he needed a way to establish a trust for his grandchildren. He turned to the Shipper Brotherhood, which served as an active loan bank. The four *Schaffers* should receive any money from his testament which would normally go to his daughters and hold it until his grandchildren reached maturity. He did, however, specify that the daughters could receive the yearly 'fruits' of the trust fund.[142]

A final source of income came from donations of money, grain and other supplies which foreign shippers sometimes left for the poor upon their successful arrival in Emden. Money-pouches for the poor hung in the hostels, and shippers would sometimes donate a portion of their freight to the poor 'out of thankfulness for a fortunate journey'. A dispute over the donations from foreign shippers was arbitrated by the consistory in 1591. On 15 February, representatives of the Gasthaus, *haussitzenden* deacons, the Clementiner Shippers and the *fremdlingen* deacons appeared before the consistory, each claiming a portion of these 'thanksgiving' donations to the poor. The consistory ruled that the goods given in general to the poor should be divided in thirds between the Clementiners, the Gasthaus and the *haussitzenden* poor (the *fremdlingen* were to receive only what was donated explicitly by name to them).[143] As the policy was recorded in the 1594 Emden Church Ordinances, the Shippers' Brotherhood could keep for its own poor all the 'white grain' given by the shippers, but the rye and the money from the hostels should be divided in thirds with the other institutions.[144]

Not only administrators of the Clementiners' finances, the *Schaffer* were also to oversee the Brotherhood's poor; specifically they were to help those in the Brotherhood who 'had done good for the poor for some time ... one should help them just like they had previously [helped]

---

[141] For a list of testaments to the Shipper poor, see Fehler, 'Social Welfare', p. 406, note 172.

[142] The testament also made a charitable donation to the poor: a quarter ton of red butter to the *haussitzenden* poor and a quarter ton to the Shipper poor. The original testament was written on 6 February 1588 (EKP 18/590–92); it was slightly revised (though no changes to this grandchildren's 'trust fund' section) on 2 January 1589 (ibid. 18/807–9).

[143] KRP, p. 868.

[144] Sehling (ed.), *Kirchenordnungen*, pp. 509f.

the poor'.[145] The *Schaffer* would provide them with weekly allotments of butter in a bowl (*Schöttel*) and bread on Sunday afternoons.[146] The ordinances also stipulated that the *Schaffer* should make special visitations three or four times a year in order to determine eligibility for relief among those receiving the food from the Brotherhood. If a person was in need, the *Schaffer* should 'let him hold the bowl'; if he is no longer needy, 'one should take the bowl from him and give it to another who is needy'.[147] The assistance provided by the Clementiner *Schaffer* extended beyond the members of the Brotherhood. They also took care of any other homebound people who did not normally receive alms but fell into poverty through sickness or some other occurrence, as well as foreign sea-faring people who had some emergency at sea and landed in Emden or were passing through the city.[148] With these responsibilities, the Shippers' Brotherhood helped to care for the poverty-stricken and encourage order, especially around the harbour portions of town. Since shipping and commerce was Emden's primary industry, these endeavours by the Clementiners were significant in helping to keep the burden of poor relief down among the *haussitzenden* deacons and the Gasthaus.

Unlike the other institutions which provided 'outdoor' relief, the Grain Reserve did not distribute aid to any particular group of poor. The administrators maintained stockpiles of grain but did not personally provide for the poor. In times of grain shortage, the Grain Reserve administrators offered their reserves at 'tolerable' prices to those citizens of Emden who could not afford the high prices. It appears that the utterly poor turned mainly to one of the city's other relief institutions for assistance; the primary recipients of the Grain Reserve's assistance were those in the middle and lower classes who were on the verge of poverty. The Grain Reserve enabled them to endure times of distress without falling into abject poverty.

With the creation of formal statutes in 1565/66, the administrative practices of the Grain Reserve became fixed.[149] Four administrators would oversee the affairs of the Grain Reserve.[150] A regular cycle of elections was also implemented. Each year at Easter, the Grain Reserve would elect two new supervisors and the two longest-serving

---

[145] StaE, I. Reg., no. 425.

[146] From 1594 Church Ordinance, Sehling (ed.), *Kirchenordnungen*, p. 509.

[147] StaE, I. Reg., no. 425.

[148] From the 1594 Church Ordinance, Sehling (ed.), *Kirchenordnungen*, p. 509.

[149] The statutes were established by 'us, the Burgermeisters and city council with the advice of the wealthiest citizens'. The statutes consist of seven Articles and are reprinted in Fehler, 'Social Welfare', pp. 520–22; Helias Loesing, *Geschichte der Stadt Emden* (Emden, 1843), pp. 123–6.

[150] Article 1.

administrators would rotate out of service after their two-year term.[151] Only Emden citizens who contributed to the Grain Reserve could vote for or be elected as an administrator.[152] The four 'old' administrators were obliged to review the accounts with the newly elected supervisors in the presence of some citizens who had contributed to the Grain Reserve.[153] Oversight of the Grain Reserve's accounts was not given to the city or church leadership, only to those involved with this communal initiative. 'One of the oldest administrators' was to keep in his house the Reserve's money chest, for which each of the four administrators would have a key.[154]

The administrators were to provide oversight and stewardship of the stockpiles of grain, which throughout the rest of the century were stored in the old Gasthaus chapel.[155] The statutes established regulations to protect the integrity of the Grain Reserve. First, at least 10 *Lasten* of rye were to be stockpiled in the Reserve at any time. Moreover, as the Grain Reserve improved and grew, it might attempt to handle '20 or 30 Lasten or even more yearly'.[156] Since the Grain Reserve sold its grain to the citizenry only in times of shortage and emergency, a routine had to be established to rotate the stockpiled grain so that it did not spoil. Thus the statutes stipulated that the administrators handle the stockpiled grain 'in a timely fashion and turn it to money'. Here is where the financial savvy of the administrators would be important. In order to prevent damage or losses, the administrators were given authority to sell the Grain Reserve's stockpiles 'to certain merchants', and of course thereafter they were to devote themselves in the most profitable way to filling 'the storehouse with fresh, good rye'.[157]

They were not given unlimited authority, however. A number of speculative practices, with either the reserves or with the finances, were prohibited. A limitation of 'one month approximately', for instance, was placed on the making of loans of either grain or money, and the

---

[151] Article 2. A list of the 'Vorratsherren' exists in a manuscript collection of Emden city and church officials, STAA, Dep. 1, Msc. no. 41, II, 269ff. The list goes back to the elections of 1573 ('soo veele men heeft naeslaen konnen' when the list was compiled in 1739). Therefore, from 1573 onwards the Grain Reserve elected two new administrators virtually every year.

[152] Articles 1, 4 and Conclusion.

[153] Article 3.

[154] Article 7.

[155] Article 5. This was the old location of Gertrude's Gasthaus on the 'new marketplace' before it moved into the former monastery.

[156] Article 3.

[157] Article 5.

administrator himself was to stand as security for the loan: 'everything to the end that the Grain Reserve may be prudently handled to increase and improvement and not to deficit and decrease'.[158]

Of course, prudence did not always guarantee the success of the administrators' policies. Because grain was to be kept in the stockpiles at all times, unanticipated events might cause the value of grain to decrease faster than the administrators could sell off their reserves. For instance, 'it could well be that, after an "expensive time", the grain suddenly faces a great unforeseen drop in price'. Since such an event would lead to 'great damage and losses to the Reserve', the administrators, with the help of the Burgermeisters and city council, should at such times negotiate with the Baker Guild so 'that they take the grain at a fixed price'.[159]

We first see the policies of the Grain Reserve tested during an 'expensive time' in 1565. As the price of grain climbed with the influx of refugees into Emden, the consistory, at the urging of the *fremdlingen* deacons, sent a commission of five to approach the administrators of the Grain Reserve in September to ask 'how much for our poor brothers [can] the congregation actually look forward to' in assistance from the Grain Reserve.[160] The administrators of the Grain Reserve responded that since their stockpiles were as large as they were going to get, they did not want to begin disbursements 'before the greatest distress is at hand'. The Reserve managers feared even greater inflation in grain prices and wanted to protect their supplies against shortfall by keeping their storehouses closed for a while longer. The consistory made clear to the *fremdlingen* that it was not their opinion but that of the Reserve administrators 'that the greatest distress is not yet at hand'. The consistory recognised the current crisis and sought 'to attain enough conciliation against the bitter lingering distress'.[161] Finally, at the end of November, the consistory announced that the 'Grain Reserve of the city poor' was finally distributing its grain: an allotment of rye cost 12 schap, for which 'the common price' was normally 22 schap.[162] In the meantime, before the Grain Reserve opened its stockpiles, the consistory had deemed it necessary on 1 October to call together a meeting 'of all the deacons of the entire city' to work out an appropriate strategy for caring for the poor, in the time of distress; and in order to extend their limited grain resources for the poor the deacons considered on 12 November mixing

---

[158] Article 4.
[159] Article 6.
[160] KRP, p. 216 (17 September 1565).
[161] Ibid. (21 September 1565).
[162] Ibid., p. 221 (26 November 1565).

beans and barley with the rye when they contracted for bread to be baked for the poor.[163]

A similar, yet modified, distribution policy was followed six and a half years later. On 3 March 1572, the four administrators of the Grain Reserve answered the consistory's summons and appeared before them. They stated that they were prepared to disburse their grain at a tolerable price 'to the neediest' – 'as long as the main stockpiles are not lessened'. Those who brought in vouchers from the ministers would be served from the Grain Reserve. However, 'to open the Reserve in general', thought the administrators of the Reserve, would not yet be advisable because they feared still more distress.[164]

As before, the Grain Reserve administrators were slow to open their stockpiles during a time of crisis because they feared a worsening of the situation and wanted to ensure that their supplies would outlast the emergency. Yet the administrators were a bit more accommodating of the consistory than they had been in 1565, allowing the ministers to authorise certain people in great distress access to the Grain Reserve. A possible explanation for this modification of the earlier policy can be found in the composition of the Grain Reserve's administration at the time. Two of the four administrators, Gerdt van Gelder and Jacob Dinclaghe, were former deacons of the *haussitzenden* poor; and Gerdt van Gelder had been one of the five-member delegation appointed by the consistory in 1565 to entreat the Grain Reserve to open its stockpiles.[165] A third member of the Grain Reserve administration, Albert van Haren, served concurrently as an overseer of the Shipper Brotherhood, and was probably sensitive to the demands on those disbursing outdoor relief to the poor.

The combination of deacons, *Schaffer* and Grain Reserve administrators worked to provide almost all of the outdoor relief to the poor in Emden. Although a number of Gotteskammern continued to provide housing to the poor in Emden, the Gasthaus was the primary provider of institutional in-house poor relief. With the expansion of its facilities into the complex of the former Franciscan monastery, the Gasthaus was furthermore able to expand its relief activities and house many more residents, on both a short-term and long-term basis.[166] The Gasthaus

---

[163] Ibid., p. 218, 220.

[164] Ibid., pp. 434f.

[165] Ibid., p. 216 (21 September 1565).

[166] The number of residents that the Gasthaus could house at once remains a mystery. The Gasthaus in Aurich had 19 beds in 1560; Heinrich Reimers, 'Das Auricher Gasthaus im 16. und 17. Jahrhundert', p. 32. The Emden Gasthaus must have had at least twice that space, given the much larger complex and the relatively high number of administrators and workers there (Aurich's Gasthaus was administered by four men and a married

provided long-term care to orphans, the elderly and the mentally ill. Foreign travellers who became ill or were detained in town, due to bad weather, for instance, could also receive short-term assistance in the Gasthaus. The largest category of the Gasthaus's residents were probably orphans and foundlings.

By mid-century, the surviving contracts of the Gasthaus reveal that at least four men administered the finances. Most of the administrators around mid-century served in that position for quite some time, almost all more than ten years, a couple more than twenty years.[167] Only after 1575 did regular yearly elections begin: typically, one or two new administrators were chosen to serve terms of office from roughly four to six years.[168] Between 1566 and 1579, five administrators oversaw the affairs of the Gasthaus. In 1579, two of the current administrators were named aldermen of the Gasthaus, and a new administrator was elected, giving the Gasthaus the administrative board that was described in the 1594 Church Ordinance.[169] Similar to the Shipper Brotherhood, the Gasthaus leadership was made up of four administrators who served roughly four-year terms in office and two aldermen whose appointments were permanent.[170]

The first description of the election procedure of the Gasthaus administrators is provided in the Church Ordinance of 1594. There is no indication that the method described in 1594 was new to the Gasthaus. Following the departure of the longest-serving administrator, the remaining administrators and aldermen chose a successor from among the citizenry of Emden. The vote was conducted with the 'assistance' of the ministers and was ratified by the city council. Thus both the city and the church held rights of supervision of the choice of the administrators

---

couple, the Gasthaus father and mother, who lived in the Gasthaus). Weber, 'Kirche und Gesellschaft', I, 93, note 97, cites a brief analysis of the residents of the Gasthaus in the late eighteenth century in Karl Heinz Bokeloh, 'Emder Wirtschaftsgeschichte 1744–1806. Preußischer Absolutismus der zweiten Hälfte des 18. Jahrhunderts in einer Randprovinz' (Ph.D. thesis, Tübingen, 1984), p. 141. Bokeloh found 133 Gasthaus residents in 1769 and 163 in 1773. Of the 158 individuals housed during 1788, he counted 45 men and women, 30 sick, 2 deserted girls, 8 deserted boys, and 61 orphans.

[167] Fehler, 'Social Welfare', p. 416 note 198.

[168] A list of Gasthaus administrators and aldermen after 1566 exists in STAA, Dep. 1, Msc., no. 41, II, 273–6v. The elections were not yet regular by 1575 since no elections were held in 1576, 1577, 1578, 1584 or 1585.

[169] Sehling (ed.), *Kirchenordnungen*, p. 505.

[170] In reality, the four-year term of office was never as regularly enforced as in the Shippers' Brotherhood. In the last quarter of the sixteenth and the first quarter of the seventeenth centuries, the term of office remained four or five years (sometimes up to seven). By the late 1640s, however, it fluctuated widely once again with terms lasting up to 20 years (perhaps due to turmoil caused by the Thirty Years' War).

as well as of the yearly review of the Gasthaus's accounts.[171] The ministers were also to accompany the administrators in their door-to-door alms collections, which took place three times a year.[172]

The Gasthaus had a more complex organisation than most of the other relief agencies. While the six administrators oversaw the business affairs of the Gasthaus, bought and sold property, and made contracts on its behalf, several additional people carried out the daily activities of the Gasthaus. Earlier, at St Gertrude's Gasthaus, a 'Gasthaus father' managed the daily expenditures, overseeing necessary repairs or handling the purchase of cattle and grain or a butcher's services to provide food for the poor in the Gasthaus. The 1594 Church Ordinance specified the duties of this 'father of the Gasthaus': he was to be an honourable and energetic man, who with his wife would take care of the daily cooking and maintain good supervision of all the residents, making sure that those able to work did so; the 'father' was to report any shortage or defect within the Gasthaus to the administrators who supposedly met three times a week; he was to be the highest authority in the Gasthaus and provide an example of piety and good order to the servants, maids and everyone else in the house.[173]

In addition to the 'Gasthaus father and mother', some other women were involved in the daily operation of the Gasthaus. In a few of the records from the second half of the sixteenth century, women called 'Gasthaus mothers' (*Gastmoeder*) appear in service of the Gasthaus poor. The descriptions of these women and their activities prove that they were, in fact, additional officials of the Gasthaus and not merely the wives of the 'Gasthaus fathers'. As her 1549 testament was notarised, the 'experienced widow Fenne Krachtz' was praised by the administrators of the Gasthaus for having 'served the poor in the Gasthaus sincerely for many years out of Christian love and duty'; she continued that commitment by leaving all remaining goods to the poor in the Gasthaus. Following her death in 1559, she was referred to as 'Fenne Krachtz *Gastmoder*' in a legal settlement between the Gasthaus and her brother's grandson.[174] Whether or not she was a widow at the time of her appointment (perhaps she had been the wife of the '*Gasthaus* father'), it is clear that she was a widow for at least the last decade of her service.

---

[171] Sehling (ed.), *Kirchenordnungen*, pp. 505f. The yearly accounts were to be presented before representatives of the city council, the preachers, elders and citizens; during the presentation 'praying and exhortations [would be given] from the pulpit' while the 'secretary of the city signed the accounting'.

[172] Ibid., p. 505.

[173] Ibid.

[174] EKP 8/518–20, 9/104.

Her work therefore would have supplemented that of the 'Gasthaus father' and his wife. Because she held her position in the Gasthaus 'for many years' prior to 1549, Fenne Krachtz demonstrates that this position for widows within the Gasthaus leadership existed long before the reorganisation of the late 1550s.

Additional references to women in the daily operations of Gasthaus poor relief exist in the contracts. The position titles vary enough in the sources to cause confusion as to the number of distinct offices held by women. In the 1560s and early 1570s, Tybe Reiners was referred to as the 'orphan mother in the Gasthaus in Emden' (Weßemoder).[175] In 1578, a testament included a 50-gulden donation to the Gasthaus poor, and the donor described explicitly how the money was to be distributed: immediately after the donor's burial, the 'general mothers in the Gasthaus' (gemeine Modern) should provide a free meal for the poor in the Gasthaus, and the remaining money should then be distributed to them by the 'general mothers'.[176] This distinction between the 'orphan mothers' and the 'general mothers' parallels a distinction which was sometimes made by supporters of the Gasthaus, between the orphans and the other Gasthaus poor. For instance, Catarina Cosmans's testament from 1570 specified that the poor orphans in the Gasthaus would get the first 10 gulden from her remaining goods, and anything left over was to go to the other poor, the haussitzenden or the Gasthaus poor, as the executor of the testament saw fit.[177]

At least two distinct positions existed for women administrators: the 'orphan mother' (wesekynder-moeder) and the 'mother in the Gasthaus' (moeder yn't gasthus) worked closely together in the Gasthaus. Indeed, concern over how the other one carried out her duties must have led to disagreement as to how best to provide for the poor in the Gasthaus. The dispute escalated and caused the two of them to come to blows in March 1560. The case also illustrates that the holders of the positions were free of any requirements to be members of the 'household of faith', proving less than complete control of the Gasthaus by the consistory. On 18 March 1560 the 'orphan mother' appeared before the consistory and was admonished for provoking the 'Gasthaus mother'. The 'orphan mother' was a member of the 'household of faith' and

---

[175] She had made her testament in June 1562 and decided in 1570 to donate her stipulated sum of 20 gulden to the haussitzenden poor while she was still living, EKP 13/22; ArchGK no. 1117, p. 40. By January 1574, she had died, and her daughter and son-in-law Evert van Pewsum (who was just completing his term as a Clementiner Schaffer) arranged to pay the Gasthaus the 117 gulden from her estate, EKP 13/707.

[176] Ibid. 15/162v–3 (23 November 1578).

[177] Ibid. 12/213–15.

admitted her fault in the matter; because of her acknowledgement, the consistory decided that her public admonishment should be read without giving her name, as follows, '[In a case] where two women have struck each other, one of them is a member of the congregation'. The 'orphan mother' further desired that 'her disposition', which had caused her to become so angry, should 'disappear'.[178]

By 1594, the different administrative functions of the 'Gasthaus mothers' were recorded in the Church Ordinance. In addition to the wife of the 'Gasthaus father', 'four honourable widows and godly matrons' were to live in the Gasthaus and be responsible for the 'beds, linen, flax, and whatever else belongs' in that category.[179] These widows were given special supervisory responsibilities of women and girls to ensure that they were working. The widows were also to meet the Gasthaus personnel three times per week to discuss the daily household activities.[180] These descriptions suggest that Emden's Gasthaus provided its residents with flax and other raw materials in order to have them perform some of the work necessary for the maintenance of the Gasthaus.[181] The 'Gasthaus mothers' also provided some financial leadership as they made their own annual rounds 'house-to-house' through the town in order to make a special collection for the orphans and the linen and household supplies of the Gasthaus. This collection, according to the 1594 Church Ordinance, supplemented the door-to-door collections of the administrators and the weekly alms collections after the sermons which were preached in the Gasthaus church.

---

[178] KRP, p. 109.

[179] See Figure 5.2 for a mid-seventeenth-century depiction of the Emden Gasthaus widows performing their duties: receiving an orphan, recording his name, and measuring and cutting the cloth for the bed sheets of the Gasthaus.

[180] The organisation of the widows had evolved by the nineteenth century so that the four 'honourable burgher-widows' provided the aforementioned oversight of the beds and clothing; these were the so-called 'Buiten-moeders'. Additionally, two 'Onder-' or 'Binnen-moeders' now lived in the Gasthaus; each was responsible for a specified portion of the Gasthaus and was to visit the poor and sick there. The former male visitors of the Gasthaus were not mentioned at this time; see Helias Meder's introduction to the *Openlijke Tafel-Gebeden tot gebruik in het Gast- en Wees-Huis der Stadt Emden* (Emden, 1802), pp. 7f. Also at this time, all members of the Gasthaus administration and staff were to be members of the Reformed congregation.

[181] Any work done by the poor residents of the Emden Gasthaus was on such a small scale that the intent was mainly to furnish the Gasthaus with inexpensive supplies. There is no evidence that the Emden Gasthaus administrators attempted to establish an industry, as was done, for example, by the Aumône générale in Lyon when they attempted to establish a silk industry by putting their poor residents to work; see Natalie Zernon Davis, 'Poor Relief, Humanism, and Heresy', in *Society and Culture in Early Modern France* (Stanford, 1975), pp. 43ff.

5.4 The 'Gasthaus Mothers' (by Alexander Sanders, c. 1650, Ostfriesisches Landesmuseum und Emder Rüstkammer, Emden). This seventeenth-century painting depicts Emden's Gasthaus widows performing their duties of receiving an orphan, recording his name, and measuring and cutting the cloth for his bedsheets in the Gasthaus.

The consistory spent much of December 1575 haggling with the city council over the right to hold a Sunday sermon and service in the Gasthaus church.[182] Finally, on Christmas Day 1575, the first such sermon was preached in the Gasthaus church by the pastor Dominus Ogerus Althes 'with the good satisfaction' of the city council.[183] Most significant about this development is the role of the city council in regulating, or at least approving, church services in the Gasthaus. It further demonstrates the general administrative independence of the Gasthaus from total control by either church or city.

The importance of religious guidance to the poor in the Gasthaus, coupled with independence from the church, dates back to the original St Gertrude's Gasthaus with its adjacent chapel, independent beneficed priest and lay administrators. After the Reformation, the religious instruction of the poor continued, now under the guidance of one of Emden's three ministers. Returning to *Gastmoder* Fenne Krachtz's testament from 1549, we discover that it was written down by one of Emden's ministers, Thomas Bramius, who was 'a servant of the Gospel in the same poor house' where Fenne worked.[184] This phrase 'in the same poor house' is ambiguous: did Bramius simply minister in the Gasthaus or did he live there as well? By the 1560s, after the relocation of the Gasthaus to the former Franciscan monastery, one of Emden's ministers received free housing in the Gasthaus.

When Pastor Cornelis Colthunus arrived in Emden in the spring of 1559 to replace Hermannus Brass, who had died in January, a process had to be developed to deal with the surviving widow of the pastor who had lived in the Gasthaus. Shortly after Colthunus's arrival, the consistory decided that the administrators of the Gasthaus should be consulted, perhaps to inquire if both the widow of the former pastor and the new pastor and his family could live in the Gasthaus.[185] Apparently, the Gasthaus was unable or unwilling to provide free housing to both. Ultimately a decision by the Countess Anna on 16 February 1561 instructed Brass's widow to leave the Gasthaus residence in favour of Colthunus.[186] Prior to the Reformation, the church and the city did not need to concern

---

[182] KRP, pp. 576f, 580, 582 (5, 9, 16, 19 December 1575).

[183] Ibid., p. 584. For Emden's preaching schedule as outlined in the 1594 Church Ordinance, see Sehling (ed.), *Kirchenordnungen*, pp. 484–9. Eight sermons in German were to be preached each week (three in French). On Sundays five German sermons would be given – at six o'clock in the morning in the Grosse Kirche, at noon in the Gasthaus church, at nine o'clock in both churches, and in the afternoon a catechism sermon. Three additional sermons were to be preached over the course of the week.

[184] EKP 8/519.

[185] KRP, p. 91 (5 June).

[186] StaE, I. Reg., no. 403a, fol. 1.

themselves with the support of priests' widows. Now, for the first time, they were confronted with a minister's widow and children who had little personal wealth. The situation was complicated by the death of Pastor Gellius Faber in 1564. Although neither widow was completely impoverished, the issue came to the forefront when the sons of these deceased ministers wished to pursue their studies (both ultimately became ministers). Those in the church leadership felt that education was a worthy goal for the heirs of their pastors, even if it was not exactly poor relief.

Early in 1565, the elder Gert Smit met with Countess Anna to discuss the financial support of incoming foreign ministers as well as that of the families of the deceased pastors of Emden's church. The countess agreed to provide some money to help the sons of Gellius and Hermannus in their studies. In the case of Hermannus's son, Egbert, the countess felt obliged to help him 'because his mother is not wealthy'. Thus, Gellius's oldest son Petrus received a one-time gift of 30 dalers to support his studies in Bremen, while Hermannus's son Egbert would receive support as long as he proved himself worthy in his exams.[187] The work of Gert Smit did not end there: he continued to work for some special provisions for the surviving families of dead ministers. The church's account book reveals an entry later in 1565 that 'the Burgermeister and city council ordered that the surviving widows of the preachers [be] provided for in the future with free apartment rent for the rest of their lives; [ordered] in the presence of Gert Smit'.[188]

The means for financing this special plan for ministers' widows is not explicitly spelled out. The city council did transfer a 100–gulden endowment to the church bookkeepers in 1565 to provide for Gellius's family.[189] Since the interest on this investment would provide only half of the year's rent, which the church paid to Gellius's widow, the church must have provided the balance of the mandate not funded by the city council.[190] It is possible, however, that the Gasthaus also provided some of the funding for this endeavour. It was they who precipitated the 'crisis' by not being able to provide housing for the widows; perhaps they now picked up a portion of the bill. A suggestive piece of evidence for this hypothesis is the fact that the same Gert Smit who helped establish the fund late in 1565 was elected as an administrator of the Gasthaus in 1566 where he served until 1575.[191] Moreover, it was Gert

---

[187] KRP, p. 193 (12 January 1565).

[188] ArchGK no. 347 (Karkenbock by tyden 1564–71), p. 130v.

[189] Ibid., p. 145v.

[190] Ibid., pp. 144v, 146v, 149, 149v, 152v, 155, 159, 167v, 169v, 171v; ibid., no. 364, pp. 9, 11, 24.

[191] Gert received the first rent payment for Gellius's widow in November 1565; ArchGK no. 347, p. 144v.

who actually continued, at least through 1568, to receive the half-yearly payments for Gellius's widow in order to deliver them to her.

The Gasthaus continued to furnish free housing to the newest minister in Emden, who was to provide 'spiritual food' to the poor in the Gasthaus as well as pastoral visitations to the sick. When the newest pastor in town, Johannes von Hatzum, died in 1566 after only one year in Emden, the Gasthaus brought concerns before the consistory regarding who would take Johannes's place in visiting the sick in the Gasthaus.[192] By 1568, two 'visitors of the sick' (*krancken visitatoeren*) had been chosen to ease the burden on the pastors.[193] Yet the Gasthaus administrators (or the workers in the Gasthaus) apparently continued to exert pressure on the minister who lived in the Gasthaus to visit the sick in the house. As recorded on 20 August 1576, the consistory had to commission a minister and three elders to admonish the Gasthaus administrators so that 'they would nevertheless provide relief to their sick with a *visitator*', beginning immediately with the two men already appointed for that purpose, 'and lighten the load on the preachers'.[194] That the *visitators* were expected to provide pastoral care to the sick suggests that they may have had some ministerial training. As seen earlier, when the city was divided into five *Klufts* for the purpose of church discipline by the elders and poor relief by the *haussitzenden* deacons in 1576, one of the *visitators* filled the spot which would have been filled by a fifth pastor if Emden had had five ministers. The *visitators* were not required to live in the Gasthaus, but according to the 1594 Church Ordinance were to visit everyone in it twice a week.[195]

One of the Gasthaus's major goals was to provide education and apprenticeships to the orphans and children in its care, so the administrators also hired a schoolmaster to teach in the Gasthaus. We first see a 'Gasthaus schoolmaster' when the consistory entreated the schoolmaster Johannes in the Gasthaus to attend the catechism sermon with his youths in order to prevent disorder and disturbances.[196] When Master

---

[192] KRP, pp. 258f (16 September 1566). They decided that Colthunis would be responsible at first while a search was conducted.

[193] Eduard Meiners, *Oostvrieschlandts kerkelyke geschiedenisse* (Groningen, 1738), I, 418.

[194] KRP, p. 634 (20 August 1576).

[195] Sehling (ed.), *Kirchenordnungen*, p. 506.

[196] EKP, p. 834 (6 November 1587). Youthful mischief during the sermons was not limited to the Gasthaus poor. On 29 April 1577 (KRP, p. 667), in order to prevent the disorder of the children in church, the consistory suggested that in the Grosse Kirche the schoolmasters, sexton and gravedigger should keep watch over the doors so that the disorderly youngsters could be kept out of the church. Similarly, the administrators of the Gasthaus were instructed to appoint a man to oversee the doors of the Gasthaus church; the omission of a schoolmaster to watch the doors of the church, unlike the

Wolter, one of the eight schoolteachers in Emden's German schools, finally left town in 1593 after a long conflict over his relationship with a 'dishonourable' woman, the hitherto 'Gasthaus schoolmaster' Johannes substituted for him. The Burgermeisters soon confirmed Johannes in his new post at the head of one of Emden's German schools, but we are left with no indication about his replacement in the Gasthaus.[197] The 1594 Church Ordinance suggests that the schoolmaster lived in the Gasthaus: his duties were described as diligently teaching and urging 'the children in piety, reading, writing, and discipline'.[198]

Since no Gasthaus account books survive before 1595, a few contracts between the Gasthaus administrators and those entering the Gasthaus (or their families) must suffice to illustrate the types of people who received care there. The elderly often had no other choice but to enter the Gasthaus. After the death of her husband in 1580, the old widow Aleit Rademaker was burdened with numerous debts. Obligations had been incurred during her husband's life, but without his income 'and in her old age she knew no other direction for her maintenance than that she must make her way into the Gasthaus'. The Gasthaus administrators arranged the sale of her house. After her debts were settled, the remaining sum of money was enough that the Gasthaus agreed to take her in for the rest of her life and provide her with a room and full board.[199]

Otto van Ruil and his wife negotiated a contract with the Gasthaus in 1599. Both of them would live there for the remainder of their lives and receive support, but the contract made significant stipulations. Otto and his wife had to bring in their own bed and sheets, along with all their necessary household effects. Everything they brought in with them became the property of the Gasthaus after both of them had died (Otto died in 1606). Moreover, they had to bring in the large sum of 750 gulden.[200] The terms of this agreement seem quite beneficial to the Gasthaus. The couple was not poor, for they were able to provide a sizeable sum of money. The fact that Otto's brother and sister-in-law provided security for the final payment of 350 gulden (the Gasthaus allowed Otto and his wife to reside after bringing only the first 400 gulden) indicates the involvement of Otto's family in the decision. Otto or his wife might have proven too difficult for their family to care for, due perhaps to sickness or age.

---

instructions for this task in the Grosse Kirche, suggests that a 'Gasthaus schoolmaster' had not yet been appointed.

[197] KRP, pp. 869, 890 (29 March 1591, 12 March and 26 March 1593).
[198] Sehling (ed.), *Kirchenordnungen*, p. 506.
[199] 13 January 1580, EKP 15/245 (also 247v).
[200] StaE, Gasth. Rep. GII, 3/1, pp. 7f.

A central function of the Gasthaus was to care for orphaned children until they were old enough to enter a trade or get married. The Gasthaus also provided a permanent residence for other adults or young adults whose care was beyond the reach or endurance of their families, especially the mentally ill and the physically disabled. The guardians of 17- or 18-year-old Hayteth Nonnenn, for instance, recognised that with no relatives or friends who would take him in and personally care for him, he had no hope of care outside of the Gasthaus. Hayteth was 'almost sick in his understanding and intelligence and was also so physically deformed that he could neither understand his duties nor earn his own support'. As remuneration for his maintenance, the Gasthaus would keep his inheritance of a moderately sized plot of land if Hayteth died while still in the Gasthaus. The Gasthaus also received the rights to any additional property that Hayteth should inherit while living there. The yearly rent income from this plot of land would go to the Gasthaus to support him. It is a pity that there is no description of the type of care provided to Hayteth or other similar mentally ill residents in the Gasthaus – only an explicit stipulation in Hayteth's contract that the Gasthaus must look after him in *all* his needs and emergencies.[201]

In a similar situation, the two sisters of the infirm and fragile Agatha Freitz decided to place their sister in the Gasthaus following the death of their uncle. The Gasthaus was to provide maintenance and clothing for the rest of Agatha's life. In exchange, the Gasthaus administrators took over title to Agatha's portion of her parents' and uncle's estate as well as claim to any future inheritances that Agatha might receive.[202]

The Gasthaus did not accept every request for residence, and a final example demonstrates some of the factors that the administrators considered in making their decision on whether to house someone or not. In 1580 the Gasthaus received from Anna Duemcken the bequest of an investment which would bring the Gasthaus 6 gulden per year in interest payments, a moderate-sized bequest to the poor compared to most testaments of the second half of the century. The donor, however, attached a condition to the bequest: 'if a relative of Anna [happened to] fall into poverty or be fragile of body or mind, then he or she should be maintained in clothing and subsistence in the Gasthaus for life from the legacy'. When the Gasthaus administrators learned that there was such a disabled child (Anna's niece), they attempted to modify the terms of the testament, claiming that they could not take in such a child for only 6 gulden per year. The administrators suggested to the executor of the will (Rolef Wyner, Anna's nephew) that

---

[201] EKP 10/565–6 (4 January 1567).
[202] Ibid. 14/65–6 (19 May 1574).

they be allowed to begin receiving the yearly interest payments immediately, but that he should care for the child himself for the next ten years. After ten years, the child would be old enough and the revenues better, and they would accept the child. Rolef protested that the testament came with a condition, and if the Gasthaus did not want to accept the child, they could not receive the specified legacy. Ultimately, the protest was arbitrated by one of the Burgermeisters, and the Gasthaus administrators finally accepted the argument of Rolef and declined to accept the child and the bequest.[203]

Perhaps the greatest change in the Gasthaus services over the course of the sixteenth century results from the consolidation of the Gasthaus's properties in the former monastery. With its greater size, the Gasthaus increased its administration and the varieties of poor people that it accepted into its care. The large endowments that had belonged to St Gertrude's Gasthaus were increased over the century. With them, the Gasthaus was financially active throughout the second half of the century and was able to remain independent of direct civic or church control, though its administrators frequently had connections with the leadership of both.

Finally, we find that long-term housing in the form of Gotteskammern continued to be offered to the poor in Emden throughout the second half of the sixteenth century. Private Gotteskammer foundations existed in addition to those operated by some of the aforementioned poor relief institutions. The Gasthaus continued to maintain a number of Gotteskammern. The old 'Boelhardus Gotteskammern', from 1509 on the New Marketplace, were still mentioned in 1565 after the relocation to the Franciscan monastery.[204] With the additional room in the more spacious monastery, the Gasthaus administrators probably had less need to use Gotteskammern to house their residents. They did, however, keep using some of their old Gotteskammern and even built new ones. In 1574, for instance, the administrators sold one of their old Gotteskammern in order to finance the construction of two new ones by the entrance to the new Gasthaus.[205] The use of Gotteskammern allowed for increased segregation among the residents of the Gasthaus (short-term from long-term, sick from well, etc.).

The Emden church had acquired the old Gotteskammern of St Anthony's Brotherhood. The Gotteskammer in which Imke Campes lived in 1580 was probably one of those under the administration of the church. The church elder Peter de Loose admonished Imke, 'who had lived for a

---

[203] Ibid. 16/119–21 (23 December 1580).
[204] Ibid. 10/244.
[205] Ibid. 12/992–3 (5 August).

long time in the Gotteskammer', because of fornication with a man she had been letting sleep in the Gotteskammer.[206] A contract from 1578 reveals that the *haussitzenden* deacons were operating at least two kammern, and the deacons and the consistory functioned together in the oversight of some of the Gotteskammern.[207] Unfortunately, the relationship between the Gotteskammern of the church and those operated by the deacons is not clear.

A number of independent Gotteskammern also existed. The so-called 'Aylt Kannegeter's Gotteskammern' were located on Schulstrasse in the late 1540s.[208] The reference is unfortunately not detailed enough to determine whether these were independent Gotteskammern, or if, like the 'Boelhardus' Gotteskammern', they had been bequeathed to another relief institution. The establishment of a Gotteskammer was one way in which a donor could receive long-term recognition for a charitable act. When one donated a sum of money to the *haussitzenden* poor, by contrast, it became an anonymous part of the deacons' activities. Thus Gerth and Gretha Reminck decided in their 1567 testament to designate the house in which they lived as 'a Gotteskammer for a poor old person' after both of them had died. It should remain 'in perpetuity' a Gotteskammer 'to the glory of God'.[209] The fact that they provided no endowment with which to maintain the Gotteskammern indicates that its administration must have been taken over by another organisation or foundation, if it was indeed to remain in service.

Gerth and Gretha's memory did not continue in Emden 'to eternal days' since there is no additional surviving reference to a 'Reminck's Gotteskammer'! However, the largest independent Gotteskammern in Emden did continue throughout the century. The well-endowed Gotteskammern of Herman Wessels (the priest who had died in 1507) kept up their activities as loan banks and maintained at least five residences for the poor.[210] By mid-century, the administrative board had

---

[206] KRP, p. 746 (12 September 1580). Imke had apparently been given promises of marriage by the 'young man' and the consistory dealt with the matter a couple of times later that year, ibid., pp. 747, 752 (3 October, 19 December). Finally, on 8 July 1582, the consistory publicly proclaimed that Imke had been admonished and had acknowledged her guilt – of falling into fornication 'although out of the hope of marriage' – and if no complaints were brought to the consistory, she would be reinstated at the next communion; ibid., p. 781.

[207] EKP 15/121 (21 February 1578). See section on 'Gaalke' in Chapter 7 below.

[208] Ibid. 3/201v (3 October 1546).

[209] Ibid. 5/206 (1555), 10/713–14 (24 September 1567).

[210] The endowment does not seem to have increased much over the course of the second half of the century. None of the surviving testaments from that time left goods to the Wessels Foundation. Even the investments of capital remained relatively small and infrequent; EKP 5/264 (32 gulden), 5/264v (34 gulden), 266v (50 gulden), 293 (34

evolved to include one of Emden's ministers. In 1555, the money for a loan from the Wessels Foundation was given 'from the hands of the preacher Hermannus Brass' and the two other administrators of the charitable foundation.[211] Again in 1580, a pastor (this time Ogerus Althes) was named as an administrator of the Wessels Gotteskammern, and the investment was made with the pastor's 'previous knowledge and consent'.[212] Although none of the other administrators of the Wessels Foundation can be located in any positions of leadership within the church or the city government, it is significant that the church, through one of its ministers, developed a supervisory role in respect of the activities of Herman Wessels's Gotteskammern.

Thus it can be seen that the administration of Emden's system of provision underwent a phenomenal transformation during the second half of the sixteenth century. The variety of institutional development and the speed with which changes were introduced in a short time during the 1550s was remarkable. With the rapidly reconstituted system of provision and an actual heightening of social and economic problems caused by the continued influx of refugees in the 1560s and 1570s, Emden's social welfare system faced rather daunting prospects. Yet somehow Emden kept its system from breaking. Indeed, the Emden civic and church leaders demonstrated a remarkable effort of provision, coming up with practical responses to a steady stream of practical problems. To be sure, there was apparently no shortage of money about (remember the construction of the elaborate new Rathaus!), but nevertheless as a way of managing a situation which might otherwise have occasioned exceptional disruption, Emden's social welfare system offers an extraordinarily successful example of imaginative urban government.

The wide range of services provided by the various deacons was expanded to meet the new needs that inevitably arose with Emden's ever-increasing population of poor. The amazing flexibility of the institutions and their administrators in attempting to deal with individual circumstances resulted in much time and discussion being spent grappling with sticky problems and particular cases. The poor relief administrators put great emphasis on health care, education and training in their attempts to prevent as much as possible the fall over the edge of poverty. The deacons hired doctors and midwives and provided

---

gulden); the last loan was purchased by another individual for 30 gulden in 1580, but at an interest rate of 9 per cent instead of the previous 6 per cent (EKP 15/272).

[211] Ibid. 5/266v (18 December 1555).
[212] Ibid. 5/293 (13 May 1580).

medicine and other treatments to both the regular poor relief recipients of the city as well as those on the precipice of poverty who became sick. When one became too old or ill (physically or mentally) to care for himself or herself (or to be cared for by the family), the Gasthaus provided an alternative to completely draining the family's resources. All the institutions also put great emphasis on apprenticeships, schooling and other methods (including provision of work tools or loans to start a business), and in these ways sought to reduce future levels of poverty.

Quite effectively, it seems, the deacons developed management methods to handle the large amounts of money and supplies necessary to provide for the poor. Whether by dividing the town into districts (*Klufts*), as the *haussitzenden* deacons did, or by taking advantage of the refugees' communication networks from home, as the *fremdlingen* did, the deacons attempted to develop better supervision of the poor. The justification for this increased oversight was, of course, two-fold: first, they wanted to ensure that the most needy were provided for; and second, an emphasis on discipline, and increasingly *church* discipline, became more typical as Emden's church became more clearly Reformed. Yet purely theological distinctions among the poor were still not popular in Emden, as the failure of the *Becken* diaconate demonstrates. Nevertheless, those who were clearly 'outside' the city's faith would have faced severe difficulties in obtaining poor relief (at least regularly) from Emden's social welfare institutions.

CHAPTER SIX

Social Welfare and Minority Groups in Calvinist Emden

That [the counts] retain the true Christian religion, which they have had from the beginning of the Reformation now 70 years through God's exceptional grace in unity and peace ... And that everything which is contrary to [the true Christian Religion] might be abolished – namely the Jewish synagogue, the [Lutheran] separation at the Neuen Münze, and various gatherings of the Anabaptists.

The 'ecclesiastical complaint of the common citizenry of the city Emden', presented to the East Frisian *Landtag* in 1590[1]

Although in reality the East Frisian Reformation was anything but united, by this point in Emden's religious development, its Protestantism and that of the ruling house of East Frisia were not much in question, although some undesirable religious minorities remained. Rather, the debate that heated up was over the confessional nature of Emden's city church. Emden's Reformed tradition from Lasco and the Dutch refugees began to come into conflict with the Lutheran rulers of the territory. Similar to the process of confessionalisation across Europe, Emden's fixing of confessional boundaries in the aftermath of the Reformation had important societal, institutional and political results. A marked acceleration of confessionalisation in East Frisia and an increased radicalism taken by both sides in Emden were the consequence, in large part, of three trends in the last quarter of the sixteenth century: the energy of the strict Calvinist minister Menso Alting, the territorial dynastic dispute of the East Frisian counts, and the emergence of new civic institutions and a sense of communal mentality in Emden.

As much as the year 1554 marked the advent of a new stage in Emden's history with the arrival of the first Dutch refugees, so too was 1575 a watershed year. The most significant beacon, the arrival of Menso Alting, was precipitated by the social instability brought about by a massive plague. Emden had recently faced seasons of plague,

---

[1] The Emden Apology for the Norden Landtag in 1593 began with the same complaints, E. R. Brenneysen (ed.), *Ost-Friesische Historie und Landes-Verfassung* (Aurich, 1720), I, 413. The original draft of the complaints was made in 1589–90; StaE, I. Reg., 910, no. 19.

especially with the ever-increasing population density caused by the arrival of refugees: between August and October 1566 there were days in which 21 and 35 people died of the plague; in August 1568 (just after Alva's victory at Jemgum) the plague returned to Emden and persisted well into December.[2] However, in 1575 an extremely virulent plague raged in Emden between Easter and November; one source claimed that 6 000 people in the city died, with 45, 52, 56, even as many as 70 people dying in single days in August and September.[3] The Emden church leadership was not spared from the disaster, as all three of Emden's ministers died within a three-week period in August.[4]

In the upheaval, the consistory struggled to get two ministers from local communities, and in October they were able to recruit Menso Alting. Alting was a native of Drenthe in the Netherlands, though he had spent the previous decade in the Palatinate, most recently as minister in Heidelberg. He was an unyieldingly orthodox Calvinist from one of the international centres of Calvinism, and he himself had an international reputation. He chose to come to Emden over competing calls to Delft, Middelburg and Frankenthal. Perhaps the proximity of his wife's family in nearby Groningen was a factor in his decision. Alting began very quickly to renovate and, in some cases, to reorganise Emden's ecclesiastical institutions.

Menso Alting and his associates also began a renewed attack on persisting Anabaptism in Emden. In 1578, the leaders of the Flemish, Frisian and Waterlander Anabaptists from the Netherlands and Friesland had chosen Emden as a meeting place to discuss internal disputes, obviously a sign of their perception of the relatively friendly climate of East Frisia. The Emden consistory took advantage of their presence and challenged the Anabaptists to a public disputation. From 27 February to 25 May 1578 the two sides met in 124 public sessions in which they discussed 14 points of doctrine.[5] Although the peaceful disputations did

---

[2] A contemporary reported that 'on every day 20 people, more or less, died' in the 1568 plague; it spread through almost all of East Frisia; from the so-called 'Emder Chronyk', published in part by Hemmo Suur as 'Zur Geschichte der Stadt Emden', in *Jahrbüchlein zur Unterhaltung und zum Nutzen zunächst für Ostfriesland und Harlingerland auf das Jahr 1837*, ed. G. W. Bueren (Emden, 1836), pp. 90f, 104.

[3] On the plague in cities of Lower Saxony, see Neithard Bulst, 'Vier Jahrhunderte Pest in niedersächsischen Städten: Vom Schwarzen Tod (1349–1351) bis in die erste Hälfte des 18. Jahrhunderts', in *Stadt im Wandel*, ed. Cord Meckseper, vol. 4 (Stuttgart–Bad Cannstatt, 1985), pp. 251–70.

[4] KRP, pp. 566f (8, 10 and 27 August).

[5] The significance of these disputations for the consistory is evidenced by the fact that the consistory suspended its meetings for most of the duration of the disputations. On 24 February they explained, 'Haec intermißiio propter colloq[uium] cum Anabapt[istis]' (KRP, p. 690). The next consistory meeting was not held until 9 April, and thereafter

not lead to any formal agreement, the local ministers circulated their version of the proceedings, and Alting felt that the doctrines of Emden's church had been justified and that the most doubtful members of the community had been strengthened in their faith.[6]

Alting's role in two other incidents shortly after his arrival further illustrated his commitment to Calvinism and a Reformed church polity. Near the end of 1575, Menso began negotiating a long-standing dispute within Emden's French Reformed church. By June 1576 he had arranged a settlement between the strict Calvinist minister of the French church, Jean Polyander, and a number of his liberal opponents from his French congregation. When the minister's opponents refused to go along with the settlement, Alting was able to secure their excommunication and the victory of the Calvinist Polyander (over some attempts by the count and the town council to interfere in the church matter). In a second example, Alting, as president of the Assembly of the East Frisian ministers (the so-called *Coetus*), initiated the creation of a '*Coetus* Ordinance' for the East Frisian churches. The Ordinance established the *Coetus* as the governing church body in the territory; no minister was to be appointed to a church without first being examined by the *Coetus*. The Ordinance then mandated a series of fundamental teachings by which an examinee was to be evaluated. One of these standards was to be the Emden Catechism of 1554 (drawn up by Lasco and others), which previously had no official sanction in East Frisia and which Alting now elevated to a standard of faith. The impact of this *Coetus* Ordinance did not, however, extend to all of East Frisia because Lutheran ministers refused to sign. Count Johan approved the ordinance, but his Lutheran brother Count Edzard II would not. Although Edzard wanted to establish a unified territorial church, he did not want to go in Alting's theological direction. From the very beginning of Menso Alting's ministry in Emden, he was involved with the ruling counts and their dynastic squabbles. One of his first responsibilities after his arrival had been to deliver the eulogy at the funeral of Countess Anna, who had died in October 1575. Her influence had helped insulate the Reformed church in Emden from the conflict within the ruling house. With her death, the brothers Edzard and Johan were free to escalate the intensity of their quarrel, although Johan still offered a certain protection to Emden.

The political and religious development of East Frisia during the last half of the century was dominated by the ever-growing dynastic dispute

---

only on 28 April and 19 May, before returning to their weekly meeting schedule at the beginning of June after the disputations were over.

[6] This was Alting's account to Beza in Geneva; see H. Klugkist Hesse, *Menso Alting: Eine Gestalt aus der Kampfzeit der calvinischen Kirche* (Berlin, 1928), pp. 230–44.

within the Cirksena house. The regency of Countess Anna ended in 1561, and the East Frisian territory was divided among her three sons. The oldest son Edzard II had married the daughter of the Swedish king in 1559, which led to a vast increase in his social prestige and that of the Cirksena house. Yet none of the three brothers was content with the tripartite division. When the youngest brother, Christoph, became ill and died while fighting the Turks in 1566, the two surviving brothers divided the territory. But a simmering feud between Count Edzard II and his brother Count Johan had great importance for Emden in the last quarter of the century. Edzard sought to maintain full hereditary control over all of East Frisia; Johan, on the other hand, with the support of his mother, Countess Anna, continued to fight for his half. Edzard became a strict Lutheran, and Johan was Reformed; each worked toward the goal of establishing an exclusive confessional church within his own territory. Edzard appointed a Lutheran court preacher in 1568. He converted during the political confrontation with his brother Johan; the confessional stance of his Swedish wife and her family might have contributed to Edzard's strict Lutheranism.

Count Edzard II, whose portion of East Frisia included Emden, moved his residence from the castle in Emden to the town of Aurich in 1561.[7] While Edzard worked from Aurich to strengthen Lutheran absolutism throughout his territory, Alting and his colleagues in Emden retained a political alliance with Count Johan. The process of confessionalisation was accelerating to full force. Under Count Edzard, much of East Frisia shifted to Lutheran orthodoxy; under Alting's leadership, Emden's town church shifted to rigid Calvinism. The Reformed theology of Bucer largely disappeared from Emden in the course of the last quarter of the century.

Edzard became more and more active in trying to counter the influence of Alting. In 1580, he moved his residence from Aurich back to his castle in Emden.[8] In 1583, he banned the meeting of the Emden *Coetus* because of its almost exclusive Reformed character. Count Johan quickly countered by initiating the *Coetus* in his own portion of the territory. Edzard ordered in 1583 that the Gasthaus church be given over to the Lutheran congregation for its worship services, but the majority in Emden fought the order, claiming that the right of disposal of the church belonged to the civic community and not to the count. As patron of the Lutheran congregation, Edzard granted them the use of

---

[7] Harm Wiemann, *Die Grundlagen der landständischen Verfassung in Ostfriesland: Die Verträge von 1595 bis 1611* (Aurich, 1974), p. 10.

[8] Menno Smid, *Ostfriesische Kirchengeschichte* (Pewsum, 1974), p. 229.

one of his own properties, the New Mint (*Neuen Münze*, just to the north of the castle), where official Lutheran services were held in 1586.

Parallel to the formation of a corporate and self-governing congregation which was emerging under Alting's Calvinist ecclesiastical constitution, there also arose a growing sense among citizens of independence from the count in matters of civic involvement. Although the count still fully controlled Emden's town council, the use of civic committees (e.g. the *Bürgerausschuß* and the Committee of Twenty-four) in the 1540s and 1560s to handle certain customs questions allowed for greater citizen autonomy. From the mid-1580s, Count Edzard and his town council exercised increasing control over the committee by dismissing and appointing deputies at will. Growing civic self-awareness can be seen in the deputies' demands for the right of election. Early in 1589, an assembly of citizens met without authorisation of the count and created its own representative committee to replace the old Twenty-four; the Council of Forty (*Vierziger Collegium*) claimed full rights of representation for the citizenry, not only in financial but also in political affairs. Because neither the count nor his council recognised the Council of Forty, their activities remained limited for a while.

Other evidence of growing civic involvement began to emerge about mid-century. The poor relief institutions of the Grain Reserve (*Kornvorrat*) and the diaconate offered means by which the citizens could control their own affairs, largely independent of the count. The Forty, however, demonstrated the extent to which the political aspirations of Emden's citizenry had developed by the end of the century; its creation was a small act of defiance against the count's control of civic matters. Similarly, as Count Edzard attempted to exert increasing control over Emden's church, Emden's citizens began acting more defiantly.

When Edzard's daughter Margarethe died in September 1588, Edzard announced his intention to have his Lutheran court minister preach the funeral sermon at her burial in the Grosse Kirche. Although the choir of the Grosse Kirche was the traditional burial place for the Cirksena house, the Reformed ministers, led by Alting, of course, protested that *the* Grosse Kirche was a civic parish church under the administration of the citizenry: unless the citizenry consented to it, the ministers could not allow 'false teaching' to take place in the church. When put to a vote before a gathering of citizens, the question was answered unanimously in favour of the ministers' position. Count Edzard accepted a compromise in which his daughter would be buried in the Grosse Kirche, but without any sermon. The count even had to agree to the presence of a large citizen militia to ensure that no Lutheran preaching took place.

Tensions were already high in Emden when Count Johan died childless on 29 September 1591. His death enabled Edzard to wrest back control of all of East Frisia. Moreover, the bit of protection afforded by Count Johan to Menso Alting and Emden's church disappeared with their ally. Edzard moved quickly to prohibit the *Coetus* in Johan's former territories, and political and confessional relations simmered for the next three years. Beginning in the summer of 1594, the confrontation reached boiling point.

Following the Dutch States-General's victory in recapturing Groningen in July 1594, Menso Alting was invited to Groningen to preach the first sermon and to assist in the organisation of the newly restored Reformed church there. Despite Count Edzard's explicit prohibition, Alting made the journey and preached the sermon. As a reprisal, Edzard removed Alting from his office and ordered the city council to ban him from the town's pulpit. Tensions increased as the conflict remained unresolved in early 1595. In March, Count Edzard continued on the offensive to impose his authority. First, he forbade all gatherings of the citizenry; this included meetings of those regulating the dykes and sluices (*Deich-und Sielachtsversammlungen*) as well as all religious services and gatherings. On 3 March, he prohibited the meetings of the consistory and the deacons. Then, on 17 March, he demanded an inspection of the poor relief accounts of the deacons (the count already had the right to inspect the church's general accounts).

This final mandate proved to be the last straw. Interestingly, after all the conflicts and confrontations between Emden and the count which led up to the Revolution, the issue which finally provoked the direct showdown was poor relief and the count's attempt to exert his jurisdiction over the independence of the town's poor relief. On that same afternoon, the ministers, elders and deacons, along with a number of respected citizens, about 70 in all, met in the consistory chamber of the Grosse Kirche and deliberated over the count's demand. They argued that they had nothing in general against revealing the poor relief accounts, but in this situation they feared that it might lead to 'dangerous changes' in their constitutional rights. Another meeting took place on the afternoon of 18 March; so many people attended the meeting that it had to be moved from the consistory chamber into the choir of the church. Menso Alting described the situation and offered his resignation since he was the principal source of the count's anger. At that point Gerhard Bolardus, an elder and a member of the Forty, spoke to the gathering and challenged them to armed opposition to the count's authority in Emden. The crowd approved and elected six officers, including Bolardus.

Thus began the Emden Revolution. The citizenry armed itself and quickly occupied all the strategic locations in Emden, including the town hall (Rathaus) and the gates of the city, without any fighting. The old town council and Burgermeisters, as officials of the count, were discharged, and on 24 March 1595, Gerhard Bolardus became the first new Burgermeister. One of the new council's first acts was to ban the Lutheran services in the New Mint and expel the count's court preacher from the city. Despite all his attempts to resist and to get outside help, Count Edzard was forced to accept the Treaty of Delfzyl (Delfzyler Vertrag) on 15 July 1595. The first article of the treaty stipulated that

> in the old city of Emden, in Faldern, and in the suburbs, be it in the Mint or anywhere else, there should publicly be no other Religion taught, practised or tolerated than that which is presently preached in the Grossen and the Gasthaus Churches. Nevertheless, no one should be encumbered or investigated in his conscience. The count is permitted, when he holds court in his castle, to allow his court preacher to preach.[9]

Henceforth, only the Reformed religion was to be practised in the town, and both the city and church administrations were to function independently of the count. When Edzard died in 1599, Emden was able to negotiate with his son Count Enno III in the Concord of Emden (Emder Konkordate) to obtain the same basic terms.

The Emden Revolution of 1595 was the culmination of confessionalisation and the rise of a corporate mentality in Emden, and it marked a revolution in the civic constitution of the city. The confessional boundaries in East Frisia were now fixed. The Emden citizenry established a Calvinist city church and gained constitutional autonomy and independence from the Lutheran count and his territorial church. East Frisia became the first territory in the Empire where a recognised Calvinist confession existed alongside the Lutheran confession of the ruler. Thus poor relief was a central issue in the Emden Revolution – an issue which bridged both confessional and civic interests among the citizens, and which had become so important in both their confessional and civic attitudes.

Relief Activities of the Minority Groups

As Emden became more clearly 'Reformed' in its confessional outlook, tensions increased between the authorities and minority groups. A frequent flashpoint of dispute between the city officials and these groups was, in fact, on the issue of poor relief. Thus, by looking at the

---

[9] Emil Sehling (ed.), *Die evangelischen Kirchenordnungen des XVI. Jahrhunderts* VII/2/1(Tübingen, 1963), pp. 414f.

questions arising from social welfare issues, we can gain some interesting insights into the conflicts over the proliferation of cultural as well as religious minority groups in the increasingly Reformed city of Emden. Now, the surviving information on the sixteenth-century minority groups in Emden is scanty indeed. Nevertheless, the clues and suggestions uncovered present a compelling picture of some of the practical concerns that faced city and church leaders as they attempted to deal with unpopular, if not legally prohibited, minority groups.

While much of Emden's population could qualify as recipients of the city's elaborate system of poor relief, certain groups found themselves on the fringes of society in late sixteenth-century Emden. By the last quarter of the century, as the Emden church grew increasingly Calvinist in its confessional outlook, church records cite Anabaptists, Lutherans and Jews as disturbing the confessional unity of the city. But these were not the only minority groups in Emden that raised concerns. Of much greater concern to the general population of Emden, who seemed much less anxious than the church and town leaders about the presence of confessional minorities, were the large number of cultural and linguistic minorities who had found in Emden a city of refuge and who were competing legally for jobs and housing. These Dutch, French and English congregations, though confessionally identified with the Reformed Emden church, constantly struggled to gain acceptance in the Emden community.

Confessionally, the French and the English churches in Emden did not differ from Emden's own Reformed church. The English and the French-speaking exiles, along with the Dutch refugees, had to flee England when King Edward VI died and was succeeded by his sister Mary. Unlike most of the Dutch refugees, however, who were able to assimilate into Emden's church, the French and the English exiles had to, and were allowed to, establish their own congregations due to language differences. Although much smaller than the Emden church, these two congregations seem to have established a typical Reformed church structure. Despite their size, both congregations were very important to Emden. The French church and its minister Jean Polyander, for example, played the key local role in the staging of the Emden Synod of 1571, especially since the leadership of Emden's church kept itself removed from the synod's proceedings.[10] The English-speaking

---

[10] Of the 29 participants in the synod, three were from Emden: all of them from the French church, namely Polyander, who served as secretary, and two of the French elders. The records of the Emden Synod were edited as *Die Akten der Synode der Niederländischen Kirchen zu Emden vom 4.–13. Oktober 1571*, by J. F. Gerhard Goeters (Neukirchen, 1971).

congregation helped make Emden a printing centre for Marian exile literature.[11]

The French-speaking religious refugees had been fleeing persecution in the southern Netherlands under Charles V and Philip II since 1521, heading first to England and then to Emden following Mary's accession.[12] The East Frisian Countess Anna legally recognised their congregation in Emden in 1554,[13] and they were authorised to hold their worship services in the ground-floor room of the large *Stadthalle*, which was located to the east of the Franciscan monastery on the outer edge of Middle Faldern (see Map 2.3). Although the Dutch-speaking refugees were allowed no separate institutions besides their diaconate, the French congregation, due to language necessities, were allowed to have their own minister, elders, deacons, consistory and school.[14] The French consistory was responsible for handling internal congregational problems. Yet representatives of the quarrelsome French congregation frequently appeared before Emden's consistory for help in resolving disputes. On one occasion, the actions of the French minister so angered one of the congregants that he asked the Emden consistory if he might be permitted to participate in communion with the Emden congregation; with the French congregation, he wanted 'to hold no further fellowship, neither in the Word, nor in communion, nor in alms'.[15]

Although the Walloon community was comparatively small, a number of influential and wealthy refugees were members of the congregation. Most important were the rich grain merchants who were members of the grain cartel run by the Commelin and du Gardin families.[16] While such

---

[11] At least 20 clandestine English Protestant works were published in Emden between 1554 and 1558; Andrew Pettegree, *Emden and the Dutch Revolt* (Oxford, 1992), p. 55, also his Appendix of Books Printed in Emden.

[12] Timothy Fehler, 'The French Congregation's Struggle for Acceptance in Emden', in *Out of New Babylon: The Huguenots and their Diaspora*, ed. Bertrand van Ruymbeke (University of South Carolina Press, forthcoming). Brief histories of Emden's French church were written by two of the congregation's ministers in the nineteenth century; J. N. Pleines, 'Die französisch reformirte Kirche in Emden', *Geschichtsblätter des Deutschen Hugenotten-Vereins*, 2 (1894), which was basically a reprint of his 'Kurze Geschichte der französisch reformirten Kirche in Emden', *EJb*, 1, 1 (1875), pp. 37–54; Pleines, *Troisième Jubilé Séculaire de la Fondation de l'Eglise Réformée française d'Emden* (Emden, 1855); Philipp Wenz, *Reformations-Jubel-Rede nebst Geschichte der französisch-reformierten Kirche in Emden* (Emden, 1819). See also the surviving documents in StaE, I. Reg., no. 405.

[13] StaE, I. Reg., no. 405, fol. 1; reprinted by Pleines, 'Französisch-reformirte Kirche', pp. 14f.

[14] KRP, pp. 496, 584 (15 February 1574, 23 December 1575); Sehling (ed.), *Kirchenordnungen*, pp. 514–16; ArchGK nos 1100, 1090.

[15] KRP, p. 563 (6 June 1575).

[16] Bernhard Hagedorn, *Ostfrieslands Handel und Schiffahrt im 16. Jahrhundert* (Berlin, 1910), pp. 125f.

members added an important level of prestige to the French exile community, they could also stir up animosities both within and especially without the congregation. The activities of some of the leaders of the Walloon grain cartel caused such problems in 1563. A rise in refugee immigration into Emden in 1562 and 1563 had both created an economic strain and raised tensions between the exiles and local residents. Perhaps in recognition of the need to preserve local acceptance of the refugees, the Emden consistory stepped in and began to legislate business practices, in this case ruling against the immoral practices of some of the members of the Walloon grain cartel. The consistory accused them of selling tainted grain (and mixing it with good grain) and of seeking undue profit during a time of scarcity. Such activities no doubt also had a harmful effect on the local Grain Reserve. In order to stem the tide of complaints against these foreign merchants, the consistory ordered them to provide restitution as well as additional money for the poor.[17]

Representatives of the French church underscored their modest size when faced with an overwhelming poor relief problem in 1568. Following the Duke of Alva's crushing victory against the Dutch rebel forces on East Frisian soil in nearby Jemgum on 21 July, many people in Emden were terrified that Alva would continue his march northward to Emden, which to that point had been openly supportive of the Dutch cause. Although by early August the Emden church was able to give prayers of thanksgiving 'for the deliverance for a time from the bloody tyrant', the city was faced with a stream of poor and wounded soldiers from the battle.[18] Many of the wounded soldiers were placed in the Gasthaus, and the refugee deacons were expected to pay for their care.[19] Apparently a considerable number of the soldiers were French-speaking, and on 4 August, the French congregation presented its concerns to the consistory regarding its limited ability to provide poor relief to the wounded soldiers. The disproportionate number of French-speaking soldiers made the relief responsibilities of the French church's deacons impossible since 'their wealth, because of their small congregation, is very small'. The French church 'hoped that one would not impose upon them the entire burden of their nation'. They asked for assistance in providing special relief – at the least, for a provision that the soldiers be cared for 'without distinction according to nation'.[20]

---

[17] KRP, pp. 160–61 (29 March 1563); Pettegree, *Emden*, p. 52.

[18] KRP, p. 319 (2 August).

[19] In the month of August, the *fremdlingen* deacons provided assistance to some 18 individuals cited as soldiers (*Landsknecht*) in their account book, *Fremdlingen I*, fols 233–33v.

[20] KRP, p. 319 (4 August 1568).

Interestingly, most of the references to the French church's poor relief involved jurisdictional disputes with the *fremdlingen* deacons.[21] Given the special status of the French church and possible rivalries between the two groups, it is not surprising that jurisdictional disputes arose between the French and Dutch deacons. The problem is best illustrated by a case before the Emden consistory on 29 November 1568. Four deacons, two from the French congregation and two from the Dutch congregation of the *fremdlingen*, asked the consistory to settle a dispute between them. The complication arose over the provision of poor relief for two orphans of a French lacemaker named Mathys. It seems that Mathys, 'although born a Frenchman', had participated not in the French congregation, but rather the Dutch. Now that he had died, the French deacons did not want to support his orphaned children from their purse, for he had not been part of their congregation. The *fremdlingen* deacons, on the other hand, argued that the French should support their French poor just as the Dutch must support theirs.

The consistory's response was important in establishing the future precedent for such disputes. In order to prevent future arguments, the consistory argued that the deacons should hold to the 'oldest rule of all' and decide jurisdictional disputes on the basis of the 'tongue' of the recipient.[22] This rule would be especially important in determining the responsible poor relief party in cases involving orphans, because the parents might not have been active in or faithful to any congregation. In the case of Mathys, the consistory exhorted the deacons of both congregations 'to the liberal collection of alms' in order to ensure that the two children were provided for by the refugee deacons, because 'it was not established that [Mathys] was in our congregation, but it is certain that he was from their community'. Whatever the resolution of this particular conflict, the consistory was certain that the care of these orphans was not to be the responsibility of the local (*Becken?*) deacons.

---

[21] No independent French poor relief records survive for Emden, but for a comparative overview of the system practised by French-speaking exile churches (primarily in England), see Andrew Spicer, 'Poor Relief and the Exile Communities', in *Reformations Old and New. Essays on the Socio-Economic Impact of Religious Change c. 1470–1630*, ed. by Beat Kümin (Aldershot, 1996), pp. 237–55; see also W. J. C. Moens, 'The Relief of the Poor Members of the French Churches in England', *Proceedings of the Huguenot Society of London* (10 January and 14 March 1894); for the elaborate system established for the French refugees in Geneva (strikingly similar to Emden's *fremdlingen* diaconate), see Jeannine Olson, *Calvin and Social Welfare: Deacons and the Bourse française* (London, 1989).

[22] KRP, p. 330 (29 November 1568).

Another interesting jurisdictional dispute between these two 'foreign diaconates' arose over a testament made to the *vrembdelingen* poor.[23] Hans de Brander, who would later serve as a *haussitzenden* deacon, and his wife Mary had determined in their testament that 50 gulden would be given to the *vrembdelingen* poor on the death of the first spouse.[24] The problem emerged after Mary's death in 1574, and the *fremdlingen* deacons requested the 50 gulden. The wording of the testament had earmarked the money to the 'expelled foreign poor of the Dutch congregation in Emden'.[25] Yet, after being shown the testament, Hans complained that it had not been written properly because it was the desire of both him and his wife that both the Dutch and the Walloon poor divide the 50 gulden; it was simply through carelessness that the Walloon poor had been forgotten. He supported his claim by pointing out that his wife had been from the Walloon congregation and he was from the Dutch.

The positions of the deacons of 'both churches' were so rigid and the arguing so fierce that the Emden consistory thought it most useful for both sides to present their cases before two impartial legal scholars. On 1 March 1574 the consistory ordered the French and the Dutch deacons to arbitrate the dispute.[26] The Walloon deacons argued that they should receive half of the bequeathed 50 gulden on the basis of Hans's confirmation; moreover, they claimed, the fact that he belonged to the Dutch congregation added credence to the impartiality of his statement. While the Walloon deacons wanted the case settled with 'justice and love according to the conscience', the *fremdlingen* deacons maintained 'the letter of the testament'. One cannot simply go around changing testaments; with the death of the testatrix, they argued, the testament was fixed and could not thereafter be modified.[27]

That such acrimony should develop over the relatively small sum of 25 gulden is curious.[28] The extreme positions and the willingness to go

---

[23] Though very few testaments of French refugees in Emden survive, studies of other French exile congregations indicate that bequests provided an important source of the congregation's poor relief revenues: 60 per cent of the testaments made by members of the London congregation between 1550 and 1580 included some sort of bequest to the poor; Andrew Pettegree, *Foreign Protestant Communities in Sixteenth-Century London* (Oxford, 1986), pp. 198, 201. Spicer, 'Exile Communities', p. 247, has found a similar pattern among the French communities in Sandwich, Canterbury and Southampton.

[24] ArchGK no. 3194, pp. 259–60.

[25] ArchGK (Nellner) 320B, no. 15.

[26] KRP, p. 498.

[27] ArchGK (Nellner) 320B, no. 15.

[28] The income of the *fremdlingen* deacons in 1574 exceeded 3 300 gulden; they received 464 gulden from testaments alone; *Fremdlingen II*, fols 423–30.

to legal arbitration suggest that underlying issues were at stake. This case clearly demonstrates deep-seated friction between the Dutch and the French refugee churches. Long-running theological and congregational disputes within the French church, now reaching their apex, might have alienated those outside the congregation in addition to many within it. The *fremdlingen* deacons had no desire to share even a portion of the bequest with the French congregation. Of course, there was always competition between poor relief agencies, especially over bequests in testaments, but the fighting was fiercest between the most closely related institutions. Just as the *haussitzenden* deacons quarrelled with the *Becken* deacons, questioning their existence, so also the *fremdlingen* deacons might not have considered the separate institutions and congregation of the French Walloons to be legitimate. Despite the religious and political similarities between the French and Dutch exiles in Emden, the minority status of the French congregation gave it an atmosphere of a voluntary church. Because the Dutch refugees had assimilated into the Emden congregation, perhaps they began to ostracise their French-speaking fellow exiles and did not want to encourage the continued 'special status' of the French congregation when they felt that their numbers should give the Dutch speakers a special status.

In the end, the legal decision came down in favour of the *fremdlingen* deacons, and they received the full 50 gulden on 16 March.[29] When the French deacons next appeared before Emden's consistory to inquire about Hans de Brander's bequest and one other testament (that of Andres Bolens), the consistory quietly explained to them the decision of the jurists in the case of Hans's testament, and said that they could not yet respond about Andres's testament.[30] It so happened that Andres Bolens had left his bequest in general to 'the foreign' poor to be divided 'according to the executors' of the will. The consistory finally decided 'according to their best wisdom' to distribute the entire bequest to the French congregation.[31] The exchange reveals not only the tension between the minority groups, but also the local authorities' desires to moderate between them and to avoid any outright disturbances among them. Perhaps the consistory tried to soothe hurt feelings and balance matters after the legal decision in Hans de Brander's case. In the event, the consistory minutes report that 'the brothers of the French congregation were contented', though the French deacons expressed their concern that they be informed in the future when deliberations took place about them in the consistory. Despite such conflicts with the *fremdlingen* deacons, the French

---

[29] ArchGK (Nellner) 320B, no. 15; *Fremdlingen II*, fol. 427.
[30] 5 April 1574 (KRP, p. 501).
[31] 7 June (ibid., p. 505).

seem to have maintained good relations with the local *haussitzenden* deacons, who recorded expenditures to French poor from time to time.[32]

Sixteenth-century sources say even less about the smaller English church than about the French congregation.[33] The English church, too, experienced controversy within its congregation. In 1558, some complaints arose regarding their minister 'John the bishop'.[34] Apparently, among the complaints of one of the English church's members was that the minister was not sufficiently diligent in visiting the sick.[35] The existence of an English diaconate was confirmed when the Emden elder Anthony Asch approached the 'deacons of the English poor' to ask how 'things stood with their poor, if they had distress'.[36] Asch would leave shortly on a trip to England, and this inquiry into the English church's poor relief was probably to determine whether or not he should try to procure some additional assistance for them while in England.[37] An eighteenth-century church history of East Frisia states that the English exile church in Emden had, in addition to their minister, five elders, four deacons and two schoolmasters. The church was given use of a particular house somewhere in town for their worship services, which were held Sundays, Wednesdays and Fridays.[38] Most of the English exiles returned to England in 1559, but it is not clear if the remnant in Emden maintained any church structure. In 1576, there was no longer an English minister in Emden.[39] An English church was later reconstituted, however, since we find mention in 1584 of the English preacher and of a baptism taking place in the English congregation.[40]

The Walloon and the English churches were minority churches, separate from the town church, but confessionally they were accepted as 'sister

---

[32] For instance, ArchGK no. 3194, p. 10. The deacons gave 7.5 schap to two French children for their travel expenses in 1580. Obviously in such a case, the *haussitzenden* deacons were willing to pay the one-time expense since the children were leaving the city and would not become a regular burden.

[33] Andrew Pettegree, 'The English Church at Emden', in *Marian Protestantism: Six Studies* (Aldershot, 1996), pp. 10–38.

[34] For instance, KRP, pp. 31, 45, 47 (21 February, 14 April, 2 May)

[35] Ibid., pp. 63f (18 August 1558); ArchGK (Nellner) 320A, no. 6.

[36] KRP, p. 72 (27 February 1559).

[37] Questions involving Asch's trip (including the financing of it) begin to appear in the consistory minutes on 13 March and continued on 8 May and into the summer (for instance, ibid., pp. 76f, 85f).

[38] Eduard Meiners, *Oostvrieschlandts Kerkelyke Geschiedenisse* (Groningen, 1738), I, 329f; KRP, p. 64 (18 August 1558).

[39] KRP, p. 609 (6 April 1576).

[40] Ibid., p. 798 (6 January 1584).

congregations' of the Emden church. This was not the case, however, with the Lutherans, the Anabaptists and the Jews. As the Emden church became more confessionally fixed during the last quarter of the century, the complaints against the latter minority religious groups became especially hostile. The so-called 'ecclesiastical complaint of the common citizenry of the city Emden', which was presented before the regional East Frisian diet (Landtag) in 1590, opened with the petition (quoted at the opening of this chapter) that the minority religious groups be eradicated from the territory: namely, the Jews, Lutherans and Anabaptists. In light of this attitude, it is important to determine how poor members of these groups, those who were generally excluded from the broad range of social welfare which has been so far described, were cared for.

Of the three 'outcast' groups disparaged by the 'common citizenry of Emden' around 1590, the Lutheran congregation had the best prospects to overcome the limitations of its minority status – its patron was Count Edzard himself.[41] The Lutheran church was dominant in much of East Frisia, particularly the north and in the larger towns of Norden and Aurich.[42] As church institutions and discipline in Emden became more distinctly Reformed during the influx of thousands of Dutch Protestants, the situation for Emden Lutherans became less agreeable. Yet the Emden Lutheran community grew after 1567 due to the arrival of numerous Lutherans, most of whom were folks of little means, who had been expelled from Antwerp.[43]

After the arrival of Menso Alting in 1575, the confessional dispute between Emden (led by Alting) and Count Edzard grew at an ever-increasing rate. In 1586, the count established an official worship service in the Neuen Münze through his court preacher, and complaints quickly rose from the Emden consistory against the polemical Lutheran sermons being given in the Neuen Münze.[44] But since the Lutheran

---

[41] On the Lutheran congregation in Emden, see Heinrich Garrelts, *Die Reformation Ostfrieslands nach der Darstellung der Lutheraner vom Jahre 1593* (Aurich, 1925), which includes the contemporary argument for a Lutheran territorial church in 1593; A. Frerichs, 'Die Neubildung der evangelisch–lutherischen Gemeinde zu Emden zur Säkularfeier am 9. Juli 1875' (Emden, 1875), pp. 3–4 describes the situation in the sixteenth century before turning to 'Die Anfänge, 1664–1744'; Smid, *Kirchengeschichte*, pp. 229–42.

[42] When one compares the confessional boundaries of East Frisia at the end of the sixteenth century with the old diocesan boundaries, one notes a striking similarity. Virtually all of what had belonged to the bishopric of Bremen was now Lutheran, and the primary Calvinist areas of East Frisia were located in the region that had been part of the bishopric of Münster. Perhaps the medieval ecclesiastical traditions which had developed in East Frisia also affected the inclination toward one confession or the other.

[43] Frerichs, *Neubildung*, p. 3; Brenneysen, *Ost-Friesische Historie*, I, 393f.

[44] KRP, pp. 835ff (30 December 1587, 2 January and 22 January 1588).

congregation had the full support of the count, the Calvinist ministers and leaders were powerless to stop the sermons.

As Lutherans came to Emden from Hamburg and Saxony, the Neuen Münze was soon overcrowded during the Lutheran services. Just as a previous attempt by the count to appropriate the Gasthaus church for Emden's Lutherans failed due to civic opposition, so too did new attempts to gain a permanent church home, this time in the old chapel of St Gertrude's Gasthaus (now called the 'Fleischhaus').[45] Count Edzard found a way, however, to assist the Lutheran congregation, which as a voluntary church had no endowment from which to draw income. He granted the Lutherans control over some of the church properties of which he still had some claim, dating back to his father Enno II's seizure of church properties after the Reformation. Edzard also granted the Lutheran church some money and church lands, which had been given to the Emden church by his mother the Countess Anna. Consequently, the Reformed church complained that they now had difficulty maintaining their own ministers and schools.[46] Despite the protestations, the Lutheran church had for the first time some financial stability.

The Lutheran congregation in Emden clearly had a moderately sized congregation during the last two decades of the century, and it was not without a powerful patron in the person of the count. Such circumstances proved especially troublesome to the leaders of the Reformed church, and complaints soon surfaced accusing the Lutherans of breaking into the sphere of public collections for poor relief. In a letter to Count Edzard's son Enno (an apparently unsuccessful attempt to influence the father through the son) on 11 December 1592, Menso Alting described the theological 'problems' caused by those at the Neuen Münze and the dispute over the church properties. Alting then turned to offences which the Lutherans committed 'against the almost 17-year-old Alms-Ordinance which had been an example to the neighbouring towns'. The 1576 Poor Relief Ordinance contained a section which explicitly forbade any collections around the houses in Emden without the consent of the *haussitzenden* deacons.[47] The Burgermeister and city council (as well as the count's bailiff) had expressly granted the *haussitzenden* deacons this special oversight control.

---

[45] Hesse, *Alting*, pp. 165ff; Smid, *Kirchengeschichte*, p. 230.

[46] The Emden citizenry wrote two letters to Edzard on 24 and 30 April 1589 protesting against the transfer of some of the properties from the Reformed church over to the Lutherans; Meiners, *Oostvrieschlandts Kerkelyke Geschiedenisse*, II, 271ff, 276ff. The complaints were also made before the Landtage in 1590 and 1593 (in each case being the second point, right after the desire to maintain the true Christian religion); StaE, I. Reg., 910, no. 19; Brenneysen, *Ost-Friesische Historie*, I, 413.

[47] Article 4. ArchGK no. 3001, p. 4.

Worse yet, Alting continued, the administrators of the Gasthaus and the *haussitzenden* poor had 'benevolently reconciled' with the Lutherans: the Lutherans were 'allowed' to collect alms at the Münze during their services in order to support their poor communicants, but the Gasthaus and *haussitzenden* administrators were to retain all other revenues. The Lutherans broke both the Poor Ordinance and their agreement with the deacons and Gasthaus in making collection rounds through the city at the houses of citizens, in addition to hanging their donation pouches in the taverns and inns.[48] According to Alting, the Lutherans were 'leaving nothing undone' in their march to bring 'what had been good order to demolition'.

Complaints against the Lutherans continued, and on 14 May 1593, all the preachers and two head-deacons went before the city council to protest a number of points of disorder in the town, including the illegal activities of the Lutherans 'against the Poor Ordinance'. Through his own commands, the count had been acting 'inequitably' and violating the ordinances. The deacons and Reformed ministers appealed to the fact that it had been the city council which had ratified the Poor Ordinance in 1576, and now the count was trying to undermine it. The city council decided to investigate further the regulation of disorderly taverns and the question of the Lutheran poor. The deacons were instructed to present documentation about exactly where the Lutherans were hanging their alms-pouches in violation of the ordinance, and the city council would then take responsibility for the matter.[49]

Although the only surviving evidence concerning the poor relief of Emden's Lutheran church lacks any description of the manner of administration or the number of poor within their congregation, the evidence conveys this minority congregation's attitudes toward poor relief. Despite the Lutheran congregation's status, it behaved like an established church, at least in its collections for poor relief; perhaps the support of the count and the Lutheran majorities in much of East Frisia gave Emden's Lutheran congregants confidence in the face of fierce protests of the Reformed ministers. Theirs was a voluntary congregation, but the Lutherans did not limit themselves to collecting alms within their own group. Instead, they followed the example of the city's established poor relief institutions and placed collection pouches throughout the city and made door-to-door collections, and in so doing the Lutherans were able to seize a portion of the donations which had been going to the Reformed deacons and the city Gasthaus as well as the

---

[48] Brenneysen, *Ost-Friesische Historie*, I, 411.
[49] KRP, p. 891 (14 May 1593).

other agencies. Adding to Alting's theological complaints against the Lutherans were the Lutherans' social activities. Alting clearly could not control his temper over the fact that, according to him, 'nothing good' (here referring to both Emden's poor relief and school systems) 'can remain unappropriated by them'.

No further references regarding the issue of Lutheran poor relief survive, so we do not know how or if the issue was resolved to either side's satisfaction. Nevertheless, the issue became moot in less than two years, for in March of 1595 the Emden Revolution took place and led to an immediate prohibition of Lutheran worship services in Emden and the establishment of an autonomous Calvinist city church. No Lutheran services were allowed in Emden for 90 years. In 1685, the Burgermeisters and city council authorised a tightly regulated Lutheran congregation: it could meet only four times a year for communion services, and each service was to be attended by a Reformed pastor and one or two deacons. Moreover, the Lutherans were to have no poor relief fund of their own; instead, the Reformed deacons were to receive all the Lutherans' collected alms immediately after the communion service, and their poor relief would be administered by the Reformed deacons.[50]

While the Lutherans with their political patronage of the count were the most serious threat to Emden's Reformed ministers and congregation, the city and territory were also home to a great many radical Protestant sects during the sixteenth century.[51] Melchior Hoffman baptised 300 people in a service in the Grosse Kirche in 1530; Andreas Karlstadt, Menno Simons, David Joris, Dirck Philips and Hendrick Niclaes all lived in or visited East Frisia during the middle decades of the century. A robust Anabaptist minority, though not necessarily in one congregation, seems to have existed in Emden throughout much of the century, despite numerous edicts from the counts and countess that

---

[50] See the opening pages of the 'Kirchenprotokoll 1685–1772' of the Emden Lutheran church; it is kept in the offices of the Lutheran church. Thanks to Dr Menno Smid for his advice as to the Kirchenbuch's existence and its whereabouts.

[51] See, J. Müller, *Die Mennoniten in Ostfriesland vom 16. bis zum 18. Jahrhundert* (Amsterdam, 1887); J. Müller, 'Die Mennoniten in Ostfriesland', *EJb*, 4/2 (1881), pp. 58–74 and 5/1 (1882); S. Blaupot ten Cate, *Geschiedenis der Doopsgezinden in Groningen, Overijssel en Oost-Friesland*, 2 vols (Leeuwarden, 1842); J. ten Doornkaat Koolman, 'De Anabaptisten in Oostfriesland ten Tijde van Hermannus Aquilonontanus (1489–1584)', *Nederlands Archief vor Kerkgeschiedenis*, Part XLVI (1963/64), p. 87–99; Andrew Pettegree, 'The Struggle for an Orthodox Church: Calvinists and Anabaptists in East Friesland, 1554–1578', *Bulletin John Rylands University Library of Manchester*, 70 (1988), p. 45–59; Erich von Reken, *Zur Geschichte der Emder Taufgesinnten (Mennoniten) 1529–1750* (Aurich, 1986).

they be expelled or face property confiscation or even death. There were, moreover, two major disputations in Emden during the century, both against the Anabaptists, one by Johannes a Lasco in 1544 and one by Menso Alting in 1578. Neither disputation yielded any sort of 'ecumenical' unity, but the Emden Reformed church acquired a much sharper focus of its own doctrines as a result of the challenge provided by the Anabaptist congregations.[52]

No records from the Emden Anabaptists themselves survive from the sixteenth century.[53] Three sixteenth-century references to their poor relief activities are available, and they provide some insights. The Emden consistory frequently addressed questions regarding Anabaptists and Anabaptism, for the Reformed church frequently lost members to the Mennonite congregation; or it had to 'correct' someone who was leaning toward Anabaptist beliefs. The consistory case of Jacob and Proene de Boer provides the earliest mention of Anabaptist poor relief in Emden.

Jacob and Proene, refugees from Ypres, had received alms from the *fremdlingen* deacons as early as 1559, and by 1560 they were involved in a consistory dispute lasting for six years over their beliefs.[54] Proene had written a 'slanderous letter' to the consistory; when she was summoned in May 1560 to prove her charges, her only response to the consistory was, 'Examine the scripture!'[55] In August both were called before the consistory to account for the grave accusations which they had made against the ministers and the deacons: Jacob and Proene were happy with neither the doctrines nor the poor relief of the church.

Because of this discontent, the Anabaptist congregation must have been especially alluring. On 22 February 1563, the couple appeared before the consistory and were accused of receiving alms from the Anabaptists. This was their first appearance before the consistory since August 1561, after no fewer than six appearances in 1560–61 and before at least 17 appearances in 1565–66. Perhaps their 'disappearance' into the Anabaptist congregation had kept them from the attention of the consistory. After a long disputation they were asked if they would remove themselves from the Anabaptists and thereafter receive no more alms from them. For a long time neither gave a clear response, but finally the wife, Proene, answered contemptuously that she did not consider perishing to be a good option and would therefore continue

---

[52] Pettegree, 'Calvinists and Anabaptists', p. 59.

[53] Any documentation which had survived into this century was destroyed in the final days of World War II when the tiny village in which the Emden Mennonite church's library had been stored for safe-keeping came under sudden attack as the war ended.

[54] *Fremdlingen I*, fols 9v, 10v, 13v, 21v, 47v, 50v, 67v.

[55] KRP, p. 112 (27 May 1560).

receiving alms from 'our adversaries', as the consistory's secretary noted, because Jacob and Proene had not left the congregation, rather 'we had left them'.[56] Proene justified their continued reliance on the Anabaptists' alms by the fact that the congregation had 'left them'. Yet examination of the *fremdlingen* deacons' account books reveals that Jacob, Proene and their child had received relief from the refugee deacons for several years, as well as every month between August 1562 and their current consistory appearance in February 1563.[57] But they must have considered the amount of the alms offered by the *fremdlingen* deacons to be inadequate. Thus the Anabaptists possessed a poor relief system for their members which was so well developed that it could draw members from Emden's Reformed church when the alms received there were not considered adequate by the recipient.[58]

The other two indications of a developed Mennonite system of poor relief come from testaments. The first reference to the 'Poor of the Mennonite congregation' is striking because of the massive size of the bequest. In August 1578 (three months after Alting's disputation), the Emden citizen Hinrich van Coeßvelde and his wife made their testaments. Hinrich specified 600 gulden to be divided up: 250 gulden between four relatives, 50 gulden to the 'poor orphan boys who are apprenticed by the citizenry', and, most surprisingly, 300 gulden to the poor of the Mennonite congregation.[59] Such a sum of money was virtually unheard of in bequests to the poor at the time, and it demonstrates the potential size of the Mennonite congregation in Emden around the time of Menso Alting's disputation.

The second testament dealt with a much smaller sum, but the bequest made an extraordinary association between poor relief institutions. Johan Claesen and Schwane, also citizens, drew up their testament on 8 March 1583. For his part, Johan stipulated that after his death 15 gulden should be given to the poor: the Gasthaus poor 5 gulden, the *haussitzenden* poor 5 gulden, and the Mennonite poor 5 gulden. Schwane used the same combination of poor relief agencies, giving 4 gulden to each.[60] Despite

---

[56] Ibid., p. 159 (22 February 1563).

[57] *Fremdlingen I*, fols 50v, 67v.

[58] Charles H. Parker has noted similar complaints against the Anabaptists by the Reformed Church at Delft. For instance, the Delft consistory denied assistance to one woman because she had sought it from both the Mennonites and the city almoners; in another case, a woman had incurred some sort of debt from a Mennonite congregation before returning to the Reformed church; Parker, 'Moral Supervision and Poor Relief in the Reformed Church of Delft, 1579–1609', *ARG*, 87 (1996), pp. 347, 356.

[59] His wife Geßke left 70 gulden between a niece and a nephew and 50 gulden to the 'orphans in the Gasthaus'; EKP 14/673.

[60] Ibid., 15/498–98v.

the accelerated confessionalisation of Emden's church at this time, we must always bear in mind that the entire citizenry did not fully accept strict confessional boundaries, just as this couple considered the Reformed *haussitzenden* deacons, the Gasthaus and the Mennonite poor to have an equal standing.

After the Emden Revolution, the Emden city council began to require the payment of 'protection money' (*Schutzgeld*) from the Mennonites and Jews who lived in the city; this policy was in contrast to that in the rest of East Frisia where Mennonites were still outlawed (except between 1625 and 1628). *Schutzgeld* meant a certain degree of toleration for the Mennonites, although a free public exercise of their religion was still not allowed. Exactly when this policy began is not known, but *Schutzgeld* lists for 1601 and 1602 exist and can provide us with a little insight into the size of the Mennonite congregation.[61] In 1601, 158 Mennonite heads of households (it was not indicated if those on the list were individuals or families) paid the Emden *Schutzgeld*; in 1602, the number had climbed to 171 despite the loss of 24 from the 1601 list (19 had moved away, 5 had died). The amount of the *Schutzgeld* payment was based upon one's assets. The 1602 list provides valuable information concerning those who were too poor to make a payment, or at least had fallen temporarily into poverty and were unable to make their full required payments, using such phrases as 'Pauper', 'fallen into poverty' (*verarmt*), and 'could give no more because of insolvency'. In 1602, 11 Mennonites were identified as being poor (4 with the term 'pauper'); 7 paid no *Schutzgeld*, while 4 paid a portion but not their full assessment. Of course the city's definition of pauper for the purpose of abstaining from the *Schutzgeld* must have differed from that used by the congregation to provide relief to those in need. Nevertheless, these numbers are suggestive of the size of the Mennonite congregation and numbers of their poor.

In 1800, Emden's Burgermeisters and city council required that all poor relief agencies inform the city of the size of their poor relief fund and the manner of administration of it. In response, the Mennonite community's report explained that the present congregation maintained no fund through regular collections. Instead, the congregation's needy were maintained by the completely voluntary contributions of the well-to-do members. Moreover, the fund for the poor was distributed through the deacons with no further administration or calculation for accounting.[62] The Mennonite minister continued,

---

[61] StaE, I. Reg., 415; Erich von Reeken, 'Zur Geschichte', pp. 20–24 (for 1601), 25–31 (for 1602).

[62] For a description of the Anabaptist office of deacon as illuminated in a church order drawn up by the Waterlander Anabaptists during their meeting in Emden in September

> this institution is as old as the existence of our congregation, and we may appeal, without timidity, to the public testimony, that our poor have never before had to ask for support from some other place; on the contrary, we have moreover extended donations, which were often not insignificant, to the churches and poor-relief of other religious societies.[63]

While no external evidence survives to prove that the system described in 1800 was truly 'as old as the existence of our congregation', the description of Anabaptist poor relief does not contradict the few sixteenth-century references that survive. Moreover, the description parallels the original Mennonite alms-giving practice in Holland during the sixteenth century: alms were not collected during worship services nor were alms-boxes placed at the door of the meeting house.[64]

By all accounts, the Anabaptists maintained a dependable system of poor relief. As a marginal community that was frequently on the verge of expulsion, the Anabaptists seem to have tried to avoid placing a burden on the local poor relief system. Indeed, their level of provision to the poor was high enough that they could even attract members of the main church into their midst with alms. To be sure, the Emden Mennonite pastor in 1800 made a similar point in his report to the city council and stated that there was 'no probable cause' to fear any burdening of the public poor relief institutions 'through poor members of our congregation'.[65]

The only minority religious group that did not have the character of a voluntary church was the Jewish community.[66] While there is evidence of a small Jewish settlement outside Emden's walls in Grosse Faldern about 1530, the first significant appearance of a Jewish community was noted about 1570.[67] By this time, Emden's population was

---

1568, see J. G. de Hoop Scheffer, 'Oude gemeente verordeningen', *Doopsgezinde Bijdragen* (1877), pp. 62–93, esp. 71–2 (Articles 8–14). Thanks to Dr Heinhold Fast for advising me of this publication and for the free reign in his extensive library.

[63] StaE, II. Reg., 1177, 2nd letter in file (26 June 1800).

[64] *Mennonite Encyclopedia* (Hillsboro, KS: Mennonite Brethren Publishing House, 1955), I, 66.

[65] StaE, II. Reg., 1177.

[66] For an excellent attempt to reconstruct the very obscure sixteenth-century history of Emden's Jewish community, see Jan Lokers, *Die Juden in Emden 1530–1806* (Aurich, 1990), esp. pp. 20–44. Lokers builds upon Bernhard Brilling's original study of the topic, 'Die Entstehung der jüdischen Gemeinde in Emden (1570–1613)', *Westfalen. Hefte für Geschichte, Kunst und Volkskunde*, 51 (1973), pp. 210–24.

[67] During construction of Emden's *Judenstrasse* in 1589, an adviser informed Count Edzard that over 60 years before, the Jews had not lived inside the city but outside the gates in Faldern which was not yet part of the city. The oldest surviving record of a money transaction of an Emden Jew is from 26 December 1571; Lokers, *Juden*, pp. 22, note 60; 23.

already overflowing into the Faldern suburbs, and as Emden began to incorporate Faldern into the city limits (and walls) cries of protest arose against Jews being allowed to live inside the city. Already by 27 February 1570, the consistory met with the city council and complained that to 'allow the Jews into the city with residences is not agreed to everywhere'.[68] In 1589, the Emden citizenry constructed a street in Grosse Faldern to centralise the Jewish quarter in one portion of the city. While the city acknowledged that it might be dangerous for the Jews as 'protected subjects' (*Schutzuntertanen*) of the count to live outside the city walls as before, it nevertheless argued the Jews should in no instance be allowed to live in 'the best streets' with 'eminent neighbourhoods'.[69]

The same attitude is often echoed in the consistory records. In May and June 1582, the widow Aelke Wittbackers was admonished for renting out her house to a 'Jew, who, like all of them, without doubt gravely blaspheme the Lord Jesus Christ'. She argued that she had only taken in the Jew, 'in order to receive a little more rent, because otherwise she had no means in order to live'. The consistory ordered her to settle the accounts as soon as possible, at least before winter, so that the Jew would be let go, 'because a Christian is not free to have any fellowship with such blasphemers of Jesus Christ'.[70] Other church members were also called before the consistory because of their business or mere conversations with people from the Jewish community.[71] When the animosity toward the Jewish community was not rooted in religious arguments, it was based on economic arguments, such as the 'wicked usury of the Jews'. For example, the so-called 'ecclesiastical complaint of the common citizenry of the city Emden' to Count Edzard in 1590 was accompanied by 'the citizenry's proof articles' to supplement each complaint. The supporting 'proof' for the complaint against the Jews contained most of the aforementioned arguments:

> 20 years ago there were only one or two Jews living here in Emden
> – outside the city gates, and not in the city – and otherwise none in
> the whole territory. However, from around the year 1570, the Jews
> were not only admitted [into Emden] abundantly with their grave
> usury to suck out the poor subjects, but also allowed their public
> exercise of religion and to hold synagogue.[72]

---

[68] KRP, p. 375 (27 February 1570).

[69] Lokers, *Juden*, pp. 23, 31.

[70] KRP, pp. 778ff (7 May, 18 and 25 June 1582).

[71] For example, ibid., pp. 640, 658, 691f, 878, 897f (24 September 1576, 4 February 1577, 9 April, 2 June 1578, 20 March 1592, 11 January, 8 February 1594).

[72] StaE, I. Reg., 910, no. 3.

Despite protestations to the contrary, the size of the Jewish community probably remained quite small during the sixteenth century. In 1593, Count Edzard confirmed that there were 'not more than six' Jewish families under his protection in Emden. Moreover, in the aftermath of the Emden Revolution, at least three of the families left the city out of uncertainty following the reduction of the count's authority in the town. When the city began its own *Schutzgeld* policy for the Mennonites, it included the Jews. In fact, the *Schutzgeld* lists of the Mennonites contained the payments of the Jews as well.[73] In the 1601 list, seven Jewish individuals or heads of families paid *Schutzgeld*; in 1602, eight were on the list. Two of the eight Jews recorded in 1602 were listed as 'paupers' and paid no *Schutzgeld*.

It is a pity that absolutely no allusion to the method of poor relief used by this small community to care for these paupers in its midst can be found in the Emden sources. One puzzling reference does exist in the records of expenditures from the Reformed church's *Becken* fund in 1558: 'The Jew Joannes Tobias received one gulden.'[74] How could it be that the consistory, from which a great deal of hostility toward any interaction with Jews had been witnessed, would give alms from the fund intended strictly for 'the household of faith'? A possible explanation could be that the payment was in connection with a baptism. Evidence from other northern German towns describes the practice of 'Jewish baptisms', in which a Jewish convert would be baptised, usually with the city council standing in as sponsor and letting the baptised receive a small gift of money.[75] It would have been extraordinarily surprising, given the attitude toward the Jews in the town, to find any of Emden's social welfare institutions providing poor relief to someone in the Jewish community.

Of course, given the confessional composition of the town and the attempts to impose confessional uniformity, we would expect there to be a difference between the status of the confessional minorities and that of the foreign refugees of the local confession in sixteenth-century Emden. Most interesting, however, is the somewhat more complex situation which is revealed when we look at these groups' poor relief. The French and Dutch exiles were allowed by the local authorities to maintain their own institutions, but their refugee status led to intense competition as they competed for the favour of the local church.

---

[73] Ibid., Reg., 415; von Reeken, 'Zur Geschichte', pp. 20–31. Jews are included on the Mennonite *Schutzgeld* lists only until 1638, after which time they must have had their own lists.

[74] KRP, p. 66 (19 September 1558).

[75] Lokers, *Juden*, p. 22, note 58. He notes that there are numerous examples of such 'Judentaufen' in Lüneburg, for example.

By the same token, the city and church authorities' dislike or even prohibition of the confessional minority groups, like the Lutherans and Anabaptists, did not necessarily find full support across the town. Local residents, at least as Emden began to become more Calvinist, seem to have often been supportive of these confessionally despised groups. The Reformed ministers and deacons were scandalised by the social welfare activities of the Lutherans, but what is perhaps most telling to us is the fact that they were able to gain support from across the town, and the local deacons felt some of their revenues slipping away. The Lutherans had a political status that was clearly affected by the support of the count, but even the prohibited Anabaptists were able to support their own members and occasionally attract new members with their poor relief.

CHAPTER SEVEN

Church Discipline, Social Disciplining and Poor Relief

> [The *haussitzenden* deacons] should also secure, that those who eat the alms and receive from the church should give no offence with sins and disgrace, but instead carry themselves in faith and behaviour as the proper poor of Christ, because it is both against God's word and against all respectability that public whores and rogues should be bolstered in their depravity with the alms.
>
> From Emden's Poor Relief Ordinance (1576)[1]

Underlying much of Menso Alting's activity was the desire to reinvigorate church discipline and moral order which some felt had decayed since the late 1560s. The Dutch refugees had indeed infused the Emden church with greater aspirations toward church discipline. Yet the social and economic situation brought about by the continuous flood of refugees into the city (as well as the piracy and fighting of the Dutch Revolt) soon overwhelmed the still relatively weak church leadership of Emden. Therefore, the supervision of morals in the town had begun once again to decrease after about 1568. This decline can be observed by a survey of discipline cases heard by the consistory over the period. Many Dutch Protestants noted the lack of discipline in Emden.[2] The desire for tight church discipline of the congregation might have been one of the major enticements into Emden's relatively large and disciplined Anabaptist community. In 1573 the consistory called a special meeting in which the town was divided into seven special *Klufts* (districts) to be supervised by the elders 'with the assistance of other pious, enthusiastic brothers' in order that 'the church discipline might be resumed and be better nurtured' because discipline had 'now almost completely decayed'.[3]

Immediately after the arrival of Alting, the consistory began procedures to elect new elders; many elders had succumbed to the plague.[4] Up to this point, Emden's attempts at church discipline had been aimed

---

[1] ArchGK no. 3001 (Article 3); Emil Sehling (ed.), *Die evangelischen Kirchenordnungen des XVI. Jahrhunderts*, VII/2/1 (Tübingen, 1963), p. 456.

[2] See, for instance, the stinging criticism of Emden in a long, detailed letter from Delft in 1573, 'Emden in niederländischer Beleuchtung aus dem Jahre 1573' [ed. A. A. van Schelven], *EJb*, 20 (1920), pp. 174–93.

[3] KRP, pp. 479f (3 July 1573).

[4] Ibid., pp. 573f, 578 (25 November, 11 December 1578).

exclusively at the members of the congregation. Under Alting's direction the consistory became ever more interested in using the influence of the church in establishing proper moral behaviour throughout the city. A number of the ecclesiastical developments early in Alting's ministry indicate that this was his aim. The consistory began negotiations in December 1575 to allow the ministers to hold Sunday services in the Gasthaus church (of the old Franciscan monastery) as well as the Grosse Kirche. Emden's topography suggests the reasons for this plan. The Grosse Kirche was located in the far south-western corner of the city, but over the last two decades especially, the town had expanded far to the east to include the former Faldern suburbs. By holding regular sermons in the Gasthaus church, now located in Emden's topographic centre, the ministers might have wished to extend the church's influence more directly into the 'new town' (see Map 2.3 and Figure 2.1).

To this end, the town's partitions were redrawn in February 1576 in order to contain the new town. Previously Emden (without the Faldern suburbs) had been divided into seven *Klufts* for church discipline (administered by elders) and three *Klufts* for poor relief (administered by deacons). With the reorganisation, the entire city with its suburbs was divided into five *Klufts* for both church discipline and poor relief (each *Kluft* was assigned a minister, three elders and six deacons). Accompanying this reorganisation, Emden's first Poor Relief Ordinance ('An Ordinance of the Beggars') was confirmed by the Burgermeisters, city council, and bailiff of Emden on 13 March 1576. The Poor Relief Ordinance's title claimed that it was the work of the ministers, elders and deacons in Emden, but the driving force behind its creation was Alting. In addition to expressly banning all begging in the city and creating two officials (*Armenvögte*) to oversee the policing of the poor on the streets, the ordinance explicitly described the standards of behaviour and church discipline which were expected of the poor and which were to be enforced by the deacons.

Reformed church discipline was aimed particularly at maintaining the reputation of the faithful by prohibiting members from activities that would dishonour God or tarnish the communion table.[5] If Herman

---

[5] For an analysis of the connections between poor relief and Dutch Reformed discipline, see Charles H. Parker, 'Moral Supervision and Poor Relief in the Reformed Church of Delft, 1579–1609', *ARG*, 87 (1996), pp. 334–61. For some of the most important recent studies on Reformed church discipline, see for the Netherlands and Emden the titles by Heinz Schilling in note 8 below; Herman Roodenburg, *Onder censuur: de kerkelijke tucht in de gereformeerde gemeente van Amsterdam, 1578–1700* (Hilversum, 1990), esp. p. 145; Rab Houston, 'The Consistory of the Scots Church, Rotterdam: An Aspect of "Civic Calvinism", c. 1600–1800', *ARG*, 87 (1996), p. 362–92. For Switzerland and France, see Robert M. Kingdon, 'The Control of Morals in Calvin's Geneva', in *The Social History of*

Roodenburg's study of the Reformed church in Amsterdam is an accurate model, members were keenly familiar with their neighbours' activities and were often quite willing to inform the consistory of them.[6] After the arrival in Emden of the London Dutch refugee church under Johannes a Lasco in 1554, the Emden church showed increasing interest in church discipline. The Emden church sought to stimulate church discipline so as to separate the 'pure' congregation from the rest. With the creation of a special diaconate to fulfil the biblical mandate of Galations 6:10 to 'do good to all men, and especially those who are of the household of faith' came an inherent push for church discipline of the poor by these *Becken* deacons. Indeed, recipients from the *Becken* fund were defined, first and foremost, by the proper belief and behaviour which made them part of the 'household of faith'.

Proper moral behaviour and proper belief were always important attributes in the eyes of the Dutch *fremdlingen* deacons caring for the refugee poor. The earliest leaders of the Dutch congregation in Emden came from a congregation in London which was composed of members who wished to submit themselves to examinations proving their legitimate membership of the congregation of true Christians. The *fremdlingen* deacons in Emden recognised the difficulty of ensuring that all the incoming refugees were truly 'right-believing' Reformed Protestants, and it was suggested that the deacons request from the poor certificates of membership which a 'proper Christian' would have received from his or her minister at home in the Netherlands (or from another exile church). Their objective in stressing church discipline was to protect the reputation of the pure congregation – to make sure that 'no swindlers and rogues' were among the recipients of relief.[7] Of course, the practical reality of providing poor relief to a massive refugee community,

---

the Reformation, ed. Lawrence P. Buck and Jonathan W. Zophy (Columbus, 1972), pp. 3–16; Kingdon, 'The Control of Morals by the Earliest Calvinists', in *Renaissance, Reformation, Resurgence*, ed. Peter de Klerk (Grand Rapids, 1976), pp. 95–106; Ulrich Pfister, 'Reformierte Sittenzucht zwischen kommunaler und territorialer Organisation: Graubünden, 16.–18. Jahrhundert', *ARG*, 87 (1996), pp. 287–332; Raymond A. Mentzer, 'Disciplina nervus ecclesiae: The Calvinist Reform of Morals at Nîmes', *SCJ*, 18 (1987), pp. 89–115; Mentzer, 'Ecclesiastical Discipline and Communal Reorganisation among the Protestants and Southern France', *European History Quarterly*, 21 (1991), pp. 163–83. For discussions of Geneva, France, Germany and Scotland, see the essays in *Sin and the Calvinists: Morals Control and the Consistory in the Reformed Tradition*, ed. Raymond A. Mentzer (Kirksville, MO, 1995) and in *Kirchenzucht und Sozialdisziplinierung im frühneuzeitlichen Europa*, ed. Heinz Schilling (Berlin, 1994); see also Ronnie Po-chia Hsia, *Social Discipline in the Reformation: Central Europe 1550–1750* (London/New York, 1989), pp. 27–8, 124–9, 137–8, 164–6.

[6] Roodenburg, *Onder censuur*, pp. 350–69.

[7] KRP, p. 277 (1 May 1567).

many of the members being completely new to the city and frequently on the move, made the oversight responsibilities of the Dutch deacons all the more difficult. In practice, strict church discipline was probably limited primarily to the 'regular' recipients of poor relief from the *fremdlingen* deacons; it would have been impossible to discipline all who needed extraordinary relief or who were merely passing through Emden on the way to some other city of refuge.

The minutes of Emden's consistory meetings are the most important source for investigating the exercise of church discipline.[8] Of course, the church council handled more than just cases of church discipline: more than half of their activities concerned issues such as church government, finance and administration, theological concerns, marriage and the family, and education. Heinz Schilling has divided the activities of Emden's consistory between the years 1557–62 into the following general categories:

State, Politics, and Society	7.1%
Calvinist Congregation	34.8%
Res Mixtae	13.2%
Church Discipline	44.9%[9]

---

[8] See Heinz Schilling's statistical studies of the work of Emden's consistory. The first study focused on a statistical analysis of the individual cases before the consistory from 1557 to 1562, 'Reformierte Kirchenzucht als Sozialdisziplinierung? Die Tätigkeit des Emder Presbyteriums in den Jahren 1557–1562', in *Niederlande und Nordwestdeutschland. Studien zur Regional- und Stadtgeschichte Nordwestkontinetaleuropas im Mittelalter und in der Neuzeit*, ed. Wilfried Ehbrecht and Heinz Schilling (Cologne Vienna, 1983), pp. 261–327. Schilling continued this statistical approach with a 'longue durée' analysis of the consistory minutes into the nineteenth century (he used detailed analyses of five-year periods every 50 years, hence 1557–62, 1596–1600, 1645–49, 1695–99, 1741–45, 1791–99, 1821–25). This study was first published as 'Sündenzucht und Frühneuzeitliche Sozialdisziplinierung: Die Calvinistische Presbyteriale Kirchenzucht in Emden vom 16. bis 19. Jahrhundert', in *Stände und Gesellschaft im Alten Reich*, ed. Georg Schmidt (Stuttgart, 1989), pp. 265–302. For a slightly modified analysis of these statistics, 'Calvinism and the Making of the Modern Mind: Ecclesiastical Discipline of Public and Private Sin from the Sixteenth to the Nineteenth Century', in *Civic Calvinism*, pp. 40–68. Schilling has also recently used the Emden consistory records for a study of discipline in early modern family life, 'Reform and Supervision of Family Life in Germany and the Netherlands', in *Sin and the Calvinists*, ed. Raymond Mentzer (Kirksville, MO, 1994), pp. 15–61; and 'Frühneuzeitliche Formierung und Disziplinierung von Ehe, Familie und Erziehung im Spiegel calvinistischer Kirchenratspropkolle', in *Glaube und Eid: Treuformeln, Glaubensbekenntnisse und Sozialdisziplinierung zwischen Mittelalter und Neuzeit*, ed. Paolo Prodi (Munich, 1993), pp. 199–235. For a comparative analysis of church discipline, see 'Die Kirchenzucht im frühneuzeitlichen Europa in interkonfessionell vergleichender und interdisziplinärer Perspektive – eine Zwischenbilanz', in *Kirchenzucht und Sozialdisziplinierung im frühneuzeitlichen Europa*, ed. Heinz Schilling (Berlin, 1994), pp. 11–40.

[9] Schilling, *Civic Calvinism*, p. 43. In his first analysis of the consistory activities

The category *Res Mixtae* includes issues that were considered by contemporaries to be neither purely political/social nor purely ecclesiastical, including marriage and the family, school and education, and poor relief and health/sickness matters.

Although the deacons were not members of the consistory, they frequently attended consistory meetings, and the consistory often addressed poor relief issues and other such cases. This was especially true in the early years of Emden's renovated consistory (after around 1557), when certain elders were given the responsibility to oversee the *Becken* fund for the poor relief of the 'household of faith', which meant that the consistory was for a time in direct control of the provision of members of the 'household'. Schilling's study found that three-quarters of the *Res Mixtae* cases concerned social welfare; thus, about 10 per cent of the consistory's activities between 1557 and 1562 involved some question or instance of poor relief.[10] Of course, most 'disciplining' of the poor took place in the field, by decisions of the deacons and other poor relief administrators themselves, especially, as mentioned above, by the *Becken* and the *fremdlingen* deacons. Only cases which became especially difficult or intractable were brought before (or taken over by) the consistory.

During the last quarter of the sixteenth century, the number of relief-related cases before the consistory declined dramatically. This trend corresponded to the increased authority given to the *haussitzenden* deacons in church discipline in the 1576 Poor Relief Ordinance: because these deacons were now expressly responsible for church discipline, there may have been less need to consult with the consistory on individual cases. The 'new emphasis' on church discipline in poor relief by the *haussitzenden* deacons can be detected soon after the arrival of Menso Alting. Church discipline of local poor relief recipients had until this time been limited to those of the *Becken* deacons or the poor of the congregation. On 16 January 1576, Alting's interest in expanding church discipline was demonstrated as two elders were assigned to contact the head-deacons (referred to as the three 'oldest' deacons, indicating the hierarchical progression from serving as under-deacon to head-deacon). These head-deacons were to instruct their under-deacons to go about in their *Kluft*, 'earnestly investigate the great sexual offence of adultery and prostitution, etc.', and then bring in their written reports to the consistory.[11]

---

during this same time period, Schilling found a slightly different statistical breakdown: 5 per cent, 26 per cent, 14 per cent and 55 per cent respectively; 'Reformierte Kirchenzucht', p. 281. Apparently, these broad categories underwent some refinement in definition. The basic picture of the consistory's activites remains, nevertheless, unchanged.

[10] Schilling, 'Reformierte Kirchenzucht', p. 286.

[11] KRP, p. 592.

This investigation proved to be the precursor of a campaign to increase the role of the *haussitzenden* deacons in relation to discipline. A month later the consistory concluded the complete reorganisation of Emden's *Klufts* and the *haussitzenden* diaconate, ordering a new division of the town into five *Klufts*, consolidating the previous three poor relief *Klufts* and seven church discipline *Klufts*. To each of the new *Klufts* were assigned three elders and six *haussitzenden* deacons (one head-deacon and five under-deacons).

The pinnacle of Alting's large-scale restructuring was the March 1576 Poor Relief Ordinance.[12] In addition to outlining the manner of selecting the deacons, describing the deacons' duties, prohibiting begging and forbidding any public alms-collections without the consent of the deacons, the ordinance also instructed the *haussitzenden* deacons frequently to visit the poor in their *Klufts* to ensure proper behaviour. The *haussitzenden* deacons were also directed to refuse aid to those who gave 'offence with sins and disgrace' so that no one 'be bolstered in their depravity with the alms'.[13] Thus the Poor Relief Ordinance made clear the new role of the *haussitzenden* deacons in church discipline. Further evidence of the consistory's drive to include the entire city in its discipline can be found in May, as the consistory decided to ask the city council for assistance in controlling misbehaviour in public places and on Sundays and during sermons: namely, such activities (or inactivities) as laziness, ball-playing on the Sabbath and during the sermons (in the streets, in the churchyard and other places) as well as 'the great disorder in the church services caused by the conversations of married couples'.[14]

Church discipline in general was not a simple process, and it was certainly made more complex when charity issues were added to the equation. A three-step process of discipline in the Reformed churches in the Netherlands has been outlined by Charles Parker: investigation into charges (either exoneration or suspension from communion while the person repented, rectified the consequences of the conduct and demonstrated improved conduct); a more permanent exclusion from communion for repeat transgressors with readmission only after confession and a demonstration of improvement during a probationary period; the final step of formal excommunication was reserved for those who consistently

---

[12] A copy exists at the front of the 'ceremonial' book of the *haussitzenden* deacons which runs from around 1576 to about 1650; ArchGK no. 3001. It has been edited in Sehling (ed.), *Kirchenordnungen*, pp. 455–69.

[13] See full quotation from a passage at opening of chapter. A concluding reference to the 'earnest law of the Christian emperors against such beggers' was to that from A.D. 382 (it can be found in Codex Justinius, XI, 26); ArchGK no. 3001 (Article 3); Sehling (ed.), *Kirchenordnungen*, p. 456, note 12.

[14] KRP, p. 618 (21 May 1576).

failed to comply with the consistory's demands. While most of Emden's discipline cases did not go beyond the first two steps and do not seem to have proceeded to formal excommunication, as in the Dutch Reformed churches 'for all practical purposes disciplined members of the church experienced a temporary excommunication since they were banned from Holy Communion until they satisfied the demands of the consistory'.[15]

Emden's deacons themselves left no specific records of their role in church discipline. Thus the accounts of the consistory provide the clearest view into the practical connections between poor relief and church discipline. Balancing these two concerns could prove to be quite complex. The process rarely involved a simple exclusion of obstinate sinners from poor relief. Rather, the process often involved long negotiations, frequent visitations and compromises as the Reformed consistory attempted to reconcile its moral ideals with the needs of the poor. A number of examples have been mentioned throughout this study, but a fuller investigation of the following five cases will illustrate some of the complexities of the disciplining process for poor recipients.

The case of Gaalke, 'who fell into adultery', shows that the deacons viewed withdrawal of alms as a drastic measure in church discipline and was often the end result of a long process of church discipline. In April 1568, two deacons brought Gaalke before the consistory, where she was reproved for her adulterous life and her various extra-marital affairs. The consistory sternly admonished her, but also had compassion for Gaalke because they thought that she was too trusting of 'bad' people. In fact, subsequent references still referred to Gaalke as a 'sister of the congregation'. The consistory ordered that alms should be withheld temporarily, to get her attention, so that they could speak to Gaalke and teach her until she learned the proper way of living. In the meantime, however, the deacons were to provide assistance for her small son.[16]

The consistory showed special concern for Gaalke's spiritual growth: six meetings with ministers and elders over the next year were recorded in the consistory minutes and one wonders how many took place outside the consistory meetings.[17] Yet in May 1569, Gaalke was evicted from the Gotteskammer in which she had been living because of her continued adulterous lifestyle.[18] Thus, although the consistory had earlier withdrawn Gaalke's poor relief stipend, she was still allowed to live in a Gotteskammer without charge (the administrators of the

---

[15] Parker, 'Moral Supervision', pp. 341–2, note 31.

[16] KRP, pp. 307, 308, 343 (12 and 26 April 1568, 14 March 1569).

[17] Ibid., pp. 327, 343, 351, 352, 362 (18 October 1568, 14 March, 23 May, 6 and 13 June, 11 September 1569).

[18] Ibid., p. 351 (23 May).

Gotteskammer are not identified). The withdrawal of poor relief from Gaalke was essentially intended to encourage her to greater moral discipline. The consistory tried to withdraw enough of the alms to get her attention and persuade her to act in the manner it wanted. Since the immediate goal was to persuade her to change her lifestyle and not solely to punish her, the consistory maintained some of the support so as to retain her allegiance. In this particular case, the consistory's piece-by-piece withdrawal of poor relief and personal talks with the accused did not produce the desired discipline. Finally, in September 1569, after a year and a half of instruction and exhortations, the consistory excommunicated Gaalke because of 'her life of adultery and prostitution, from which she cannot be drawn away through any exhortation; indeed, even more, she is leading her daughter into it'.[19]

Of course, the presence of children in a family made even more complex the questions of poor relief and discipline, and the deacons had to grapple with how to provide for poor children whose parents lost their alms as a result of disciplinary action. The church records make no further mention of Gaalke's daughter, but a second case demonstrates the way in which the deacons grappled with the problem. Galein Thorens and his wife Peterken, refugees from Oudenaarde in Flanders, were initially called before the consistory in March 1582 because of their 'injustice and disorderly living'. The consistory provided no description of what injustice they had caused but did admonish them 'most diligently to work' so that they and their household might understand 'how they have hitherto devoted themselves to injustice'.[20] Obviously, their 'injustice' had some connection with lack of diligence in their work. Later, they were directed to 'reconcile with the people they had harmed', these harmed people having been 'shorted' on 'interest'.[21]

This case raised exceptional concerns for the deacons. Since Galein and Peterken required poor relief, the deacons asked the consistory if the couple should continue to receive alms while they were being disciplined; and if not, what should be done about their children?[22] The

---

[19] Ibid., p. 362 (11 September).

[20] Ibid., p. 776.

[21] 11 May 1582 (ibid., p. 778); compare 29 July 1583 (ibid., p. 792).

[22] The family received frequent aid from the *fremdlingen* deacons between 1568 and 1575 (when the account book ends). Their extraordinary requests involved such needs as a bed, rent, rye and payments during sickness, the plague and periods of unemployment. The family was on the deacons' regular relief rolls from 1571 to 1575. References from 1568 to 1572 mention two children; those from 1573 to 1574 mention three children. For the records of the disbursements to the couple in the surviving account books, see *Fremdlingen I*, fols 233v, 235v; *Fremdlingen II*, fols 47 (2), 28 (2), 49, 51, 53, 127, 131, 133, 142, 143, 144, 146, 148 (2), 191, 290, 370, 469, 480, 544, 555.

consistory decided that the deacons should 'in no way' serve Galein and Peterken with poor relief. However, it determined that the children should not be punished because of the sins of their parents. The consistory instructed the deacons to try to 'find some way by which the children will be helped to some extent, but that the relief to the children remain as much as possible unknown to the parents so that they are not strengthened in their depravity'.[23] This last phrase ('that they are not strengthened in their depravity') came directly out of the 1576 Poor Relief Ordinance. Unfortunately, the deacons left no record of the plan they devised, and one wonders if they were able to keep the children's provision secret from the parents. Nevertheless, it is clear that while the parents were being taught the consequences of not working, the children were not to be punished by having their assistance totally withdrawn.

Two months later, the consistory ordered two elders to look into the case of Galein and Peterken Thorens.[24] On 11 May 1582 the couple appeared before the consistory and were asked to speak. Galein answered by apologising for his role in the affair. Peterken also acknowledged her guilt and promised 'to better herself and in the future to act more carefully and honestly through God's grace'. Both of them then appealed to the consistory that they lift the punishment which, of course, included the withdrawal of poor relief. The consistory ruled that the couple must still reconcile themselves with the people they had harmed, and assigned an elder to inquire into the matter and confirm if they had yet been reconciled.[25] A year later, the Thorenses had still not made matters right when their case was again brought to the attention of the consistory. In July 1583 the consistory received word that Galein and Peterken wanted very badly to be readmitted to communion. The consistory dispatched a minister to check to see 'if they had yet satisfied the people who were shorted through them'. The minister reported back to the consistory that the people involved still complained 'about their interest'.[26]

By the following spring, however, matters must have been resolved because Peterken was again receiving poor relief of 1 daler a week.[27] But her reunion with the congregation and with the poor relief rolls was

---

[23] 5 March 1582 (KRP, p. 776).

[24] Ibid., p. 778 (7 May). Both of the elders, coincidentally, had previously been deacons, so that they would have had special experience in the issues involving poor relief; Harmen Eilertz had been a *Becken* (and a *haussitzenden* deacon following the 1578 merger), Detleff Karstens a *Becken* deacon.

[25] Ibid.

[26] Ibid., p. 792 (29 July).

[27] Ibid., p. 801 (18 May).

short-lived. On 18 May 1584, Peterken (alone this time) was summoned before the consistory. They admonished and punished her 'very sternly out of God's word because of her grave sin of dishonesty which she has committed again'. Peterken acknowledged her guilt and again promised improvement, but the consistory was not satisfied. They decided that 'because her sin is so great and troublesome' she should be refused communion. The rest of the punishment was apparently a decision to expel Peterken from Emden (although it may have been a threat to prevent further misbehaviour): first the deacons, because they were familiar with her from their poor relief disbursements, were to try to get her to 'leave from here with love', but if she would not go, then the deacons were to petition the government for help.[28] However, the sources fail to disclose what ultimately happened to Peterken or her children.

Like the examples of Gaalke and the Thorenses, the case of Hermes de Grave demonstrates the use of poor relief as a tool to try to build church discipline. It also further suggests the complexities of providing relief for families whose 'head' was to receive no more alms. The schoolmaster Hermes de Grave was a poor refugee from Oudenaarde in Flanders. He, his wife and two children had received poor relief from the *fremdlingen* deacons on a fairly regular basis for several years, since at least 1567.[29] He also received extraordinary relief when he was sick, or when he and his wife had needed shoes, for example. When his wife was pregnant with her third child in 1570, the deacons gave Hermes extraordinary alms on ten separate occasions, including help for a midwife in November. Hermes and his family were, therefore, no strangers to the Dutch *fremdlingen* deacons.

Something, however, must have triggered a conflict between Hermes and the congregation. Perhaps the instigating event was the birth of the third child. Hermes had married a widow (apparently with one child) in 1568. She gave birth to her second child around August 1568, but it is not clear from the account books if this was Hermes's child or not. Thus this third child in 1572 was plausibly Hermes's first biological child. In any event, he was suddenly called before the consistory in June 1572 'because of his errors'. The consistory admonished him because of 'his slander, as he called the congregation a devilish congregation'. The consistory later recounted that he had called them devilish 'only because we baptise children'.[30] The church clearly already had enough

---

[28] Ibid.; compare ibid., p. 799 (4 May).

[29] For the records of the deacons' disbursements to Hermes and his family, see *Fremdlingen I*, fols 185v, 211; *Fremdlingen II*, fols 22, 134, 135 (2), 138, 139, 140, 142, 143, 144 (2), 145, 147, 148, 169, 279, 362, 442, 480, 550, 554, 555.

[30] KRP, pp. 449, 450 (6, 16 June).

problems with Anabaptists without a member criticising them too. Hermes's vocation as a schoolmaster probably gave him added credibility in the community, and in order to ensure that no one joined with him, the consistory decided to publicise his case before the congregation.[31] Moreover, the consistory suggested that *fremdlingen* deacons should not provide him with assistance.[32] The consistory attempted on a couple of other occasions to prevail on him to change his view, but to no avail. Thus on 11 July the consistory decided to publicly discredit Hermes as an apostate from the true doctrine and a slanderer of the congregation.[33]

Though the case ends here in the consistory records, the account books of the *fremdlingen* deacons provide further insights into the story of Hermes. A number of surprising things occurred concerning Hermes's poor relief from the *fremdlingen*. First of all, it was not terminated as the consistory had wanted; the deacons continued his family's regular, bi-weekly alms disbursement for every period throughout 1572, 1573 and into 1574.[34] Moreover, the amount of the alms remained unchanged. In the following year and a half after the consistory heard the case, the deacons continued every two weeks to give Hermes's family 1.6 gulden almost without exception. Though the consistory's desire for a complete withdrawal of alms did not result even in a reduction by the deacons, there was one change in the manner of relief provided them by the *fremdlingen* deacons: the deacons changed their manner of recording the poor relief given to Hermes's family. In every one of the previous 16 references to Hermes in the account books (before June 1572), the heading written by the deacons reads 'Hermes de Grave' or 'Hermes de Grave with wife [and children]'. Beginning immediately with Hermes's confrontation with the consistory, the deacons altered the identifying heading to read 'the wife of Hermes de Grave'.

Hermes had clearly not died; in such cases the deacons immediately began to alter their lists to use the word 'widow' (*weduwe*) and not 'wife' (*huusfrouw*). And, while he might have been forced to leave the town, as happened with Peterken Thorens, his family stayed in Emden and continued to receive the same amount of relief that the entire family had been receiving previously. The deacons had neither withdrawn nor reduced the amount of poor relief to the de Grave family, but they sanctioned Hermes by removing him as the recognised head of his

---

[31] The deacons identified him as 'schoolmaster' twice in 1570; *Fremdlingen II*, fols 134, 135.

[32] KRP, p. 449 (6 June).

[33] Ibid., pp. 450, 452 (23 June and 11 July 1572).

[34] *Fremdlingen II*, fols 279, 362, 442.

family and identifying his wife as the one who handled the money (although still only recognising her by his name!). Whether this symbolic move had any impact, psychologically or otherwise, on Hermes or on others who might have been tempted to follow his ideas, we cannot be sure. We do know that the 'wife of Hermes de Grave with 3 children' continued to receive regular bi-weekly alms until 9 August 1574, with gradual reductions in the amount during the middle of 1574, when she was 'dismissed' (*afgedanct*) from the relief rolls of the *fremdlingen*. With special approval, 'the wife of Hermes' received two more gifts to help with rent in October 1574 and April 1575. Hermes apparently died later in 1575, as 'the widow of Hermes de Grave' received rent money in November of that year.[35]

In contrast to these first three cases where discipline failed to unite the poor relief recipient with the congregation and which resulted in the withdrawal of alms (and even expulsion from a Gotteskammer and the city by the deacons), the example of Rogier van Aetdael resulted in a more 'successful' implementation of church discipline – at least from the perspective of the consistory. That is, the sinner was reunited with the congregation. By the time that Rogier van Aetdael appeared before the consistory in August 1567 he had already been excommunicated from the congregation for almost four years.[36] He had left his wife several years earlier and was living with another woman, with whom he had three children.[37] Perhaps he had been living in another town in his adulterous relationship and just recently returned to Emden. In any case Rogier himself had initiated this new appearance before the consistory because he wanted to be reconciled and admitted to the congregation. The consistory decided that he first had to meet certain conditions. Above all, he was to uphold his marriage vows with his original wife and bestow great care upon her; this meant completely cutting off relations with the other woman as long as his wife lived. Moreover, Rogier was to continue the support of his young children and to live a disciplined life for a time to prove his readiness to be taken back into the congregation.[38] Such probationary periods were a common step in the discipline process. The central goal during this time would be for the transgressor to earn back his or her good reputation and demonstrate an improvement in conduct.

Despite his own desire for reconciliation with the church and despite the orders of the consistory, Rogier was still with the 'other' woman

---

[35] *Fremdlingen II*, fols 442, 550, 555.
[36] KRP, p. 176 (13 May 1563).
[37] Ibid., p. 282 (7 August 1567).
[38] Ibid., pp. 282–3.

three months later. In November the deacons asked the consistory if they should now distribute alms to Rogier 'in his poverty with his adulteress because his previous wife was still alive'. That Rogier had not bothered to heed their instructions angered the consistory, and they answered, 'He may not be helped with our alms, because he wants to continue in the adultery, and because he has brought the other woman, the adulteress, here against our advice.'[39]

Naturally, we have no way of knowing which of the punishments (in this case, denial of communion or denial of poor relief) had the desired effect. But after three more years of excommunication, Rogier approached the consistory and 'confessed with tears that he had fallen into the pit of damnation'.[40] He entered a sort of probationary period, and in the following March, the consistory agreed to accept Rogier back into the congregation as long as there had not been any complaint against him during the preceding month.[41]

The combination of poor relief and church discipline could also result in a negotiated settlement between the deacons and the relief recipient. The final case study to be analysed here brings to light the importance of poor relief for the pure exercise of church discipline. In the case of Willum the Blind, the decisions of the consistory regarding questions of sin and discipline were influenced by some concerns about the costs of maintenance from the coffers of the poor. Sometimes the consistory was willing to compromise church discipline when poor relief was involved.

Willum the Blind earned his money and maintenance as a musician and singer.[42] As a blind man, he had few other opportunities for work. Because Blind Willum's work was not regular and the playing of music probably did not bring in a great deal of money, he had already borrowed money at least once from the *Becken* fund of the poor.[43] In December 1559 and July 1560, the consistory felt the need to admonish

---

[39] Ibid., p. 290 (20 November 1567).

[40] Ibid., p. 401 (11 December 1570).

[41] Ibid., p. 406 (9 March 1571). Thirty years later in Holland, the Delft consistory found itself in a similar situation with Lieven van Vijven who, after his first wife had died, had married the 'other woman' with whom he already had a child. Despite his public repentance, the consistory referred the matter to the South Holland Synod at The Hague and denied his requests until the issue was resolved by the higher ecclesiastical body. The synod ruled against Lieven, and, unlike Rogier in Emden, he was never readmitted to Holy Communion; Parker, 'Moral Supervision', pp. 352–3.

[42] For a short description of the life of a musician in early modern Emden and of the cultural role of music in the town, based on the life of 'Willum de blinde', see Louis Hahn, 'Wilhelm, der blinde Sänger. Ein Emder Kulturbild aus dem Reformationsjahrhhundert', *Ostfriesland. Mitteilungsblatt der Ostfriesischen Landschaft und der Ostfriesischen Heimatvereine*, 2, 2 (1952), pp. 4–7.

[43] KRP, p. 66 (19 September 1558).

Willum because of his playing of music at wedding celebrations, which often became rowdy; they did not mind if he played 'spiritual songs or others to which one did not know unsavoury words'. Yet the consistory realised at the time that if it exercised strict church discipline in Willum's case and prohibited him from making dance music, then Willum would lose the means of supporting himself. The consistory was in a bind: 'the congregation could not tolerate his dances in general as good; they could also not completely damn him'. Therefore, the consistory made a compromise with Willum. He could play music, but should not play all dances. In this way, the congregation 'could let him earn his own maintenance, because without the playing of dances, the congregation would have to feed him immediately from the poor purse'.[44]

This compromise prevailed for ten years, until January 1570, when complaints were brought before the church council that Willum had done 'great misbehaviour' in social gatherings, and an elder was dispatched to talk to Willum to avoid future public problems. In January and February, Willum made a couple of appearances before the consistory, saying that he must be allowed to play at weddings and other celebrations because he did not know any other calling through which he could 'nourish himself [in a] godly' manner. The consistory decided once again, 'with prudence', to let the matter stand according to the old understanding. This decision provoked the protestation of the three ministers who insisted that the consistory must not simply overlook such misbehaviour, but the 'majority of the brothers' decided not to revise the old agreement.[45]

On 30 October 1570 Willum was once more summoned before the consistory for 'frivolous playing at bawdy dances'. Willum again promised that he would avoid all new frivolous songs and dances. This time, however, church discipline stood in the foreground, and the consistory was stronger in its admonition:

> Because unavoidable, wicked scandal would arise from such music and dance, it is therefore seen as the most useful and safest, that Willum from now on avoid absolutely all playing, godly support himself, and hold himself moderately in his household; and if he is wanting in anything, the brothers will not leave him in distress.[46]

The consistory here used the promise of poor relief as a motivation for Willum to behave properly. A week later the consistory publicly announced that Willum had confessed his sins and had said that he was sorry that he had transgressed by the frivolity of his playing at lewd

---

[44] Ibid., pp. 101, 113–14 (4 December 1559, 15 July 1560).
[45] Ibid., pp. 371, 373–4 (2 and 5 January, 6 February 1570).
[46] Ibid., p. 397.

dances and had promised not to do such things any more.[47] This combination of church discipline bolstered by poor relief apparently had the
desired effect for the consistory as there were no further complaints
against Willum the Blind in the records.[48]

Thus it can be seen that church discipline was no simple matter for
Emden's poor relief officials. The deacons (and elders) were clearly
prepared to give much time and effort to dealing with such painstaking
care with these damaged lives. They looked at the individual circumstances of each case, and fully withdrew alms only as a last resort. They
used alms to encourage greater church discipline, yet they were also
willing to negotiate when the individual case required it. Such was the
case with Willum: the deacons recognised that he was a blind man with
limited work opportunities and that he was willing to work using his
musical skills, but how could they keep him from supporting himself by
playing that bawdy music? And even more complex than the case of
Willum were the situations when other family members, especially children, would be affected by a withdrawal of poor relief. The deacons
had to measure carefully their dual motivations of providing relief to
the needy and maintaining discipline and order in the town.

Unfortunately, little personal information survives about the deacons
to help portray the sort of men they were and discern their motivations
in devoting such effort to the poor. However, a limited prosopographic
analysis of the *haussitzenden* deacons during the second half of the
sixteenth century sheds some light on the types of civic activities in
which they were often involved.[49] For many of these sixteenth-century
officials, their position as *haussitzenden* deacon was a preparation for
entering the civic élite. Of the 201 identified deacons, more than 28 per
cent (57) men also served as administrators of either the Gasthaus, the
Clementiner Brotherhood, or the Grain Reserve (16 of these men administered at least two of the other three institutions, and three men
had tenures with all four institutions). Around 85 per cent of this group
served as deacons before serving with the other institution, although
some later returned as deacons again. For instance, Jacob Dinclaghe
served as an 'under-deacon' until becoming a 'deputy' in the city government for a couple of years in the late 1560s; in 1573 he began

---

[47] Ibid. (6 November).

[48] On 20 November (ibid., p. 399), the consistory decided to help Willum by asking
the city council if he could work as a messenger or crier since he had given up playing at
weddings and there was not much else he could do to support himself.

[49] Timothy Fehler, 'Social Welfare in Early Modern Emden' (Ph.D. thesis, University
of Wisconsin-Madison, 1995), pp. 533–42; compare Marion Weber, 'Emden – Kirche
und Gesellschaft in einer Stadt der Frühneuzeit', part II, *EJb*, 69 (1989), pp. 39–81.

working both as a Clementiner *Schaffer* and as an administrator of the Grain Reserve; his four-year term of office as *Schaffer* ended in 1577, but in the meantime, Jacob became a Gasthaus administrator in 1575. After completing his administration with the Gasthaus, Jacob returned to the *haussitzenden* diaconate in 1583 as a head-deacon for another four to six years. Jacob spent most of the rest of his life (died 1606) in the city government, serving on the Council of Forty in 1589, as the tensions with the count were beginning to rise, and then serving on the newly independent city council after the Emden Revolution in 1595.

The connections of the *haussitzenden* deacons with positions in the church and city government were more striking than those with the other poor relief institutions. Some 40 per cent of the deacons (80 different men) also held positions as elder (21), in a civic committee as a deputy (14) or on the Forty (59), or as city councilman (21). Once again, almost all of these men had used their diaconal work as a stepping stone for later church and civic positions. One of the most surprising findings, however, is that only two of the 21 who were also city councilmen held the position before 1595; a full 90 per cent entered the magistracy only after the Emden Revolution broke the count's domination of the city council. Clearly, therefore, the diaconate, as a form of service which was regarded highly in the city, became a much more prominent entry into the city council after the council ceased to be a mere appointed office of the count. More than one-third of Emden's city councillors in the decade after the Revolution also served as *haussitzenden* deacons.[50] Moreover, the large number of former deacons (only six of the 59 were 'Fortymen' *before* becoming deacons) on the citizen-created Council of Forty illustrates well the high esteem in which the citizenry held the *haussitzenden* diaconate. Three former *haussitzenden* deacons also became Burgermeisters of the city.[51]

---

[50] Weber, II, 70. Although there are problems with some of the name lists used by Weber, this percentage is sound.

[51] Each of the three illustrates the wide range of civic activities in which those in the city's elite could participate. Gerhard Bolardus, the hero of the 1595 Revolution, began as a head-deacon before retiring from the diaconate to become an elder; he served with the Grain Reserve and as a deputy and 'Fortyman', and became one of the first elected Burgermeisters after the Revolution. Bartholomaeus Hinrics was a churchwarden before becoming a head *haussitzenden* deacon: he administered the Grain Reserve and the Gasthaus before serving on the Forty and later as Burgermeister. Arend Schinckel is in the minority as he became a deacon *after* holding several other important positions; he served on the Grain Reserve and as a Clementiner *Schaffer* before becoming a head-deacon in 1590; Arend worked as a deacon until elected as an elder on the eve of the 1595 Revolution; but he never actually served as an elder; he gave up that position shortly after the Revolution since he was elected to the new city council; five years later he became Burgermeister.

Despite the clear association that could exist between many of Emden's deacons and the higher civic circles in the city, the results are actually mixed. Indeed, a full 60 per cent (122) of the known *haussitzenden* deacons cannot be confirmed in an additional church or civic office (52 per cent appear in no other poor relief, church or civic offices). Thus the majority of deacons held no other formal offices in the town. Some men, such as Jacob Dinclaghe, were certainly quite active in Emden's social élite, and the diaconate was obviously looked upon with great esteem. As Emden's civic awareness and pride burst forth during the later sixteenth century, the diaconate provided many of those with ambition a spring-board into civic offices. Of course, a prosopographic analysis cannot determine individual motivations, but this breakdown indicates that mere political ambition was not the driving force for a significant portion of the deacons. Rather, the deacons' activities, account books and meticu-lous care taken with so many individual poor people suggests strongly that the diaconate required a heavy commitment of both time and energy (and money, since the deacons often had to cover some expenses them-selves, at least initially). The size of the *haussitzenden* diaconate made the job of canvassing the city to investigate the needs and circumstances of the poor a less burdensome task for each deacon, and deacons could probably serve without greatly detracting from their other occupations. While the result of service as a *haussitzenden* deacon was often a rise in social prestige, most deacons seem to have been motivated primarily by a combination of civic and Christian duty.

Social Discipline: the 'Poor-wardens' and the 'Workhouse'

Closely related to the exercise of early modern church discipline was a growing interest in 'social discipline'. Gerhard Oestreich developed his idea of 'social disciplining' in an attempt to understand monarchical absolutism in Europe and the ways in which obedient and orderly sub-jects were created by European élites.[52] Orderliness in the state depended

---

[52] Oestreich, 'Strukturprobleme des europäischen Absolutismus', *Vierteljahrschrift für Sozial- und Wirtschaftsgeschichte*, 55 (1968), pp. 329–47. This essay was originally given as a lecture in 1962. For a short sketch of his development of the concept see his introduction in *Strukturprobleme des frühen Neuzeit*, ed. Brigitta Oestreich (Berlin, 1980), pp. 7–9. Two works in particular provide helpful summaries of the development and reception of Oestreich's theories: Winfried Schulze, 'Gerhard Oestreichs Begriff "Sozialdisziplinierung in der frühen Neuzeit"', *Zeitschrift für Historische Forschung*, 14 (1987), pp. 265–302; Stefan Breuer, 'Sozialdisziplinierung. Probleme und Problem-verlagerungen eines Konzepts bei Max Weber, Gerhard Oestreich und Michel Foucault', in *Soziale Sicherheit und soziale Disziplinierung*, ed. Christoph Sachße and Florian Tennstedt (Frankfurt am Main, 1986), pp. 41–69.

upon the necessary preconditions of obedience and discipline, not only of the subjects but of the ruling class itself. Oestreich's 'social disciplining' process progressed through a gradual development from its first clear manifestations in the police ordinances of the early modern cities to the eighteenth century, when it was fully in operation (from *Sozialregulierung* to *Fundamentaldisziplinerung*). Sixteenth-century cities reacted with laws and regulations against the increasing population densities and the concomitant general social and economic problems; it had become necessary to improve the social life of the city in an ever tighter living space and an increasing number of negative social and economic circumstances.[53] Scholars from different disciplines have identified a heightened concern about discipline, control and deviance in the early modern period.[54] Given their role in compelling compliance with their moral standards, the Reformed consistories of Europe were obviously quite active in establishing discipline. Nevertheless, recent work on the Emden consistory, for instance, has attempted to detach church discipline from analysis of criminalisation by discriminating between the state's power to punish crime and the church's authority to discipline sin.[55] Just as the clear parallels between church and social discipline have been investigated, so too have recent scholars attempted to stretch the analysis of early modern discipline to include its specific connections with work and social welfare.[56]

---

[53] Breuer, 'Sozialdisziplinierung', pp. 52–5, provides a summary description of Oestreich's chronology; see also Schulze, 'Oestreichs Begriff', p. 268.

[54] For instance, Michel Foucault, *Folie et déraison. Histoire de la folie à l'âge classique* (Paris, 1961); Foucault, *Surveiller et punir. Naissance de la prison* (Paris, 1975); Pieter C. Spierenburg, *The Spectacle of Suffering: Executions and the Evolution of Repression from a Pre-Industrial Metropolis to the European Experience* (Cambridge, 1984).

[55] Schilling, 'Reformierte Kirchenzucht', p. 284; Schilling, '"History of Crime" or "History of Sin"? – Some Reflections on the Social History of Early Modern Church Discipline', in *Politics and Society in the Reformation Europe. Essays for Sir Geoffrey Elton on his 65th Birthday*, ed. E. J. Kouri and Tom Scott (London, 1987), pp. 289–310. This concern has also been echoed by Ole Peter Grell, 'The religious duty of care and the social need for control in early modern Europe', *Historical Journal*, 39 (1996), pp. 262–3. On the work of the Amsterdam consistory, see Roodenburg, *Onder censuur*, pp. 17–27.

[56] Robert Jütte has been the leading historian to develop this approach in evaluating sixteenth-century civic poor relief. See the following titles by Jütte: 'Poor Relief and Social Discipline in Sixteenth-Century Europe', *European Studies Review*, 11 (1981), pp. 25–52; *Obrigkeitliche Armenfürsorge in deutschen Reichstädten der frühen Neuzeit. Städtisches Armenwesen in Frankfurt am Main und Köln* (Cologne, 1984); 'Disziplinierungsmechanismen in der städtischen Armenfürsorge der Frühneuzeit', in *Soziale Sicherheit und soziale Disziplinierung. Beiträge zu einer historischen Theorie der Sozialpolitik*, ed. Christoph Sachße and Florian Tennstedt (Frankfurt, 1986); see also Thomas Fischer, 'Der Beginn frühmoderner Sozialpolitik in deutschen Städten des 16. Jahrhunderts', *Jahrbuch der Sozialarbeit*, 4 (1981), pp. 46–68; H. C. M. Michielse, 'Policing the Poor: J. L. Vives and the Sixteenth-Century Origins of Modern Social Welfare Administration', *Social Service Review*, 64 (1990), pp. 1–21.

Robert Jütte has identified several procedural 'disciplining' aspects of social welfare: supervision, control, examination, education and punishment.[57] He argues that poor relief served as one of the earliest 'experiment fields for social control' in early modern urban society. The early modern poor were also expected to uphold such values as diligence, obedience, humility, self-control and, above all, work in order to receive their alms. Jütte's attempt to utilise the 'social disciplining' paradigm in the study of poor relief has, however, drawn criticism. Martin Dinges has questioned the ability of the paradigm to capture the full range of early modern poverty: regardless of the extent of administrative changes which emphasised greater discipline, the poor maintained a complex range of relief strategies of their own which frequently sidestepped governmental control, and which are therefore easily overlooked by the 'social disciplining' paradigm.[58] Though this study has focused on institutional developments, its limited investigation into the activities of the poor themselves seems to confirm Dinges's caution.

The development of Emden's poor relief institutions reveals two general strands of 'social disciplining' which go beyond church discipline: first, the broad range of discipline features connected with the begging prohibition and attempts to limit foreign beggars; second, the role of work and education, especially with respect to young boys. Both of these strands demonstrated the active concerns of both ecclesiastical and secular officials.

From the very first East Frisian Church Ordinance in 1529, territorial authorities attempted to limit relief to the local poor only. Of course to meet such a goal required not only social disciplining to expel (or minimise the number of) foreign beggars, but also the practical development of local institutions to provide relief to the local poor. Such was the case in Emden: the first effect of the Church Ordinance's strategy of poor relief was the creation of a new institution that would later become the *haussitzenden* diaconate. The emphasis on banning foreign beggars came later. Whereas the 1529 Church Ordinance fixed the poor relief on the poor of the individual parish, the Police Ordinance of 1545 actually recognised that without a ban on foreign beggars, the funds available to maintain the local poor would be too small to support them.

Moreover, the Police Ordinance required the expulsion of foreign beggars from East Frisia, on the additional ground that social order needed to be preserved. Thus began the task of identifying the source of

---

[57] Jütte, 'Poor Relief and Social Discipline', esp. pp. 34–42.

[58] Dinges, 'Frühneuzeitliche Armenfürsorge als Sozialdisziplinierung? Probleme mit einem Konzept', *Geschichte und Gesellschaft*, 17 (1991), pp. 5–29.

social danger and attempting to reduce it. The Police Ordinance identified foreign beggars roving around in gangs as 'mostly murderers and wicked rogues'. Yet despite its call for wider social discipline, this Police Ordinance had little effect on the removal of foreign beggars. With no administrative officers to enforce the mandate, there was frequently little chance of it being carried out. The sheer number of foreign refugees that soon flooded into Emden made it even more difficult to prohibit foreigners from begging. Soon a new distinction between the worthy and unworthy foreign poor was created, based on church discipline. Yet the most prominent example of attempts to implement such a distinction, the *Becken* diaconate, did not last.

Upon the arrival of Alting, one notes an expansion of church discipline to cover public disorder. For example, the consistory approached the city council in May 1576 to ask for help in the elimination of disorderly conduct, indicating their desire to control public order but noting their own lack of 'discipline authority' to act alone.[59] Then, with the Poor Relief Ordinance of 1576, the push toward social discipline had advanced enough that the ordinance did not simply prohibit begging, but mandated the hiring of a new official to police the poor.[60] Alting, like most Calvinist reformers, was strongly opposed to begging because it violated the scriptural mandate to 'not let anyone eat if he refused to work' (2 Thessalonians 3:10, cited at the opening of the Poor Ordinance). The Poor Ordinance went on to provide detailed instructions, summarised below, for the duties of the new poor-wardens (*Armenvögte*), the important new arrivals on Emden's social welfare scene.[61]

(a) The two *Armenvögte* were to be chosen by the administrators of the Gasthaus and the *haussitzenden* poor, each of which maintained one warden; they also wore a special jacket to identify themselves and their official office.[62]

---

[59] KRP, p. 618 (21 May 1576).

[60] On the Reformed Delft consistory's concerns about begging among its relief recipients, see Parker, 'Moral Supervision', p. 348.

[61] The Poor Relief Ordinance very probably formalized a position that had recently evolved. The *haussitzenden* deacons' accounts from late 1574 and 1575 include payments to 'Ecke der armen voeget' for salary and clothing for the poor; Ecke apparently did not continue in the position after it was reshaped by the ordinance, however, as he disappears from the records; ArchGK no. 1118, pp. 35, 36, 36v, 37v, 38, 40v. The articles dealing with the *Armenvogt* office were extracted from the original Poor Ordinance and separately ratified on 17 July 1576, ArchGK no. 3001, pp. 12–15.

[62] One of the first two *Armenvögte*, Berent, was also 'Gasthaus father', so he had a great deal of experience in poor relief. Although the ordinance indicates a salary of 50 gulden plus clothing, the records of the *haussitzenden* deacons reveal that 'their' poor warden received only 40 gulden a year in 1579–82; ArchGK no. 3194, pp. 24, 52, 86, 184, 188, 191, 206, 216, 232, 233.

(b) Their job was to look after the poor in the entire city, day and night, to make sure that the poor did not go into the streets to beg.

(c) If the poor-warden found people in the street, he was to examine them and ask their name and surname.

(d) If the person were foreign, the *Vogt* should ask the person where he or she came from and what he or she was doing, and then lead the person to the next deacon. And if this occurred at night, the *Vogt* should take the person to the Gasthaus for the night, then return to the Gasthaus at a certain time on the following morning and lead the healthy foreign poor out of the city with a customary sum of money; he should leave the sick in the Gasthaus until they were stronger.

(e) If the person who was found begging in the streets was local, then he or she should be admonished for begging and directed home; afterwards, the *Vogt* should give the person's name to the head-deacon, or whoever was administering the *Kluft* at the time – in this way the person could be admonished once more by the deacons and when opportune, punished with the withdrawal of alms.[63]

(f) When the *Armenvögte* patrolled the streets at night, they were to watch for poor relief recipients who were drinking or wasting their alms; if they discovered someone being foolish with their alms, the *Armenvögte* had the right to enter their residence and investigate their situation and activities; the next day the *Vogt* was to report to the head-deacon so that he and his helpers could judge the situation.[64]

(g) Nevertheless, the *Armenvögte* had no right to judge the poor themselves, and they could neither dispense nor withhold alms; this was the job solely of the deacons.

The poor-wardens became the poor relief employees in Emden who worked most closely in enforcing social discipline. Adhering to Alting's aspirations of ensuring discipline, the Poor Relief Ordinances of 1576 emphasised both a church and a social discipline. While the deacons distributed the poor relief and helped the elders to regulate or monitor church discipline, the poor-wardens were almost entirely responsible for the general supervision of the poor in the streets, ensuring that the potential sources of social danger to the congregation were minimised. The poor-wardens were not active in inspecting the beliefs of the poor relief recipients; their role was specifically aimed at controlling begging.

---

[63] The *haussitzenden* deacons reimbursed Arent the *Vogt* for the costs incurred for 'placing a wicked young man (*boeßgeselle*)' in 1579, ArchGK no. 3194, p. 4.

[64] Despite the obvious concern of Emden's officials about the proper use of alms by the recipients, the Emden accounts record few complaints of misuse of alms. The deacons were, however, sensitive to suggestions or evidence that the recipient might be able to make do without assistance from the poor fund. Compare with the situation in Delft; Parker, 'Moral Supervision', pp. 347–8.

Such 'inspectors' were not unique to Emden but were apparently common in the Dutch and French Reformed churches, although other cities usually involved a more specific mandate to report on the beliefs of alms recipients (as well as their behaviour).[65] Punishment for misbehaviour of a poor relief recipient could be severe and could call for expulsion from the city or withdrawal of alms. The position of the *Armenvogt* was only supervisory, however, because he had no authority to dispense alms or punish the poor who misbehaved. He was merely to report the results of his patrols to the head-deacons. Despite this restriction on the deacons' activities, the account books of the deacons indicate that the poor-wardens were one of the primary distribution conduits of clothing to the poor in the *Klufts* with significant amounts of money reimbursed to the poor-wardens for clothing (and occasionally for rye) to the poor.[66] Berent, the poor-warden, also received bi-annual support from both the *haussitzenden* deacons and the Gasthaus for his role as foster father to an orphan.[67]

The ever-increasing effort to mobilise administrators of poor relief to act in areas of social discipline continued after the Poor Relief Ordinance. In October 1580, a pastor told the two poor-wardens that they should instruct each deacon to investigate the types and behaviours of disorderly people and make a record of his findings. The head-deacons would then bring in their lists, 'so that one may finally implore the government for help against [such behaviour]'.[68] Because the church and the state were working toward the similar ends of controlling and improving behaviour, the trend toward increasing social discipline gradually merged with the Reformed confessionalisation which soon could be described as 'civic Calvinism' in Emden.[69]

Appeals to the town government by the poor-wardens or the deacons in cases of obstinacy were usually intended to arrange for the expulsion of the poor relief recipient from town. But the simple policy of expulsion was not always considered the best solution in the sixteenth century. When placing great emphasis on social discipline and punishment, we should remember that other ideals were often more important to

---

[65] Compare, for instance, the *opsienders* in Delft; Parker, 'Moral Supervision', p. 340.

[66] For instance, ArchGK no. 3194, pp. 7, 47, 52, 65, 93, 98, 119, 129, 139, 148, 168, 169, 182, 191, 192, 200, 202, 209, 214, 216, 223, 227, 232, 234, 246, 251, 258, 260.

[67] For instance, ibid., p. 232 (September 1582).

[68] KRP, p. 748 (24 October 1580).

[69] 'The secular process of social disciplining was attended and assisted by the religious disciplining of the new confessional churches'; Thomas Winkelbauer, 'Sozialdisziplinierung und Konfessionalisierung durch Grundherren in den österreichischen und böhmischen Ländern im 16. und 17. Jahrhundert', *Zeitschrift für historische Forschung*, 19 (1992), p. 320.

contemporaries. For instance, Emden leaders realised that if they did not care adequately for the poor in the city, these poor would ultimately leave and become a hardship to another city; each locality had the responsibility to avoid shifting the burden on to some other place. The description of the new office of 'poor-warden' in the Emden Poor Ordinances of 1576 ended with a citation from the second Council of Tours in 1567 which demonstrated this other important ideal: 'Let every single city feed the poor and needy inhabitants with suitable nourishment according to men; let both the vicars of the presbyteries and all citizens not deviate from the maintenance of their own poor: who will themselves [otherwise] become the poor throughout other cities.'[70]

That early modern cities were as interested in maintaining this other ideal as in enforcing discipline by means of expulsion is evidenced by the case of the son of Belhasen Goltsmit. Belhasen was a citizen of Bremen, and his son Hans Bußenschutte had been living in Emden. According to a letter sent from the Emden city council to the Bremen city council on 26 May 1571, Hans had been wandering about the town causing a tumult 'because of his insanity and his sick comprehension'. This problem was taking place at the very height of refugee immigration into Emden, when the city was overcrowded and the poor relief institutions were stretched to their limits. Yet, instead of simply expelling Hans from Emden, causing him to wander to some other city for them to deal with, the Emden council wrote to Bremen and asked that the father take his son back into his home. But Bremen's response was not the answer that Emden had hoped for. The Bremen council wrote that the father Belhasen was too poor at the present time to take Hans in and fully support him. They asked if it would not be possible for Emden to keep Hans for a while longer, in the hope that perhaps Hans would get better through God's grace.[71]

The newly accentuated work ethic certainly permeated much of Emden's social welfare system. The consistory frequently exhorted church members 'to work diligently', and deacons oftentimes specified at the onset of a particular case that the recipient should work as hard as possible and then the deacons would help out with the rest; as we saw in the case of Willum the Blind, 'The brothers will not leave him in distress.' The deacons demonstrated the value placed on work in their keenness to help the poor to help themselves, especially by providing

---

[70] The complete citation for the reference in the Poor Ordinance can be found in Joannes Dominicus Mansi (ed.), *Sacrorum Conciliorum* (Florence, 1763), IX, 790–806 (here p. 793, Canon 5).

[71] The exchange of letters is preserved in StaE, I. Reg. 424 (the first three pages).

workers with the tools of their trade and loans to help start a business.[72]

Beyond the emphasis on work for adult recipients, Emden's poor relief system also attempted to make sure that the youth were educated and taught a trade. Previous chapters have examined the importance given to education both in theory (the church ordinances) and in practice. The account books of the deacons revealed numerous expenditures of 'school-money' (*Schulgeld*) to pay schoolmasters to teach poor children. Great efforts were also made to arrange apprenticeships for young boys. Parents' poor relief stipends would sometimes be delayed or withheld if the parents did not see to it that their children were placed in apprenticeships or as domestic servants. But in addition to this impetus for educating the youth and/or providing them with work, there was also an ever-growing concern to control and discipline basic misbehaviour and rowdiness, especially among young boys.

In the 1570s, the consistory complained a number of times about the disorder caused by the youth in the church services or during the catechism sermon. Two special attempts were made to discipline the poor youth. In 1573, the Countess Anna gave one of her properties, the Old Mint (*Olde Münze*), to the 'general citizenry' of the town. She had intended to sell the building, but the Burgermeisters and council of the city, and all the ministers, elders and schoolmasters heard of her plans and asked her to convert it into a 'a general school and a workhouse (*Tuchthuß*) for the young boys', which she approved.[73] Another attempt to guard the behaviour of the young boys was made in September 1579, when the preachers and deacons issued a supplemental order to the Poor Relief Ordinance containing 13 articles to provide better supervision and discipline of the youth.[74] Included among these articles were requirements to attend school, serve a master craftsman as an apprentice and attend catechism lessons. The deacons were also given detailed instructions regarding the diverse methods which should be employed to oversee and keep a register of the youth in the city.

Such concern with orderliness and discipline led the church and city fathers to consider the construction of a city workhouse at the beginning of the seventeenth century. Anna's converted building had served as a school since the mid-1570s, but the authorities remained concerned about the growing 'pernicious lifestyles and wickedness' and wanted to instil 'discipline and decency'. On 26 January 1607 the consistory agreed

---

[72] For example, *Fremdlingen II*, fols 50, 228 235, 328 (work tools); 136, 328, 419 (business loans).

[73] ArchGK (Nellner) no. 90 (1 September 1573).

[74] ArchGK no. 3001, pp. 28–32.

with representatives of the 'three poor institutions' (these would be the *haussitzenden* deacons, the Gasthaus, and the Shippers) that it would be useful to construct a workhouse. Yet when they approached the city council later that week, they were informed that there were not enough municipal funds for its construction, although the idea truly pleased the city council. 'If the poor institutions can see to the financing, [the city council] would do all the authorisation, but they fear that it is not to be here with the workhouse. They would nevertheless do their best to punish wickedness.'[75]

The idea of municipal workhouses was a popular one in northern Europe at the turn of the century. No doubt the Emden officials had heard of the workhouses recently built in Amsterdam, and Emden's deliberations pre-date the creation of workhouses in Germany.[76] The Amsterdam *tuchthuis* for men (1589) and *spinhuis* for women (1596) clearly served as the most influential model for such institutions in the Netherlands and northern Germany.[77] These workhouses were to be 'houses of correction' where sturdy beggars, vagrants and rogues would be punished and taught to work hard and live an honest life. This policy of confinement gained momentum throughout the seventeenth century and later became one of the dominant means in the attempt to repress vagrancy and begging.[78]

---

[75] KRP, pp. 972, 973 (26 January and 1 February 1607).

[76] *Zuchthäuser* were founded in Bremen (1609–13), Lübeck (1613), Hamburg (1614–22), Danzig (1629); Vienna (1670), Frankfurt am Main (1679), Königsberg (1691); most German institutions were founded in the eighteenth century. The southern Netherlands also followed the model, for instance Antwerp (1613); Robert Jütte, *Poverty and Deviance in Early Modern Europe* (Cambridge, 1994), p. 174.

[77] Similar late sixteenth-century trends can be traced in England, Spain and Italy. Bridewell palace in London was converted for the punishing of idle poor and vagabonds in 1553; this was followed by other towns in the 1560s and a Poor Relief Act of 1576 ordered the creation of 'houses of correction' in all counties and corporate towns. In Spain and Italy, beggars hospitals were constructed to discipline and punish beggars who would otherwise have been expelled or put on galleys: Toledo (1581), Madrid (1582), Barcelona (1583), Turin (1583), Rome (the Ponte Sisto founded by Pope Sixtus V in 1587), Modena (1592), Venice (1594), Florence (1621); Jütte, *Poverty and Deviance*, pp. 169–74.

[78] Michel Foucault has entitled this programme of social engineering 'the Great Confinement' and argued that this new form of discipline went far beyond economic necessity or providing assistance. Historians have questioned whether Foucault's discursive *grand renfermement* corresponds to historical 'reality'. See, for instance, J. Gutton, *La société et les pauvres en Europe* (Paris, 1974), pp. 122–57; H. C. Midelfort, 'Madness and Civilization in Early Modern Europe: A Reappraisal of Michel Foucault', in *After the Reformation. Essays in Honor of J. H. Hexter*, ed. Barbara C. Malament (Philadelphia, 1980), pp. 247–65; Bronislaw Geremek, 'Renfermement des pauvres en Italie (XIVe ... XVIIIe siècles): remarques preliminaries', *Mélanges en l'honneur de Fernand Braudel* (Toulouse, 1973).

The Emden church and city officials took up the question of such a workhouse on at least two occasions in subsequent years. One of the pastors reported to the consistory on 8 February 1608 that a Burgermeister and his council had given an encouraging answer regarding the workhouse and that representatives of the poor relief agencies, the consistory, the city council and even the Council of Forty should consider how to raise funds for its construction and maintenance. The consistory's discussions the next month illustrate the urgency they felt: it appeared that the aforementioned delegation was accomplishing little in its discussions, so some in the consistory suggested an increase in their own proposed funding in order to move the others so that 'the work of the workhouse will no longer be suppressed'.[79] The city fathers were still working on the issue a year later when the Council of Forty resolved that 'a workhouse may be built in this good city for the maintenance of good discipline among wicked and common folk'. To that end they established a 'commission on the construction of a workhouse' to deliberate 'if, and through what means and in what place, a workhouse with its annex might be constructed and established in this good city'.[80] In the end, the city and church records include no further evidence of the ultimate construction of any workhouse in the early seventeenth century. Although the city and church leaders thought the issue urgent enough to consider in some detail, they determined to leave any such discipline to Emden's current poor relief institutions rather than follow the trend throughout the region and construct a workhouse.

As we have seen, there was a significant increase in the number of social discipline policies within Emden's poor relief throughout the second half of the sixteenth century. Emden's creation of the 'poor-warden', for example, was an effective way to reduce the amount of begging and misbehaviour on the part of transients. By mandating policing of the city's streets 'day and night', the Poor Relief Ordinance added teeth to the previous prohibitions against begging. Nevertheless, in the same passage that Emden recognised the need to expel certain poor from their midst, the city also recognised that the poor-wardens should be mindful that the poor for whom Emden did not provide 'will become themselves the poor throughout other cities'. The consistory was particularly interested in maintaining proper church discipline among the town's relief recipients, and the deacons exerted much effort in

---

[79] KRP, pp. 989–90 (8 February and 20 March 1608).

[80] StaE, I. Reg., no. 424 (14 February 1609). The 12 members of the commission included two representatives each from the city council, the council of Forty, the church elders, the Clementiner Shippers, the administrators of the *haussitzenden* poor and the Gasthaus.

attempting to balance the complex concerns of discipline and charitable provision. The effects (though apparently unsuccessful) to construct a city workhouse demonstrate the common interest in proper behaviour, shared by city, church and poor relief administrators.

CHAPTER EIGHT

Emden and the Development of 'Reformed' Social Welfare

When you ask, if people are worthy of the ecclesiastical community, who, although they have opportunity, do not apply themselves to the support of the poor, I answer thus: here friendly exhortations, not sharp orders, are in order. For we see that Paul moderated himself and extorted nothing from such people who did not want to [give alms], rather only graciously beseeched that they would help poor brothers: and this not under compulsion, rather each after the kind disposition of his heart, that it be a blessing and not scanty; because God loves a joyful giver. So it is right to make this charitable duty clear through exhortation, but benevolence must remain voluntary (II Cor. 8:9ff).

John Calvin, letter to Menso Poppius (1559)[1]

In light of Calvin's response to a question about East Frisian charity, the criticisms made by Emden's church bookkeeper at the end of the century appear quite surprising (see Chapter 1). Nevertheless, the bookkeeper articulated the practical frustrations of an accountant trying to balance the books with revenue sources split between competing charitable institutions. He harked back to the 'good old days' before the town's remarkable poor relief innovations. Of course, the innovations in the town's social welfare system, which he so disliked, were not unique to Emden. They were part of developments seen over much of western Europe. Yet what was achieved in Emden was remarkable – both for the multiplicity of institutional innovations and particularly for the speed and apparent effectiveness of the responses to the problems of the century. In a town whose city fathers had so little experience in contending with such problems, the social welfare institutions underwent exceptional transformations as church and city leaders struggled to cope with demographic and economic crises. That the system created in the midst of these sixteenth-century crises remained largely intact into this century (with significant changes or additions only in the nineteenth century) attests to the relative success of the early modern reforms.

Emden was a sixteenth-century boom town. Its population exploded from perhaps 3 000 at the start of the century to as much as 25 000 by the early 1570s. Such a demographic expansion not only stimulated

---

[1] *Calvini Opera* 17:453–4 (26 February 1559).

economic activity but also raised the spectre of social and political crisis. Most of the new arrivals were economic and religious refugees from the revolt in the neighbouring Netherlands. Some of these exiles were wealthy and contributed to Emden's economic boom. Many, however, arrived in Emden with quite limited prospects. The account books of the foreign deacons list some 5 000 welfare recipients for the first five years of the 1570s. Thus the augmentation of a more extensive and sophisticated system of poor relief was a necessity if the city's institutions were not to break down under the strain of new demands placed on local resources.

Emden's case immediately draws attention to itself by the variety of its institutions for poor relief. The developmental path that these agencies took is also striking. The first half of the sixteenth century witnessed rather slow changes and few innovations in Emden's system of social welfare provision, despite the dramatic religious transformation brought about the introduction of Protestantism. Only after the 1550s did dramatic change take place, change caused most obviously by social and economic pressures, but change which occurs in an increasingly 'Reformed' city.

Before returning to an analysis of the 'causes' of Emden's reforms, it would be beneficial to look back over the multiplicity of relief organs that developed over the course of the century. The sixteenth century began with a consolidation of the St Gertrude Gasthaus properties as they expanded their facilities by moving to the outskirts of town where they could build an entire complex including individual apartments (Gotteskammern). The institution's independent and lay administration remained so after the Reformation, though it had the help and interest of both countess and city, as the Gasthaus (note the loss of 'St Gertrude' in the name) renovated its facilities by taking over the former Franciscan monastery. Despite the explicit religious differences between the friars and the now Protestant territory, the friars were allowed to remain active for more than three decades after the introduction of Protestantism. The final reason given for the ouster of the friars and the transfer of their properties to the Gasthaus was the mid-century emergency caused by the influx of refugees and the problems of food and housing shortages: the Franciscans were no longer able to continue their charitable work adequately and were certainly not as efficient as a large, centralised Gasthaus with endowments, administrators and staff aimed solely at that end.

As the Gasthaus moved into its larger, reconstructed complex, it appears to have broadened the range of services that it offered its residents. By this time it had obviously evolved from just a temporary residence for transient poor to a long-term residence for orphans, the elderly and the mentally and physically disabled. Administrators and the 'Gasthaus mothers' expected the residents to provide as much of their own support as possible: the administrators ensured that residents' property and inheritance flowed into the Gasthaus accounts to offset expenditures; the 'Gasthaus mothers' expected the children to work with flax and help in other ways to provide for their daily needs, and the Gasthaus sought to place orphans in apprenticeships to learn their craft. Though the Gasthaus encouraged work and work-related activities, its residents were never engaged directly in industrial production, which, for instance, was encouraged by the administrators of Catholic Lyon's Aumône générale.[2]

Perhaps the most unusual discovery about Emden's early post-Reformation social welfare is the survival of the religious confraternities. Martin Luther's condemnation of confraternities' spiritual functions notwithstanding, Emden's adoption of Protestantism did not result in the demise of the late medieval confraternities. The confraternities were gradually replaced by other relief institutions, but not all declined in equal measure. The Reformation did not bring radical change in the administrations of these confraternities. Nor did it immediately end their spiritual functions, particularly of the two whose activities were centred on the still-operating Franciscan monastery (Our Lady's and St Ann's). Only in the 1540s do references to the confraternities as spiritual brotherhoods disappear from the sources. By the 1540s, St Clement's had become the primary organisation, and by the 1550s it had absorbed the assets and administrations of the other confraternities and modified its charter. Originally founded as a religious guild of shippers and merchants to provide spiritual assistance to its members, St Clement's finally evolved into a poor relief brotherhood, chartered to assist the families of its members and those who lost their goods or relatives at sea. The Catholic spiritual functions disappeared. The fact that it was the Shippers' Brotherhood which was allowed to survive reflects the

---

[2] Lyon proposed establishing a silk industry using orphans; Natalie Zemon Davis, 'Poor Relief, Humanism, and Heresy', in *Society and Culture in Early Modern France* (Stanford, 1975), p. 43. The refugee poor administrators in England likewise took advantage of the French cloth industry in England to help support exile Huguenot congregations; Andrew Spicer, 'Poor Relief and the Exile Communities', in *Reformations Old and New*, ed. Beat Kümin (Aldershot, 1996), pp. 244–5. Despite the large size of Augsburg's economy, its Lutheran and Catholic orphanages, like Emden's, did not use its residents in a direct attempt to build an in-house industry; Thomas Max Safley, *Charity and Economy in the Orphanages of Early Modern Augsburg* (New Jersey, 1997), pp. 209–73.

central role that the harbour and the seafaring professions played in Emden's social and economic development. In the reorganisation of social welfare, the town wisely maintained the institution which had traditionally provided assistance to its most important trades. Another of the conventional methods of poor relief – the provision of Gotteskammern – continued throughout the early modern period. Many of the early establishments were preserved, and an analysis of testaments from the later sixteenth century yields the occasional new foundation.[3]

It is a pity that no Gasthaus or confraternity account books from the early period survive. Such evidence would allow us to measure the financial impact of the initial Reformation decades. Yet increasing evidence for the confraternities' contractual obligations in the field of poor relief indicates that they played an important role before their merger, especially as Emden parish finances became tighter following Count Enno's confiscation of ecclesiastical property with the Reformation. The count made no attempt to compensate the parishes with some form of common chest, and overseers could only appeal to 'Christian love' to finance their efforts. The traditional tax, the *huusdelinge*, was also stretched further than customary: whereas it had previously been used to supplement pastor and church, it was now expected to cover poor relief expenses as well.

The Lutheran Church Ordinance of 1529 called for new poor relief overseers to administer the *huusdelinge* and other poor funds. Yet closer examination of Emden's sources indicates that several of the ostensibly new 'administrators of the poor' simultaneously held the traditional medieval office of churchwarden. This suggests that the Emden church simply added a new function to an existing position when carrying out the 1529 Church Ordinance.

Emden's recently created 'administrators of the poor' evolved into a new, more extensive institution in the middle of the century. Although the exact date is uncertain, the major points of transformation can be detected around the time of Johannes a Lasco's tenure as superintendent in the 1540s. Lasco's most enduring institutional contribution was the 1544 creation of the Emden church consistory, intended as a tool to oversee and deliberate matters of congregational church discipline. The consistory's earliest lay members appear to have been churchwardens, who were now also, it seems, in charge of poor relief activities.[4] It soon became evident, however, that they could not cope with this additional

[3] For later *Gotteskammern*, see EKP 10/244, 10/713–14, 12/992–3, 15/121, 15/272, and KRP, p. 746.

[4] Menno Smid, *Ostfriesische Kirchengeschichte* (Pewsum, 1974), p. 166.

burden, and their duties were thus entrusted to two new lay offices: 'elder' for church discipline and 'deacon' for poor relief.[5] Whether the reorganisation occurred during Lasco's tenure cannot be determined, but by the time of the earliest surviving consistory minutes (July 1557), it was clear that approximately 20 local deacons of the church existed (so-called *haussitzenden* deacons), each of whom was responsible for a specific part of the town. It is at this time that the first account books of the deacons appear. With the increasing organisation of the church came increased interest in rationalised recordkeeping, and Emden's relief institutions began showing the common sixteenth-century tendency of rationalising their administration by dividing the town into districts, keeping lists of recipients and improving accounting procedures. Dividing the town into neighbourhoods enabled poor relief administrators increased personal knowledge about recipients.[6]

Emden's Reformed deacons were not civic or secular officials like those in Geneva, where the deacons were appointed directly by the city and funded from the city budget (from confiscated ecclesiastical wealth).[7] Nor did Emden's deacons share the functions that were frequently given to French deacons, who were involved in catechism instructions and might even replace the minister and conduct services.[8] The first official description of election procedures for the *haussitzenden* deacons comes from the Poor Relief Ordinance of 1576. These regulations, which were ratified by the count's bailiff and by Emden's Burgermeisters and city council, stated that the deacons were to be chosen by the pastors and elders and presented to the congregation; they make no mention of any

---

[5] Compare Calvin's view of the offices of the church in his Ecclesiastical Ordinances (1541) for Geneva: *Calvin: Theological Treatises*, vol. xxii, trans. J. K. S. Reid (Philadelphia, 1954), pp. 58–72. See also Elsie Anne McKee, *John Calvin on the Diaconate and Liturgical Almsgiving* (Geneva, 1984), ch. 5 (esp. after p. 127; pp. 133–7 on the Reformed doctrine of the plural ministry).

[6] For instance, for Zürich, see Lee Palmer Wandel, *Always Among Us: Images of the Poor in Zwingli's Zürich* (Cambridge, 1990), p. 149; for Delft, see Charles H. Parker, 'Moral Supervision and Poor Relief in the Reformed Church of Delft, 1579–1609', *ARG*, 87 (1996), p. 340; for Groningen, see J. van der Ploeg, 'Armoede en diakonale armenzorg in de stad Groningen, 1594–1650' (Masters thesis, Groningen, 1978), p. 19.

[7] Robert Kingdon, 'The Deacons of the Reformed Church in Calvin's Geneva', in *Mélanges d'histoire du XVIe siècle offerts à Henri Meylan* (Geneva, 1970), pp. 83–5. E. William Monter, *Calvin's Geneva* (New York, 1967), pp. 156, 220.

[8] Such diaconal functions were necessitated by persecutions and shortages of pastors because the Reformed churches were illegal and often operating under ground; Robert Kingdon, *Geneva and the Consolidation of the French Protestant Movement 1564–1572* (Geneva, 1967), p. 41. Compare Glenn Sunshine, 'From French Protestantism to the French Reformed Churches: the Development of Huguenot Ecclesiastical Institutions, 1559–1598' (Ph.D. thesis, University of Wisconsin-Madison, 1992), pp. 157, 160–61, 166, 173–85.

approval by civil authorities.[9] While the city maintained no official oversight role in the examination of the yearly accounts – the ordinance required only that the head-deacons provide a 'yearly accounting before the elders and deacons, indeed, before everyone who wants to hear, and this accounting shall be announced from the pulpit to the entire congregation' – the annual accounts were always signed by the pastors, head-deacons, two to four elders, and a few leading citizens (frequently city councilmen).[10] Thus the functions of the deacons remained largely under the control of Emden's ecclesiastical authorities. Although the deacons regularly reported problems to the consistory, they were not members of the consistory with the elders and pastors. By-laws governing consistory meetings ('the gathering of pastors and elders') do not include the deacons in the consistory's weekly Monday meetings at 1 o'clock; the only mention of the deacons is in the requirement that the presiding pastor with his assigned elders should interact 'weekly and monthly with the deacons in order to advise with the most useful help in their difficulties'.[11] According to the 1576 Poor Relief Ordinance, 'out of the consistory one pastor and some elders shall come along' to the meeting of the *haussitzenden* deacons on the Thursday before communion: here 'they should discuss with each other the service and needs of the poor and, where there is a shortcoming, better it'.[12] A subsequent set of by-laws governing the meetings of the deacons indicates that a pastor should be available for the weekly Sunday afternoon diaconal meetings when possible.[13]

The convergence of religious motivations and economic concerns in the late 1550s led to a branching out into a new poor relief organ, the *Becken* deacons. At the height of the economic crisis of 1557, the Emden deacons struggled to ensure support of the members of the congregation, the so-called 'household of faith'. The consistory's solution was to create a special fund – named after the collection dish, the *Becken* – to provide for the godly poor. Despite the religious motivations,

---

[9] ArchGK no. 3001, fol. 1; Emil Sehling (ed.), *Die evangelischen Kirchenordnungen des XVI. Jahrhunderts*, VII/2/1 (Tübingen, 1963), p. 455.

[10] ArchGK no. 3001, fol. 7; Sehling (ed.), *Kirchenordnung*, p. 457. Copies of these signed annual reports beginning with 1576 can be found in the second section of ArchGK no. 3001. An earlier account book provides the actual annual accounting for 1575, which was signed by only the four ministers; ArchGK no. 1118, p. 49. Thus the 1576 Ordinance might have established more extensive oversight of deacons' accounts than had previously been in operation.

[11] Sehling (ed.), *Kirchenordnung*, pp. 452–4, esp. Articles 1 and 17. These regulations probably came from either 1564 or 1573.

[12] ArchGK no. 3001, pp. 6–7; Sehling (ed.), *Kirchenordnungen*, p. 457.

[13] StaE, I. Reg., no. 424; Sehling (ed.), *Kirchenordnungen*, pp. 464–5.

this new innovation went forward in fits and starts. The implementation of this new category of poor faced stiff opposition from the *haussitzenden* deacons; the elders, who already worked closely with the congregation in matters of discipline, had to take over these new charity functions. Although an official *Becken* diaconate was finally inaugurated, it proved to be a short-lived experiment which never gained enough donor support, and after two decades the *Becken* deacons and their poor were merged back into the *haussitzenden* diaconate.

Perhaps the refugees' most direct effect on Emden's social welfare was the creation of the special diaconate of the foreign poor between 1554 and 1557. This enabled the wealthier Dutch refugees to finance and administer assistance for their poorer compatriots, and seems to have been modelled on Geneva's Bourse française, which was created after Calvin's arrival (probably in the 1540s) to provide a mechanism for support of Geneva's French poor without straining the city's local institutions.[14] Especially during the first two decades of its existence, the office of the *fremdlingen* deacon was vital in establishing Emden's place as 'mother church' for the struggling Reformed congregations in the Netherlands by easing the economic strain on local institutions caused by the tremendous influx of refugees. During much of this period, the expenditure of the foreign deacons was far greater than that of their local *haussitzenden* equivalents. Through the mid-1570s, for instance, the latter spent around 500–1 000 gulden per annum, while the *fremdlingen* deacons' disbursements shot up to over 3 500 gulden a year at the height of the refugee influx after 1570. Indeed, following the return of most of the wealthy Dutch merchants to the Netherlands after 1575, the *fremdlingen* deacons saw a marked decline in their finances, and the local deacons' expenditures show a dramatic increase: the *haussitzenden* expenditures jumped to 3 000 gulden in 1577 and steadily increased each year so that, after 1587, they were consistently providing over 10 000 gulden to the local poor (see Tables 8.1 and 8.2 and Figure 8.1). The *fremdlingen* deacons' effective care of thousands of immigrants during the height of the Dutch Revolt allowed Emden to prosper as an exile centre. By absorbing much of the financial pressure, the foreign deacons made it politically and socially acceptable to take in so many Dutch refugees, and the city profited greatly from the additional shipping and trade activities that they generated in turn.

Without a doubt, Emden's *fremdlingen* deacons, under the local church consistory's watchful eye, established a highly rationalised system of poor relief which took advantage of the various geographic connections

---

[14] On its origins, see Jeanine Olson, *Calvin and Social Welfare: Deacons and the Bourse française* (Selinsgrove, 1989), pp. 32ff.

Table 8.1   Yearly expenditure (in round gulden) of the city, the *haussitzenden* deacons and the church of Emden, 1575–95

Year	City	*Hauss.* Deacons	Church
1575	15 114	414	1 916
1576	16 049		1 768
1577	17 065	3 049	2 313
1578	12 339	4 496	2 278
1579	23 019	4 215	1 839
1580	12 171	6 256	2 242
1581		7 761	2 545
1582		7 943	3 433
1583		8 009	3 263
1584	25 482	8 928	3 167
1585	20 009	8 735	2 806
1586		9 938	3 835
1587		10 759	3 620
1588	19 954	9 666	2 475
1589	38 189	11 493	3 106
1590	33 525	10 639	3 619
1591	21 070	10 305	2 917
1592	21 107	9 716	2 655
1593	21 659	9 932	2 962
1594	31 557	10 423	3 093
1595	23 835	12 473	2 935

Sources: City: StaE, Alte Kamerei, 2/18, 2/20, 2/23, 2/24, 2/25; *haussitzenden* deacons: ArchGK no. 3001; church: ArchGK no. 364.

Table 8.2   Yearly expenditure (in round gulden) of the *fremdlingen* deacons, 1558–75

Year	*Fremdlingen* deacons	Year	*Fremdlingen* deacons	Year	*Fremdlingen* deacons
1558	726	1564	574	1570	2 936
1559	638	1565	764	1571	3 240
1560	350	1566	948	1572	3 563
1561	372	1567		1573	3 021
1562	407	1568		1574	2 853
1563	599	1569	2 210	1575	2 207

Source: *Fremdlingen I* and *II*.
Note: The city budget was characterised by extreme variations (note the peak in 1589–90, caused by extraordinary building projects); church spending remained more or less stable, while the *haussitzenden* deacons disbursed nearly three times as much in 1595 compared to 1578.

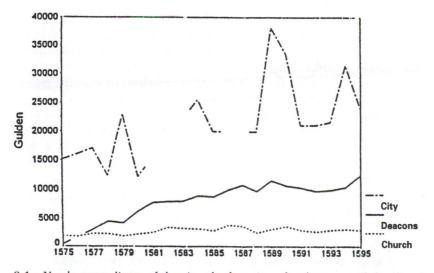

8.1 Yearly expenditure of the city, the *haussitzenden* deacons and the church of Emden, 1575–95

and social networks that the refugees brought with them. This operating principle was a common feature among exile communities of the mid-sixteenth century. From the deacons of Geneva's Bourse française to the poor relief provided by the French refugees in England, we find evidence that a sophisticated and effective system of poor provision was a fundamental necessity to the continued survival of exile communities. Becoming a burden on local institutions could be the death blow to foreigners seeking refuge. Such was the experience of foreigners in Geneva before the creation of the Bourse française. The Genevan magistrate ordered the city to be cleared of foreigners section by section because of the massive strains placed on the local hospital by the burden of large numbers of foreign poor in both 1540 and 1543. 'These rulings seem to have sprung from a pragmatic decision that the strangers could not be cared for by the city rather than a specific dislike or fear of the foreigners.'[15]

The Reformed exile congregations in England 'offered a more coherent system of welfare than that evolving within their host communities'.[16]

---

[15] William Naphy, *Calvin and the Consolidation of the Genevan Reformation* (Manchester, 1994), pp. 122–3. In crediting the Genevan Bourse, Jeannine Olson, *Social Welfare*, p. 183, writes, 'The refugee funds may have saved Geneva as a city of refuge by taking the burden off the indigenous welfare system and the general hospital. The deacons' funds dissipated at least some of the hostility that native Genevans felt toward the influx of foreigners.'

[16] Spicer, 'Poor Relief', p. 255.

But this was not necessarily so in Emden. The Emden church and civic leaders not only encouraged the operation of the *fremdlingen* deacons, but also worked to establish a strikingly coherent and broad-ranging local system. Another innovation of the 1550s was the creation of the Grain Reserve. This independent civic charity helped to stem the tide of high prices during times of need. Though it was controlled by neither church nor city, there is evidence of co-operation (and some conflict) between the Grain Reserve and the other relief institutions in provisioning the city with inexpensive grain. Such an institution was usually a temporary, stop-gap measure in early modern cities, yet Emden's permanent Grain Reserve represented a growing communal awareness in much the same way as the emerging ecclesiastical structures indicated a growing confessional identity in Emden.

The prime catalysts for the proliferation of poor relief organs were social and economic pressures, rather than moral and religious pressures. One indication of the relative importance of these pressures is the gradual transformation of the confraternities. We would expect an end to their spiritual activities as an early result of the Reformation. Yet Emden's confraternities continued to function throughout the first three Reformation decades. The citizens still remembered them in their wills, but from the 1520s for increasingly different reasons. Whereas the pre-Reformation language reflected the importance of the charitable deed to the salvation of the donor's soul, references to the poor relief activities of the confraternities become much more prominent in the wills and contracts of the post-Reformation period. It is evident, therefore, that in response to the new theological climate, the confraternities shifted their emphasis from traditional religious activities to the care of the poor. This, no doubt, allowed them to survive the first Reformation challenge largely unchanged.[17]

By the 1550s, large-scale institutional reform became inevitable for a city that was undergoing dramatic socio-economic changes. The flood of Dutch refugees was a pivotal event in Emden's religious, political, social and economic history. Housing and food shortages occurred, shipping boomed as many of the wealthier Dutch emigrants brought their trading contracts with them, but at the same time increasing

---

[17] Confraternal evolution did not require the introduction of Protestantism. Nicholas Terpstra, *Lay Confraternities and Civic Religion in Renaissance Bologna* (Cambridge, 1995), has demonstrated that Bologna's confraternities evolved from voluntary charities into civic institutions sometimes due to political struggles and sometimes due to necessities of famine and plague.

numbers of less prosperous labourers arrived. The poor of Emden were no longer simply the local *haussitzenden*, and the structures of social welfare which had gradually evolved throughout the first half of the century were suddenly tested and found wanting. Hastened by the demographic and economic crisis of the late 1550s, the trend towards centralisation of traditional relief institutions spread to Emden's Gasthaus properties, and the city also saw the formation of a grain reserve and new diaconates (*fremdlingen* and *Becken*). Thus after very gradual institutional evolution over the first half of the century, and despite major religious changes, dramatic upheavals suddenly occurred in Emden's social welfare landscape almost simultaneously. The next wave of institutional modifications and renovations occurred at the same time as the growing crisis brought about by an escalation of the Dutch Revolt in the mid-1560s.

To identify the social and economic pressures as the primary catalysts is not to argue that religious motivations did not play a vital part in shaping the changes. Religious arguments were certainly made for the ouster of the Franciscans, and may indeed have motivated a number of leading officials (including Lasco in the mid-1540s), but it took the crisis of 1557 to bring their expulsion. The creation of the Reformed church office of 'deacon' to handle most of Emden's poor relief demonstrates that city's new ecclesiology provided a new shape to the earlier 'administrators of the poor'. Even the fascinating example of the 'deacons of the household of faith', whose creation was driven almost entirely by a Bucerian theological concept, is an exception which proves the rule. Struggling with insufficient financial endowment and a lack of voluntary support, it remained but a temporary phenomenon. Many of the citizens viewed it not as a new institution created out of economic necessity but as a theological invention, and despite their commitment to the Reformation and church discipline, most were more interested in supporting institutions which cared for a larger segment of the civic community. Rather than being inherently Protestant, Emden's pattern of social welfare reform responded to specific socio-economic needs, maintained as much continuity with the traditional institutions as possible, and combined the current religious (the Reformed diaconates) with civic (the citizen committee of the Grain Reserve) priorities.

Due to the rather slow evolution of the civic magistracy's autonomy from the count, Emden's magistracy played only a small direct role in Emden's poor relief operations early in the century. Emden's deacons of the *haussitzenden* poor were clearly ecclesiastical officers who reported problems first to the consistory. Even in Calvin's Geneva, the deacons were usually important civic officials called *procureurs de l'hôpital*, appointed directly by the city and funded from the city budget. Emden's civic authorities played primarily a supervisory role. Members of the city council sometimes signed the deacons' annual accounts, oversaw the general activities of the Gasthaus, and after the Emden Revolution (1595) ordered the rewriting of guild ordinances to include the poor guild members.

Due probably to the lack of autonomy of Emden's magistracy which was under the control of the count throughout the Middle Ages and the sixteenth century, Emden's city leaders were not directly involved with the town's poor relief, and the town developed a highly organised, though not centrally administered, social welfare system. Recent research has demonstrated how political circumstances compelled Reformed leaders to implement poor relief in different ways throughout Europe. There does not, therefore, seem to be a set pattern of interaction across Protestant Europe between church and city leaders in questions of social welfare. The provision of poor relief in both Geneva and Zürich involved high levels of co-operation between church officers and the local magistracy, bringing the care of the poor under the supervision of a single administration.[18] On the other hand, religious and political arrangements in France caused Nîmes's Calvinist leaders to maintain an ecclesiastical poor relief largely independent of civic control.[19] In the 'great cities' of Holland, the introduction of Calvinism in the aftermath of the Dutch Revolt triggered quarrels over the borders of civic and ecclesiastical jurisdictions: Calvinists intended to establish independent diaconates primarily to relieve poor church members; opponents of Calvinism expected church deacons to work under municipal authority and objected to favouritism shown to the church poor.[20] The

---

[18] Kingdon, 'Deacons', pp. 82–6; Wandel, *Always Among Us*, p. 145.

[19] See Raymond Mentzer, 'Organizational Endeavor and Charitable Impulse in Sixteenth-Century France: The Case of Protestant Nîmes', *French History*, 5 (1991), p. 7. Of course, the *decision* of Nîmes's Reformed leaders to direct poor relief through their ecclesiastical channels rather than through the municipal channels was not an option for exile churches. For exile congregations such ecclesiastically directed relief was a *necessity*; see the works by Spicer and Olson, and the discussion of Emden's *fremdlingen* above.

[20] From about 1573 to 1614, for instance, the Delft Reformed consistory controlled poor relief and its church discipline independently from the magistrates. In 1614 financial and religious tensions compelled the church officials to merge the diaconate with the municipal charitable institution; Parker, 'Moral Supervision', pp. 338–43. For details on the controversy in the six 'great cities' of Holland (Dordrecht, Haarlem, Delft, Leiden, Amsterdam and Gouda), see Charles H. Parker, *The Reformation of Community: Social Welfare and Calvinist Charity in Holland* (Cambridge, 1998), pp. 155–88; I thank Professor Parker for sending me his manuscript before publication.

traditional underdeveloped nature of Emden's magistracy kept civil officers from direct involvement in the town's charity, and not until the last quarter of the sixteenth century do we find explicit evidence of extensive civic activity as town leaders struggled with the count for autonomy.

A growing civic identity throughout the century resulted in the production of a city Poor Relief Ordinance, ratified by the city council and Burgermeisters in 1576 with additional poor legislation and amendments in the subsequent few years. Prior to this point, official regulation of poor relief activities depended on the brief references in the territorial church and police ordinances, and in the practical decisions and precedents formed especially by the church consistory. By the end of the century – especially after the Emden Revolution – the city's magistracy was attempting to exert regulatory control over Emden's social welfare institutions.

Recent scholarship has underscored that Catholics, Lutherans and Reformed Protestants were deeply interested in stemming the tide of moral decay. For instance, as the existence of the Lutheran church in the territory of Brandenburg–Ansbach–Kulmbach became more secure, government mandates 'began to probe deeper and deeper into parish affairs and the conduct and belief of the parishioners became central issues.'[21] The early modern church and state frequently worked with a common purpose: to control and reform the behaviour of parishioners and subjects. Given the similarity between the Catholic and Protestant movements with respect to the essential linkage between the religious and secular aspects of society, scholars have developed the concept of 'confessionalisation', which attempts to describe the changes brought to the broader institutions of society when efforts to reform religion were made.[22] With like purposes, then, Emden's early modern church and

---

[21] C. Scott Dixon, 'The Reformation and Parish Morality in Brandenburg–Ansbach–Kulmbach', *ARG*, 87 (1996), p. 260.

[22] For an overview of confessionalisation, see Heinrich Schmidt, *Konfessionalisierung im 16. Jahrhundert* (Munich, 1992). Heinz Schilling and Wolfgang Reinhard developed the concept of confessionalisation, building on the work of Ernst Walter Zeeden who suggested the similarities within the Protestant and Catholic Reformations. See the following works by Heinz Schilling: 'Die Kirchenzucht im frühneuzeitlichen Europa in interkonfessionell vergleichender und interdisziplinärer Perspektive – eine Zwischenbilanz' in H. Schilling (ed.), *Kirchenzucht und Sozialdisziplinierung im frühneuzeitlichen Europa* (Berlin, 1994), pp. 11–40; 'Die Konfessionalisierung im Reich: Religiöser und gesellschaftlicher Wandel in Deutschland zwischen 1555 und 1620', *Historische Zeitschrift*, 246 (1988), pp. 1–45; H. Schilling (ed.), *Die reformierte Konfessionalisierung in Deutschland – Das Problem der 'Zweiten Reformation'* (Gütersloh, 1986). See the following works by

state worked together: the 'social disciplining' by the territorial government (e.g. police ordinance) and the emerging, autonomous city government was assisted by the 'religious disciplining' of the new confessional church. The institutional developments in Emden's social welfare system can shed some light on this general institutionalisation of Reformation culture that was occurring across early modern Europe.

In the later sixteenth century, fights over confessional boundaries became central to the political control of Emden and the East Frisian territories. As the city became increasingly Calvinist, Emden's Reformed leaders attempted to establish a jurisdiction separate from that controlled by the Lutheran count. The town's poor relief institutions also became entwined in the confessional conflicts. Alting in particular was explicitly interested in church discipline which could delineate the community of faith. The religious motivations behind the increasing emphasis on church discipline are revealed in the Poor Relief Ordinance (1576) which highlights biblical justifications for limiting alms to the 'worthy' poor and excluding charity from those who could be thereby encouraged in their immoral lifestyles. This ordinance also provided scriptural and theological underpinnings for the prohibition on begging, whereas the earlier begging prohibitions in the Police Ordinance had been based on practical and financial arguments.

Yet Emden's poor relief also bears the impression left by the interplay of politics and religion within East Frisia's confessional fight. One of the Reformed ministers' chief complaints in Emden's battle with the Lutherans and count decried the poor relief activities of the Lutherans in the town. The Reformed ministers wanted to halt the Lutherans' poor relief collections throughout the city, and in doing so argued that Reformed charity was to be the only lawful poor relief in the city. Poor relief was certainly an important symbol of both confessional and civic devotion at the end of the century. Indeed, the final issue which sparked the Emden Revolution against Count Edzard II in 1595 was his mandate which included the right to oversee the deacons' accounts (his officials already oversaw the church and city accounts).

Although categories of the worthy and unworthy poor existed before the Reformation, Emden's Reformed leaders increased the emphasis on such distinctions. And the definitions of worthiness became more

Wolfgang Reinhard: 'Reformation, Counter-Reformation, and the Early Modern State: A Reassessment', *Catholic Historical Review*, 75 (1989), pp. 383–404; 'Zwang zur Konfessionalisierung?', *Zeitschrift für historische Forschung*, 10 (1983), pp. 257–77; 'Konfession und Konfessionalisierung in Europa' in W. Reinhard (ed.), *Bekenntnis und Geschichte: Die Confessio Augustana im historischen Zusammenhang* (Munich, 1981), pp. 165–89.

explicitly connected with Reformed discipline and beliefs. This is not surprising, as confessional boundaries closed in the city. As the community defined itself more clearly, the poor bridged the civic and religious spheres (their care promoted civic harmony, and charity provided evidence of Christian brotherly love).[23] In order to protect the Reformed community's integrity, church leaders felt it imperative that the poor maintain the moral standards being enforced throughout the congregation. Just as Reformed discipline promoted the social conventions of civil society and sought to reinforce orthodox beliefs, attempts were made by Emden's leaders to correlate poor relief with Reformed discipline.

Of course, our initial investigatory forays into the practice of poor relief and church discipline suggest that the addition of Reformed discipline to poor relief did not yield simple solutions. In particular, the generosity of the deacons themselves might thwart the exercise of pure discipline; evidence suggests that they were reluctant to turn the needy away.[24] The *haussitzenden* deacons' distrust of the *Becken* diaconate illustrates their hesitance to accept a definition of worthiness based solely on Reformed discipline. Withdrawal of alms seems to have been only a final event in the disciplining process, and deacons frequently continued providing relief while the recipients met with pastors and elders. The mandate in the Poor Relief Ordinance of 1576 that the deacons provide no alms to the poor living immoral lives demonstrates the aims of the church and city leaders to curb the deacons' generosity.[25]

There is also evidence that local interests among Emden citizens could supersede religious motivations. This was certainly the case with the *Becken* diaconate. Between 1558 and 1578, dozens of surviving wills left bequests to the support of the Gasthaus and the *haussitzenden* poor, while only a handful bequeathed money to the *Becken* – despite the fact that the *Becken* deacons had been chartered to provide for the 'proper and most pious poor'.[26] This suggests that most Emden testators favoured the town's traditional poor relief systems rather than the new concept of the 'pure' congregation. Similarly, a testament from 1583 (at the heart of Emden's 'Calvinisation') that divided its bequest equally between the Reformed *haussitzenden* deacons, the Gasthaus

---

[23] Wandel has shown that the poor of Zurich helped define the basis of a new Protestant Christian community; *Always Among Us*, pp. 170–73

[24] Olson found this to be true in Geneva as well; *Social Welfare*, p. 139.

[25] Such mandates against refusing alms to 'all unneedy beggars, as they continue in undisciplined, ungodly lives and laziness' are also found in the Poor Relief Ordinance mandated for the Lutheran city Aurich by Count Edzard II in 1578; Sehling (ed.), *Kirchenordnungen*, p. 668.

[26] Ibid., pp. 461–2.

and the Mennonite poor demonstrates that confessional motivations could take a back seat to generosity motivated by local concerns.[27]

We have also seen that provisioning of poor relief was a negotiated process between the recipient and the welfare administrators. Just as the deacons and consistory used poor relief as an incentive to help achieve positive discipline results, the poor themselves frequently asserted their own claims and promised moral behaviour in order to continue receiving alms. The case of Willum the Blind provides one good example of this process as he made forceful appeals to the circumstances of his poverty and convinced the consistory that he needed alms in exchange for a cessation of his 'frivolous playing [of music] at bawdy dances'.[28] Despite such fluctuations in the correlation between poor relief and church discipline, there does not seem to be evidence that the Calvinist leaders used poor relief to entice a reluctant population to accept the Reformed religion.[29] While they did want to influence behaviour and were willing to use poor relief as a tool to that end, Emden's pastors, who were the ones most interested in instituting Reformed discipline, seem to have been unwilling to compromise too much to gain converts.

Though economic pressures drove the institutional changes, Emden's religious climate shaped them. Under the earlier influence of Lasco and the later influence of Dutch refugees, the reforms took on one key Reformed characteristic – that of the 'deacon'. The minor poor relief innovations in the Lutheran Church Ordinance of 1529 led to an evolution from traditional church position of churchwarden into a new administrator of the *haussitzenden* poor. This was the office which evolved into the Reformed deacons of the same name.[30] Calvin's

---

[27] Testament of Emden citizens Johan Claesen and Schwane; EKP 15/498–98v.

[28] Parker relates the case of Anna Gillis who seems to have used a potential affiliation with the Mennonite congregation as a strategy to advance her poor relief request before the Delft consistory; 'Moral Supervision', p. 356.

[29] L. J. Rogier in particular has made this claim regarding Calvinist charity; *Eenheid en scheiding. Geschiedenis der Nederlanden* (Utrecht, 1968), p. 107. Arie Th. van Deursen has successfully challenged this claim regarding the Dutch Reformed congregations by illustrating that their limited resources and small memberships (with Amsterdam's larger congregation being the only exception) would have severely limited the practical exercise of such a motivation; *Bevianen en Slijkgeuzen. Kerk en Kerkvolk ten tijde van Maurits en Oldenbarnevelt* (Assen, 1974), pp. 102–7.

[30] See note 5 above. While the 1578 Poor Relief Ordinance for the Lutheran city of Aurich is essentially a restatement of the key poor relief points of the 1529 Church Ordinance for East Frisia, it used the term 'deacon' three times to refer to the town's poor relief administrators; it also makes references to Aurich's Gasthaus and a new *Armenvogt*; Sehling (ed.), *Kirchenordnungen*, pp. 668–70. On common sixteenth-century usage of the term, see McKee, *Diaconate*, pp. 129–30.

teaching on the need for this new church office stimulated the reshaping of Emden's charity administrator to fit into Reformed ecclesiology.

The place of almsgiving in the Reformed worship service, particularly in German-speaking Reformed worship, is a complex problem with little explicit evidence.[31] Clearly the understanding of 'Christian love' as the principle behind almsgiving can be detected in East Frisia's 1529 Lutheran Church Ordinance, and the Lutheran liturgy included an exhortation by the pastor either before or after the sermon to remember the poor with alms.[32] Elsie McKee has judged as 'extremely probable' the view that Reformed deacons collected alms at the door following the pastor's exhortation to charity as a final blessing. While Emden's evidence does not allow us to shed any additional light on this liturgical question, the *haussitzenden* deacons collected weekly alms at the Sunday services in addition to those gathered in alms-pouches placed across the town and in extraordinary collections.[33] Thus sometime after the Reformation, an alms collection became part of the regular worship service.

Calvin himself emphasised the importance of charity in demonstrating the church's compassion. In a sermon on 1 Timothy 3:8–13, he rhetorically asked, 'Do we want to show that there is reformation among us? We must begin at this point, that is, there must be pastors who bear purely the doctrine of salvation, and then deacons who have the care of the poor.'[34] As Emden became more closely connected with Dutch Calvinist refugees in the 1550s, on at least one occasion Calvin was consulted regarding East Frisian charity. Menso Poppius, the minister from the nearby East Frisian village of Manslagt, made at least one appearance before the Emden consistory around the time he wrote to John Calvin in 1559. No doubt he had also asked the Emden ministers the same question he posed to Calvin in Geneva, namely, should someone who did not give charitably be excluded from the communion table? Calvin responded that although charitable giving is extremely important, it must be voluntary, and hence the reluctant giver should not be excluded from communion (see quotation at opening of chapter). Calvin ended his letter to Poppius with the following reminder, 'The healthy understanding of people commands not to support from alms the poor to whom religious benevolence becomes an invitation to

---

[31] See notes 45 and 46 in Chapter 3 above. McKee, *Diaconate*, ch. 2, discusses the variations involved in the place of almsgiving in worship.

[32] Sehling (ed.), *Kirchenordnungen*, pp. 367, 380.

[33] The weekly collection totals for 1561–67 are recorded in ArchGK no. 1117, pp. 2–34.

[34] Quoted in McKee, *Diaconate*, p. 184.

laziness. Paul also says this clearly because he commands to exclude lazy brothers and idlers from the community and adds: whoever will not work, should not eat (2 Thess. 3:10)'.[35] The Emden consistory also described how the congregation's treatment of the poor should go beyond alms. In a long letter to Antwerp offering advice on the role and function of the pastor, Emden's consistory at one point instructed the Antwerp church to maintain peace and order between the rich and poor; the richer members of Antwerp's Reformed congregations were trying to keep to themselves and apparently despised their poor brothers enough to try to hold special services without the poor in attendance. The Emden consistory wrote that 'it would be better that the rich should have no sermon' than for such divisiveness to continue.[36]

The changes of the sixteenth century increased the financial responsibilities of the people of Emden. Count Enno's confiscation of church properties shortly after the Reformation created the first major burden: more than ever before the parishioners were called upon to subsidise the church and the poor. After the middle of the century, the magnitude of the system demanded yet greater resources from the citizenry: there were simply more poor to provide for and, thus, more institutions to support. Donors met the increased financial burden with surprisingly little protest. In fact, the few surviving complaints were aimed not at the cost of maintaining the poor but at the use of poor relief funds to support the preachers.[37] The amounts involved were substantial, and welfare costs grew at a steadier and faster rate than either the church or city budgets throughout the last quarter of the century – hence the church bookkeeper's complaints (see Tables 8.1 and 8.2 and Figure 8.1).

Emden's population clearly heeded the exhortations to charity. In surprisingly few years during the second half of the sixteenth century did the institutions fail to take in enough revenues to cover their expenses, and when they did run into deficits, special collections around the town or loans from another institution generally met their needs. (There is, of course, the notable exception of the *Becken* deacons who had no revenues from traditional property holdings, no compulsory

---

[35] Poppius made an appearance in the Emden consistory minutes on 27 February 1559 (KRP, p. 72). Calvin's response to him is found in *Calvini Opera*, 17:453–4.

[36] ArchGK 320A, fol. 86 (23 March 1558); A. Arnout van Schelven, *De Nederduitsche Vluchtelingenkerken der XVIe Eeuw in Engeland en Duitschland in Hunne Beteekenis voor de Reformatie in de Nederlanden* (The Hague, 1908), p. 337. The consistory deliberated over their response on 7 March 1558; see KRP, p. 36.

[37] See pp. 83–4 above for those who did not approve of their *huusdelinge* going to the pastor any longer; see pp. 179–81 for complaints over the maintenance of the refugee ministers from the funds of both the *fremdlingen* and *Becken* deacons.

rate, and far from enough voluntary contributions.) Only the *fremdlingen* deacons seem to have had to impose a compulsory rate on the wealthier refugees – calling it a 'voluntary assessment' – and they were forced to increase the frequency of its collection and to rely on assistance from international sources as the refugee influx intensified.[38] Individual deacons were also expected to cover expense overruns at least on a short-term basis, until they could be reimbursed from other income. The trend of generally operating with end-of-year surpluses ended for the *haussitzenden* deacons in 1609, from which time (with the exception of 1619) they constantly gave out more than they took in.[39]

What makes Emden's history so remarkable is the fact that the ecclesiastical developments within the church coincided with the timing of similar communal developments that were occurring within the separate secular framework of political organisation.[40] The mutual influences of these separate movements resulted in increasing self-confidence among Emden's citizens, and this case demonstrates the interdependence of social, political, economic and ecclesiastical factors which were at play in early modern Europe. After the city and church continued to define themselves more clearly and exert their authority at the end of the century, Emden's church issued a new church ordinance in 1594. Here they explicitly stipulated the administrative structures and duties of the Gasthaus, *haussitzenden* deacons, Shippers' Brotherhood and *fremdlingen* deacons. The consistory had frequently mediated with and consulted these poor relief organs, but they had never before claimed authority over the Gasthaus or the Shippers' Brotherhood.[41] As the conflict with the count grew, Emden's Reformed consistory asserted control over most of the poor relief in the city. Only the Grain Reserve was not mentioned in the 1594 Church Ordinance – a recognition perhaps of the fully civic motivations behind its foundation.

The 1595 Revolution resulted from the convergence of Emden's growing civic consciousness and confessional identity. Following the Revolution the city clearly defined itself as 'Reformed'; the church had

---

[38] Timothy Fehler, 'Social Welfare in Early Modern Emden' (Ph.D. thesis, University of Wisconsin-Madison, 1995), pp. 352–71; Fehler, 'The Burden of Benevolence: Poor Relief and Parish Finance in Early Modern Emden', in Beat Kümin (ed.), *Reformations Old and New* (Aldershot, 1996), pp. 234–6.

[39] ArchGK no. 3001 (the account book ends in 1648).

[40] Heinz Schilling, *Civic Calvinism in Northwest Germany and the Netherlands* (Kirksville, MO, 1992), p. 27.

[41] It would be interesting to have evidence of any effect this Reformed church ordinance might have had on the Gasthaus residents and their property. On confessional conformity in Augsburg's Lutheran and Catholic orphanages, see Safley, *Charity and Economy*, pp. 140–42.

just defined as 'Reformed' almost all the city's poor relief in its church ordinance. Similar to the trend of confessionalisation across Europe, the political and religious impulses of city and count are impossible to separate completely in this case. As an issue that was neither purely political nor purely ecclesiastical, poor relief became a vital expression of the developing political and confessional boundaries. Emden's poor relief changes – frequently stimulated by social and economic stress over the century – finally became institutionalised in the heated confessional climate of the last quarter. New theological ideals (such as the 'household of faith') sometimes failed in Emden's testing ground of poor relief.

In the complex interplay of religious ideals, political struggles and economic exigencies, Emden's exceptionally detailed and varied institutions of poor provision became both weapons in the political/confessional struggles and outward expressions of the theological underpinnings of the Reformed community. Here Emden's story is especially instructive, for it provides a window to a point of intersection of these varied and sometimes competing motivations. Religious and socio-economic concerns were inextricably linked in the period. When we as historians look at early modern poor relief, we cannot neatly separate the motivations because they were not separated in the minds of contemporaries. To come back to Grell's call for a revision of the study of early modern poor relief, we certainly cannot understand the Reformation, nor the major institutional changes of the period, without religion, but we also cannot comprehend fully the motivations of the reformers without recognising the social and political context. Emden's poor relief changes were usually driven by socio-economic crises, yet often shaped by religious ideology with a mix of practical good sense. The motivations of the city's poor relief administrators included varying combinations of civic pride, concern for good social order, personal ambition, Christian duty, and sincere (sometimes paternalistic) interest in the lives of those in need. Indeed, what makes the Reformation era so interesting and dramatic is that sixteenth-century people linked these issues so closely. The story of Emden's social welfare serves as a reminder of the tightly woven web of early modern religious, political and socio-economic concerns.

Appendix: About the Currency

The standard currency in East Frisia throughout most of the sixteenth century was the gulden; smaller currencies such as schap, krumstert, stüber and witten were also frequently used. Because a complicated system of currency existed, I have tried to simplify all my references into a basic unit of gulden. Various currency reforms and frequent inflation changed the relationships between the units of currency. For instance, Count Edzard I issued a currency reform in 1491 which yielded the following relations:

1 rheinische gulden = 1 Emden gulden = 36 krumstert = 24 stüber
1 krumstert = 4 witten
1 stüber = 6 witten
1 Arensgulden = 15 krumstert

Inflationary forces affected the relationships; for example, by 1503 a rheinische gulden was worth about 40 krumstert. In 1507, a new 'currency ordinance' indicated that a krumstert should be valued at 3.5 witten and 1 schap at 18 witten. Between 1510 and 1530, a gulden was generally valued at about 42 to 47.5 krumstert.[1]

During the last two-thirds of the sixteenth century, the 'Emden gulden' was standardised to 10 schap or 200 witten. A daler was introduced which equalled 1.5 Emden gulden. As a general rule, I have attempted to convert other currencies (such as the 'daler', 'thaler', or other foreign currencies) into their basic gulden equivalents.

The following examples of wages, salaries and prices gleaned from surviving city and church account books give some feel for the value of a gulden at various points in the sixteenth century.[2]

---

[1] See the works by Anton Kappelhoff, 'Beiträge zur Geldgeschichte Ostfrieslands', *EJb*, 37 (1958), pp. 33–78; 'Eine Inflation und Währungsreform in Ostfriesland gegen Ende des 15. Jahrhunderts', *Ostfriesland*, 3 (1956), pp. 11–18; *Die Münzen Ostfrieslands seit dem Auftreten von Häuptlingen*. Some of the results are summarised by Christian Lamschus, *Emden unter der Herrschaft der Cirksena* (Hildesheim, 1984), p. 161.

[2] See also Bartels, 'Gehalts-, Löhnungs- und andere Preisverhältnisse um 1550', *EJb*, 2, 2 (1877), pp. 160–62.

Day-Labourer's Wages

During the first two decades of the century, the average daily wage of those who performed manual labour for the city was about 4.1 krumstert; the range was generally between 3 and 5 krumstert. If one were to work 300 days a year, this wage would yield a maximum of about 30 rheinische gulden.[3] Of course, seasonal variations in labour needs limited the work opportunities of most manual day-labourers, and yearly earnings of 5–10 gulden are not surprising. For example, the street-cleaner and caulk-layer Tyadtmer Kalckstoter earned 10.1 rheinische gulden in wages from the city in 1512; the total fell to 2.5 gulden throughout all of 1513.

By 1577, the church usually paid carpenters and other day-labourers who worked on building repairs between 4 and 5 schap per day. If a labourer worked every day, the yearly maximum would have been about 120 gulden, so we might expect the average yearly income to have been around 30–60 gulden. By 1593, the church was paying about 7.5 schap for a day's wage to the master craftsman; his assistants were paid about 5–5.5 schap per day.[4]

Salaries

The account books recorded a wide range of salaries of city and church officials, and frequently cash payments were supplemented with rent and housing costs, or with a regular allowance of grain, beer or clothing. Yet the range of the cash salaries paid in Emden gives some impression as to the value of the gulden. The pastors' salaries were usually provided in addition to housing expenses. In the mid-1540s, Johannes a Lasco received 200 gulden as superintendent of the East Frisian churches, and Emden's two additional pastors received 100 gulden each (at the same time, one of Emden's Burgermeisters, Petrus Medmann, received a yearly salary of 150 gulden). By 1554 the three pastors each received 140 gulden a year. In 1572, the three pastors were paid 250, 200 and 200 gulden; by 1577 the salaries had climbed to 300, 250 and 250 gulden, with a fourth minister receiving 50 gulden. By 1595, all the pastors' salaries were over 500 gulden, with the chief preacher, Menso Alting, receiving 600 gulden per year.

---

[3] Lamschus, *Herrschaft der Cirksena*, p. 189; Schnedermann, 'Emder Stadtrechnungen aus den ersten Jahrzehnten des 16. Jahrhunderts', *EJb*, 1, 3 (1874), p. 111.

[4] These figures come from the church's account book, ArchGK no. 364.

The salary range of other officials was generally much lower than that of the ministers and the Burgermeisters. The rector of Emden's Latin school received a salary of 20 gulden in 1550 (66 gulden in 1572, 90 in 1577, and 150 in 1595), but this was in addition to the tuition fees (*Schulgeld*) paid him by the students. The church's organist was paid a salary of 25 gulden in 1572, 30 in 1577, and 40 in 1595; the 'choir-master' or 'song-master' of the church was slightly better paid with salaries of 55, 60 and 100 gulden in the same years. The very low salaries of the church's sexton and grave-digger (usually between 5 and 20 gulden in the last half of the century) were probably supplemented with fees for their services.

We know the salaries of a number of Countess Anna's servants around 1550. Her chancellor's salary was over 300 gulden, while the secretary to the chancellor received between 20 and 30 gulden. The wagon-driver's salary was 6 gulden, the messenger's was 14 gulden, and the butcher in the castle received about 25 gulden. The court tailor was paid only 5 gulden, but received his clothing and shoes free of charge; the cook's salary was 28 gulden, but did not include clothing. The female servants of the countess received between 4 and 18 gulden per year.

Prices

The prices of foodstuffs, animals and clothing are even more difficult to determine. In the second half of the century, roughly 1 gulden could generally buy a shirt, pants or shoes. A pair of boots usually cost a bit more, 1.5–3 gulden; a jacket cost still more. Around mid-century one could buy a horse for anywhere between 40 and 60 gulden. Countess Anna bought young Count Edzard II a stallion for about 70 gulden. The prices paid for meat ranged from 8 gulden for a 'fat beast' to 15 gulden for an ox (for butchering).

In times of great price fluctuation, some contemporaries made notes which recorded the change in grain and butter prices.[5] One writer noted 1482, 1483, 1490, 1492, 1493 and 1494 as years of extremely high prices for agricultural products (and listed 1495, 1496 and 1510 as years of unusually low prices). Table A.1 lists prices in rheinische gulden for a

---

[5] Especially Eggerik Beninga, *Chronica der Fresen* (up to 1557), and the writer of the *Emden Chronyk* (during the second half of the sixteenth century), which was partially transcribed by Hemmo Suur as 'Zur Geschichte der Stadt Emden', in *Jahrbüchlein zur Unterhaltung und zum Nutzen zunächst für Ostfriesland und Harlingerland auf das Jahr 1837*, ed. G. W. Bueren (Emden, 1836).

Tonne (approximately a metric ton) of rye, butter and beer; the figures in Emden gulden from later in the century use the additional unit of measure of the *Last*, which was about two *Tonnen* (a *Last* was originally the amount in a wagon which could be pulled by two horses).[6] These price comparisons give an indication as to the extreme fluctuations that could take place in Emden due to insufficient harvests or frequent floods.

Table A.1   Sample prices in Emden

Year	Rye	Butter	Hamburg beer
1482	3.5 rh. gulden		
1483	3.7	10.0 (white butter)	
		13.5 (red butter)	
1490	5.0	10.0	
1492	5.0	12.0	
1493	6.0	12.0	
1494	0.6	4.0	
1495	0.6		3.0
1509		7.0	
1513			1.5
1515		13.5	
1518			1.0 to 2.6
1520		10.0	
1525			3.0
1526	1.7		2.8 to 3.0
1527			3.0
1528			3.4 to 3.5
1529			3.3 to 3.8
1530		8.0 to 15.0	

Month/year	Rye (per *Last*)	Butter (per *Tonne*)	Wheat (per *Last*)
1546	*c.* 50 Emd. gulden	17	
11/1565	124		100
2/1570	27	45 (red)	
5/1570	37.5		
2/1571	55.5	34.5	
5/1571	42	33	
2/1572	111		150
4/1572		28.5 (red)	
		19.5 (white)	
2/1573	108		
4/1573	52.5		
1/1574		57	
1580	124.5		

---

[6] The first portion of the table was compiled from Lamschus, *Herrschaft der Cirksena*, pp. 159–60.

Bibliography

I. Primary Sources

A. Archival Materials

Archiv der Grossen Kirche in Emden

Number	Description
1–102	Testaments, contracts, donations, and similar documents involving the church. The pre-1500 documents have been printed in *OUB*, but the archival numbers given in *OUB* do not correspond to the current numbers
120	Printed manuscript of J. Conrad's *Gedenkschrift zur Gasthaus- und Gasthauskirchenfrage*, 1919
315	Inventory of church properties and rent incomes in 1546
320A, B, C	Collection of correspondence
329–31	Consistory minutes (Kirchenratsprotokolle)
344–68	Church account books covering much of sixteenth century
1090	The 'Confession' and 'Discipline' of French Reformed church, 1611
1100	Protocol book of French church's consistory meetings, 1611–1718
1117	Account book of the Deacons of the *Haussitzenden* Poor, 1561–73
1118	Account book of the Deacons of the *Haussitzenden* Poor, 1573–79; has been badly damaged and restored
3001	Account book and protocol book of the Deacons of the *Haussitzenden* Poor, 1578–1657; divided into four sections: 1) alms ordinances and statutes, 2) yearly revenues and expenditures, 3) standing loans of capital, 4) bequests to the poor
3007	Revenues of the Deacons of the *Haussitzenden* Poor, 1674–1703
3013	Expenditures of the Deacons of the *Haussitzenden* Poor, 1674–1704
3041	Protocol book of the meetings of the *Haussitzenden* Deacons, 1619–1776

3042	Register of bequests and testaments to the *Haussitzenden* Poor, 1617–41
3043	Register of loans, contracts, and obligations of the Deacons of the *Haussitzenden* Poor, 1674
3048	Register of distributed clothing, sheets, and cloth, 1694–1773
3051	*Haussitzenden* deacons' memorial book of burial cloths, 1658–79
3052	Register of apprenticeships for youth and 'derde parts kinderen' 1651–1780
3053	Lists of gifts to incoming and departing poor travellers, 1669–1774
3194	Expenditure account book of the Deacons of the *Haussitzenden* Poor, 1579–83
No number	Account books of Deacons of *Fremdlingen* Poor, 1558–68 (on microfilm) and 1569–75

Stadtarchiv Emden

Reg., number	Description
I. Reg., 292	Mandates regarding the plague in Emden and East Frisia, 1565–1730
405	French Reformed church correspondence, 1576–1743
406	Disputes between Lutheran and Reformed in Emden, 1656–1719
407	Dispute over Count Edzard II's demand for his court preacher to hold the sermon at his daughter's funeral, 1588
412a	Deals with the Lutheran worship services in Emden, 1588–1745
413	Deals with Roman Catholics in Emden, 1685–1732
414	Protocol of disputation between Emden ministers and Flemish Anabaptists, 1578
415	Contains mandates against Anabaptists and the *Schutzgeld* lists of the Mennonites and Jews, 1534–1737
417	File dealing with Jewish affairs, 1572–1745; although listed in register, could not be located by Archive staff
419	Collection of documents regarding the administration of the properties of the Grosse Kirche, 1483–1747

421	Documents touching on school matters, such as the hiring of the rectors and other teachers, 1573–1746
423	Deals with the Gasthaus, 1557–1752; includes Anna's correspondence with city and the monk's petition
424	Miscellaneous documents which deal with poor relief; for instance, mandates against begging, deliberations about a 'Tucht-haus'
425	Documents from Clementiner Shippers' Brotherhood, including transcription of foundation ordinances and a printed version of the revised post-Police Ordinance statutes
426	Various charitable donations to the city
427	Marriage and baptism mandates, 1575–1707
458, a–pp	Individual files on Emden's guilds and craft organizations in the sixteenth and seventeenth centuries; see also nos 457, 460, 846, 954
846	Emden Protokollbuch, 1483–1522
912	Tax collection (*Schattinge*), *c.* 1524
II. Reg.,1177	Letters from the various religious organizations and poor relief institutions in Emden in response to the city councils request for descriptions of their poor relief practices, 1800
GII, 3/1	(Gasthaus Repertorium) Gasthaus account book, 1595–1620
GIII, 53	Mandates from Burgermeister and city council, 1618–1789
GIII, 135u	Leases of the Gasthaus's lands and householdings, 1585–1607
AK 2, 1–30	(Alte Kamerei) Various income and expenditure account books of the city's 'Rentmeister' from the sixteenth century. A number of them have been lost, i.e. 1, 2/1, 12–14, 19 and 21.
AK XXV, 1–4	('Schatzungregister') Tax collections, 1555, 1556, 1562/63, 1565/66
Prot. I, 7	Contains list of names of most civic office-holders, usually from the late sixteenth century onward; also the under-deacons from 1588, the head-deacons from 1583, and the churchwardens from 1581

Prot. IV, 1–4	Diaries of the Emden Magistracy, 1595–96, 1601–3; 1599–1602; and 1612–30 (no. 3 is missing)
Prot. XIX, 1–3	Books of Citizens (Bürgerbücher), 1512–54, 1554–66, 1571–95
HS, 44	Sixteenth- and seventeenth-century guild record books; see also nos 154–9, 164–7, 198, 199, 219, 227, 241–5, 267, 272, 380, 443, 444
MS, 6	Large collection of craft guild rolls; see also no. 3

Staatsarchiv Aurich

Rep.	*Description*
135, 7	(Konsistorium Aurich), various letters from the period of the Reformation, *c.* 1548
135, 12	Documents dealing with the secularisation of the monasteries in East Frisia, *c.* 1555; contains some of the correspondence with the countess regarding the conversion of the Franciscan monastery in Faldern
135, 146	Count Edzard II's Lutheran Church Ordinance, 1593
135, 174	The early documents contain complaints of the Emden citizenry and church to the count in the early 1590s
234	Emden Kontraktenprotokoll; volume 1 begins in 1509
241, Msc. A168	Querimoniale Civitatis Emedense, criminal complaint book, 1510–57
241, Msc. A190	Contains lists of deacons, poor relief administrators, and city government and church officials from the late sixteenth century into the eighteenth century

B. Printed Sources

Die Akten der Synode der Niederländischen Kirchen zu Emden vom 4.–13. Oktober 1571, ed. J. F. Gerhard Goeters (Neukirchen, 1971)

Althusius, Johannes, *Politica Methodica Digesta* (3rd edn, 1614), ed. Carl Joachim Friedrich (Cambridge, MA, 1932)

Barghorn, E., 'Kirchliche Zeugnisse der ev.-ref. Gemeinde zu Emden 1562–1886', *QuF*, 13 (1964), 61–111

Beninga, Eggerik, *Chronica der Fresen*, ed. Heinz Ramm (2 vols, Aurich, 1961–64)

Beninga, Eggerik, *Volledige Chronyk van Ostfrieslant [...] geschreven van [...] Heer Eggeric Beningha, Hooftling te Grimersum, Raad van het Ostfriese Regeerhuis en Drost op Leeroohrt, nu met Rand en Kanteikeningen oude Versegelingen en andere Stukken verrykt*, ed. Eilhardus Folkardus Harkenroht (Emden, 1723)

Brenneysen, E. R. (ed.), *Ost-Friesische Historie und Landes-Verfassung. Aus denen im Fürstlichen Archiv vorhandenen und sonst colligirten glaubwürdigen Documenten [...] zusammengetragen* (2 vols, Aurich, 1720)

'Ein Brüchteregister des Amtes Emden aus dem 15. Jahrhundert', ed. G. Liebe, *EJb*,7,1 (1886), 19–92

Buma, Wybren Jan and Ebel, Wilhelm (eds), *Das Emsiger Recht* (Göttingen, 1967)

Ebel, Wilhelm (ed.), *Ostfriesische Bauernrechte* (Aurich, 1964)

Ecke, Karl (ed.), *Ein 'Emder Adressbuch' aus den Jahren 1562/63* (Aurich, 1978)

Emmius, Ubbo, *De Statu reipublicae et ecclesiae in Frisia orientali*, bound in *De Frisia et Frisiorum republica* (Leiden, 1616)

Emmius, Ubbo, *Tractat von Ostfriesland, ins Hochteutsche übergesetzet und mit Anmerckungen und Documenten erlaeutert [...]*, trans. E. R. Brenneysen (Aurich, 1732)

Eppens, Abel, *De Kroniek van Abel Eppens tho Equart*, ed. J. A. Feith and H. Brugmans (2 vols, Amsterdam, 1911)

Friedlaender, Ernst (ed.), 'Eine ostfriesische Gildenrolle des 16. Jahrhunderts', *EJb*, 1, 2 (1875), 67–75

Generale Ordre van de Diaconie, der Gemeente Jesu Christi in Groningen (3rd printing, Groningen, 1730)

Haenisch, Pastor (ed.), 'Bettelgedicht des Studenten Simon Petri in Emden 1600', *EJb*,14 (1902), 306–8

Die Kirchenratsprotokolle der Reformierten Gemeinde Emden 1557–1620, ed. Heinz Schilling and Klaus-Dieter Schreiber (2 vols, Cologne and Vienna, 1989–92)

Kohlmann, Dr (ed.), 'Emden im Jahre 1617', *EJb*, 8, 1 (1888), 95–8

Kuyper, Abraham (ed.), *Joannis a Lasco opera* (2 vols, Amsterdam, 1866)

Niederländische Akten und Urkunden zur Geschichte der Hanse und zur deutschen Seegeschichte, ed. Rudolp Häpke (2 vols, Munich, 1913–23)

Ostfriesisches Urkundenbuch 787–1500, vols I and II, ed. Ernst Friedlaender (Emden, 1878–81)

Ostfriesisches Urkundenbuch, vol. III, ed. Günther Möhlmann (Aurich, 1975)

'Polizeiordnung' of Edzard I for Emden, *EJb*, 2, 1 (1875), 115–18

Reershemius, Peter Friedrich, *Ostfriesländisches Prediger-Denkmal* (Aurich, 1796)

Schelven, A. A. van (ed.) 'Emden in niederländischer Beleuchtung aus dem Jahre 1573', *EJb*, 20 (1920), 174–93

Sehling, Emil (ed.), *Die evangelischen Kirchenordnungen des XVI. Jahrhunderts* (Seibenter Band: Niedersachsen, II. Hälfte: Die außerwelfischen Lande, 1. Halbband), prepared by A. Sprengler-Ruppenthal (Tübingen, 1963)

Stracke, Johannes, 'Querimoniale Civitatis Emedense'(first 59 folios), typewritten transcription in Johannes a Lasco Bibliothek Grosse Kirche Emden: 'Stracke Nachlaß'

Stracke, Johannes (ed.), 'Unser lever vrouwen register', in his 'Geistliche Laienbruderschaften im ausgehenden Mittelalter', *EJb*, 51/52 (1971/72), 53–64

'Testament der Moetke von Diepholz 1593', ed. Ernst Friedlaender, *EJb*, 14 (1902), 294–9

Toorenenbergen, J. J. van (ed.) *Stukken betreffende de Diaconie der Vreemdelingen te Emden, 1560–1576*, Werken der Marnix-Vereeniging, 1st series, part II (Utrecht, 1876)

Ubbius, Henricus, 'Beschreibung von Ostfriesland vom Jahre 1530', ed. F. Ritter, *EJb*, 18 (1913), 53–141; German translation by G. D. Ohling, *Feriae Auricanae* (Aurich, 1933), pp. 1–16

Vries, J. Fr de, 'Besoldungsklage eines Predigers in der zweiten Hälfte des XVII Jahrhunderts', *EJb*, 12 (1897), 172–5

Vries, J. Fr de, 'Schreiben des Landsknechts Hans Bloemhoff aus der Zeit des dreisigjährigen Krieges an Bürgermeister und Rat der Stadt Emden', *EJb*, 12 (1897), 172–3

Wiemann, Harm, *Die Grundlagen der landständischen Verfassung in Ostfriesland. Die Verträge von 1595 bis 1611* (Aurich, 1974)

Wicht, Matthias von, *Das Ostfriesische Land-Recht nebst dem Deich- und Syhlrechte, mit verschiedenen der aeltesten Handschrifften zusammen gehalten und von vielen Schreibfehlern gesaeubert* (Aurich, [1746])

C.   *Published Sixteenth-Century Poor Relief Treatises*

Bucer, Martin, *A Treatise, How by the Worde of God, Christian mens Almose ought to be distributed* (?, 1557?; reprinted, Amsterdam, 1976)

Hyperius, Andreas, *De publica in pauperes beneficentia*, in *Varia opuscula theologica* (Basel, 1570), pp. 870–965

Hyperius, Andreas, *The Regiment of the Povertie. Compiled by a learned divine of our time D. Andreas Hyperius and now serving very fittly for the present state of this realme*, trans. Henry Tripp (London, 1572)

Krimm, Herbert (ed.), *Quellen zur Geschichte der Diakonie* (3 vols, Stuttgart, 1960–65)

'Liber vagatorum', German translation: *Von der falschen Betler buberey. Mit einer Vorrede Martini Luther. Und hinden an ein rotwelsch Vacabularius, daraus man die wörter, so yn diesen büchlein gebraucht verstehen kann* (Wittenberg, 1528)

Karlstadt, Andreas, '"There Should be No Beggars Among Christians": An early Reformation Tract on Social Welfare by Andreas Karlstadt', trans. Carter Lindberg, in Carter Lindberg (ed.), *Piety, Politics and Ethics Reformation Studies in Honor of George Wolfgang Forell* (Kirksville, MO, 1984), pp. 157–66

Luther, Martin, *Ordenung eyns gemeynen kastens*, in D. *Martin Luthers Werke*, Kritische Gesamtausgabe, vol. 12, pp. 11–30 (Weimar, 1891)

Salter, Frank Reyner (ed.) *Some Early Tracts on Poor Relief* (London, 1926) [Contains translations of Vives's *De Subventione Pauperum*; the Ypres *Forma Subventionis*; Luther's *Ordinance for a Common Chest*; Zwingli's *Ordinance and Articles Touching Almsgiving*; *Les Pauvres des Rouen*; the English Legislation of 1531 and 1536]

Villavicentio, Laurentius de, *De oeconomia sacra circa pauperum curam a christo instituta ... libra tres* (Antwerp, 1564)

Vives, Jan Luis, *On Assistance to the Poor* (*De subventione pauperum*), trans. Alice Tobriner, in *A Sixteenth-Century Urban Report*, Part II, Social Service Monographs, 2nd Series (School of Social Service Administration, University of Chicago, 1971)

II.   Secondary Materials

A.   *Regional Studies: Emden, Northern Germany, and the Netherlands*

Antholz, Heinz, *Die politische Wirksamkeit des Johannes Althusius in Emden* (Aurich, 1955)

Bartels, Petrus, 'Miscellanea. Gehalts-, Löhnungs- und andere Preisverhältnisse um 1550', *EJb*, 2, 2 (1877), 160–62

Bernoulli, W., *Das Diakonenamt bei J. a Lasco* (Greisensee, 1951)

Blaupot Ten Cate, S., *Geschiedenis der Doopsgezinden in Groningen, Overijssel en Oost-Friesland* (2 vols, Leeuwarden, 1842)

Blockmans, W. P. and Prevenier, W., 'Poverty in Flanders and Brabant from the Fourteenth to the Mid-Sixteenth Century: Sources and Problems', *Acta Historiae Neerlandicae*, X (1978), 20–57

Brilling, Bernhard, 'Die Entstehung der jüdischen Gemeinde in Emden (1570–1613)', *Westfalen*, 51 (1973), 210–24

Buhr, Hermann de, 'Die Entwicklung Emdens in der zweiten Hälfte des 16. Jahrhunderts' (Ph.D. thesis, University of Hamburg, 1967)

Bulst, Neithard, 'Vier Jahrhunderte Pest in niedersächsischen Städten. Vom Schwarzen Tod (1349–1351) bis in die erste Hälfte des 18. Jahrhunderts', in Cord Meckseper (ed.), *Stadt im Wandel*, vol. 4 (Stuttgart–Bad Cannstatt, 1985), pp. 251–70

Buss, Harm, *Letztwillige Verfügungen nach ostfriesischem Recht* (Aurich, 1966)

Buurman, Heinrich, *Die Apotheken Ostfrieslands von den Anfängen bis zur Gründung des Deutschen Reiches, 1871* (Aurich, 1990)

Cantzler, Gerhard, *Altes Handwerk in Ostfriesland. Von der Zunft zur Innung* (Aurich, 1991)

Conrad, Pastor J., 'Gedenkschrift zur Gasthaus- und Gasthauskirchefrage' (typescript, ArchGK no. 120/Nellner, Emden, 1919)

Dalton, Hermann, *Johannes a Lasco* (Gotha, 1881; reprint, Nieuwkoop, 1970)

Der Ploeg, J. van, *Armoede en diaconale Armenzorg in de stadt Groningen, 1594–1650* (thesis, University of Groningen, 1978)

Duke, Alastair, *Reformation and Revolt in the Low Countries* (London, 1990)

[No name], 'Emdens Einrichtungen zu wohlthätigen Zwecken', *Ostfriesisches Monatsblatt für provinzielle Interessen*, 2 (1874), 165–73, 371–5, 400–404

Emmius, Ubbo, *Menso Altings Leben*, trans. Erich von Reeken (Emden, 1982)

Engelbrecht, Jörg, *Die reformierte Landgemeinde in Ostfriesland im 17. Jahrhundert. Studien zum Wandel sozialer und kirchlicher Strukturen einer ländlichen Gesellschaft* (Frankfurt, 1982)

Fehler, Timothy G., 'The Burden of Benevolence: Poor Relief and Parish Finance in Early Modern Emden', in Beat Kümin (ed.), *Reformations Old and New. Essays on the Socio-Economic Impact of Religious Change c. 1470–1630* (Aldershot, 1996), 219–36

Fehler, Timothy, 'Social Welfare in Early Modern Emden: The Evolution of Poor Relief in the Age of the Reformation and Confessionalization' (Ph.D. thesis, University of Wisconsin-Madison, 1995)

Frerichs, A., *Die Neubildung der evangelisch-Lutherischen Gemeinde zu Emden. Zur Säkularfeier am 9. Juli 1875* (Emden, 1875)

Fritzschen, Günther, 'Die Entwicklung des Emder Stadtrechts bis zum Beginn des 16. Jahrhuderts' (Ph.D. thesis, University of Göttingen, 1958)

Fürbringer, Leo, *Die Stadt Emden in Gegenwart und Vergangenheit* (Emden, 1892)

Garrelts, Heinrich, *Die Reformation Ostfrieslands nach der Darstellung der Lutheraner vom Jahre 1593 nebst einer kommentierten Ausgabe ihrer Berichte* (Aurich, 1925)

Hagedorn, Bernhard, 'Betriebsformen und Einrichtungen des Emder Seehandelsverkehrs in den letzten drei Jahrzehnten des 16. Jahrhunderts', *Hansische Geschichtsblätter*, 16 (1910), 187–284

Hagedorn, Bernhard, *Ostfrieslands Handel und Schiffahrt im 16. Jahrhundert* (Berlin, 1910)

Hagedorn, Bernhard, *Ostfrieslands Handel und Schiffahrt vom Ausgang des 16. Jahrhunderts bis zum Westfällischen Frieden (1584–1648)* (Berlin, 1912)

Hahn, Louis, 'Emdens älteste Schulordnung', *EJb*, 25 (1937), 62–5

Hahn, Louis, 'Wilhelm, der blinde Sänger. Ein Emder Kulturbild aus dem Reformationsjahrhundert', *Ostfriesland. Mitteilungsblatt der Ostfriesischen Landschaft und der Ostfriesischen Heimatvereine*, 2 (2nd quarter, 1952), 4–7

Herwerden, P. J. van, 'Geschiedenis van het Sint Geertruids- of Pepergasthuis te Groningen', *Economisch–Historisch Jaarboek*, 28 (1961), 149–217

Hesse, H. Klugkist, *Menso Alting. Eine Gestalt aus der Kampfzeit der calvinischen Kirche* (Berlin, 1928)

Hindrichs, Ernst and Zon, Henk van (eds), *Bevölkerungsgeschichte im Vergleich: Studien zu den Niederlanden und Nordwestdeutschland* (Aurich, 1988)

Houston, Rab, 'The Consistory of the Scots Church, Rotterdam: An Aspect of "Civic Calvinism", *c.* 1600–1800', *ARG*, 87 (1996), 362–92

Houtrouw, O. G., *Ostfriesland. Eine geschichtlich-ortskundige Wanderung gegen Ende der Fürstenzeit* (Aurich, 1889)

Israel, Jonathan I., 'Dutch influence on urban planning, health care and poor relief: the North Sea and Baltic regions of Europe, 1567–1720', in Ole Peter Grell and Andrew Cunningham (eds), *Health Care and Poor Relief in Protestant Europe* (London, 1997), 66–83

Janssen, Antoon E. M. and Nissen, Peter J. A., 'Niederlande, Lüttich', in Anton Schindling and Walter Ziegler (eds), *Die Territorien des Reichs im Zeitalter der Reformation und Konfessionialisierung. Land und Konfession 1500–1650*, vol. 3 (Münster, 1991), pp. 200–235

Jütte, Robert, 'Health care provision and poor relief in early modern Hanseatic towns: Hamburg, Bremen and Lübeck', in Ole Peter Grell and Andrew Cunningham (eds), *Health Care and Poor Relief in Protestant Europe* (London, 1997), 108–28

Kappelhoff, Anton, 'Beiträge zur Geldgeschichte Ostfrieslands', *EJb*, 37 (1957), 33–78

Kappelhoff, Bernd, 'Die Reformation in Emden' (2 parts), *EJb*, 57 (1977), 64–143; 58 (1978), 22–67

Knetsch, F. R. J, '"De armen hebt gij altijd bij U". Religieus gemotiveerde armenzorg in de stad Groningen', in G. van Halsema Thzn, Jos. M. M. Hermans, et al. (eds), *Geloven in Groningen* (Kampen, 1990), pp. 11–27

Kochs, Ernst, 'Die Anfänge der Ostfriesischen Reformation' (3 parts), *EJb*, 19, 1 (1916), 109–72; 19, 2 (1918), 173–273; 20 (1920), 1–125

König, Joseph, *Verwaltungsgeschichte Ostfrieslands bis zum Aussterben seines Fürstenhauses* (Göttingen, 1955)

Lahn, Louis, *Emdens Apotheken und Apotheker in fünf Jahrhunderten* (Aurich, 1954)

Lamschus, Christian, *Emden unter der Herrschaft der Cirksena. Studien zur Herrschaftsstruktur der ostfriesischen Residenzstadt 1470–1527* (Hildesheim, 1984)

Leistikow, Dankwart, 'Mittelalterliche Hospitalbauten Norddeutschlands', in Cord Meckseper (ed.), *Stadt im Wandel*, vol. 4 (Stuttgart–Bad Cannstatt, 1985), pp. 223–49

Lengen, Hajo Van, *Geschichte des Emsiger Landes vom frühen 13. bis zum späten 15. Jahrhundert* (Aurich, 1973)

Lengen, Hajo Van, 'Land und Stadt im ostfriesischen Küstenraum während des späten Mittelalters und der frühen Neuzeit', in Cord Meckseper (ed.), *Stadt im Wandel*, vol. 4 (Stuttgart–Bad Cannstatt, 1985), pp. 39–62

Loesing, Helias, *Geschichte der Stadt Emden bis zum Vertrage von Delfsyhl 1595* (Emden, 1843)

Lokers, Jan, *Die Juden in Emden 1530–1806* (Aurich, 1990)

McCants, Anne E. C., *Civic Charity in a Golden Age: Orphan Care in Early Modern Amsterdam* (Champaign, 1997)

Meder, Helias, *Openlijke Tafel-Gebeden tot gebruik in het Gast- en Wees-Huis der Stad Emden* (Emden, 1802)

Meier, Hermann, 'Das Gasthaus und das Privilegium der "Särgemacherei"', *Ostfriesisches Monatsblatt für provinzielle Interessen*, 1 (1873), 480–87

Meiners, Eduard, *Oostvrieschlandts Kerkelyke Geschiedenisse of een historisch en oordeelkundig verhaal van het gene nopens het Kerkelyke in Oostvrieschlandt, en byzonder te Emden, is voorgevallen, zedert den tydt der Hervorminge, of de jaren 1519, en 1520, tot op den huidigen dag* (2 vols, Groningen, 1738–39)

Minolts, M., 'Die Clementiner Brüderschaft in Emden', *Ostfreesland. Ein Kalender für Jederman*, 20 (1933), 151–2

Minolts, M., 'Emdens Bysejaager', *Ostfreesland. Ein Kalender für Jederman*, 23 (1936), 157–8

Mülder, J., *Die Diakonie der Fremdlingen-Armen 1558–1858* (Emden, 1858; reprint Emden, 1958)

Muller, Scheila D., *Charity in the Dutch Republic. Pictures of Rich and Poor for Charitable Institutions* (Ann Arbor, 1985)

Murken, Axel Hinrich, 'Von der ersten Hospitälern bis zum modernen Krankenhaus – Die Geschichte der Medizin und ihrer Institutionen vom frühen Mittelalter bis der Neuzeit unter besonderer Berücksichtigung Niedersachsens', in Cord Meckseper (ed.), *Stadt im Wandel*, vol. 4 (Stuttgart–Bad Cannstatt, 1985), pp. 189–222

Nauta, D., 'Tien Jaren uit de geschiedenis van Emden als centrum van gereformeerde activiteit', *Gereformeerd Theologisch Tijdschrift*, 57 (1957), 128–36

Nijenhuis, W., 'Die Bedeutung Ostfrieslands für die Reformation in den Niederlanden', *EJb*, 62 (1982), 87–102

Parker, Charles H., 'Moral Supervision and Poor Relief in the Reformed Church of Delft, 1579–1609', *ARG*, 87 (1996), 334–61

Parker, Charles H., *The Reformation of Community: Social Welfare and Calvinist Charity in Holland, 1572–1620* (Cambridge, 1998)

Pettegree, Andrew, *Emden and the Dutch Revolt* (Oxford, 1992)

Pettegree, Andrew, 'The English Church at Emden', in his *Marian Protestantism: Six Studies* (Aldershot, 1996), pp. 10–38

Pettegree, Andrew, 'The Exile Churches and the Churches "Under the Cross": Antwerp and Emden during the Dutch Revolt', *Journal of Ecclesiastical History*, 28, 2 (April 1987), 187–202

Pettegree, Andrew, *Foreign Protestant Communities in Sixteenth-Century London* (Oxford, 1986)

Pettegree, Andrew, 'The Struggle for an Orthodox Church: Calvinists and Anabaptists in East Friesland', *Bulletin of the John Rylands Library*, 70 (1988), 45–59

Pleines, J. N., 'Die französisch reformirte Kirche in Emden', *Geschichtsblätter des Deutschen Hugenotten-Vereins*, I. Zehnt, Heft 2 (1894)

Pleines, J. N., 'Kurze Geschichte der französisch-reformirten Kirche in Emden', *EJb*, 1, 1 (1875), 37–54

Pleines, J. N., *Troisième Jubilé Séculaire de la Fondation de l'Eglise réformée française d'Emden* (Emden, 1855)

Poppen, G. V., 'Urkunde. Niedergelegt in dem Grunstein des neuen Armen- und Arbeitshauses zu Esens, am Freitag den 23ten September 1864', *Ostfriesland Zeitschrift für Kultur, Wirtschaft und Verkehr* (1965, 4), 11–12

Reeken, Erich von, *Zur Geschichte der Emder Taufgesinnten (Mennoniten) 1529–1750* (Aurich, 1986)

Reimers, Heinrich, *Die Gestaltung der Reformation in Ostfriesland* (Aurich, 1917)

Reimers, Heinrich, *Die Säkularisation der Klöster in Ostfriesland* (Aurich, 1906)

Roodenburg, Herman W., *Onder censuur: de kerkelijke tucht in de gereformeerde gemeente van Amsterdam, 1578–1700* (Hilversum, 1990)

Schaer, Friedrich W., 'Öffentliche Fürsorge im Dreißigjährigen Krieg. Aus den Registern des Auricher Armenhauses', *Ostfriesland Zeitschrift für Kultur, Wirtschaft und Verkehr* (1965, 4), 25–6

Schelven, A. Arnout van, *De Nederduitsche Vluchtelingenkerken der XVIe Eeuw in Engeland en Duitschland in Hunne Beteekenis voor de Reformatie in de Nederlanden* (The Hague, 1908)

Schilling, Heinz, *Civic Calvinism in Northwest Germany and the Netherlands: Sixteenth to Nineteenth Centuries* (Kirksville, MO, 1991)

Schilling, Heinz, 'Frühneuzeitliche Formierung und Disziplinierung von Ehe, Familie und Erziehung im Spiegel calvinistischer Kirchenratsprotokolle (Emden und Groningen)' in P. Prodi (ed.), *Glaube und Eid: Treuformeln, Glaubensbekenntnisse und Sozialdisziplinierung zwischen Mittelalter und Neuzeit* (Munich, 1993), pp. 199–235

Schilling, Heinz, Introduction to *Die Kirchenratsprotokolle der reformierten Gemeinde Emden 1557–1620*, vol 1, eds H. Schilling and K.-D. Schreiber (Cologne and Vienna, 1989), pp. IX–XXVIII

Schilling, Heinz, *Niederländische Exulanten im 16. Jahrhundert* (Gütersloh, 1972)

Schilling, Heinz, 'Reformation und Bürgerfreiheit. Emdens Weg zur calvinistischen Stadtrepublik', in Berndt Moeller (ed.), *Stadt und Kirche* (Gütersloh, 1978), pp. 128–61

Schilling, Heinz, 'Reformierte Kirchenzucht als Sozialdisziplinierung?: Die Tätigkeit des Emder Presbyteriums in den Jahren 1557–1562', in Wilfried Ehbrecht and Heinz Schilling (eds), *Niederlande und Nordwestdeutschland. Studien zur Regional- und Stadtgeschichte Nordwestkontinentaleuropas im Mittelalter und in der Neuzeit* (Cologne and Vienna, 1983), pp. 261–327

Schilling, Heinz, 'Sündenzucht und Frühneuzeitliche Sozialdisziplinierung. Die Calvinistische Presbyteriale Kirchenzucht in Emden vom 16 bis 19. Jahrhundert', in Georg Schmidt (ed.), *Stände und Gesellschaft im alten Reich* (Stuttgart, 1989), pp. 265–302

Schmidt, Heinrich, *Politische Geschichte Ostfrieslands* (Leer, 1975)

Schöningh, Wolfgang, 'Emden. Ein Stadtgeschichtlicher Rückblick', in

Günther Möhlmann (ed.), *Ostfriesland. Weites Land an der Nordseeküste* (Essen, 1961), pp. 108–19

Schöningh, Wolfgang, 'Westfälische Einwanderer in Ostfriesland 1433 bis 1744', *Westfälische Forschungen*, 20 (1967), 5–57

Schulz, Walter, 'Studien zur Genese und Überlieferung des Ostfriesischen Landrechts', *EJb*, 72 (1992), 81–169

Siebern, Heinrich, *Die Kunstdenkmale der Stadt Emden* (Hannover, 1927)

Smid, Menno, 'Die geschichtliche Entwicklung der konfessionellen Verhältnisse in Ostfriesland', *Jahrbuch der Gesellschaft für niedersächsische Kirchengeschichte*, 89 (1991), 201–14

Smid, Menno, 'Jan Laski', in *TRE*, vol. XX, pp. 448–51

Smid, Menno, 'Johannes Laski', in *Neue Deutsche Biographie*, 13, pp. 657–8

Smid, Menno, 'Kirche zwischen Burg und Rathaus. Ein Beitrag zur Emder Stadtgeschichte und zum Verhältnis von Staat und Kirche in Emden', in *Res Frisicae. Beiträge zur ostfriesischen Verfassungs-, Sozial- und Kulturgeschichte* (Aurich, 1978), pp. 131–50

Smid, Menno, 'Kirchliche Beziehungen zwischen Groningen und Ostfriesland im 16. Jahrhundert', in G. van Halsema Thzn., Jos. M. M. Hermans, et al. (eds), *Geloven in Groningen* (Kampen, 1990), pp. 28–42

Smid, Menno, *Ostfriesische Kirchengeschichte* (Pewsum, 1974)

Smid, Menno, 'Ostfriesland', in Anton Schindling and Walter Ziegler (eds), *Die Territorien des Reichs im Zeitalter der Reformation und Konfessionalisierung. Land und Konfession 1500–1650*, vol. 3 (Münster, 1991), pp. 162–80

Soly, Hugo, 'Continuity and change: attitudes towards poor relief and health care in early modern Antwerp', in Ole Peter Grell and Andrew Cunningham (eds), *Health Care and Poor Relief in Protestant Europe* (London, 1997), 84–107

Spaans, Joke, *Haarlem na de Reformatie. Stedelijke cultuur en Kerkelijk Leven 1577–1620* (The Hague, 1989)

Sprengler-Ruppenthal, Anneliese, 'Einleitung' to the Kirchenordnung der Grafschaft Ostfriesland, in Emil Sehling (ed.), *Die evangelischen Kirchenordnungen des 16. Jahrhunderts*, vol. 7/II/i (Tübingen, 1963), pp. 307–56

Sprengler-Ruppenthal, Anneliese, *Mysterium und Riten nach der Londoner Kirchenordnung der Niederländer* (Cologne, 1967)

Stracke, E., 'Emder Künstler des 16. und 17. Jahrhunderts', *EJb*, 13 (1899), 164–83

Stracke, Johannes, 'Geistliche Laienbruderschaften im ausgehenden Mittelalter', *EJb*, 51/52 (1971/72), 35–65

Stracke, Johannes, 'Goldschmiede in Emden von 1400 bis 1860', *EJb*, 61 (1981), 9–90

Stracke, Johannes, 'Die Maler und Glaser in Emden seit dem Mittelalter', *EJb*, 54 (1974), 23–46

Stracke, Johannes, 'Das Pestbuch eines Emder Arztes', *Ostfriesland. Zeitschrift für Kultur, Wirtschaft und Verkehr* (1959, 1), 13–14

Stracke, Johannes, 'Das St.-Gertruden-Gasthaus in Emden', *EJb*, 51/52 (1971/72), 126–31

Swart, F., *Zur Friesischen Agrargeschichte* (Leipzig, 1910)

Tanis, James, 'East Friesland and the Reformed Reformation', *Calvin Theological Journal*, 26 (November 1991), 313–49

[No name], 'Über Lazarus Haus (in Misc. Sammlungen)', *EJb*, 14 (1902), 479–81

[No name], 'Ursprung des Fremdlingen-Armen-Institutes zu Emden', *Frisia*, III (1844), 162–3

De Vries, J. Fr., 'Gilden und Zünfte Emdens', *Ostfriesisches Monatsblatt für provinziellen Interessen*, 4 (1876), 292–305

De Vries, J. Fr., 'Schul-Chronik. oder Nachrichten über Gründung, Entwicklung und gegenwärtigen Zustand des Elementarschulwesens in der deutsch-reformierten Gemeinde Emdens', *Ostfriesisches Monatsblatt für provinzielle Interessen*, 5 (1877), 559–68

Wagner, Dr, 'Beiträge zur Geschichte der Armenpflege und des Gasthauses in Norden', *EJb*, 15, 1 (1905), 138–60

Weber, Marion, 'Emden – Kirche und Gesellschaft in einer Stadt der Frühneuzeit' (2 parts), *EJb*, 68 (1988), 78–107; 69 (1989), 39–81

Weerda, Jan, 'Der Emder Kirchenrat und seine Gemeinde' (Habilitationsschrift, Münster, 1948)

Weerda, Jan, 'Das ostfriesische Experiment. Zur Entstehung des Nebeneinander lutherischer und reformierter Gemeinden in der ostfriesischen Territorialkirche', *Zeitschrift für evangelisches Kirchenrecht*, vol. 5, no. 2/3 (1956), 159–96

Wenz, Philipp, *Reformations-Jubel-Rede nebst Geschichte der französisch-reformierten Kirche in Emden* (Emden, 1819)

Wiemann, Harm, 'Die Bauern in der ostfriesichen Landschaft im 16.–18. Jahrhundert', in Günther Franz (ed.), *Bauernschaft und Bauernstand 1500–1970* (Limburg, 1975), pp. 153–64

Zmyslony, Monika, 'Die geistlichen Bruderschaften in Lübeck bis zur Reformation' (Ph.D. thesis, University of Kiel, 1974)

B. *Studies of Poor Relief, Confessionalisation, Church Discipline, and Social Discipline*

Allweyer, Franz, 'Der Einfluß der Reformation auf das württembergische Armenwesen' (Ph.D. thesis, University of Erlangen, 1929)

Alves, Abel Althouguia, 'The Christian Social Organism and Social Welfare: The Case of Vives, Calvin and Loyola', *SCJ*, 20 (1989), 3–21.

Andrew, Donna T., *Philanthropy and Police: London Charity in the Eighteenth Century* (Princeton, 1989)

Barge, Herman, 'Die älteste evangelische Armenordnung', *Historisches Vierteljahreschrift*, 11 (1908), 193–225, 296

Barry, Jonathan and Jones, Colin (eds), *Medicine and Charity before the Welfare State* (New York, 1991)

Beier, A. L., *Masterless Men: The Vagrancy Problem in England 1560–1640* (London, 1985)

Bernoulli, W., 'Von der reformierten Diakonie in der Reformationszeit', in Herbert Krimm (ed.), *Das diakonische Amt der Kirche* (2nd edn, Stuttgart, 1965), pp. 197–242 [1st edn, Stuttgart, 1953, pp. 193–230]

Boldt, Annette, *Das Fürsorgewesen der Stadt Braunschweig in Spätmittelalter und Früher Neuzeit. Ein exemplarische Untersuchung am Beispiel des St. Thomae-Hospitals* (Hildesheim, 1988)

Bonolas, Philippe, 'La Question des Etrangers à la fin du XVIe Siècle et au Début du XVIIe Siècle', *Revue d'Histoire Moderne et Contemporaine*, 36 (1989), 304–17

Bosl, Karl, 'Armut, Arbeit, Emanzipation', in *Beiträge zur wirtschafts- und sozialgeschichte des Mittelalters* (Cologne and Vienna, 1976)

Bosl, Karl, *Armut Christi: Ideal der Mönche und Ketzer, Ideologie der aufsteigenden Gesellschaftsschichten vom II. bis zum 13. Jahrhundert* (Munich, 1981)

Bosl, Karl, 'Potens und Pauper. Begriffsgeschichtliche Studien zur gesellschaftlichen Differenzierung im frühen Mittelalter und zum "Pauperismus" des Hochmittelalters', in his *Frühformen der Gesellschaft im mittelalterlichen Europa. Ausgewählte Beiträge zu einer Strukturanalys der mittelalterlichen Welt* (Munich–Vienna, 1964), pp. 106–34

Brucker, Gene, 'Bureaucracy and Social Welfare in the Renaissance. A Florentine Case Study', *Journal of Modern History*, 55 (1983), 1–21

Bulst, Neithard, 'Zum Problem städtischer und territorialer Kleider-, Aufwands- und Luxusgesetzgebung in Deutschland (13.–Mette 16. Jh.)', in A. Gouronu and A. Rigaudière (eds), *Renaissance du pouvoir legislatif et genèse de l'état* (Perpignan, 1988), pp. 29–57

Callahan, William J., 'Corporate Charity in Spain: the *Hermandad del Refugio* of Madrid, 1618–1814', *Histoire Sociale*, 9 (1976), 159–86

Chabot, Isabelle, 'Poverty and the widow in later medieval Florence', *Continuity and Change*, 3, 2 (1988), 291–311

Chill, Emmanuel, 'Religion and Mendicity in Seventeenth-Century France', *International Review of Social History*, VII (1962), 400–425

Chrisman, Miriam Usher, 'Urban Poor in the Sixteenth Century: the Case of Strasbourg', in Miriam Usher Chrisman and Otto Gründler (eds), *Social Groups and Religious Ideas in the Sixteenth Century* (Kalamazoo, 1978), pp. 59–67, 169–71

Davis, Barbara Beckerman, 'Poverty and Poor Relief in Sixteenth-Century Toulouse', *Historical Reflections*, 17 (1991), 267–96

Davis, Barbara Beckerman, 'Poverty and Poor Relief in Toulouse, ca. 1474–ca. 1560: The Response of a Conservative Society' (Ph.D. thesis, University of California, Berkeley, 1986)

Davis, Barbara Beckerman, 'Reconstructing the Poor in Early Sixteenth-Century Toulouse', *French History*, 73 (1993), 249–85

Davis, Natalie Zemon, 'Economie et Pauvreté aux XVIe et XVIIe Siècles: Lyon, Ville Exemplaire et Prophétique', in M. Mollat (ed.), *Etudes sur l'Histoire de la Pauvreté*, vol. 2 (Paris, 1974), pp. 747–822

Davis, Natalie Zemon, 'Poor Relief, Humanism, and Heresy', in her *Society and Culture in Early Modern France* (Stanford, 1975)

Demandt, Karl E., 'Die Anfänge der staatlichen Armen- und Elendenfürsorge in Hessen', *Hessisches Jahrbuch für Landesgeschichte*, 30 (1980), 176–235

Depreeuw, Wim Charles, 'Landloperij, Bedelarij en Thuisloosheid: Een Sociohistorische Analyse van Repressie, Bijstand en Instellingen' (Ph.D. thesis, Catholic University of Louvain, 1986)

Dinges, Martin, 'Frühneuzeitliche Armenfürsorge als Sozialdisziplinierung? Probleme mit einem Konzept', *Geschichte und Gesellschaft*, 17 (1991), 5–29

Dinges, Martin, 'Materielle Kultur und Alltag – Die Unterschichten in Bordeaux im 16. und 17. Jahrhundert', *Francia*, 15 (1987), 257–79

Dinges, Martin, *Stadtarmut in Bordeaux 1525–1675. Alltag, Politik, Mentalitäten* (Bonn, 1988)

Dixon, C. Scott, 'The Reformation and Parish Morality in Brandenburg–Ansbach–Kulmach', *ARG*, 87 (1996), 255–86

Ehrle, Franz, *Beiträge zur Geschichte und Reform der Armenpflege* (Freiburg im Breisgau, 1881)

Ehrle, Franz, 'Die Armenordnungen von Nürnberg (1522) und Ypern (1525)', *Historisches Jahrbuch*, 9 (1888), 450–79

Elton, Geoffrey, 'An Early Tudor Poor Law', *Economic History Review*, 2nd series, 6 (1953), 55–67

Fairchilds, Cissie, *Poverty and Charity in Aix-en-Provence* (Baltimore, 1976)

Favier, Ren, 'L'Eglise et l'Assistance en Dauphine sous l'Ancien Regime: La Vingt-Quatrième des Pauvres', *Revue d'Histoire Moderne et Contemporaine*, 31 (1984), 448–64

Feuchtwanger, Ludwig, 'Geschichte der sozialen Politik und des Armenwesens im Zeitalter der Reformation' (2 parts), *Jahrbuch für Gesetzgebung, Verwaltung und Volkswirtschaft*, 32 (1908), 167–204; 33 (1909), 191–228

Feuß, R., *Kurzgefaßte Geschichte der Armenpflege, die künftige Armenfürsorge und die Einrichtungen eines Wohlfartsamtes in Bremen* (Bremen, 1919)

Fideler, Paul A., 'Christian humanism and poor law reform in early Tudor England', *Societas*, 4 (1974), 269–85

Fischer, Thomas, 'Armut, Bettler, Almosen – Die Anfänge städtischer Sozialfürsorge im ausgehenden Mittelalter', in Cord Meckseper (ed.), *Stadt im Wandel*, vol. 4 (Stuttgart–Bad Cannstatt, 1985), pp. 271–82

Fischer, Thomas, 'Der Beginn frühmoderner Sozialpolitik in den deutschen Städten des 16. Jahrhunderts', *Jahrbuch der Sozialarbeit*, 4 (1981), 46–68

Fischer, Thomas, *Städtische Armut und Armenfürsorge im 15. und 16. Jahrhundert. Sozialgeschichtliche Untersuchungen am Beispiel der Städte Basel, Freiburg i.Br. und Straßburg* (Göttingen, 1979)

Flynn, Maureen, 'An Approach to Family Welfare: the Confraternities of Early Modern Castile' (M.A. thesis, University of Wisconsin-Madison, 1979)

Flynn, Maureen, *Sacred Charity: Confraternities and Social Welfare in Spain, 1400–1700* (Ithaca, 1989)

Forschl, Thomas, 'Rahmenbedingungen des Stadtbürgerlichen Alltags im 16. Jahrhundert', A. Kohler and Heinrich Lutz (eds), *Alltag im 16. Jahrhundert* (Vienna, 1987), pp. 174–94

Förstl, Johan Nepomuk, *Das Almosen. Eine Untersuchung über Grundsätze der Armenfürsorge in Mittelalter und Gegenwart* (Padeborn, 1909)

Fries, Ottmar, 'Luthers Schrift "Ordnung eines gemeinen Kastens"', *Schweizer Beiträge zur allgemeinen Geschichte*, 11 (1953), 27–42

Funk, M. J., *Geschichte und Statistik des Bremer Armenwesens* (Bremen, 1913)

Gavitt, Philip, *Charity and Children in Renaissance Florence: The Ospedale Degli Innocenti, 1410–1536* (Ann Arbor, 1990)

Geremek, Bronislaw, 'Il Pauperismo nell'età preindustriale (secoli XIV–XVII)', in R. Romano and C. Vivanti (eds), *Storia d'Italia*, vol. V (Turin, 1973), pp. 669–98

Geremek, Bronislaw, 'Renfermement des pauvres en Italie (XIVe …
    XVIIIe siècles): remarques preliminaries', *Mélanges en l'honneur de
    Fernand Braudel* (2 vols, Toulouse, 1973)
Goldsmith, Leslie Henry, 'Poor Relief in Sixteenth-Century Orléans'
    (Ph.D. thesis, University of Wisconsin-Madison, 1980)
Grell, Ole Peter, 'The Protestant imperative of Christian care and neigh-
    bourly love', in Ole Peter Grell and Andrew Cunningham (eds), *Health
    Care and Poor Relief in Protestant Europe 1500–1700* (London,
    1997), 43–65
Grell, Ole Peter, 'The religious duty of care and the social need for
    control in early modern Europe', *The Historical Journal*, 39 (1996),
    257–63
Grell, Ole Peter and Cunningham, Andrew (eds), *Health Care and Poor
    Relief in Protestant Europe 1500–1700* (London, 1997)
Grimm, Harold, 'Luther's Contribution to Sixteenth-Century Organiza-
    tion of Poor Relief', *ARG*, 61 (1970), 222–34
Gutton, Jean-Pierre, *La société et les pauvres. L'exemple de la généralité
    de Lyon 1534–1789* (Paris, 1971)
Gutton, Jean-Pierre, *La société et les pauvres en Europe (XVIe–XVIIIe
    siècles)* (Paris, 1974)
Habermas, Jürgen, *Strukturwandel der Öffentlichkeit. Untersuchungen
    zu einer Kategorie der bürgerlichen Gesellschaft* (Neuwied/Berlin,
    1962)
Hanawalt, Barbara, 'Keepers of the Lights: Late Medieval English par-
    ish gilds', *Journal of Medieval and Renaissance Studies*, 14 (1984),
    21–37
Henderson, John, 'The parish and the poor in Florence at the time of
    the Black Death: the case of S. Frediano', *Continuity and Change*, 3,
    2 (1988), 247–72
Henderson, John, *Piety and Charity in Late Medieval Florence* (Chi-
    cago, 1997)
Henderson, Robert W., 'Sixteenth-Century Community Benevolence:
    An Attempt to Resacralize the Secular', *Church History*, 38 (1969),
    421–8
Herlan, Ronald, 'Relief of the Poor in Bristol from Late Elizabethan
    Times until the Restoration Era', *Proceedings of the American Philo-
    sophical Society*, 126 (1982), 212–28
Hsia, Ronald Po-chia, 'Civic Wills as Sources for the Study of Piety in
    Münster', *SCJ*, 14 (1983), 321–48
Hsia, Ronald Po-chia, *Social Discipline in the Reformation: Central
    Europe 1550–1750* (London/New York, 1989)
Hudemann-Simon, Calixte, 'Wohlfahrts-, Armen- und Gesundheitswesen

in der Saarregion 1794–1813', *Jahrbuch für westdeutsche Landesgeschichte*, 17 (1991), 129–58

Johnston, Alexandra F., 'English Guilds and Municipal Authority', *Renaissance and Reformation*, 13 (1989), 69–88

Jordan, T. K., *Philanthropy in England 1480–1660* (New York, 1959)

Jütte, Robert, *Abbild und Sozialle Wirklichkeit des Bettler- und Gaunertums zu Beginn der Neuzeit* (Cologne, 1988)

Jütte, Robert, 'Andreas Hyperius (1511–1564) und die Reform des frühneuzeitlichen Armenwesens', *ARG*, 75 (1984), 113–38

Jütte, Robert, 'Disziplinierungsmechanismen in der städtischen Armenfürsorge der Frühneuzeit', in C. Sachße und F. Tennstedt (eds), *Soziale Sicherheit und soziale Disziplinierung* (Frankfurt, 1986), pp. 101–18

Jütte, Robert, 'Die "Küche der Armen" in der Frühen Neuzet am Beispiel von Armenspeisungen in deutschen und Westeuropäischen Städten', *Tel Aviver Jahrbuch für Deutsche Geschichte*, 16 (1987), 24–47

Jütte, Robert, *Obrigkeitliche Armenfürsorge in deutschen Reichsstädten der frühen Neuzeit: Städtisches Armenwesen in Frankfurt am Main und Köln* (Cologne, 1984)

Jütte, Robert, 'Poor Relief and Social Discipline in Sixteenth-Century Europe', *European Studies Review*, 11 (1981), 25–52

Jütte, Robert, 'Prolegomena zu einer Sozialgeschichte der Armenfürsorge diesseits und jenseits des Fortschritts', *Geschichte und Gesellschaft*, 17 (1991), 92–101

Jütte, Robert, Review of *Stadtarmut in Bordeaux 1525–1675* by Martin Dinges, *SCJ*, 20 (1989), 496–7

Jütte, Robert, 'Stigmasymbole: Kleidung als identitätsstiftendes Merkmal bei spätmittelalterlichen und frühneuzeitlichen Randgruppen (Juden, Dirnen, Aussätzige, Bettler)', in Robert Jütte and Neithard Bulst (eds), *Zwischen Sein und Schein: Kleidung und Identität in der ständischen Gesellschaft* (Freiburg-im-Breisgau, 1993), pp. 65–89

Kalberlah, Gerhard, 'Der soziale Gedanke in Bugenhagens Braunschweiger Kirchenordnung', *Jahrbuch der Gesellschaft für niedersächsische Kirchengeschichte*, 51 (1953), 113–17

Kamen, Henry, *The Iron Century. Social Change in Europe, 1560–1660* (London, 1976)

Kingdon, Robert, 'Calvinism and Social Welfare', *Calvin Theological Journal*, 17 (1982), 212–30

Kingdon, Robert, 'Calvin's Ideas about the Diaconate: Social or Theological in Origin?', in Carter Lindberg (ed.), *Piety, Politics and Ethics: Reformation Studies in Honor of George Wolfgang Forell* (Kirksville, MO, 1984), pp. 167–80

Kingdon, Robert, 'The Control of Morals in Calvin's Geneva', in

Lawrence P. Buck and Jonathan W. Zophy (eds), *The Social History of the Reformation* (Columbus, 1972), pp. 3–16

Kingdon, Robert, 'The Control of Morals by the Earliest Calvinists', in Peter de Klerk, *Renaissance, Reformation, Resurgence* (Grand Rapids, 1976), pp. 95–106

Kingdon, Robert, 'The Deacons of the Reformed Church in Calvin's Geneva', in *Mélanges d'histoire du XVIe siècle offerts à Henri Meylan* (Geneva, 1970), pp. 81–90

Kingdon, Robert, 'Social Welfare in Calvin's Geneva', *American Historical Review*, 76 (1971), 50–69

Knetsch, F. R. J., 'Diakonaat als Ambtelijke Armenzorg, I: Inleidende Operkingen bij een Verwaarloosd Gebied uit de Kerkgeschiedenis', *Nederlands Archief voor Kerkgeschiedenis*, 64 (1984), 144–59

Knobler, Abby Phyllis, 'Luther and the Legal Concept of the Poor in the Sixteenth Century German Church Ordinances' (Ph.D. thesis, University of California, Los Angeles, 1991)

Kölmel, Wilhelm, 'Apologia Pauperum. Die Armutslehre Bonaventuras da Bagnoregio als soziale Theorie', *Historisches Jahrbuch*, 94 (1974), 46–68

Lane, Franz Peter, 'Poverty and Poor Relief in the German Church Orders of Johann Bugenhagen 1485–1558' (Ph.D. thesis, Ohio State University, 1973)

Laslett, Peter, 'Family, Kinship and Collectivity as Systems of Support in pre-industrial Europe: a consideration of the "nuclear-hardship" hypothesis', *Continuity and Change*, 3, 2 (1988), 153–76

Leeuwen, Marco. H. D. van, 'Logic of Charity: Poor Relief in Pre-Industrial Europe', *Journal of Interdisciplinary History*, 24 (1994), 589–613

Lindberg, Carter, 'La Theologie et L'assistance Publique: le cas d'Ypres (1525–1531)', *Revue d'Histoire et de Philosophie Religieuses*, 61 (1981), 23–36

Lindberg, Carter, '"There Should Be No Beggars Among Christians": Karlstadt, Luther, and the Origins of Protestant Poor Relief', *Church History*, 46 (1977), 313–34

Lindgren, Uta, 'Europas Armut: Probleme, Methoden, Ergebnisse einer Untersuchungsserie', *Saeculum*, 28 (1977), 378–418

Locher, Gottfried, 'The Theology of Exile: Faith and the Fate of the Refugee', in Miriam Usher Chrisman and Otto Gründler (eds), *Social Groups and Religious Ideas in the Sixteenth Century* (Kalamazoo, 1978), pp. 85–92

Lombardi, Daniela, 'La Demande d'Assistance et les Reponses des Autorités Urbaines Face à Une Crise conjoncturelle: Florence 1619–

1622', *Mélanges de L'Ecole Française de Rome: Moyen Age – Temps Mondernes*, 99 (1987), 935–45

Martz, Linda, *Poverty and Welfare in Hapsburg Spain. The Example of Toledo* (Cambridge, 1983)

Maschke, Erich, 'Obrigkeit im spätmittelalterlichen Speyer und in anderen Städten', *ARG*, 57 (1966), 7–23

Maurer, Wilhelm, 'Die hessischen Kastenordnungen', *Jahrbuch der Hessischen Kirchengeschichtlichen Vereinigung*, 4 (1953), 1–37

McIntosh, Marjorie K., 'Local responses to the poor in late medieval and Tudor England', *Continuity and Change*, 3, 2 (1988), 209–46

McKee, Elsie Anne, *John Calvin on the Diaconate and Liturgical Almsgiving* (Geneva, 1984)

Menning, Carol Bresnahan, *Charity and State in Late Renaissance Italy: The Monte di Pietà of Florence* (Ithaca, 1993)

Mentzer, Raymond A., Jr, 'Organizational Endeavor and Charitable Impulse in Sixteenth-Century France: the Case of Protestant Nîmes', *French History*, 5 (1991), 1–29

Metz, K. H., 'Staatsraison und Menschenfreundlichkeit. Formen und Wandlungen der Armenpflege im Ancien Regime Frankreichs, Deutschlands und Großbritanniens', *Vierteljahrsschrift fur Sozial- und Wirtschaftsgeschichte*, 72 (1985), 1–26

Michielse, H. C. M., 'Policing the Poor: J. L. Vives and the Sixteenth-Century Origins of Modern Social Administration', *Social Service Review*, 64 (1990), 1–21

Moeller, Berndt, 'Frömmigkeit in Deutschland um 1500', *ARG*, 56 (1965), 5–30

Moeller, Ernst V., *Die Elendsbrüderschaften. Ein Beitrag zur Geschichte der Fremden Fürsorge im Mittelalter* (Leipzig, 1906; reprint, Leipzig, 1972)

Moens, W. J. C., 'The Relief of the Poor Members of the French Churches in England', *Proceedings of the Huguenot Society of London* (10 January and 14 March 1894)

Mollat, Michel, *The Poor in the Middle Ages*, trans. by Arthur Goldhammer (New Haven, 1986) [originally published as *Les Pauvres au Moyen Age* (Hachette, 1978)]

Mollat, Michel, (ed.), *Etudes sur l'histoire de la pauvreté* (2 vols, Paris, 1974)

Mone, Franz Joseph, 'Über die Armenpflege vom 13. bis 16. Jahrhundert (in Konstanz, Güntersthal, Straßburg, Bretten, Baden, Bruchsal)', *Zeitschrift für die Geschichte des Oberrheins*, 1 (1850), 129–63

Mone, Franz Joseph, 'Über die Krankenpflege vom 13. bis 16. Jahrhundert (in Wirtenberg, Baden, der baier. Pfalz und

Rheinpreußen)', *Zeitschrift für die Geschichte des Oberrheins*, 2 (1851), 257–91

Moore, Carol, 'Poor Relief in Elizabethan England: a New Look at Ipswich', *Proceedings and Papers of the Georgia Association of Historians*, 7 (1986), 98–119

Moritz, Werner, *Die bürgerlichen Fürsorgeanstalten der Reichsstadt Frankfurt a.M. im späten Mittelalter* (Frankfurt, 1981)

Mueller, Reinhold C., 'Charitable Institutions, the Jewish Community, and Venetian Society. A Discussion of the Recent Volume by Brian Pullan', *Studi Veneziana*, 14 (1972), 37–82

Münch, Paul, *Zucht und Ordnung, Reformierte Kirchenverfassung im 16. und 17. Jahrhundert: Nassau-Dillenburg, Kurpflaz, Hessen-Kassel* (Stuttgart, 1978)

Nobbe, H., 'Die Regelung der Armenpflege im 16. Jahrhundert nach den evangelischen Kirchenordnungen Deutschlands', *Zeitschrift für Kirchengeschichte*, 10 (1889), 569–617

Norberg, Kathryn, *Rich and Poor in Grenoble 1600–1814* (Berkeley, 1985)

Oberman, Heiko, '*Europa afflicta*: The Reformation of the Refugees', *ARG*, 83 (1992), 91–111

Oehmig, Stefan, 'Der Wittenberger Gemeine Kasten in den ersten zweieinhalb Jahrzehnten seines Bestehens (1522/23 bis 1547): Seine Einnahmen und seine Finanzielle Leistungsfähigkeit im Vergleich zur vorreformatorischen Armenpraxis', *Jahrbuch für Geschichte des Feudalismus*, 12 (1988), 229–69

Oestreich, Gerhard, 'Die antike Literatur als Vorbild der praktischen Wissenschaften im 16. und 17. Jahrhundert', R. R. Bolgar (ed.), *Classical Influences on European Culture A.D. 1500–1700* (London, 1976), pp. 315–24 [reprinted in Gerhard Oestreich, *Strukturprobleme der frühen Neuzeit* (Berlin, 1980), pp. 358–66]

Oestreich, Gerhard, *Strukturprobleme der frühen Neuzeit* (Berlin, 1980)

Oestreich, Gerhard, 'Strukturprobleme des europäischen Absolutismus', first published in *Vierteljahrsschrift für Sozial- und Wirtschaftsgeschichte*, 55 (1968), 329–47; then printed in his *Geist und Gestalt des frühmodernen Staates. Ausgewählte Aufsätze* (Berlin, 1969), pp. 179–97

Olson, Jeannine E., *Calvin and Social Welfare: Deacons and the Bourse française* (Selinsgrove, 1989)

Pelling, Margaret, 'Healing the Sick Poor: Social Policy and Disability in Norwich, 1550–1640', *Medical History*, 29 (1985), 115–37

Pelling, Margaret, 'Illness among the poor in an early modern English town: the Norwich census of 1570', *Continuity and Change*, 3, 2 (1988), 273–90

Petri, Franziscus, *Unser Lieben Frauen Diakonie. Vierhundert Jahre evangelischer Liebestätigkeit in Bremen* (Bremen, 1925)

Peukert, D., *Grenzen der Sozialdisziplinierung. Aufstieg und Krise der deutschen Jugendfürsorge 1878–1932* (Cologne, 1986)

Pfister, Ulrich, 'Refomierte Sittenzucht zwischen kommunaler und territorialer Organisation: Graubünden, 16.–18. Jahrhundert', *ARG*, 87 (1996), 287–332

Pound, John, *Poverty and Vagrancy in Tudor England* (London, 1971)

Press, Volker, *Calvinismus und Territorialstaat. Regierung und Zentralbehörden der Kurpfalz 1559–1619* (Stuttgart, 1970)

Pugh, Wilma, 'Catholics, Protestants, and Testamentary Charity in Seventeenth-Century Lyon and Nîmes', *French History*, 11 (1980), 479–504

Pugh, Wilma, 'Social Welfare and the Edict of Nantes: Lyon and Nîmes', *French Historical Studies*, 8 (1974), 349–76

Pullan, Brian, 'Catholics and the Poor in Early Modern Europe', *Transactions of the Royal Historical Society*, 26 (1976), 15–34

Pullan, Brian, *Poverty and Charity: Europe, Italy, Venice, 1400–1700* (Brookfield, VT, 1994)

Pullan, Brian, 'Poverty, Charity and the Reason of State', *Bollettino dell'Istituto di Storia della Società e dello Stato Veneziano*, 2 (1960), 17–60

Pullan, Brian, *Rich and Poor in Renaissance Venice: The Social Institutions of a Catholic State to 1620* (Cambridge, MA, 1971)

Pullan, Brian, 'Support and redeem: charity and poor relief in Italian cities from the fourteenth to the seventeenth century', *Continuity and Change*, 3, 2 (1988), 177–208

Rapley, Elizabeth, *The Devotees: Women and Church in Seventeenth-Century France* (Cheektowaga, NY, 1990)

Ratzinger, Georg, *Geschichte der kirchlichen Armenpflege* (Freiburg im Breisgau, 1884)

Reinhard, Wolfgang, 'Konfession und Konfessionalisierung in Europa', in W. Reinhard (ed.), *Bekenntnis und Geschichte: Die Confessio Augustana im historischen Zusammenhang* (Munich, 1981), pp. 165–89

Reinhard, Wolfgang, 'Reformation, Counter-Reformation, and the Early Modern State: A Reassessment', *Catholic Historical Review*, 75 (1989), 383–404

Reinhard, Wolfgang, 'Zwang zur Konfessionalisierung?', *Zeitschrift für historische Forschung*, 10 (1983), 257–77

Riis, Thomas (ed.), *Aspects of Poverty in Early Modern Europe* (3 vols, Stutttgart, 1981; Odense, 1986–90)

Roche, Daniel, 'Paris Capitale des Pauvres: Quelques Réflexions sur le

Pauperisme Parisien entre XVIIe et XVIIIe Siècle', *Mélanges de l'Ecole Française de Rome: Moyen Age – Temps Modernes*, 99 (1987), 829–59

Rotzoll, Ursula, *Kasten-Ordnungen der Reformationszeit. Von der mittelalterlichen zur neuzeitlichen Armenpflege* (M.A. thesis, University of Marburg, 1969)

Rushton, Peter, 'Lunatics and Idiots: Mental disorder, the Community, and the Poor Law in North-East England 1600–1800', *Medical History*, 32 (1988), 34–50

Rushton, Peter, 'The Poor Law, the Parish and the Community in North-East England, 1600–1800', *Northern History*, 25 (1989), 135–52

Sachße, Christoph and Tennstedt, Florian (eds), *Geschichte der Armenfürsorge in Deutschland vom Spätmittelalter bis zum 1. Weltkrieg* (Stuttgart, 1980)

Sachße, Christoph, and Tennstedt, Florian (eds), *Soziale Sicherheit und soziale Disziplinierung. Beiträge zu einer historischen Theorie der Sozialpolitik* (Frankfurt, 1986)

Sachße, Christoph, and Tennstedt, Florian (eds), *Jahrbuch der Sozialarbeit* 4 (Hamburg, 1981)

Sakrausky, Oskar, 'Die Klagenfurter Armenstiftung der Bürgerschaft vom 12. Juni 1588', *Carinthia I*, 171 (1981), 192–203

Schaeffer, Fr. B., *Frankfurter Armen- und Wohlfahrtspflege in alter und neuer Zeit* (Frankfurt, 1927)

Scherpner, Hans, *Theorie der Fürsorge* (2nd edn, Göttingen, 1974)

Schiavini Trezzi, Juanita, 'Pauperismo e Assistenza negli antichi stati Italiani: Secoli XV–XIX', *Nuova Riv. Storica*, 64 (1980), 421–7.

Schilling, Heinz, 'Calvinistische Presbyterien in Städten der Frühneuzeit – eine kirchliche Alternativform zur bürgerlichen Repräsentation?', in Wolfgang Ehbrecht (ed.), *Städtische Führungsgruppen und Gemeinden in der werdenden Neuzeit* (Cologne, 1980), pp. 385–444

Schilling, Heinz, 'Das Calvinistische Presbyterium in der Stadt Groningen während der Frühen Neuzeit und im ersten Viertel des 19. Jahrhunderts. Verfassung und Sozialprofil', in Heinz Schilling and Herman Diedriks (eds), *Bürgerliche Eliten in den Niederlanden und in Nordwestdeutschland. Studien zur Sozialgeschichte des europäischen Bürgertums im Mittelalter und in der Neuzeit* (Cologne, 1985), pp. 195–273

Schilling, Heinz, 'Frühneuzeitliche Formierung und Disziplinierung von Ehe, Familie und Erziehung im Spiegel calvinistischer Kirchenratsprotokolle (Emden und Groningen)', in P. Prodi (ed.), *Glaube und Eid: Treueformeln, Glaubensbekenntnisse, und Sozialdisziplinierung zwischen Mittelalter und Neuzeit* (Munich, 1993), pp. 199–235

Schilling, Heinz, '"Geschichte der Sünde" oder "Geschichte des Verbrechens"? Überlegungen zur Gesellschaftsgeschichte der frühneuzeitlichen Kirchenzucht', *Annali dell'Istituto Storico Italo-Germanico di Trento*, 12 (1986), 169–92

Schilling, Heinz, '"History of Crime" or "History of Sin"? – Some Reflections on the Social History of Early Modern Church Discipline', in E. J. Kouri and Tom Scott (eds), *Politics and Society in Reformation Europe. Essays for Sir Geoffrey Elton on his 65th Birthday* (London, 1987), pp. 289–310

Schilling, Heinz, 'Die Kirchenzucht im frühneuzeitlichen Europa in interkonfessionell vergleichender und interdisziplinärer Perspektive – eine Zwischenbilanz', in H. Schilling (ed.), *Kirchenzucht und Sozialdisziplinierung im frühneuzeitlichen Europa* (Berlin, 1994), pp. 11–40

Schilling, Heinz, 'Die Konfessionalisierung im Reich: Religiöser und gesellschaftlicher Wandel in Deutschland zwischen 1555 und 1620', *Historische Zeitschrift*, 246 (1988), 1–45

Schilling, Heinz, *Konfessionskonflikt und Staatsbildung – Eine Fallstudie über das Verhältnis von religiösem und sozialem Wandel in der Frühneuzeit am Beispiel der Grafschaft Lippe* (Gütersloh, 1981)

Schilling, Heinz, 'Die niederländischen Exulanten des 16. Jahrhunderts. Ein Beitrag zum Typus der frühneuzeitlichen Konfessionsmigration', *Geschichte in Wissenschaft und Unterricht*, 43, 2 (Feb 1992), 67–78

Schilling, Heinz, 'Reformierte Kirchenzucht als Sozialdisziplinierung?: Die Tätigkeit des Emder Presbyteriums in den Jahren 1557–1562', in Wilfried Ehbrecht und Heinz Schilling (eds), *Niederlande und Nordwestdeutschland. Studien zur Regional- und Stadtgeschichte Nordwestkontinentaleuropas im Mittelalter und in der Neuzeit* (Cologne/Vienna, 1983), pp. 261–327

Schilling, Heinz, (ed.), *Die reformierte Konfessionalisierung in Deutschland – Das Problem der 'Zweiten Reformation': Wissenschaftliches Symposion des Vereins für Reformationsgeschichte 1985* (Gütersloh, 1986)

Schilling, Heinz, 'Religion und Gesellschaft in der Calvinistischen Republik der vereinigten Niederlande: "Öffentlichkeitskirche" und Sekularisation: Ehe- und Hebammenwesen: Presbyterien und politische Partizipation', in Franz Petri (ed.), *Kirche und gesellschaftlicher Wandel in den deutschen und niederländischen Städten der werdenden Neuzeit* (Cologne and Vienna, 1980), pp. 197–250

Schilling, Heinz, *Die Stadt in der Frühen Neuzeit* (Munich, 1993)

Schilling, Heinz, 'Sündenzucht und Frühneuzeitliche Sozialdisziplinierung. Die Calvinistische Presbyteriale Kirchenzucht in Emden vom 16 bis

19. Jahrhundert', in Georg Schmidt (ed.), *Stände und Gesellschaft im Alten Reich* (Stuttgart, 1989), pp. 265–302

Schmidt, Heinrich, *Konfessionalisierung im 16. Jahrhundert* (Munich, 1992)

Schmidt, Heinrich, 'Das Bernische Sittengericht zwischen Sozialdisziplinierung und kommunaler Selbstregulation', in H. von Rütte (ed.), *Bäuerliche Frömmigkeit und kommunale Reformation* (Basel, 1988), pp. 85–121

Schulze, Winfried, 'Gerhard Oestreichs Begriff "Sozialdisziplinierung in der frühen Neuzeit"', *Zeitschrift für Historische Forschung*, 14 (1987), 265–302

Schwartz, Robert, *Policing the Poor in eighteenth-century France* (Chapel Hill, NC, 1988)

Slack, Paul, 'Poverty and Politics in Salisbury 1597–1666', in Paul Clark and Paul Slack (eds), *Crisis and Order in English Towns 1500–1700* (London, 1972), pp. 164–203

Smiar, Nicholas Paul, 'Poor Law and Outdoor Poor Relief in Zürich 1520–1529: A Case Study in Social Welfare History and Social Welfare Policy Implementation' (Ph.D. thesis, University of Illinois-Chicago, 1986)

Snell, K. D. M., and Millar, J. (eds), 'Lone-Parent Families and the Welfare State: Past and Present', *Continuity and Change*, 2 (1987), 387–422

Sokoll, Thomas, 'Anhaltend Frischer Wind aus Cambridge: Neues über Haushalt und Familie, Eigentum und Armut', *Archiv für Sozialgeschichte*, 28 (1988), 355–65

Spicer, Andrew, '"A Faythful Pastor in the Churches": Ministers in the French and Walloon Communities in England, 1560–1620', in Andrew Pettegree (ed.), *The Reformation of the Parishes* (Manchester, 1993), pp. 195–214

Spicer, Andrew, 'Poor Relief and the Exile Communities', in Beat Kümin, *Reformations Old and New. Essays on the Socio-Economic Impact of Religious Change c. 1470–1630* (Aldershot, 1996), pp. 237–55

Stapperich, Robert, 'Martin Butzers Anteil an den sozialen Aufgaben seiner Zeit', *Jahrbuch der Hessischen Kirchengeschichtlichen Vereinigung*, 5 (1954), 120–41

Steinbicker, Carl R., Poor Relief in the Sixteenth Century (S.T.D. thesis, Catholic University of America, 1937)

Sunshine, Glenn, 'From French Protestantism to the French Reformed Churches: the Development of Huguenot Ecclesiastical Institutions, 1559–1598' (Ph.D. thesis, University of Wisconsin, Madison, 1992)

Terpstra, Nicholas, *Lay Confraternities and Civic Religion in Renaissance Bologna* (Cambridge, 1995)

Tierney, Brian, 'The Decretists and the "Deserving Poor"', *Comparative Studies in Society and History*, 1 (1958/59), 360–73

Tierney, Brian, *Medieval Poor Law: A Sketch of Canonical Theory and its Application in England* (Berkeley, 1959)

Tobriner, Alice, *A Sixteenth-Century Urban Report*, Social Service Monographs, 2nd series (School of Social Service Administration, University of Chicago, 1971)

Trexler, Richard, 'Charity and the Defense of Urban Elites in the Italian Communes', in Frederic Cople Jaher (ed.), *The Rich, the Well Born, and the Powerful. Elites and Upper Classes in History* (1973), pp. 64–109

Troeltsch, Ernst, *The Social Teaching of the Christian Churches*, trans. by Olive Wyon (2 vols, New York, 1931)

Tronrud, Thorold J., 'Dispelling the Gloom: The Extent of Poverty in Tudor and Early Stuart Towns: Some Kentish Evidence', *Canadian Journal of History*, 20 (1985), 1–21

Vieules, Evelyne, 'Le Livre de Comptes d'une Confrérie Toulousaine (1493–1546)', *Annales du Midi*, 95 (1983), 91–105

Vital, Chomel, 'De la Charité à la Philanthropie. L'Assistance à Grenoble, 1600–1814, d'Après un Livre Recent', *Cahiers d'Histoire*, 31 (1986), 171–80

Volaucnik, Christoph, 'Aspekte der Bregenzer Armenfürsorge vom 15. bis 19. Jahrhundert', *Montfort*, 40 (1988), 247–65

Wandel, Lee Palmer, *Always Among Us. Images of the Poor in Zwingli's Zurich* (Cambridge, 1990)

Weissman, Ronald, *Ritual Brotherhood in Renaissance Florence* (New York, 1982)

Willen, Diane, 'Urban Women in Tudor–Stuart England: the Value of Borough Sources', *Proceedings and Papers of the Georgia Association of Historians* (1983), 19–27

Willen, Diane, 'Women in the Public Sphere in Early Modern England: The Case of the Urban Working Poor', *SCJ*, 19 (1988), 559–76

Wilson, Norman J., 'Conceptions of Poor Relief in Sixteenth-Century Strasbourg', *UCLA Historical Journal*, 8 (1987), 5–24

Winkelbauer, Thomas, 'Sozialdisziplinierung und Konfessionalisierung durch Grundherren in den österreichischen und böhmischen Ländern im 16. und 17. Jahrhundert', *Zeitschrift für historische Forschung*, 19 (1992) 317–40

Winckelmann, Otto, 'Die Armenordnungen von Nürnberg (1522), Kitzingen (1523), Regensburg (1523) and Ypern (1525)', *ARG*, 10 (1912/13), 242–80

Winckelmann, Otto, 'Über die ältesten Armenordnungen der Reformationszeit (1522–1525)', *Historische Vierteljahrschrift*, 17 (1914/15), 187–228, 361–400

Woolf, Stuart, *The Poor in Western Europe in the Eighteenth and Nineteenth Centuries* (London, 1986)

Wright, William, 'A Closer Look at House Poor Relief through the Common Chest and Indigence in Sixteenth-Century Hesse', *ARG*, 70 (1979), 225–37

Wright, William, 'Reformation Contributions to the Development of Public Welfare in Hesse', *Journal of Modern History* (On-Demand-Supplement; Abstract in vol. 49, no. 2, 1977, p. ii), D1145–D1179

Zeeden, Ernst W., *Die Entstehung der Konfessionen. Grundlagen und Formen der Konfessionsbildung* (Munich, 1965)

Zeeden, Ernst W., *Konfessionsbildung: Studien zur Reformation, Gegenreformation und katholischen Reform* (Stuttgart, 1985)

Index